HIDDES

of
SOMERSET, AVON,
GLOUCESTERSHIRE & WILTSHIRE

Front Cover:
Lower Slaughter
by
Graham Lewis

Acknowledgments

This book would not have been compiled without the dedicated help of the following: Elaine and Hong - Administration; Joann, Les & Graham - Artists; Bob and Les - Research; Shane - Editing; and Jennie - Writing and Production.

Map origination by Paul and Simon at Legend DTP, Stockport.

All have contributed to what we hope is an interesting, useful and enjoyable publication.

Other titles in this series:

The Hidden Places of East Anglia
The Hidden Places of Dorset, Hampshire and Isle of Wight
The Hidden Places of the Lake District and Cumbria
The Hidden Places of Lancashire and Cheshire
The Hidden Places of Northumberland and Durham
The Hidden Places of North Wales
The Hidden Places of Devon and Cornwall
The Hidden Places of the Heart of England
The Hidden Places of the South East
The Hidden Places of South Wales
The Hidden Places of Scotland
The Hidden Places of Thames and Chilterns
The Hidden Places of Yorkshire and Humberside

Printed and bound by Guernsey Press, Channel Islands.
© M&M Publishing Ltd.
Tryfan House, Warwick Drive, Hale, Altrincham, Cheshire WA15 9EA.
First printed 1990.

THE HIDDEN PLACES
OF
SOMERSET, GLOUCESTERSHIRE & WILTSHIRE

Contents

Salisbury to Stonehenge

Wilton House

Salisbury Cathedral

Salisbury to Stonehenge

Near the charmingly-named village of **LOVER**, in the southeasternmost corner of Wiltshire, is **REDLYNCH**, a pleasant community noted for the fine brick-built mansion, Newhouse, which lies a short distance to the east. The mansion has a Jacobean core dating from 1619 and two Georgian wings which are arranged in the classic 'trinity' configuration. Inside, there is an interesting display of historic costumes, as well as a collection of relics relating to Admiral Nelson. Nearby there is some excellent accommodation at **Templeman's Old Farmhouse**.

Templeman's Old Farmhouse is the delightful country home of June and Peter Dabell, two fine hosts who take great delight in sharing it with guests. Set high on the Downs on the edge of the New Forest, this makes a peaceful relaxing base from which to tour the surrounding area. Inside, the guest rooms are spacious and elegant; all are beautifully furnished and equipped with good facilities. To ensure they feel totally relaxed and at home, guests are even brought tea or coffee in bed each morning.

Templeman's Old Farmhouse, Redlynch, Nr. Salisbury
Tel: 01725 20331

Continuing westwards, the next port of call is **DOWNTON**, an ancient village which is spread out on both sides of the River Avon. The nearby earthwork was originally constructed by the Ancient Britons and was later occupied by the Saxons who established a meeting place or 'moot' on the site. This event was commemorated in the 18th century when the present Moot House was constructed on the old castle foundations. The building and its garden stand opposite a small 18th-century amphitheatre which was built to resemble the original Saxon meeting place. In 1955, a Roman villa comprising of seven rooms and a bathhouse was discovered near here which is believed to date from around 300 AD.

The medieval centre of Downton, with its broad main street and distinctive grassy strip, is known locally as The Borough and was laid out by the Bishop of Winchester in 1205. Many of the thatched brick-built houses which can be seen here today date from the 18th century. There is a working tannery beside the river at the heart of the village, built in 1918. The village Church of St Lawrence stands on the site of a Saxon church which is believed to have been consecrated by St Birinus in 638. The present-day building was originally constructed in the 1100s, although it has been much altered over the centuries and inside, there are some fine carved monuments by the 18th-century Dutch sculptor, Peter Scheemaker. Downton's old manor house is the former home of the Raleigh family and for many years Sir Walter's brother, Carew, was the local member of parliament.

The Warren, Downton, Salisbury Tel: 01725 20263

Should you wish to stay in Downton then make tracks to **The Warren**. Situated in the heart of this historic New Forest village, the Warren is a charming medieval longhouse which is owned by John and Elizabeth Baxter. Here, Elizabethan panelling and oak beams are complemented by antique furniture and furnishings which help to retain the property's original character, while modern comforts such as central heating ensure guests enjoy a restful stay. There are six well-equipped bedrooms, two en-suite, plus a comfortable guest lounge, but the highlight of your stay is likely to be Elizabeth's wholesome breakfast which can be enjoyed in a beautiful room overlooking the large walled garden with the Norman village church beyond. With Salisbury Plain, Stonehenge and many other places of interest within easy reach, the Warren makes an ideal base for touring this beautiful corner of England.

Leaving Downton, cross the River Avon and turn onto the A338 Salisbury road which passes to the west of Eyre's Folly, a unique 17th-century octagonal tower which is one of the earliest follies to have been built in Britain. More commonly known as The Pepperbox, this unusual slate-roofed structure was built in 1606 and enjoys magnificent views over Salisbury and southwest Wiltshire. The tower is surrounded by 72 acres of juniper-filled downland which now belongs to the National Trust.

Continuing northwards along the A338 takes you to Longford Castle, a largely 16th-century structure which stands near the confluence of the Rivers Ebble and Avon. The building is constructed to an unusual triangular design and houses an interesting collection of paintings.

From here, drive back across the A338 to reach NUNTON, an attractive village of thatched cottages and brick residences, the most notable of which is Nunton House. The village lies in the lower valley of the Ebble, a delightful river which is said to contain some of the finest trout in the country. A mile or so upstream is the pleasant riverside community of ODSTOCK. Make a point of visiting the village church which, according to local legend, is the subject of an infamous gypsy curse. The curse surrounds the figure of Joshua Scamp, a notorious local character whose grave lies in the southeast corner of the churchyard. Scamp was a gypsy who in 1801 was wrongfully hanged for stealing horses. This made him a martyr-figure among the Romany people and each year a disorderly crowd would assemble around his grave to commemorate his death, usually after having already toasted to his memory in the nearby Yew Tree Inn.

One year, the rector resolved to put an end to the unruly gathering; he locked the door of the church and dug up a wild rose which Scamp's family had planted beside his grave. This action so incensed the gypsy people that they placed a curse on anyone who dared to bar them from the church again. Not long after, two men defying the curse met with an untimely end, occurrences which led the rector to take the key of the church and throw it into the River Ebble where it is said to remain to this day. A briar rose was then replanted on Scamp's grave which can still be seen beside the crumbling headstone.

Present-day travellers looking for an excellent place to stay in this ancient village should try **Hillside**. Set in a beautiful and tranquil spot and lying only a couple of miles from Salisbury, this appropriately-named bed and breakfast establishment is the home of Carol and Jeffrey Dodd, two fine hosts who provide first-class hospitality. Their en-suite guest rooms are all superbly equipped and located in a separate wing with its own entrance. As well as enjoying magnificent views over the surrounding countryside, this charming hillside house has a wonderful private garden. This is inhabited by a splendid peacock whose plumage adds a brilliant splash of colour to the lovely open lawns. All in all, this true haven of peace and tranquillity is an ideal place to enjoy Wiltshire at its best.

Hillside, Odstock, Salisbury Tel: 01722 329746

The charming village of **COOMBE BISSETT** lies a couple of miles further upstream at the point where the A354 Blandford Forum to Salisbury road crosses the River Ebble. This is where you will find the first-rate pub and restaurant, the **Fox and Goose**, just across the road from the village pond. The pub is a focal point for visitors and locals alike. The friendly host, Mike Chapman, has been in the catering industry all his working life and has built this charming pub and eating place into a charming establishment which is full of character and charm. Customers can choose from a fine selection of ales, wines and first-class food. The menu is varied and imaginative and is sure to satisfy. It includes such mouthwatering dishes as deep-fried Brie or spicy chicken wings, followed by mixed grill or pork fillet. There is also a special children's menu and an excellent outdoor play area.

The Fox and Goose, Blandford Road, Coombe Bissett, Salisbury
Tel: 01722 77437

From Coombe Bissett, continuing northeast along the A354 towards Salisbury brings you to the charming hamlet of BRITFORD lying within the branches of the River Avon a mile and a half to the south of the city. Here is a moated country house and the fine Saxon Church of St Peter which predates Salisbury Cathedral by several centuries. Inside, there are some fine stone carvings which are thought to date from around 800 AD, three carved door surrounds from before the Norman Conquest, and an unusual and elaborately decorated tomb believed to belong to the Duke of Buckingham who was beheaded in Salisbury in 1483.

SALISBURY stands at the confluence of the rivers Avon, Wylye, Bourne and Nadder. Originally called New Sarum, the town grew up around the cathedral which was erected on a sheltered site two miles south of its predecessor at Old Sarum. Over the centuries, the townspeople gradually followed the clergy down from the windswept hillside and today, Salisbury is a flourishing town with a twice weekly open-air market (Tuesdays and Saturdays), a corn exchange and a cattle market.

Mompesson House, Salisbury

East end, Salisbury Cathedral

The new cathedral was the inspiration of Bishop Herbert Poole who wanted to distance the church from the Norman authorities who occupied a castle on the original site. Sadly, the bishop died before his dream was realised and it fell to his brother Richard to implement his plan. Work on the new building began on Easter Monday 1220 and was completed 38 years later, a remarkably short construction period considering the scale of the project and building methods of the day. As a result, the structure has a uniformity of style which is unmatched by any other medieval cathedral in England. The spire were added in 1334 and, at a height of 404 feet, is the tallest in the country. Its construction was a remarkable architectural achievement considering the central piers stand on foundations which go down less than ten feet into marshy ground.

Set into the floor beneath the spire is a brass plate with the inscription, 'AD 1737 The Centre of the Tower'. This marks the spot where, fifty years earlier, Sir Christopher Wren calculated that the tower was leaning almost two and a half feet off-centre. His answer to the problem was to insert iron tie-rods, and when these were replaced in the 1950s, it was discovered that the lean had not worsened in over 250 years.

The cathedral is said to contain a door for each month of the year, a window for each day and a column for each hour (8760 in total). The elaborately decorated west front includes a series of niches, each of which at one time contained a statue; over the centuries many were destroyed by weathering and the ones that can be seen today are 19th-century replacements. A small statue of Salisbury's 'Boy Bishop' stands inside the cathedral's west door. According to the custom of the day, a chorister was elected 'bishop' by his comrades for a period lasting from St Nicholas Day to Holy Innocents' Day (6-28 December) each year. On one occasion during the 17th century, the incumbent was said to have been 'tickled to death' by the other choirboys, and because he had died 'in office', a statue was made showing him in his bishop's regalia.

The oldest working clock in Britain (and possibly in the world) can be found in the cathedral's fan-vaulted north transept. It was built in 1386 to strike the hour and has no clock face. Look out also for the recently-restored 13th-century roof paintings in the choir, and the 200 or so carved stone figures illustrating scenes from the Old Testament on the walls of the octagonal chapter house.

There are also several magnificent tombs in the cathedral, the oldest of which is that of William Longespere, Earl of Salisbury, whose reclining armour-clad effigy has lain here since 1226. Eleven years before, he witnessed the sealing of the Magna Carta by his half-brother, King John, and indeed one of the four remaining copies of this historic document is on display in the Charter House. This is located in the library above the east walk of the cathedral's magnificent cloisters, the largest of their type in England.

Heale House, Middle Woodford

As the cathedral was built before the town, it was necessary to construct housing for the clergy at the same time. This were arranged around a walled square which is now considered to be the finest cathedral close in the country. To enter the close it is necessary to pass through one of its medieval gateways, the least congested of which are Harnham Gate to the south and St Ann's Gate to the east. Just to the south of the cathedral lies the Bishop's Palace which was constructed in the 13th century and now houses the cathedral choir school. During the Great Plague of 1665, Charles II based his court here for several months to the escape the pestilence which was sweeping London. The bishop's residence was

12

also made famous by John Constable who painted his famous landscape of Salisbury Cathedral in the palace gardens; it now hangs in the Victoria and Albert Museum in London.

The pathway along the western side of the cathedral close, West Walk, passes two noteworthy establishments. The award-winning Salisbury and South Wiltshire Museum is located in the medieval King's House and contains a large collection of historic artefacts, including relics from Stonehenge, pottery fragments from Old Sarum and tiles from a Roman mosaic. There is also an interesting display of English china, pottery and glassware, and a mounted group of great bustards, the majestic birds which at one time were found on Salisbury Plain. (Open Mondays to Saturdays and summer Sunday afternoons; 10am to 5pm, all year round. Admission charge payable.) A few doors away, the splendid Bishop's Wardrobe houses the Duke of Edinburgh's Royal Regiment Museum; this contains an interesting collection of regimental militaria which documents the history of the Royal Berkshire and Wiltshire Regiments since 1743. (Open daily, 10am to 4.30pm between June and October; restricted opening at other times; closed December and January).

One of the finest buildings in the cathedral close stands on the northern side of Choristers' Green. The elegant Mompesson House was constructed for a wealthy Wiltshire merchant around 1701 and is now owned by the National Trust. Inside, there is a delicately carved oak staircase, a splendid collection of period furniture and some fine plaster ceilings and overmantels. The Turnbull Collection of 18th-century English china and glassware is also housed here, and to the rear, there is a delightful walled garden. (Open Saturdays to Wednesdays, 12 noon to 5.30pm between 1st April and 1st November. Admission charge payable; free to National Trust members).

Malmesbury House on the northwestern side of the cathedral close has a 14th-century core and an interior and façade which were regularly updated between 1640 and 1749. It also contains some fine 18th-century furnishings. (Open to the public on Tuesdays, Wednesdays, Thursdays and Bank Holiday Mondays between April and early-October). A row of handsome 17th-century almshouses can also be seen nearby which were built on the instructions of the Bishop Seth Ward.

Beyond the walls of the cathedral close, a walk around Salisbury's city centre reveals a wonderful range of historic inns, shops and houses which chronicle the city's development from the 13th century to the present day. Many are half-timbered or have overhanging gables or bow-windowed fronts. One of the most distinctive can be found in Queen Street, the three-storey house built in 1425 for six-times mayor John A'Port. Restoration of this half-timbered structure during the 1930s revealed that, astonishingly, none of the original 15th-century timbers needed replacing. It now operates as a retail shop, although visitors are welcome to view the interior with its Jacobean wood panelling, stone fireplace and carved oak mantelpiece.

Grasmere House, 70 Harnham Road, Salisbury Tel: 01722 338388

Other buildings in Salisbury worth mentioning are the octagonal Poultry Cross which was constructed in the 15th century to provide shelter for the market traders, and the nearby Church of St Thomas of Canterbury which occupies the site of a church which was completed twenty years before the cathedral. The present-day building contains a highly unusual 16th-century wall-painting which can be found above the chancel arch. Restored in the 19th century, this remarkable work of primitive art depicts Christ on a rainbow, the Virgin Mary, St John the Baptist, and a whole collection of saints condemning the unworthy to eternal damnation. Even the local cinema is housed in a former merchants hall dating from the 15th century.

14

Leaving the city centre behind, go in search of **Grasmere**, an impressive Victorian bed and breakfast establishment which is set back off Harnham Road on the edge of Salisbury. Standing in beautiful grounds near the confluence of the Rivers Nadder and Avon, the atmosphere is one of elegant luxury; all the rooms are beautifully furnished yet still retaining a homely feel. The five guest rooms are all en-suite, with three enjoying superb views of the rivers and the majestic cathedral beyond. There is a croquet lawn in the garden which guests are welcome to use, while those wishing to venture further afield will find the heart of historic Salisbury only a ten minute walk away.

Before leaving Salisbury behind, take a look at the windswept hillside that formed the site of the original city. **OLD SARUM** can be found a couple of miles north of the present city centre and just to the west of A345. This ancient stronghold was successively an Iron Age hill fort, a Roman settlement called Sorviodunum, and a medieval cathedral town. The Saxons named it Searobyrg meaning 'dry place', and this is perhaps another reason why the bishops decided to move their cathedral to another more hospitable site in the 13th century. Today, Old Sarum is deserted. All that remains of the once-glorious 56-acre fortifications are some ruined castle walls and an outline of the cathedral's original foundations. However, it still has a distinctive atmosphere and is well worth a visit.

Despite having an electorate which at one time numbered only ten, Old Sarum returned two MPs to Westminster before the 1832 Reform Act put an end to the so-called 'rotten boroughs'. A plaque on the site commemorates the constituency's most illustrious MP, the 18th-century orator and statesman William Pitt the Elder. Below Old Sarum lies **STRATFORD-SUB-CASTLE**, a tranquil community of 17th- and 18th-century houses lying on the banks of the River Avon.

Salisbury is filled with hotels and guesthouses, but we doubt if you will find a quieter or more pleasant place to stay than **Stratford Lodge**, the beautiful Victorian home of Jill Bayly. It is tucked away in Park Lane and has all the charm and grace of the Victorian era. Jill takes great care to ensure that her guests are well cared for; her cooking is second to none, and dinner in the lovely restaurant really is a special meal. Such dishes as 'roast duckling with black cherry and port sauce' are accompanied by fresh vegetables, straight from the garden. Dessert, often simple but always delicious, is also often prepared from fruit grown in the garden.

This is a four-star guest house offering every comfort. The bedrooms are furnished to a very high standard, using pretty pastel colours and matching fabrics. Flowers, antique furniture and pictures adorn every room, and there are lots of books to help you plan your day's sightseeing. Jill is always on hand to let you know what's going on and to advise you of the best places to visit, or if you are feeling lazy and are loath to venture far, the garden is very sheltered and secluded. Guests are very welcome to make use of it and will find it a super place to curl up with a book and just enjoy the sunshine. Jill provides an excellent breakfast and she always tries to offer some slightly unusual dish which may tempt you away from the usual egg and bacon. Mushrooms on toast or smoked haddock kedgeree make a wonderful change and will set you up for the day.

Stratford Lodge, 4 Park Lane, Castle Road, Salisbury
Tel: 01722 325177

Northeast of Salisbury is Figsbury Ring, a National Trust-owned Iron Age hill fort which enjoys some excellent views over Salisbury and the Avon Valley.

The country lanes to the southeast of here led us to the quiet hamlet of STOCKBOTTOM, near Pitton. Here, Cliff and Joan Lodge offer excellent bed and breakfast accommodation at their lovely 18th-century home, The Homestead. Renovated and refurbished to a very high standard, this lovely old house enjoys a beautiful setting with the Downs literally just over the garden fence. The guest rooms are all attractively furnished and have hot and cold washbasins and beverage making facilities, while the Stable and the Cart Shed, provide superb en-suite accommodation in a converted barn. The highlight of your stay is likely to be the fresh farmhouse food which is personally prepared by Cliff and Joan. Their four-course breakfasts and superb dinners are highly recommended by locals and visitors alike.

The Homestead, Stockbottom, Pitton, Salisbury Tel: 01980 611160

Following the A30 northwest takes you along the edge of the top secret military establishment, PORTON DOWN. Except on rare occasions, this unusual area of chalk downland has remained hidden to the public for over fifty years. Ironically, this has led to it becoming a unique nature conservation area containing a wide variety of rare plants, flowers and birds. Indeed, the great bustard has successfully been reintroduced here following its local extinction in the early 19th century. This large long-legged bird is a feature in the country's coat of arms and was once common on Salisbury Plain before before it was wiped out by over-enthusiastic riflemen.

Driving westwards along the small country roads once again, climb onto the ridge which carries the main A345 before descending into the Avon Valley. The seven-mile stretch of river between Salisbury and Amesbury is known locally as the Woodford Valley.

It contains some of the loveliest and most peaceful villages in Wiltshire, including **GREAT DURNFORD** with its Norman church, restored mill and picturesque cricket pitch, **LAKE** with its impressive Tudor mansion, and **MIDDLE WOODFORD** with the exceptional Heale House Gardens and Plant Centre. The beautifully landscaped gardens lie within the eight-acre grounds of Heale House, an elegant mansion dating from the late 16th century which was built in an idyllic position beside the River Avon. (Open daily, 10am to 5pm, all year round).

The Old Bakery, Netton, Nr. Salisbury Tel: 01722 73351

Two narrow roads, one on the east bank, one on the west, follow almost every bend in the river which along this stretch is shallow, wide and fast-flowing. Head for the only bridge which connects the villages of **NETTON** and **UPPER WOODFORD** but before crossing, make a point of calling in at the Old Bakery in Netton. Now the charming home of Valerie Dunlop, the Old Bakery offers first-rate bed and breakfast accommodation. As its name suggests, the house was converted from the former village bakery and the garden here is lovely. Guests can look out on some of the few remaining water meadows in England to be properly worked, and an evening stroll across the meadows to the village pub proves an enchanting experience. Valerie is a friendly hostess and excellent cook whose breakfasts are renowned. All three guest rooms are cosy and extremely comfortable, making this a marvellous place to stay and explore the many places of interest in the area.

Having crossed onto the western bank of the River Avon, continue north along the Woodford Valley then turn west towards Stonehenge.

Stonehenge

For one of the most famous Megalithic sites in Europe, STONEHENGE appears strangely dwarfed by the open expanse of Salisbury Plain, and it's not until it is approached on foot through the tunnel under the A360 that the true scale of this spectacular Bronze Age monument becomes clear. In fact, some of its great stones stand over twenty feet high and are embedded up to eight feet in the ground. The central area consists of an inner horseshoe and an outer ring of massive sarsen (or 'foreign') stones with lintels which are thought to have been brought all the way from the Marlborough Downs. Some time earlier, a double outer circle of eighty 'bluestones' had been erected which are believed have been quarried in the Preseli Hills in Dyfed and then transported over 200 miles to Salisbury Plain.

The largest bluestone, the Alter Stone, is set at the very centre of the formation and from here, the Heel Stone can be seen some 256 feet away. On the longest day each year, the sun rises over this stone leading experts to conclude that the site was constructed for the purpose of observing ancient sun worshipping rituals. Stonehenge is owned and managed by English Heritage. (Open daily, all year round. Admission charge payable; free to English Heritage and National Trust members).

The A360 Amesbury to Devizes road is one of the few routes across the central expanse of Salisbury Plain. Four miles northwest of Stonehenge and just to the north of this road, is the village of **ORCHESTON**, a remote community lying at the head of a small river on the edge of Salisbury Plain.

Here you will discover some charming accommodation at **Cozens House**. The hosts, Penelope and Antony Smith, are two real country lovers who offer their many guests peace and tranquillity at their detached, self-contained cottage which is fully equipped for self-catering as well as bed and breakfast. There are twin bedrooms, one of which is en-suite, and bed and breakfast is also available in the main house. The surrounding gardens are delightful and feature a superb Grade II listed grain store. As a peaceful haven from which to explore nearby Salisbury, Stonehenge, the New Forest and other such places of interest, Cozens House is hard to beat.

Cozens House, Orcheston, Salisbury Tel: 01980 620257

From Orcheston, head south once again and retrace your steps onto the A303 near **WINTERBOURNE STOKE**. This village can be easily missed, being tucked away off the main road down a cul-de-sac; however, its charming stone-built cottages, 13th-century church and flint-and stone-fronted manor house are well worth a detour. A series of about twenty burial mounds, or barrows, can be found to the east of the village, most of which were constructed by the Beaker people who migrated here from continental Europe around 2000 BC.

Three miles to the west of Winterbourne Stoke, and just to the north of the A303, lies the spectacular but little-visited Iron Age hill fort of Yarnbury Castle. Dating from the 2nd century BC, the fort's series of grassy banks and ditches enclose an area of some 28 acres which are a haven of tranquillity compared with the organised commotion of Stonehenge. The fort has an earlier earthwork fortification at its centre and enjoys spectacular views over the southern fringe of Salisbury Plain.

A couple of miles to the southwest, the village of WYLYE was once an important junction and staging post on the London to Exeter coaching route. At one time, the village boasted nine inns although today, only the 14th-century Bell Inn remains. A statue near the bridge over the River Wylye (from which Wilton and Wiltshire get their names) commemorates a post-boy who was sadly drowned after rescuing several passengers from a stagecoach which overturned at this point during a flood.

Leaving Wylye, there is a minor road which runs parallel to the A36 along the southwestern bank of the river. The six-mile stretch to the southeast of the village contains some delightful unspoilt communities, including the three LANGFORDs (Little, Steeple and Hanging) with their chequered flint houses and thatched brick cottages, and GREAT WISHFORD with its 17th-century almshouses, 18th-century village fire engine and unusual sign on the churchyard wall recording the price of bread at various points in the last 200 years (in 1800 the cost was 3s 4d a gallon, in 1904 only 10d, and in 1924 2s 8d). Each year on Oak Apple Day (May 29th), the citizens of Great Wishford celebrate their ancient right to cut and gather timber in nearby Grovely Wood by marching onto the wooded ridge and returning with freshly cut branches. Later in the day, a party from the village dance on the green in front of Salisbury Cathedral carrying bundles of sticks known as 'nitches'.

A little upstream from Great Wishford lies the attractive village of STAPLEFORD, site of the Norman castle which once was owned by William the Conqueror's chief huntsman, Waleran. The village church dates from the same period and contains some

Wilton

Royal Wilton Carpet Factory

impressive banded columns. A stone bench can be seen in the church porch which is marked out with the grid of the medieval board game, nine men's Morris.

WILTON, the capital of Saxon Wessex and third oldest borough in England, lies on the River Wylye midway between Stapleford and Salisbury. The town is renowned throughout the world for its carpets which are still woven at the Royal Wilton Carpet Factory, an enterprise which was given a royal charter by William III in 1699. The carpets are manufactured along traditional lines from local wool and indeed, four sheep fairs continue to be held each year in the town between August and November. The old part of Wilton is centred around the market square which contains a number of interesting buildings, including an 18th-century town hall and the half-ruined Church of St Mary.

On the western edge of town, Wilton House stands on a site originally occupied by an abbey which was founded by Alfred the Great. After the abbey was dissolved by Henry VIII, this superb piece of land was given to Sir William Herbert who was created Earl of Pembroke in 1551; it has remained in his family ever since. After a devastating fire destroyed the original building in 1647, the house was rebuilt by Inigo Jones who was responsible for creating the magnificent single and double 'cube' rooms with their lavish gilt decorations. At the beginning of last century, the north and west fronts were remodelled by James Wyatt who also designed the Gothic-style cloisters.

Today, Wilton House contains an outstanding collection of works of art including furniture by Chippendale and Kent, and paintings by Rembrandt, Van Dyke, Rubens and Tintoretto. There is also a famous collection of over 7000 model soldiers and a magnificent Tudor kitchen. During World War II, the house was used as an operations centre for southern command and the Normandy landings are believed to have been planned here. The grounds of Wilton House are also well worth discovering; originally laid out by Isaac de Caus, they are known for their distinctive cedar trees, Roger Morris' Palladian bridge of 1737, and Sir William Chambers' casino. (Open daily, from 11am to 6pm and from 12 noon on Sundays; Easter to mid-October. Admission charge payable.)

The lovely small village of BURCOMBE lies a couple of miles west of Wilton on the banks of the River Nadder and if you are looking for an exceptional place to stay then keep an eye out for **Manor Farm**. Your friendly hostess, Sue Combes, takes great pride in offering her guests top class accommodation and excellent home cooking. Her enthusiasm and joie de vivre is infectious and a stay here is sure to leave you revitalised and refreshed. Breakfasts here are wonderful; Sue uses only fresh local produce and provides a tasty and substantial meal that sets you up for the day perfectly. The farmhouse's walled garden is a delight, particularly in spring and autumn, as are the walks across the farm onto the Downs.

Manor Farm, Burcombe, Salisbury, Tel: 01722 742177

Four miles to the southwest of Burcombe, the A30 passes close to the famous Fovant Hill Regimental Badges which were carved into the side of the chalk escarpment by soldiers stationed nearby during the two World Wars. After taking a look at these, turn north in Fovant village to reach the two National Trust-owned properties which are located near the lovely hillside village of DINTON. The first, Little Clarendon, is a small, yet impressive early-Tudor manor house which is located quarter of a mile east of Dinton church. (Open to the public by prior written appointment only. Admission charge payable; free to National Trust members.)

The second property is situated to the west of the village on the northern side of the B3089. Philipps House is a handsome white-fronted neo-Grecian residence which was designed by architect Jeffry Wyattville in the early 19th century. It stands within the attractive landscaped grounds of Dinton Park and is administered and maintained by the Young Women's Christian Association as an arts and cultural centre. (Open to the public by prior arrangement only; contact the Warden. Admission charge payable; free to National Trust members). Dinton village also contains the 17th-century Lawes Cottage which is the former home of composer and associate of John Milton, William Lawes. Part of his score for Milton's Masque of Comus is believed to have been written here in 1634.

The final area to explore in this part of Wiltshire is the delightful upper Ebble Valley, so retrace your steps back to Fovant before continuing south along a small country lane towards the Saxon village of **BROADCHALKE**. This is the former home of the 17th-century diarist, John Aubrey, whose family owned a small estate in the village. Aubrey was a warden at the parish church and lived in the Old Rectory; he was also a keen angler and wrote of his beloved River Ebble, 'there are not better trouts in the Kingdom of England than here'.

The Queen's Head, Broadchalke, Salisbury, Tel: 01722 780344

Broad Chalke is also the home of the first-rate Queen's Head Inn. The ambience here is best described as one of peace and plenty; there is a lovely inglenook fireplace which adds warmth and character to the bar, and outside, there is a secluded patio garden where customers can enjoy a quiet drink on a fine summer's day. The superb restaurant menu often features local fish and game along with old-fashioned dishes such as jugged hare or game pie, followed by mouthwatering homemade desserts such as chocolate ripple cheesecake or walnut and treacle tart. Finally, having satisfied your appetite, what could be better than to retire to one of the four excellently equipped, self-contained guest rooms which are situated off the rear courtyard.

CHAPTER TWO

Westbury to the Dorset Border

Chalcot House

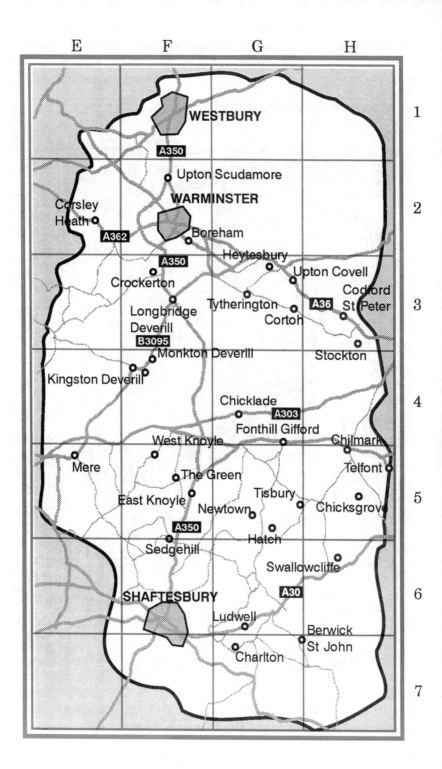

Entrance to the Main Hall, Wardour Castle

CHAPTER TWO

Westbury to the Dorset Border

The village of **BERWICK ST JOHN** lies at the head of the Ebble Valley and just to the north of the steep ridge of chalk downland known as Cranborne Chase. According to local legend, it is possible to summon the Devil by cursing at the top of one's voice while walking seven times around Winkelbury Camp, the ancient Iron Age hill fort which lies to the north of the village. When called in this manner, Satan is said to appear riding a black horse and will grant his summoner one wish.

The possible appearance of the Devil is perhaps at the root of one of Berwick St John's less unnerving customs. Thanks to a legacy left by the vicar for this purpose, the church bells were tolled for ten minutes at eight o'clock each night to direct travellers lost on the downs to safety, a custom which lasted for over 200 years between the mid-18th-century and the Second World War.

On leaving Berwick St John, head towards Ludwell on the A30, before turning south onto the country road which connects with the B3081 Shaftesbury to Tollard Royal road. This road runs along the western edge of the National Trust-owned Win Green Hill, the highest point in Cranborne Chase (and indeed, in Wiltshire) which is crowned by a copse of beech trees set around an ancient 'bowl' barrow. From the top of the hill, there are wonderful views northwest to the Mendip Hills and southeast to the Isle of Wight.

The village of **TOLLARD ROYAL** stands in the heart of Cranborne Chase a couple of miles to the southeast. The community's royal connections date back to King John who had a small estate here and often hunted on the surrounding land which at that time was densely forested. A reminder of this once-great primeval forest is the fragmented belt of woodland known as the Inner Chase which runs along the downland ridge on both sides of Tollard Royal.

The name of King John is reflected in the village inn and in King John's House, an impressive part stone, part timber-framed residence dating from the 13th century which was once a royal hunting lodge. The building's immaculate present condition is largely due to one General Pitt-Rivers, an early and highly enthusiastic English archeologist who inherited the estate in the late 19th century and spent the last two decades of his life unearthing its many Bronze Age remains. The general founded a museum in the nearby village of Farnham to display his collection of historic discoveries; however, it was closed in the 1960s and its exhibits were transferred to Oxford and to Salisbury's South Wiltshire Museum which has a gallery named after him.

Tollard Royal's late-13th-century village church is dedicated, somewhat unusually, to St Peter Ad Vincula (St Peter in chains); it contains the tomb of General Pitt-Rivers and stands within a delightful churchyard a short distance from the village centre. The general was also responsible for laying out nearby Larmer Tree Gardens, the original 'larmer' tree being the place where King John met up with his hunting party.

From Tollard Royal, retrace your steps down Zigzag Hill and continue northwest along the B3081 towards Shaftesbury. After a couple of miles make a short diversion to ASHMORE, a charming village which lies just over the Dorset border to the west of the main road. At over 700 feet above sea-level, this is the highest village in Dorset; all the more incredible, then, that Ashmore should have a gigantic village pond, 40 yards in diameter and 16 feet deep in the middle. The village is recorded in the Domesday Book as Aisemare, meaning the pond by the ash tree, and even in the most severe drought, this unlikely body of water is said never to have dried up. The inhabitants of the village celebrate its continuing presence in the Filly Loo ceremony which takes place each year around midsummer; while a band plays on a platform in the centre of the pond and teams of Morris dancers from all over the region dance around the edge.

The lovely Dorset border town of SHAFTESBURY is referred to as 'Shaston' in the novels of Thomas Hardy and the town is perhaps best known for its steep cobbled street, Gold Hill, which was featured in a famous 1980's television commercial for brown bread. Lined on one side with old cottages and on the other with an enormous medieval buttressed wall, this unique curved thoroughfare leads up to a 700 foot summit which provides some glorious views over Blackmoor Vale.

An abbey for nuns was founded in Shaftesbury by King Alfred around 888 AD, his daughter Aethelgifa being the first abbess. Some decades later, the fifteen year-old Anglo-Saxon king, Edward the Martyr, was buried here after being murdered in 978, an event which made Shaftesbury an important place of pilgrimage for many years. The abbey was finally dissolved in 1539 on the orders of Henry VIII; however, shortly before, the abbess is rumoured to have concealed the abbey's considerable treasure somewhere in the town. According to local legend, the only one to know its hiding place is the ghost of a monk who is sometimes seen walking on the site of the old abbey.

Wardour Castle

From Shaftesbury, join the A30 and drive east into Wiltshire for six miles before turning north to reach the village of **ANSTY**. The next destination is Old Wardour, a ruined 14th-century castle which is signposted from the village along a narrow lane. In 1643, the 61 year-old Lady Arundel and a garrison of fifty Royalist guards held the castle for six days against a 1300-strong Parliamentarian force. She is believed to have surrendered only after being offered acceptable terms; however, these were immediately disregarded by Cromwell's troops and the indomitable lady was thrown into the castle dungeons from where she is said to have escaped through a secret passage, probably a castle drain. To avenge the Parliamentarian treachery, her son returned to besiege the castle, an operation which eventually led to its destruction.

Present-day visitors to Wardour can view the remains of the old castle with its unique hexagonal courtyard and unusual grotto close by. The site stands within the grounds of the 'new' Wardour Castle, an 18th-century Palladian mansion which is now a girls' school and not open to the public. A exceptionally fine baroque chapel adjoins the school which has a striking interior and contains some impressive works of art.

A couple of miles further north, make a point of stopping in the village of TISBURY, home of what is claimed to be the largest surviving tithe barn in England. Tithe barns were constructed to store 'tithes', one tenth of the local farm tenants' crops, which were payable to the owners of church lands. The barn at Tisbury stands on the medieval Place Farm and once belonged to the Abbess of Shaftesbury's estate. Much of the old farmyard remains, including its impressive 14th-century double gatehouse and nearby outbuildings. The massive 190 foot long barn was built of stone in the 15th century and has thirteen pairs of storage bays. Its thatched roof covers a third of an acre and its complex structure of timber posts and beams gives it an almost cathedral-like quality.

Elsewhere in Tisbury, the 13th-century village Church of St John the Baptist has a splendid carved roof and a pulpit, pews and font cover dating from the 17th century. A tall spire stood on top of the church tower until it collapsed in 1762. The elegant Palladian-style Georgian country residence known as Pyt House lies two and a half miles west of the village; this was the scene of a famous confrontation between angry farm workers and mounted soldiers during the agricultural protests of 1830. (Open Wednesdays and Thursdays, 2.30pm to 5pm between May and September).

A number of interesting small communities lie on the northern side of the Nadder Valley to the northwest of Tisbury. The most westerly of these, CHILMARK, is the site of the famous quarry from which the stone for Salisbury Cathedral, Wilton House and many other fine buildings in the area was taken. Stone was first quarried here by the Romans and several centuries of workings have left a network of deep tunnels and vaults which are now used by the Ministry of Defence for storing arms and ammunition.

Stone from Chilmark's quarry is much in evidence in the delightful villages of TEFFONT MAGNA and TEFFONT EVIAS a couple of miles further east. The settlements take their name from the Anglo-Saxon words teo, meaning boundary, and funta, meaning brook; the name for the stream which connects them, the Teff, has similar roots. In both villages, the old thatched cottages are connected to the outside world by a series of attractive small bridges over the stream.

The Old Rectory, Chicklade Tel: 01747 89226

Just to the north of Teffont Magna, and on the western side of the minor road which connects the village with the A303, is Farmer Giles Farmstead, a 175-acre working livestock farm which is open to visitors. Attractions include a herd of 150 dairy cows, Shire horses, Highland cattle, Shetland ponies, sheep, goats, rabbits and a variety of domestic fowl, all of which can be seen at close quarters. Visitors can try their hand and milking a Jersey cow or bottle-feeding a baby lamb, or enjoy a leisurely stroll around this beautiful stretch of Wiltshire farmland. There is also an interesting exhibition on the history of farming, a pond stocked with rainbow trout, and children's adventure area containing old tractors and

35

several up-to-date pieces of playground equipment. (Open daily, 10.30am to 6pm between late-March and early-November; also weekends during November and December. Admission charge payable.)

Just on the other side of the A303 is **CHICKLADE. The Old Rectory** has been described by someone who had previously visited there, as "a place where you will experience the courtesy and charm of a gentler age; a time when life moved at a more leisurely pace". This was exactly what you will find. It is situated in this beautifully unspoilt part of Wessex, where the borders of Wiltshire and Dorset meet with Somerset.

The Rectory is a fascinating house, full of period charm and character, and parts of the building date back to the 17th century. The gardens are beatiful, having been lovingly cared for and of course with the advantage of trees and shrubs that have matured over the years.

The accomodation offers spacious and comfortable bedrooms, furnished in a traditional style, each having hot and cold water, razor points and electric heaters. If you have young children, Mr and Mrs Ballard, who own The Old Rectory, will be delighted to babysit for you. You will take your meals in a lovely sunny room, decorated in soft pinks and greys which highlight the highly polished dark wood of the tables and chairs. The Old Rectory is licensed, so you will be able to enjoy a drink if you wish.

Heading northwards once again, join the A303 for a short distance before turning northwest onto the minor road which runs parallel to the A36 Salisbury to Warminster road. This road follows the course of the upper Wylye river and passes through a series of charming small settlements. An Elizabethan merchant named Topp was responsible for building Stockton House, a handsome residence with mullioned windows and banded flint stonework; he also constructed Stockton's elegant almshouses which are set around three sides of a square courtyard a short distance away.

Next, why not have a look at the sister villages of **CODFORD ST MARY** and **CODFORD ST PETER**. The villages lie near the prehistoric remains of Codford Circle, an ancient hilltop meeting place which stands 617 feet up on Salisbury Plain. The church in Codford St Peter contains an exceptional Saxon stone carving which is said to date from the 9th century. Thought to be part of a stone cross, it features a man holding a branch who is engaged in some kind of ritual dance. It is a surprisingly powerful piece and is widely regarded as one of Wiltshire's finest treasures.

In Codford you will discover the impressive **George Hotel**, a first-rate establishment which stands in the heart of the village. Located on the edge of Salisbury Plain and within easy reach of the Marlborough Downs and the Nodden Valley, this charming hostelry is a marvellous place to stay. The restaurant here serves an extensive and varied menu which includes such mouthwatering dishes as deep-fried Camembert, homemade steak and oyster pie, and chicken Kiev. There are also various bar snacks available ranging from wholesome sandwiches to substantial hot meals. The George also offers an imaginative vegetarian menu and has a well-deserved reputation for using fresh, local produce. Whatever your tastes, this is the ideal base for touring this lovely part of the country.

The George Hotel, Codford, Nr. Warminster Tel: 01985 50270

A mile or so further upstream at UPTON LOVELL is the Prince Leopold, a lovely inn dating back to 1887 and stands on the banks of the River Wylye. It was named after Queen Victoria's youngest son who used to drink here when he lived in nearby Boyton. Today, it is a popular establishment run by Pamela and Graham Walden-Bradley which offers a wide selection of real ales and an extensive range of first-class bar meals; alternatively, you can enjoy an intimate dinner in the charming restaurant. There are also four lovely en-suite guest rooms available and at the end of the evening, you will be glad you decided to stay. The Prince Leopold also has easy access to historic Bath, Salisbury, Longleat and Stonehenge providing you with ideas for the next day's touring.

Prince Leopold, Upton Lovell, Nr. Warminster Tel: 01985 50460

Continuing up the Wylye Valley leads you to the old ecclesiastical centre of HEYTESBURY. During Norman times, the village Church of St Peter and St Paul was a collegiate institution with its own dean and chapter of canons. Much of this fine cruciform building dates from the 13th century, though like many of its rural counterparts throughout Wiltshire and Gloucestershire, the building was extensively 'restored' during the Victorian era. On this occasion, however, the refurbishment was carried out under the careful supervision of architect William Butterfield. The present-day church interior contains a number of interesting features, including some fine fan-vaulting and an intricate stone screen in the north transept. The almshouse known as the Hospital of St John was founded in Heytesbury by the Hungerford family during the 15th century. The original structure burnt down in the mid-18th-century and was replaced by the Georgian building which can be seen today.

Heytesbury's ecclesiastical past is reflected in the name of its splendid pub, the Angel Coaching Inn. Standing in the heart of the old village, this delightful establishment is run by Sue Smith and Philip Roose-Francis. A true hostelry, it preserves the tradition of good food, fine ale and first-class accommodation. Sue is a Cordon Bleu chef and the restaurant food is both mouthwatering and beautifully presented, while Philip maintains equally high standards in the bars which serve excellent real ales and a quality wine list which includes some very rare vintages. The beautifully-appointed bedrooms all have en-suite facilities and provide an atmosphere of great charm and comfort. This really is an enchanting place to stay and not to be missed.

Angel Coaching Inn, The High Street, Heytesbury,
Nr. Warminster Tel: 01985 40330

One of the strangest villages in Wiltshire lies within the Salisbury Plain military training area to the north of Heytesbury. The ghost-village of **IMBER** remains permanently out-of-bounds to the public except on the one or two occasions each year when special permission to go there is granted by the Ministry of Defence. The inhabitants were evicted from their homes by the army in 1943 on the understanding that they would be allowed to return after the War. However, the MoD failed to keep its promise and the villagers remain in exile to this day. All that remains of their community is the shell of the parish church and a collection of decaying timber and brick-built cottages, many of which have been given concrete frontages to provide more realistic conditions for training soldiers in modern street fighting. A church service is held in the village each September in commemoration of the lost community.

On leaving Heytesbury, a nine-mile direct drive leads to the small town of **MERE**, a historic community which, thankfully, is now bypassed by the A303 trunk route. The town takes its name from one John Mere, a 14th-century merchant adventurer who founded a chantry in the Church of St Michael's. The church dates back to the 11th century and has a fine Perpendicular tower, one of the pinnacles of which has been hit by lightning three times this century, belying the old saying that lightning never strikes twice in the same place. Inside, there is some fine medieval glass, an octagonal font and a pair of monumental brasses believed to date from 1398 and 1426.

Mere

The Dorset dialect poet, William Barnes, lived adjacent to the church in the handsome 15th-century Old Chantry; he also ran his own school in a room above the Old Market Hall in the town square. The square is also the site of a Victorian clock tower which was gifted to the townspeople by the Prince of Wales in 1868. Among the other distinctive buildings in Mere are its two old coaching inns, the Old Ship with its 18th-century wrought-iron sign commemorating the family crest of John Mere, and the Talbot which claims to have been visited by Charles II following the Royalist defeat in the Battle of Worcester (he is said to have gone on to stay at Zeals House, a couple of miles further west). Magnificent views over Blackmoor Vale can be enjoyed from the top of nearby Castle Hill, the site of a now-demolished fortification built by Richard, Earl of Cornwall.

STOURTON is home of the famous Stourhead House and Gardens. The village itself is a neat community of estate cottages which lies at the bottom of a steep wooded valley (cars are normally left in the car park on the ridge above). It is especially pretty during the daffodil season, and again in early-summer. The main attraction here, however, is the beautiful country house and landscaped grounds which make up the famous Stourhead estate.

The house at Stourhead was built between 1722 and 1724, with the library and picture gallery added a few years later, for a wealthy Bristol banker, Henry Hoare. It was designed in Palladian style by architect Colen Campbell and is one of the first examples of a Georgian country mansion. The interior contains a superb collection of works of art, including furniture by Chippendale the Younger, intricate woodcarving by Grinling Gibbons and a collection of paintings and sculpture by such artists as Angelica Kauffman and Michael Rysbrack.

Stourhead House and Gardens

It was the original owner's son however, the second Henry Hoare, who made the biggest impression on the estate. Between 1741 and 1780, he designed and laid out one of the finest 18th-century gardens in Europe. Using a wide range of classical and contemporary influences, he created a wonderful combination of

41

carefully designed vistas and woodland walks. Special features include the 14th-century High Cross which was brought here from Bristol in 1765, a graceful stone bridge over the lake, a neo-Roman pantheon and an exquisite white-painted stone rotunda known as the Temple of the Sun. The gardens also contain a magnificent range of rare trees and shrubs, including rhododendrons, azaleas and tulip trees, and are crisscrossed by a series of beautiful woodland walks and open pathways. In 1946, the Hoare family presented Stourhead to the National Trust who have continued the process of introducing unusual plant varieties. (House open daily, except Thursdays and Fridays, 12 noon to 5.30pm; 1st April to 1st November. Garden open daily, 8am to 7pm or dusk if earlier; all year round. Admission charge payable; free to National Trust members).

On the northwestern edge of the estate, a 160 foot triangular redbrick folly stands at the top of the 790 foot Kingsettle Hill. King Alfred's Tower was built by Flitcroft in 1772 in commemoration of the great King of Wessex who is believed to have raised his standard against the Danes at this point in 878. Those climbing to the top are rewarded with a glorious view which takes in the three counties of Wiltshire, Dorset and Somerset. The tower lies three and a half miles by road from Stourhead House. (Open daily except Mondays and Fridays, 2pm to 5.30pm between 1st April and 1st November. Admission charge payable; free to National Trust members). The National Trust also owns Whitesheet Hill, the site of an Iron Age hill fort, which can be found on the Stourhead estate some distance northeast of the main gardens.

Leaving Stourhead, heading north, a country lane leads to the ancient village of HORNINGSHAM. The village name is believed to mean 'bastard's farm' from the Early English words horning, meaning bastard, and ham meaning farm. Reference to the settlement is made in the Domesday Book of 1086, although evidence exists of earlier occupation by the Romans. Noteworthy buildings in the present-day village include St John the Baptist's church with its medieval tower, the 18th-century Bath Arms inn, a row of 14th- to 16th-century thatched almshouses, and the historic Old Meeting Place which was built in 1568 as a place of worship by Presbyterian masons who were brought down from Scotland to work at Longleat House.

Top quality farmhouse accommodation can be found at Horningsham's Mill Farm, a delightful establishment in a wonderful tranquil location. Run by John and Vera Crossman, this beautiful Georgian mill has been providing first-class bed and breakfast accommodation for more than thirty years. To the front, there is a truly picturesque mill lake with resident swans, ducks and geese which is part of the Longleat Estate. Set in a perfect picture-postcard location and built on several different levels, the converted Mill House offers attractively furnished guest rooms with superb views. The house combines the old Butcher's and Baker's farms which, together with Mill Farm, supported the self-sufficient village of Horningsham for over 250 years.

Mill Farm, Horningsham, Nr. Warminster Tel: 01985 844333

One of England's most famous stately homes, LONGLEAT, lies a mile to the north of Horningsham. This magnificent Elizabethan mansion was designed by Robert Smythson for Sir John Thynne, an ancestor of the present-day owner, the Marquess of Bath. Built to a largely symmetrical design, the imposing three-storey building was begun in 1568 and was still under construction at the time of Thynne's death in 1580. Over the centuries, the house has been furnished with some superb furniture and works of art, including tapestries, velvet and leather work, and paintings by Titian and Reynolds. Other noteworthy features include the state coach, the Victorian kitchen, the family's official robes and the waistcoat worn by Charles I at the time of this execution.

One of Longleat's most notorious inhabitants is the ghostly Green Lady who is said to wander the top-floor corridor. She is believed to be the spirit of Louisa Carteret whose husband, Thomas Thynne, the second Viscount Weymouth, is alleged to have killed her lover in a duel. He then concealed the body in the cellar where it remained until it was accidentally discovered under the stone-flagged floor earlier this century.

The grounds of Longleat House were landscaped by Capability Brown and now contain one of the best-known safari parks in the country. The famous 'Lions of Longleat' are joined by a number of other exotic animals, including elephants, rhinos, zebras and white tigers. The park also features safari boat rides, a narrow gauge railway, children's amusement area, garden centre and maze, and can be very crowded on summer weekends. (House open daily, all year round. Safari Park open daily, except during the winter months. Admission charge payable).

The Bridge House, Nunney, Frome Tel: 01373 836329

The focus of the village of NUNNEY is its picturesque ruined castle; this was begun in 1373 by Sir John de la Mare on his return from the wars in France and is thought to be modelled on the Bastille. The structure is made up of four solidly-built towers which stand on an island formed by a stream on one side and a wide ten foot deep moat on the other. The castle came under Parliamentarian artillery fire during the English Civil War despite having a garrison of only one officer, eight men and a number of civilian refugees. After two days, the building was damaged beyond repair and the gallant Royalists surrendered.

One of the thirty-pound cannonballs which helped to demolish the castle walls is on view in Nunney's 13th-century All Saints' Church. This much-altered building also contains an interesting model of the castle in its original condition, as well as a number of tombs to the de la Mare family, including a stone effigy of Sir John. Nunney's old Market Place, which was granted a trading licence by the Crown in 1260, is also worth a visit.

Visitors to Nunney should also make a point of calling in at the charming Bridge House, an absolutely delightful Grade II listed house which is situated alongside Nunney Brook in the centre of this ancient medieval settlement. Your hostess Christine Edgely welcomes you with a smile into her enchanting home with its outstanding views of the surrounding countryside. She has a number of comfortable and attractively decorated en-suite guest rooms available, while downstairs there is a lovely intimate restaurant where diners can savour a variety of mouthwatering dishes ranging from the traditional to the more creative, accompanied by a bottle from carefully selected wine list. Take time to browse in Christine's lovely antique and bric-a-brac shop before exploring the castle or venturing out to some of the many other local places of interest.

Those keen to find an exceptional place to stay on the beautiful eastern fringe of the Mendip Hills should make the trip to CHELYNCH near DOULTING, five miles further west along the A361. You would have to go a long way to beat the farmhouse accommodation at Hurlingpot Farm, an attractive working dairy farm which lies somewhat hidden in the heart of this delightful settlement. The home of Jean Keevil, her wonderful Grade II listed Jacobean farmhouse is set in a Tudor walled garden containing beautiful flowers and a 150 year-old monkey puzzle tree. Inside, there are three elegantly furnished en suite guest rooms which offer every modern facility. The lovely country-style kitchen has a warm, bright atmosphere and provides the perfect setting for the superb breakfasts Jean serves each morning.

The next port of call is WARMINSTER, a historic wool and coaching town with three old inns and some handsome 18th- and 19th-century buildings. The organ in the 14th-century minster church was originally intended for Salisbury cathedral; similarly, Warminster's famous school, which was founded in 1707, contains a doorway which was designed by Christopher Wren and was originally installed at Longleat House. Two miles to the west, the 800 foot Cley Hill forms part of the ancient Ridgeway which once ran from South Devon to the Wash.

Hurlingpot Farmhouse, Chelynch, Doulting,
Shepton Mallet Tel: 01749 880256

To the north is the small market town of WESTBURY with its fine Georgian houses, impressive town hall and pleasant little market place. However, Westbury's best-known feature lies a couple of miles to the east of the town on the side of the 755 foot high Westbury Hill. Here, Wiltshire's oldest and most famous White Horse can be found which was carved into the chalk hillside in the 18th century. (An earlier figure is believed to have been carved here to commemorate King Alfred's defeat of the Danes in 878.) The head of the White Horse stands just below the ramparts of Bratton Castle, a spectacular Iron Age hill fort which covers 25 acres and can be reached via Bratton village. Those climbing to the top will be rewarded with outstanding views over the surrounding countryside and farmland.

Two miles to the east of Bratton, the village of EDLINGTON possesses a 14th-century church of almost cathedral-like proportions. During a rebellion against Henry VI's corrupt government in 1450, the Bishop of Salisbury was dragged from here and stoned to death on top of nearby Golden Hall Hill.

46

CHAPTER THREE

Trowbridge to Chippenham

Great Chalfield Manor

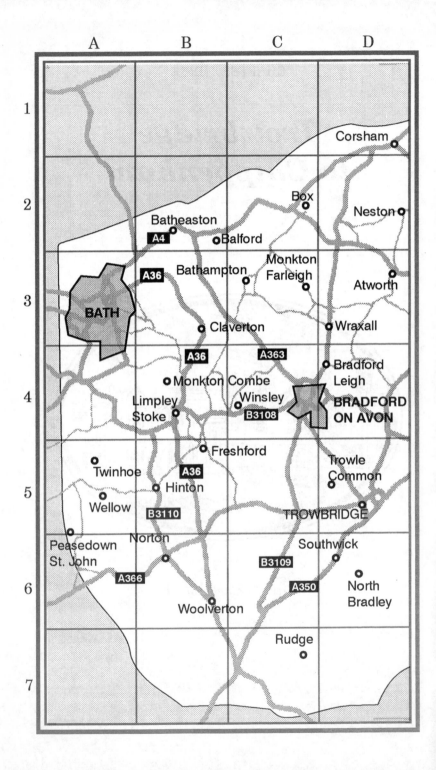

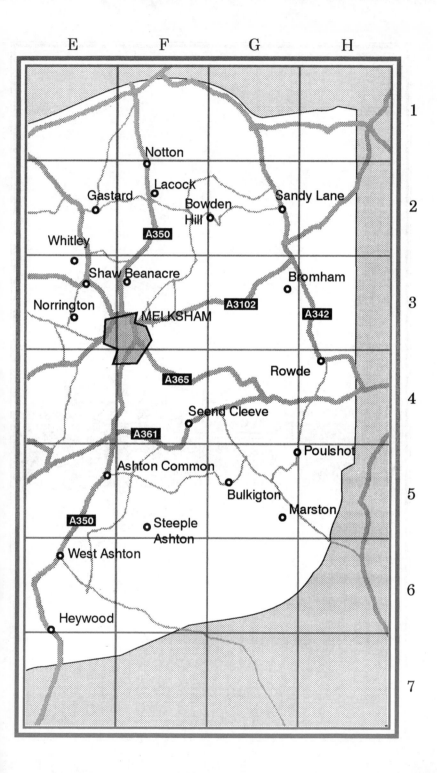

Corsham Court

CHAPTER THREE

Trowbridge to Chippenham

The first stop in the western area of central Wiltshire is the attractive village of **STEEPLE ASHTON**. Set within tranquil country lanes four miles to the southeast of Trowbridge, the most striking feature in the village is its 15th-century parish Church of St Mary the Virgin which, curiously enough, has no steeple (the original 93 foot spire was destroyed by lightning in 1670 and was never rebuilt). As well as some fine lierne vaulting and part-medieval stained-glass window lights, this impressive Perpendicular structure contains the renowned Samuel Hey Library which numbers among its catalogue the early-15th-century Book of Hours, an illustrated Latin prayer book containing recommended worship for every hour of the day.

Church Farm, High Street, Steeple Ashton, Trowbridge
Tel: 01380 870518

Other noteworthy features in Steeple Ashton include the Norman village cross with its four sundials, and the long main street with its unusual number of delightful old buildings, many of which are half-timbered and feature attractive red herringbone brickwork.

First-rate farmhouse accommodation is also available here at **Church Farm**, a working farm which is situated adjacent to Steeple Ashton's famous church. The truly unique farmhouse is largely constructed of soft red bricks set within a timber frame and has parts dating back to the 16th century. Inside, the bedrooms and reception rooms all have a marvellous quaint atmosphere yet have been tastefully updated to provide all the modern comforts. Mrs Cottle provides the warmest of welcomes including tea and farmhouse cake on arrival. Guests should make a point of finding the charming thatched summer house where they can relax and enjoy the sounds of the English countryside.

A couple of miles further west is Steeple Ashton's sister village of **WEST ASHTON**. This pleasant community is home to another excellent bed and breakfast establishment, **Ashton Hill Farm**, a lovely place to stay which can be found just off the Melksham to Westbury road. Sheena Awdry is your friendly welcoming hostess who goes out of her way to make you feel at home on her family's 400-acre working arable and beef farm. She is an excellent cook and will readily prepare a tasty farmhouse tea given prior notice. Enjoying a peaceful location on the banks of the River Biss, this is an ideal location for touring the Cotswolds, the West Country and Wiltshire. Children are welcome and guests are free to take a look around the farm, but check before you set off or you may meet up with Eric and Ernie, the pedigree bulls!

Ashton Hill Farm, West Ashton, Trowbridge Tel: 01225 760359

BECKINGTON is an attractive village with some fine attractions for visitors: a medieval castle, a 13th-century abbey, a church with a Norman tower and some lovely old gabled houses.

In the heart of the village is the locally-renowned **Woolpack Inn**, a superb 16th-century hostelry which has been sympathetically restored to provide every modern comfort in an atmosphere of mellow antiquity. The atmosphere in the bars and restaurant is cosy and welcoming. The food, too, is a sheer delight; the extensive menu offers excellent value for money and features such superb dishes as local game and fresh fish from Brixham. In fine weather, you can also eat outside in the high-walled, creeper-clad patio garden. The Woolpack's ten en-suite guest rooms are beautifully furnished and provide first-class accommodation in keeping with the age and character of the building.

The Woolpack Inn, Beckington, Nr. Bath Tel: 01373 831244

The historic village of NORTON ST PHILIP is only a short distance away. Much of the settlement's history seems to centre around the George, a wonderful old inn built in the 15th century by nearby Hinton Priory as a house of hospitality. This exceptional timber-framed building has oriel windows, a gallery to the rear, an unusual archway, and an overhanging first floor which was once used a cloth warehouse. The rebellious Duke of Monmouth made his headquarters here before the Battle of Sedgemoor in 1685, and according to legend, nine local men implicated in the ill-fated uprising were imprisoned here after the battle, in what is now the Dungeon Bar, before being burnt at the stake in a nearby orchard.

Some years earlier in 1668, there is a record of Samuel Pepys and his wife having dined at the George whilst on their way to Bath.

The village Church of St Philip was rebuilt in the 17th century and is believed to contain the grave of the Siamese-twin sisters who were born in the nearby hamlet of Foxcote. Their tombstone is now lost but is said to have been carved with a likeness of the girls who had 'two bodies upward and one stomach.'

The next stop is FARLEIGH HUNGERFORD, site of the once-impressive Farleigh Castle which was built in the late 14th century by Sir Thomas Hungerford, the first Speaker of the House of Commons. Sir Thomas had acquired the old manor house on the site and is said to have started to fortify the building without having first obtained permission from the Crown, a potentially serious offence which could have led to his disgrace. However, the Hungerfords were a powerful family who at one time owned land all the way to Salisbury and so were able to survive the king's displeasure.

In the 16th century, however, one member of the Hungerford family did succeed in upsetting royal sensibilities by locking up his wife for four years in one of the castle towers. He was eventually executed by Henry VII for 'treason and unnatural vice'. In the early 18th century, the castle changed hands, however the new owners saw the edifice more as a quarry than a place to live and removed most of the walls to build a new Gothic-style house on the opposite side of the village. Nevertheless, an impressive shell of towers and perimeter walls survived which was brought under the ownership of English Heritage earlier this century. The castle chapel of St Leonard's also remains intact; this contains an impressive 15th-century mural of St George, some striking stained glass, and a number of interesting tombs, including that of the first Sir Thomas Hungerford. (Open daily, 9.30am to 6.30pm; from 2pm Sundays and to 4pm in winter; all year round. Admission charge payable).

A minor road to the north of Farleigh Hungerford leads to the village of WESTWOOD, site of the National Trust-owned Westwood Manor. This charming stone-built manor house was constructed in the 15th century and then remodelled in the late 16th century. Its attractive landscaped grounds contain an interesting display of modern topiary and inside there are a number of impressive period features including some fine Jacobean

Lacock Abbey

plasterwork. (Open Sundays, Tuesdays and Wednesdays, 2pm to 5pm between 1st April and end-September. Admission charge payable; free to National Trust members).

Another interesting country house, Iford Manor, lies just to the west of Westwood. Although this handsome Tudor residence is not open to the public, its gardens are. Indeed, visitors come from all over the world to enjoy the grounds which were laid out in Italian style by the landscape architect Harold Peto prior to the First World War. The design is said to have been inspired by Edwin Lutyens and Gertrude Jekyll, and makes imaginative use of its idyllic setting beside the River Frome. Behind the house, the land rises sharply in a series of delightful terraces, and there are a number of pools, summerhouses and classical buildings which give the entire garden a wonderful romantic feel. (Open Wednesdays, Sundays and Bank Holiday Mondays between May and July. Admission charge payable).

Ilford Manor

Now the county town of Wiltshire, the roots of **TROWBRIDGE** go back beyond the Domesday Book. The modern town grew up around the Norman castle which belonged to the de Bohun family, the curved walls of which are indicated by the course of present-day Fore Street. For centuries it was an important weaving centre and by 1830, as many as nineteen mills were sited in the town. An unusual number of handsome stone-built townhouses can be seen in the present-day centre, most of which date from this period of prosperity.

The remodelled parish Church of St James was founded in 1483 by a wealthy cloth-maker on the site of its 12th-century predecessor and altered once again during the 19th century. It contains some lavish decorations and is crowned by one of the finest parish church spires in the county. The churchyard contains the grave of Thomas Helliber, a local weaver who allegedly led a rebellion against the introduction of cloth-making machinery; despite claiming his innocence, he was hanged in 1803 on the morning of his nineteenth birthday. The tomb of George Crabbe, one of the former church rectors, can be found in the chancel; an acknowledged poet, he was responsible for writing the work on which Benjamin Britten based his opera, Peter Grimes.

Another of Trowbridge's famous sons was Sir Isaac Pitman, the creator of the famous shorthand system, who was born in a now-demolished house in Nash Yard; Pitman Avenue, and a plaque and bust in the town hall commemorate his links with the town. An interesting collection of historic artefacts and locally-found relics are on display at the Trowbridge Museum in the civic hall. Items on show include a special collection of educational toys and children's games dating from the 18th century. (Open Tuesdays and Saturdays, 9.30am to 12.30pm, all year round).

Magnolia Lodge, 46 Wingfield Road, Trowbridge
Tel: 01225 763093

On the western side of Trowbridge David and Christine Harris, two charming hosts, run the first-rate bed and breakfast establishment, Magnolia Lodge. David is a former professional horticulturalist and his vast knowledge of plants is reflected in the many rare and exotic shrubs which can be found in the garden. The house itself is an elegant late-Victorian town villa with a bright welcoming atmosphere and a number of spacious bedrooms which are all appointed to a high modern standard. David and Christine provide their guests with warm hospitality and a first-rate Wiltshire breakfast. Given prior notice, they can also provide delicious evening meals which are served in the pleasant airy surroundings of the dining room.

Before moving on to Bradford-on-Avon have a look at **MELKSHAM**, a busy market town which is located to the northeast of Trowbridge. William the Conqueror is said to have granted the village of Melksham to his knight Britric Aluric, an event which is recollected in the name of the present-day Aloeric School. Like Trowbridge, Melksham was an important weaving centre and the large number of substantial 17th- and 18th-century merchants' houses around Canon Square stand as a testimony to this prosperous time.

Early in the 19th century, Melksham attempted to become a spa town following the discovery of a chalybeate spring and indeed a pump room was built which can still be seen on the Devizes road. However, competition from the more fashionable Bath Spa soon stifled its ambitions and by 1822 the project was abandoned. The destiny of the town turned out to lie with manufacturing and in 1819, a branch of the Wiltshire and Berkshire Canal was opened to link the town's many industrial concerns with the outside world. Although much changed, the town still retains its industrial feel.

Frane Lea Park, Church Lane, Forest, Melksham
Tel: 01225 707778

In the 13th and 14th centuries, the once densely forested countryside around Melksham was an important royal hunting area and indeed, the area to the northeast of the town is still known as Melksham Forest. Over the years, the forest has largely been cleared of trees, first for agricultural use and then, as Melksham's cloth-weaving industry continued to expand, for house building.

Today, the Forest is home to Frane Lea Park, a first-rate holiday park offering excellent self-catering accommodation. The park is situated within the landscaped grounds of a former farmhouse in Church Lane; it is a modern purpose-built development of seven single-storey cottages which is owned and immaculately maintained by Mr and Mrs Frane. The attractive luxury cottages vary in size and can accommodate either two, four or six persons. All are furnished and appointed to a very high standard with fully-equipped fitted kitchens, colour televisions and private gardens.

Returning to the centre of Melksham, join the A365 Box road and drive northwest for a couple of miles to reach the pleasant community of ATWORTH. The village Church of St Michael dates from the early-19th-century, with the exception of its saddleback tower which survives from an earlier rebuilding in the 15th century.

The Stone Barn Bed & Breakfast, Atworth Tel: 01225 706410

Atworth is also the location of a delightful place to stay, the Stone Barn at Manor Farm. Situated just three miles from Bradford-upon-Avon, this Grade II listed building has undergone extensive renovation and now provides first-class accommodation either on a bed and breakfast or self-catering basis. The rooms are all decorated and equipped to the highest standards with beautifully coordinated furnishings throughout. From the spacious breakfast room guests look out onto their own private garden, a real summer sun trap, and if they can tear themselves away, there are many interesting places within easy reach, such as historic Bath, the Kennet and Avon Canal, and slightly further afield, Stonehenge and Longleat.

The narrow country lanes to the south of Atworth lead you to the National Trust-owned Great Chalfield Manor, a superb Tudor manor house which lies three miles due west of Melksham. Begun in 1480, this delightful moated residence was built by Thomas Tropenell who also was responsible for constructing the bell tower and spire on the nearby 13th-century parish church. The house is approached through an arched gateway and across a polished stone courtyard which is overlooked by oriel windows. Inside, the many noteworthy features include an original Tudor screen, a impressive great hall and a dining room which contains a portrait of Tropenell. Great Chalfield Manor is lived in by the descendants of Major R Fuller who carried out substantial restoration work earlier this century. (Open for guided tours on Tuesdays, Wednesdays and Thursdays between 1st April and end-October. Admission charge payable; free to National Trust members).

Another National Trust-owned property lies a mile or so to the south of Great Chalfield in the village of HOLT. Known as The Courts, this was where local weavers came to settle their disputes until the end of the 18th century. The present-day building was constructed in neo-Gothic style around 1800 though it has an elegant decorated façade dating from around a century earlier. Regrettably, it is not open to the public; visitors are however welcome to tour the magnificent seven-acre garden, half of which is arranged in formal style with a lily pond, herbaceous borders and dividing yew hedges, and the rest being a wild garden with an arboretum. (Open daily except Saturdays, 2pm to 5pm between 1st April and 1st November. Admission charge payable; free to National Trust members).

Holt itself consists of a series of handsome 17th- and 18th-century houses set around a village green. The village was once a popular spa and indeed the old well can still be seen in the grounds of a local factory.

West of here is the historic market town of **BRADFORD-ON-AVON**. A settlement existed on this important riverside site long before the days of the Domesday Book; indeed, the town's oldest building, the Saxon church of St Lawrence, is believed to have been built by St Aldhelm around 700 AD. Once part of a monastery which was largely destroyed by the Danes, the building 'disappeared' for over a thousand years, during which time the townspeople used it as a school, a charnel house for storing the bones of the dead, and a residential dwelling.

Bradford-on-Avon

In 1858, a clergyman looking down from the hill above the town detected the cruciform shape of a church; further investigations on the site revealed two carved angels, a discovery which precipitated the removal of the surrounding buildings and led to the uncovering of the Saxon gem which can be seen today. Only 38 feet long and with a chancel arch only three feet wide, it is one of the smallest churches in the country.

Bradford-on-Avon also boasts an attractive Norman church which was extensively restored in the last century. Inside, it contains a number of interesting memorials including that of

61

Lieutenant-General Henry Shrapnel, an army officer who in 1785 invented the shrapnel shell.

One of the town's most distinctive features is its unique nine-arched bridge over the River Avon. Originally constructed in the 13th century for packhorse traffic, it was extensively rebuilt in the 17th century. The small, domed building towards the southern end of the bridge is a former chapel which was converted for use as the town gaol. John Wesley is said to have spent an uncomfortable night here; however, the two cells were more often required to house local drunks which led to the building being referred to as the 'Blind House'.

Another of Bradford's extraordinary buildings dates from the period when the town was under the administration of the nuns of Shaftesbury Abbey. By the 14th century, the increased output from the surrounding farms had created a problem in storing the 'tithes', one tenth of the annual farm produce. To solve this, a tithe barn 164 feet long and 33 feet wide was constructed near the river which had fourteen bays, four projecting porches and a roof consisting of 30,000 stone tiles weighing an estimated 100 tons. Today, this magnificent stone building houses an interesting agricultural museum which contains a unique collection of antique farm implements and machinery.

During the 16th and 17th centuries, Bradford-on-Avon stood at the heart of one of Britain's great sheep farming areas. As a result, the town became a major centre of the textile industry and attracted skilled weavers from all over Europe (the town is even said to have given the Bradford in Yorkshire its name). Despite protests from local self-employed cloth-workers, by the early 1800s there were thirty water-powered cloth-mills operating in the town. Within 100 years, however, all had been forced to close as the industry transferred to the industrialised North.

Lock Inn Cottage, 48 Frome Road, Bradford-on-Avon
Tel: 01225 868068

Bradford-on-Avon's prosperity was also partly due to its position on the important Kennet-Avon east-west waterway. A bridge over this famous canal is the unusual location of the Lock Inn Cottage, a unique canal-side café which is also a specialist gift shop and an efficient bike-hire service. Dick and Jane Barrow's surprising family home is filled with artefacts which are hand-painted in the characteristic rose and castle designs which have traditionally adorned British narrowboats. Bikes can also be hired here (by the hour, half-day or full-day) for journeys through the surrounding lanes or along the towpath to a Saxon church and medieval tithe barn. Dick and Jane's thriving canal-side tearoom offers a mouthwatering range of drinks, hot savouries, cream teas and ice creams which can be enjoyed inside, by the canal or taken-away.

The period of prosperity during the 16th and 17th centuries left a legacy of handsome old stone buildings in Bradford-on-Avon, the most notable of which is The Hall, a fine early-Jacobean residence which was built by John Hall in 1610 (the grounds may be visited by appointment). Other interesting structures in the town include The Shambles, a unique early shopping precinct, the Priory and Westbury House, all of which are worth a visit.

Woolley Grange Hotel, Woolley Green, Bradford-on-Avon
Tel: 01225 864705

If you are looking for a place to stay in Bradford-on-Avon you may be fortunate enough to find the **Woolley Grange Hotel and Restaurant** at **WOOLLEY GREEN**. Situated just off the B3105 one mile northeast of the town centre, this splendid Jacobean manor house was constructed of mellow bath stone in the early 17th century by the Randolph family. It stands within fourteen acres of beautiful landscaped grounds with wonderful southerly views of Salisbury Plain and the White Horse at Westbury. What

63

makes this fine country house hotel so exceptional, however, is that it actively welcomes (and makes excellent provision for) children of all ages. A further noteworthy characteristic is its superb food, prepared in distinctive country house style from produce grown in the Victorian walled garden or brought by local suppliers. Recommended.

Excellent bed and breakfast accommodation can be found at the aptly-named **Midway Cottage** in **FARLEIGH WICK**, an attractive hamlet which stands on the A363 midway between Bradford-on-Avon and the A4 at Bathford. (It also lies approximately midway between Trowbridge and Bath.) This lovely restored Victorian cottage is owned by Mrs Jayne Prole who provides her guests with comfortable accommodation and a truly splendid English breakfast. She has three letting bedrooms available, all equipped with en-suite facilities, colour televisions, telephones and tea/coffee making facilities. One bedroom is situated on the ground floor, and with only two small steps, is suitable for the less mobile. Midway Cottage is English Tourist Board two-crown commended, but is unsuitable for smokers.

Midway Cottage, Farleigh Wick, Bradford-on-Avon
Tel: 01225 782101

Not far away is the village of **MONKTON FARLEIGH** which has a lovely old church. The building dates from around 1200 and contains some fine Norman features, including the inner door and archway in the north porch. Much of the detail carries the familiar zigzag moulding which is characteristic of the period. The sturdy tower was built a little later in the 13th century to a saddleback design. Inside, there is an attractive Elizabethan carved pulpit and some fine pre-Reformation carving in the choir stalls.

Fern Cottage, Monkton Farleigh Tel: 01225 859412

There is a first-rate place to stay in Monkton Farleigh, Fern Cottage, an English Tourist Board commended bed and breakfast establishment which is owned and run by Christopher and Jenny Valentine. (For accurate directions, telephone the Valentines on 01225 859412.) Their charming stone-built residence dates from around 1680 and retains many of its original 17th-century features. Inside, it has been carefully and elegantly modernised and now offers a high standard of comfort in truly relaxed and tranquil surroundings. Christopher and Jenny are terrific hosts who offer their guests the warmest of welcomes and one of the best English breakfasts in Wiltshire.

To the northwest, following the country lanes, you will find the pleasant village of BATHFORD. Here, in Ashley Road, is a delightful bed and breakfast establishment, Bridge Cottage. This charming cottage is the home of Ros and Terry Bright, two fine hosts who offer their guests en-suite accommodation appointed to a high standard. They also serve a first-class breakfast in the guests' private dining room. Through the arches there is a lovely three-tier patio garden filled with tubs of flowers and lawns. There are wonderful views across the valley from the cottage, and from Bathford you can follow a beautiful country and canal walk across

65

the meadows to Bath - an enchanting experience which takes approximately one hour.

Bridge Cottage, Ashley Road, Bathford, Nr. Bath
Tel: 01225 852399

The straggling community of **BOX** lies on the A4 midway between Bath and Chippenham, three miles to the east of Bathford. The village has been inhabited since Roman times and building remains from this period are dotted throughout the surrounding area. High quality Bath stone is still quarried nearby; the village is perhaps best known, however, for being at the western end of Brunel's remarkable feat of civil engineering, Box Tunnel. The 1.8 mile-long tunnel took five years to build and when completed in 1841, it was the longest railway tunnel in the world. The west portal can be seen from a viewing point on the A4 where, in 1987, a plaque was erected to commemorate the completion of a major cleaning and restoration programme. According to local legend, the sun shines through the entire length of the tunnel on one occasion each year – sunrise on April 9th, Brunel's birthday.

For those keen to stay in Box, first-rate accommodation is offered at Cheney Cottage. This attractive residence is a picturesque neo-Elizabethan thatched house, nestling in four acres of beautiful gardens with outstanding views across the Box valley. Its peaceful location belies the fact that it lies only six miles from historic Bath, making it an ideal base from which to tour the magnificent local countryside and explore the historic sites of the area. The cottage provides double, twin and single rooms, all with washbasins and tea/coffee making facilities. Breakfast menus range from full English to the lighter continental, with special diets catered for by prior arrangement; packed lunches can also be supplied on request.

Cheney Cottage, Ditteridge, Box, Corsham Tel: 01225 742346

A settlement has existed at **CORSHAM** since before the days of the Romans and over the centuries it has grown to become a significant weaving and cloth-making centre. The old town High Street is filled with mellow cream-coloured Bath-stone buildings, many of which date from the 17th and 18th centuries.

75 High Street, Corsham, Wiltshire Tel: 01249 713366

Visitors to this ancient and picturesque town will find a lovely place to stay at **75 High Street**, a charming Grade II listed mid-18th-century house owned and run by Pat Rodger. Pat has been welcoming guests into her delightful home for over five years and has a knack for making them feel completely at home. Situated in the centre of Corsham, Pat's house overlooks the 16th-century Flemish weavers' cottages, giving visitors the feeling of having stepped back in time. The peace and tranquillity of this town is all pervasive, and you can't help but awake refreshed, relaxed and ready for the superb breakfast Pat prepares, wherever possible, using fresh Wiltshire produce.

Some of the most striking buildings in Corsham are the pedimented Hungerford Almshouses which were built in 1668 by the local lady of the manor, Dame Margaret Hungerford. The old warden's house, with its elegant bell tower and magnificent carved porch, is especially fine. Adjoining the almshouses is an old schoolhouse which still retains its 17th-century classroom layout, original seating and schoolmaster's pulpit-style desk.

At the other end of the High Street there is a row of gabled Flemish-style weavers' cottages which are particularly characteristic of the period. The nearby St Bartholomew's Church was built in the 12th century on the site of an earlier Saxon chapel. It was added to on a number of occasions, then extensively restored in 1874; however, it still retains a number of interesting period features, both inside and out.

Audrey's, 55 High Street, Corsham Tel: 01249 714931

Before visiting Corsham's most famous attraction, Corsham Court, why not have a bite to eat in the centre of town. Corsham High Street is lined with buildings of great architectural interest. At No. 55 there is one that dates back to 1906 and is now a spacious tearoom, Audrey's. It is situated just 100 yards along the road from Corsham Court and is open every day for morning coffee, lunch and afternoon tea. Audrey's is excellent value; everything is home-cooked and the menu includes such imaginative dishes as 'bacon hotpot'. The menu is changed regularly, but a good homemade soup is always available, along with a range of appetising dishes to tempt the palate.

Saxon monarchs visited the old royal manor at Corsham Court long before the Norman invasion. However, the present Elizabethan mansion with its imposing pedimented gateway was built in 1582 by 'Customer' Smythe, a high-ranking Collector of Customs in Queen Elizabeth I's London treasury. Additions to the building were made by Nash during the Georgian era, and the surrounding grounds were laid out by the famous 18th-century landscape gardener, Capability Brown, with later work being completed by Humphrey Repton. The gardens contain an unusual Gothic-style bathhouse and a large number of semi-tame peacocks which sometimes wander out of the grounds and strut down the High Street. Today, Corsham Court is owned by the Methuen family who originally acquired it to accommodate their outstanding collection of 16th- and 17th-century paintings and furniture. The collection has been built up over the years and is now on view to the public. (House and gardens open daily except Mondays and Fridays; 2pm to 4pm, and to 6pm between June and September. Closed mid-December to mid-January. Admission charge payable).

Those preferring farmhouse accommodation should try **Pickwick Lodge Farm** on the edge of Corsham. Go and call on Mrs Stafford, who owns the house with her husband, to see what sort of accommodation she has to offer. This warm-hearted lady will certainly ensure that anyone who stays with her is well catered for. The accommodation comprises of two letting rooms which are both warm and comfortably furnished. Children are very welcome and arrangements can be made for baby sitting if you have young ones and would like to take the opportunity of going out to one of the nearby villages for an evening meal. Mrs Stafford advises that the White Horse pub at Biddestone and The White Hart at Ford have excellent food. She herself only provides bed and breakfast.

Pickwick Lodge Farm, Corsham Tel: 01249 712207

Pickwick Lodge has quite a history; part of it is early 16th-century and the remainder 17th-century. It was once a shepherd's cottage with two rooms upstairs and two rooms downstairs, but additions and extensions have been made over the centuries without sacrificing any of its charm. Pickwick Lodge Farm provides an ideal base for exploring Corsham and the many other places of interest in the surrounding district.

69

Great Chalfield Manor

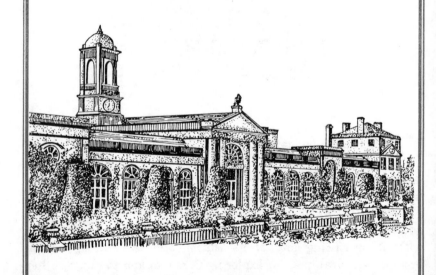

Bowood House

The network of minor country roads to the east of Corsham lead to the exquisite National Trust-owned village of LACOCK. Preserved as only an estate village can be, the buildings in Lacock are all said to be 18th-century or older. A stroll around the square of streets reveals a wonderful assortment of delightful mellow stone buildings, including the famous Red Lion Hotel in the High Street.

Another hostelry in Lacock worth a mention is The George, one of the oldest continuously licensed premises in the country. Lacock also possesses an exceptional 15th-century church, St Cyriac's, which contains a superb fan-vaulted chapel, some fine stained glass, the tomb of Sir William Sharington, and a memorial brass of Robert Baynard and his wife surrounded by their fifteen kneeling children.

The entire village once belonged to the estate of Lacock Abbey. This outstanding abbey and country mansion dates from 1232 when it was founded by Ela, Countess of Salisbury. Following the death of her father, Ela was married to Richard the Lionheart's stepbrother, William Longsword, and bore him several children. He, too, died shortly after returning from battle, and in her grief, she founded Lacock Abbey and continued to live on for another 35 years. The original cloisters, chapter house, sacristy and kitchens of the Augustinian nunnery still survive to this day.

However, much of the remainder of the present-day building dates from the mid-16th-century when the abbey was acquired by Sir William Sharington following the Dissolution of the Monasteries in 1539. He constructed an impressive country house around the abbey's core, which he left intact (with the exception of the chapel which was replaced by stables). He also built the elegant octagonal tower which overlooks the nearby River Avon.

The house remained in the Sharington family for a relatively short time, for in 1574, heiress Olive Sharington leapt from the roof into the arms of her lover, John Talbot, on hearing that permission for their marriage had been denied. Saved by her billowing undergarments and Talbot's heroic action, Olive was eventually given the go-ahead to wed her badly flattened suitor. The house then remained in the Talbot family until it was ceded to the National Trust in 1958. (Open daily except Tuesdays; 1pm to 5.30pm; between 1st April and 1st November. Admission charge payable; free to National Trust members).

Perhaps the most eminent member of the Talbot family was the photographic pioneer, William Henry Fox Talbot, who carried out most of his experiments at Lacock in the 1830s. Indeed, one of the earliest photographs ever produced shows a detail of one of the abbey's latticed oriel windows. The Fox Talbot Museum celebrates his many discoveries and is housed in the 16th-century tithe barn, a Grade I listed building which is situated near the abbey gates. (Open daily, 11am to 5.30pm between 1st March and 1st November. Admission charge payable; free to National Trust members).

Visitors who come to Lacock to view its beautiful buildings - the magnificent Abbey and the Fox Talbot Museum - should also make a point of calling in at **King John's Hunting Lodge Tearooms** in Church Street. The Hunting Lodge dates back to the 13th century and, in fact, predates the Abbey. It is also said to contain as many as six very friendly ghosts! Over the last decade, Robert and Jane Woods have built up an international reputation for serving the most delicious homemade scones and cakes, and the finest specially-blended teas. They also have two superb letting rooms available, one a family room with a four-poster and the other a medieval suite which overlooks the beautiful orchard tea gardens.

King John's Hunting Lodge, 21 Church Street, Lacock,
Nr. Chippenham Tel: 01249 730313

Marvellous farmhouse bed and breakfast accommodation can be found near Lacock at **Wick Farm**, a 15th-century manor farm which once belonged to Lacock Abbey and is now the charming home of Susan and Philip King. An absolute picture with Virginia creeper and winter jasmine climbing the walls, Wick Farm offers superb accommodation in its comfortably furnished guest rooms; it also offers one of the finest farmhouse breakfasts in the county. Wick Farm is also a coarse fishing enthusiast's paradise, with all types of fish available, including carp, chub and tench. The farm is also certified with the Camping and Caravanning Club as a 'Hideaway Site'. There are five delightful pitches and, with the ancient village and abbey of Lacock lying just down the road, an abundance of beautiful walks through the surrounding countryside.

Wick Farm, Lacock, Chippenham Tel: 01249 730244

Alternatively, those with touring caravans could try the Piccadilly Caravan Site in Folly Lane. Lying only half a mile from the centre of Lacock, this is a real haven for both caravanners and campers. Set in two and a half acres of secluded grounds in the rolling Wiltshire countryside, the site provides level ground for up to forty pitches. Excellent amenities are provided, including a shower and toilet block with hot and cold water, an Elsan disposal point, laundry room and children's play area; electric hook-ups are available for a small extra charge, gas cylinders and refills are available on site, and newspapers and milk can be delivered by arrangement. Ring for details on tel: 01249 730260.

From Lacock, continue eastwards along the country roads to the charming community of SANDY LANE.

The village contains an assortment of traditional cottages, the imposing George Inn, and one of the few thatched churches in England. Turning north onto the A342 Chippenham road and after a couple of miles you will reach Derry Hill, the entrance point to the splendid Bowood House. Concealed within the remains of Chippenham Forest, this elegantly proportioned country mansion has undergone a series of alterations since it was completely rebuilt in 1754. Designed in part by Robert Adam, the house includes an impressive library and a laboratory where Joseph Priestley first identified oxygen in 1774. Much of the building is now used to display an extensive art collection; the orangery is now a delightful picture gallery, and there are also fine displays of sculpture, watercolours, costumes and a collection of Indian relics which was accumulated by the present owner's great-grandfather when he served as the Viceroy of India between 1888-94.

The grounds of Bowood House cover an area of over 1000 acres and were laid out by Capability Brown; they include a magnificent landscaped lake with an Italianate cascade, over 150 species of well-labelled trees, and some pleasant woodland walks which are particularly spectacular during the rhododendron season. (The house and grounds are open daily, 11am to 6pm between mid-May and mid-June Admission charge payable). There is also a restaurant, shop and children's adventure play area.

Standing at a busy road junction in the sheltered valley of the River Marden, CALNE is a once-thriving weaving town which later became known as a meat-curing centre (for many decades, a Harris Bacon factory was located here). Calne also features some fine old almshouses in Kingsbury Street, an imposing 12th- to 15th-century parish church, and an impressive coaching inn, the Lansdowne Arms, which was built in the 18th century on the site of an earlier inn, the old brewhouse of which can still be seen in the yard.

The pleasant village of CHERHILL lies three miles further east along the A4. Today, this is a peaceful village with a hidden 14th- to 15th-century church and an excellent inn, the Black Horse, which is the only such establishment to survive from the days when this was an important staging post on the busy London-Bristol coaching route. The character of the village was very different in the 18th century when an infamous band of robbers known as the Cherhill Gang used to surprise passing travellers. Their intrusion was particularly startling in view of the fact that, before attacking, the gang were said to remove all their clothes to avoid being recognised.

At the Manor House in Cherhill, Trudy Oatley combines her successful interior design business with providing first-rate bed and breakfast accommodation. The present house dates back to the 15th century; however, the site has been occupied since ancient times and indeed, a fine Roman mosaic was discovered in the ruins of a villa which once stood adjacent to the present-day building. Trudy's flare for design, colour and arrangement is much in evidence throughout the house. The old manor has been beautifully and sympathetically restored, and provides accommodation and furnishings of a very high standard. Guests can make use of the outdoor swimming pool and tennis courts, or stroll round the gardens working up an appetite for the wonderful food which Trudy provides. With its beautiful views both inside and out, the Manor House is truly a delightful place to stay.

Trudy Oatley Interiors, Cherhill, Nr Calne Tel: 01249 817085

Cherhill Down, the chalk ridge to the south of the village, is the site of a famous White Horse which was cut in the hillside by Dr Christopher Alsop in 1790. The nearby Lansdowne Monument dates from 1845 and was built on the instructions of the Third Marquess of Lansdowne to commemorate his ancestor, Sir William Petty. This exposed hilltop is also the site of the ancient Iron Age earthwork, Oldbury Castle. Now owned by the National Trust, this 190-acre hill fort enjoys magnificent views of the Marlborough Downs and the Vale of Pewsey.

East Wiltshire

Devizes Castle

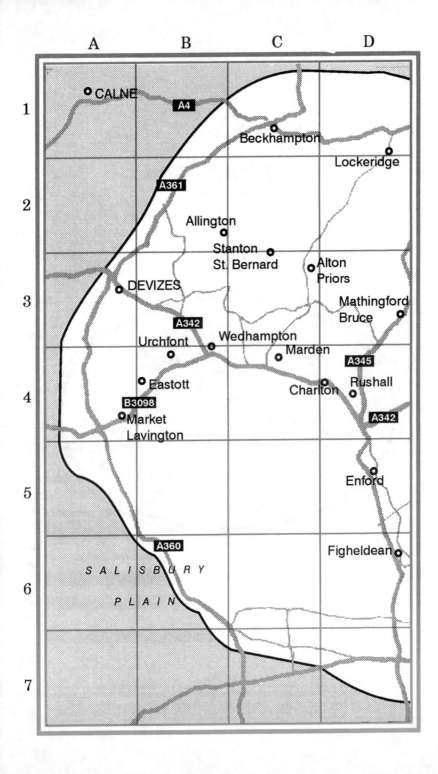

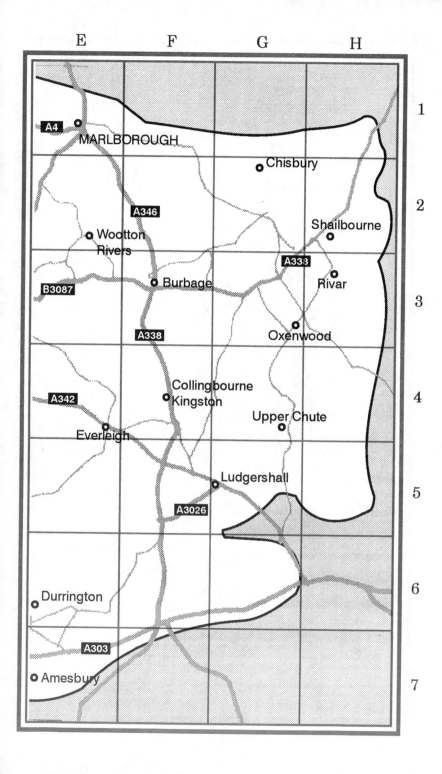

Devizes Cross

CHAPTER FOUR

East
Wiltshire

AVEBURY, in east Wiltshire, is an ancient settlement standing at the centre of one of the most important Megalithic monuments in Europe. The village stands on a 28-acre site which is completely surrounded by a ring of standing (or sarsen) stones almost a mile in circumference; this in turn is surrounded by a ditch and a raised bank which enclose almost 100 standing stones dating from around 2300 BC. These are thought to have been erected by the Beaker people, immigrants from continental Europe who brought with them sophisticated pottery-making skills (some exceptional pieces have been found in the graves of their dead chieftains).

The standing stones come in two basic shapes: the tall narrow ones are believed to represent the male form and the broad diamond-shaped ones the female form, characteristics which led archeologists to conclude that the site was probably used for the observance of fertility rituals. Megaliths weighing as much as forty tons were dragged from the Marlborough Downs and erected in three circles. Sadly, only 27 of the stones in the central area remain, the rest having been removed over the centuries only to be broken down and used as building materials; the positions of the missing stones have, however, been marked by a series of modern concrete piers.

Avebury Stone Circle was extensively excavated by Alexander Keiller during the 1930s and a museum bearing his name is located just outside the earthwork perimeter near the part-Saxon, part-Norman village Church of St James. The museum is administered by English Heritage and houses a fascinating collection of artefacts which were discovered at Avebury and at Windmill Hill, a Neolithic hill fort and later a Bronze Age burial ground which lies a mile and a half to the northwest. (Open daily from 9.30am (2pm on winter Sundays) to 6.30pm (4pm in winter), all year round.) Another attraction in the village is the Wiltshire Folk Life Society's exhibition of rural crafts which is situated in an enormous thatched barn. As well as containing a unique collection of historic farm implements, the Great Barn hosts regular demonstrations of lesser-known rural skills.

Avebury Stones

Avebury also possesses an elegant Elizabethan manor house, Avebury Manor, which was built on the site of a 12th-century priory and is now under the ownership of the National Trust. It has been much-altered over the centuries, particularly during the reign of Queen Anne and then in the Edwardian era, when major alterations were carried out by Colonel Jenner. Inside, there are some fine plasterwork ceilings and an interesting collection of antique furniture and porcelain. The manor grounds are partly laid out as a formal garden and contain a wonderful old dovecote, medieval walls and some splendid topiary. (Open daily except Mondays and Thursdays; 11am to 5.30pm; between 1st April and end-October. Admission charge payable; free to National Trust members).

The largest man-made prehistoric mound in Europe can be found on the northern side of the A4 one mile south of Avebury. The huge flat-topped cone of Silbury Hill stands 130 feet high and covers an area of five acres. Its purpose, however, remains a mystery. Recent excavations have yielded up little about the mound except that it is thought to have been constructed in four stages between around 2145 BC and 95 BC. According to local legend, the structure contains a huge gold statue which was hidden here by the Devil while on his way to Devizes; another theory suggests that it was created as a burial place for King Sil and his horse. Whatever its origins, the green cone of Silbury Hill has an uncanny presence which seems to dominate the surrounding landscape. Because of problems with erosion, however, members of the public are no longer permitted to climb to the top.

Near the hamlet of **SHEPARDS SHORE**, approximately midway between Avebury and Devizes, the road crosses the ridge which carries the ancient Wansdyke path. This spectacular earthwork is thought to have been constructed in the late 6th century by the Britons as a defence against the Saxons, and then strengthened two centuries later by the west Saxons as a defence against the Vikings. Consisting of a single raised bank and ditch, it once stretched for over fifty miles from the Berkshire border to northern Somerset. The twelve-mile eastern section from Savernake Forest to Morgan's Hill, near Calne provides one of the most spectacular archeological walks in England. (An excellent view of the Wansdyke can be enjoyed from the top of Tan Hill above the village of All Cannings.)

A mile and a half further south, we reached the old ecclesiastical community of **BISHOPS CANNINGS**, so-called because the Bishop of Salisbury once owned a manor here. Probably as a consequence, the parish church is somewhat oversized and bears a striking resemblance to Salisbury Cathedral with a tall tapering spire and some fine stone carving. The church organ was donated in 1809 by Captain Cook's navigator, William Bayley, who was born locally, and there is also an unusual meditation seat inscribed with some cautionary words in Latin on the subject of sin and death.

According to local legend, the term Wiltshire Moonraker has its origins in Bishops Cannings. During the 16th century, a government excise patrol discovered two local men combing a village pond with a rake on the night of a full moon. When asked what they were doing, they villagers pointed to the moon's reflection replied that they were trying to scrape the thick yellow cheese from the surface. Convinced that they had lost their senses, the excisemen roared with laughter and rode off into the night, leaving the local men to get on with their task of retrieving their cache of contraband liquor from the bottom of the pond.

A hollow in the Downs one mile to the west of Bishops Cannings was the scene of a bloody battle during the English Civil War. On 13th July 1643, the Royalist forces under Prince Rupert's brother, Maurice, defeated the Parliamentarian forces at Roundway Down. Local legend has it that each year on the anniversary of the battle, the cries of the dead can be heard emanating from a long-lost burial ditch beside the battlefield. One mile further south, a stroll to the beech trees on top of Roundway Hill provides some spectacular views over the surrounding downland landscape.

By the standards of most other settlements in the locality, DEVIZES is a relatively modern town having been founded by the William the Conqueror's nephew, Bishop Osmund, in 1080. He was responsible for building a timber castle between the lands of two manors, a position which gave the town its name (it comes from the Latin ad divisas, meaning 'at the boundaries'). After the original wooden structure burnt down, Roger, Bishop of Sarum, built a stone castle in 1138 which remained in place until it was compulsorily dismantled following the English Civil War. The castle which can be seen today dates from the 19th century and is not open to visitors.

Bishop Roger also built two fine churches in Devizes: St Mary's in New Park Street and St John's near the site of the old castle. The latter was built around 1130 and features a Norman tower and several original arches with characteristic zigzag carving. The churchyard contains some interesting tombs and is surrounded by a number of lovely old buildings including a 17th-century sexton's house. Beyond the church, Long Street is lined with elegant Georgian dwellings; it also contains the Wiltshire Archeological and Natural History Society's award-winning Devizes Museum with its superb collection of artefacts from such archeological sites as Avebury and Stonehenge.

Many of the finest buildings in Devizes are situated in and around the old market place; these include the town hall, the corn exchange and the handsome 16th-century coaching inn, the Bear

Hotel. The market place is also the site of an unusual market cross, one panel of which is inscribed with the sobering story of Ruth Pierce, a market stall-holder who, in 1753, was accused of swindling her customers. On announcing to the assembled throng, 'May I be struck dead if I am lying', she dropped down dead on the spot.

A good place to stay in the centre of Devizes can be found within a few yards of the Market Place on the A360 Potterne Road. Here you will find **Pinecroft**, an excellent bed and breakfast establishment which is run by May and Philip Linton. Pinecroft is a spacious part-Georgian, part-Edwardian residence standing in a huge, delightfully-planted garden. The guest rooms are large and equipped with colour televisions and beverage making facilities. The Lintons also offer a first-rate mountain-bike hire service.

Pinecroft, Potterne Road, Devizes Tel: 01380 721433

The Kennet and Avon Canal passes along the northern edge of Devizes. Designed in the early 19th century by John Rennie, this impressive feat of civil engineering once linked London with Bristol. At that time, Devizes Wharf was a flourishing commercial centre through which most of the town's goods passed. Today, the wharf is a more genteel place, though in recent years it has undergone something of a rejuvenation; several of the old warehouses have now been renovated and are occupied by such concerns as the local tourist information office, the Wharf Theatre and the Canal Interpretation Centre with its fascinating exhibition on the background and history of the canal.

A walk along the towpath to the west of Devizes to have a look at the famous Caen Hill flight of canal locks is recommended. Further west, the land falls 200 feet into a shallow valley within the space of two miles, an incline which created significant engineering difficulties for Rennie. He solved the problem by constructing a giant staircase of sixteen locks, so tightly-spaced that they scarcely seem a narrowboat-length apart. In total, a series of twenty-nine double-gated locks were needed to traverse the valley, a sequence through which the hardest working barges took half-a-day to pass. The lock gates are currently undergoing an extensive programme of restoration and it is hoped that this stretch of canal will become navigable again by the mid-1990s. An excellent view of the lock staircase can be obtained from a white-painted bridge which spans the canal a few hundred yards along the gravel towpath.

Those looking for a wonderfully tranquil place to stay within easy reach of the canal should try **Dye House** in Dye House Lane. The house lies a short walk from the Kennet and Avon Canal and is so-called because it was once the site of a silk dying mill. Victoria Heaton-Renshaw provides outstanding hospitality at her spacious Victorian home which is set within two and a half acres of beautifully cultivated gardens.

Dye House, Dye House Lane, Devizes Tel: 01380 722030

Driving southwards towards the heart of Salisbury Plain, the next stop is the lovely old village of POTTERNE, home of a unique exhibition of antique fire engines and fire-fighting equipment which is administered by the Wiltshire Fire Service. The village itself contains some noteworthy buildings, including a 13th-century church with a Saxon font and the 500 year-old Porch House, a black-and-white timbered structure which in its lifetime has served as a priest's home, an alehouse, a bakery and an army billet.

Turning west into country lanes brings you to the charming twin communities of **WORTON** and **MARSTON**. Worton's Christ Church is situated within an attractive treed churchyard and is unusual in this part of Wiltshire for not having a tower or spire.

Worton also possesses a splendid old country inn, the **Rose and Crown**. A genuine 'hidden place', this delightful village pub is tucked away on the old Melksham to Salisbury road and is well worth making the effort to find. The Saunders are friendly hosts who have turned the Rose and Crown into a popular watering hole for visitors and locals alike. Its popularity is readily understood when you sample their fine draught beers or taste their mouthwatering meals; the menu includes such house specialities as 'Worton beef and kidney pie', or 'pork in cider with Bramley apples'. The bar is full of historic artefacts and photographs, including one of a real-life local giant, while in a separate building there is a full length skittle alley where customers can complete their evening's entertainment.

The Rose and Crown, 108 High Street, Worton Tel: 01380 724202

The village of **ERLESTOKE** was much altered in the late 18th century when a new manor house was built and the surrounding land 'emparked' by the London-based landscape architect, William

Eames. About a century later, the old village church was replaced by the Gothic Perpendicular-style building which can be seen today. Today, Erlestoke provides a good sheltered base for exploring Salisbury Plain; it also offers a first-rate bed and breakfast establishment, **Longwater**

Longwater, Lower Road, Erlestoke, Devizes Tel: 01380 830095

Situated 300 yards north of the village centre, Longwater is a superb modern farmhouse which is licensed and ETB three crown commended. Mrs Pam Hampton offers luxurious en-suite bedrooms, marvellous hospitality, delicious breakfasts and, by arrangement, evening meals.

Eastcott Manor, Easterton, Devizes Tel: 01380 813313

In the delightful hamlet of EASTCOTT you will find Eastcott Manor, a splendid black and white half-timbered country residence which in the late 18th century was the home of the rumbustious Squire Wroughton. Today, the house is known more for its peace and tranquillity and for its easy access to the spectacular countryside of the northern Salisbury Plain. The building is the home of Janet Firth and her husband, Major Malcolm Firth, who offer first-rate overnight accommodation in charming historic surroundings. Janet, a trained cook, takes great pride in providing her guests with delicious meals which she prepares from the finest local produce.

The attractive settlement of URCHFONT lies a mile to the northeast. As well as possessing an exceptionally fine (and much-altered) 13th-century parish church, the village contains an elegant William and Mary manor house which once belonged to William Pitt and has since been converted to an educational institution. Look out also for the picturesque village duck pond.

Excellent facilities for campers and touring caravans are provided near Urchfont at the Bell Caravan and Camping Park at LYDEWAY. Situated on the Andover road, this attractive park offers thirty fully-equipped pitches in a secluded location at the foot of the Marlborough Downs.

The park is set in the grounds of the former Old Bell coaching inn and is ideal for touring the surrounding area. With full washing facilities, showers, a heated outdoor swimming pool, take-away service, off-licence, shop, games room and more besides, guests have everything they could wish for. The site's four-key English Tourist Board rating indicates the standards that can be expected.

Bell Caravan and Camping Park, Andover Road, Lydeway,
Devizes Tel: 01380 840230

Returning to the A360 and turning south brings you to the lovely old community of WEST LAVINGTON. The village church, which dates from the late-12th-century, stands alongside an attractive wisteria-covered manor house. In the mid-16th-century, the local lords of the manor, the Dauntsey family, were responsible for founding West Lavington's famous school. They also constructed the handsome almshouses to the northeast of the church which were subsequently rebuilt in brick during the 1830s.

Continuing south takes you across the central area of SALISBURY PLAIN. Along this stretch, much of the land on either side is owned by the Ministry of Defence; indeed some 92,000 acres make up the Salisbury Plain Training Area, 30,000 acres of which are regularly used either for live firing or as impact areas. Public access, therefore, is severely restricted. However, the MoD do make the effort to open up most of the prohibited areas on certain specified days each year. There are believed to be 17,000 archeological sites within the military training area, many of which are under the protection of special management agreements. The area also contains nine Sites of Special Scientific Interest (SSSIs) and a rich variety wild flora and fauna; in addition, over three and a half million trees have been planted here since the army took over in 1897.

The next destination is the ancient monastic town of AMESBURY. According to Mallory, Queen Guinevere withdrew to a priory here on hearing of King Arthur's death (when she herself died, her body was taken back to Glastonbury by Sir Lancelot to be buried beside the king). A more verifiable account records Queen Elfrida as having the founded the abbey around 979 in reparation for her part in the murder of her son-in-law, Edward the Martyr, at Corfe Castle. Almost two centuries later, the abbey was rebuilt by Henry II in a cruciform shape with a large central tower. Sadly, none of the original buildings remain above ground except for the old church of St Mary which was founded by the Saxons and remodelled during the Norman era. The present-day abbey buildings were completed in 1840 and are not open to the public.

Today, Amesbury is a pleasant town which is set in a bend of the Wiltshire Avon. The river is spanned by the graceful five-arched Palladian-style Queensbury Bridge which connects the town with WEST AMESBURY, site of the prehistoric earthworks, Vespasian's Camp, and the 17th-century West Amesbury House. A little further west, two lines of 100 year-old beech trees beside the A303 Amesbury bypass are said to represent the ranks of English and French ships at the Battle of the Nile.

Heading north out of Amesbury along the A345 Marlborough road and after approximately one mile, you will come to the ancient

Amesbury

site of Woodhenge. This is one of the earliest historic monuments in Britain to have been discovered by aerial photography, its six concentric rings of post holes having been spotted as cropmarks by Squadron-Leader Insall in 1925. The site is believed to date from around 2000 BC and once consisted of a series of timber uprights (now indicated by concrete posts) which, like nearby Stonehenge, were positioned to predict the sun's path across the sky on Midsummer's Day.

The one and a half acre site was extensively excavated between 1926 and 1928 and a number of Neolithic artefacts were discovered, including flint scrapers, arrow heads and two ceremonial chalk axes. Perhaps the most striking find, however, was discovered in the centre of the circle: the skeleton of a three year-old child with a fractured skull who was possibly the victim of a ritual sacrifice. The whole area is surrounded by a circular ditch some 220 feet in diameter, and is bordered to the northeast by another Neolithic structure, Durrington Walls. This once-spectacular earthwork enclosed an 80 foot ditch and is now virtually bisected by the Amesbury to Marlborough road. The two sites probably formed a single religious observatory which, for some unexplained reason, was moved to Stonehenge towards the end of the Neolithic period around 1800 BC.

For some distance to the north of Amesbury, the landscape is somewhat marred by the uniform rows of military housing. However, should you choose to follow the minor road northwards along the eastern bank of the Upper Avon, you will pass through some pleasant riverside settlements. The next stop is the village of UPAVON, an ancient Saxon river town which stands at the junction of the A345 and A342. This was the birthplace of Henry 'Orator' Hunt who became the Member of Parliament for Preston in 1830.

This is also where you will discover the renowned Braybrooke Pottery, an absolute gem of a hidden place. The proprietor, Sally Lewis, is a potter with a considerable reputation who designs all her own work, including specially commissioned commemorative pieces. On most days, visitors can watch Sally at work and admire her enviable artistic skills. A wide choice of beautiful pottery pieces are available to purchase, each of which is individually designed and handcrafted to make a very special gift at a surprisingly reasonable price. Braybrooke Pottery is also a well-known name at British craft exhibitions.

MARDEN is another ancient settlement. The 12th-century pinnacled church is thought to have one of the oldest doors in the country; the lock is known to be at least 300 years old, and the timber perhaps as old as the church itself. It is surrounded by an elaborately carved Norman doorway and inside, there is a fine chancel arch and an unusual ceiling in the nave. The village also possesses an imposing 18th-century manor house, Marden Manor, and a mill which was mentioned in the Domesday Book.

Braybrooke Pottery, Andover Road, Upavon, Nr. Pewsey
Tel: 01980 630466

Across the river to the northeast of Marden is a 35-acre oval site which is believed to have been the largest Neolithic henge in Britain. Dating from around 1900 BC, it features entrances on its northern and eastern sides, and once contained an enormous earthwork mound, Hatfield Barrow, which stood 50 feet high and 200 feet wide at the base.

The minor roads to the east of Marden lead back towards the A345 via the village of NORTH NEWNTON. Here you could stop and call in at the delightful Woodbridge Inn.

Mr Lou Vertessy and his family have made the Woodbridge Inn into a very inviting, attractive hostelry. Winners of the Best Catering Pub of the Year Award, he has successfully created an atmosphere of cosy informality where customers can enjoy mid-morning coffee, a pint of fine ale, a tasty bar snack or a delicious meal. The cosy intimate restaurant offers a superb menu which combines traditional English favourites with mouthwatering Mexican, Far Eastern and Cajun dishes. Beautiful en-suite accommodation is also available here, as well as a number of pitches in the lovely secluded caravan and camping park which adjoins the inn. With good fishing, four petanque (French boules) pistes, a children's play area and an attractive beer garden, the Woodbridge provides just about everything the visitor could wish for.

Woodbridge Inn, North Newnton, Pewsey Tel: 01980 630266

Continue northeast to the lovely old town of PEWSEY. Once under the ownership of King Alfred the Great, a statue of this 9th-century king of Wessex stands overlooking the River Avon at the crossroads in the centre of town. The main church is built on Saxon sarsen stones and has a 15th-century tower and an altar rail made from timbers belonging to the San Josef, a ship captured by Nelson in 1797. The streets contain an assortment of Georgian houses and thatched cottages and are the venue for a famous West Country carnival which takes place each year in September.

The long rambling village of MILTON LILBOURNE lies just to the south of the B3087 one and a half miles east of Pewsey. This pleasant community with its high pavements, fine cottages and handsome village church is a place of outstanding architectural and natural beauty. It also provides a good base for walks onto Milton Hill and to the Giant's Grave Neolithic long barrow.

Milton Lilbourne is also the location of a first-rate farmhouse bed and breakfast establishment, **Totteridge Farm**. A real haven for nature and animal lovers, this working farm combines a wonderful mixture of livestock and arable farming with an abundance of wildlife. There is a 100 year-old badger set on the farm's land, and rabbits, foxes, owls and many other birds and animals are all common sights here. Your charming hostess, Patricia Wells, provides very comfortable accommodation for non-smokers in her part-16th-century farmhouse home, all the guest rooms of which enjoy beautiful views over the Vale of Pewsey. A delightful place to stay, Totteridge Farm provides an excellent base for exploring the many lovely walks which crisscross the surrounding landscape.

Totteridge Farm, Milton Lilbourne, Pewsey Tel: 01672 62402

Returning to the centre of Pewsey, rejoin the A345 and continue northwards towards Marlborough. After half a mile or so you will come to the Kennet and Avon Canal so why not stop and have a look at the old wharf, canal house and warehouse which together make up Pewsey Wharf. Half a mile further on, turn west off the A345 to reach the famous white horse at **ALTON BARNES**. According to local legend, the contractor who was commissioned to carve the figure on the side of Milk Hill ran off with his £20 advance payment. Notwithstanding, work on this, the largest white horse in Wiltshire, was completed in 1812 and today, it is visible from Old Sarum over twenty miles away to the south.

A good view of the horse can be had from the wonderful old Barge Inn in **HONEYSTREET**, a short distance to the south. The inn once contained a bakery and general store which served communities throughout the area. Alton Barnes itself possesses a tiny church with a Saxon shell and a timber roof dating from the 15th-century. In 1830, a mob protesting about the introduction of agricultural machinery stormed the rectory and manor house beside the church, injuring one of the rector's colleagues and causing the militia to be called out from Marlborough and Devizes.

The road leading northwards out of Alton Barnes climbs up the slope of Walker's Hill. Just below the summit on the northern side, a path from the road leads to the New Stone Age encampment of Knap Hill; another path provides a short but fairly demanding climb to a long barrow known as Adam's Grave from which there are fine views in all directions.

Avebury Manor

Due north of here are the the twin settlements of **EAST KENNET** and **WEST KENNET**. A pleasant half-mile stroll to the west of the villages crosses the River Kennet and leads to the top of a gentle rise on which is sited the West Kennet Long Barrow, the largest sectioned burial chamber in the country. This 4500 year-old tomb is over 330 feet long, 80 feet wide and 10 feet high and is approached by way of a semicircular forecourt. The narrow entrance is guarded by number of colossal standing stones through which it is just possible to squeeze. Inside, the five burial chambers were found to contain the remains of forty-or-so people, including at least a dozen children; these were discovered in 1956 when the structure was excavated. The barrow is thought to have served as a tomb for around 1000 years, carbon dating having fixed a date of 2570 BC on the oldest remains, while the final sealing of the tomb, dated by pottery fragments, is believed to have been carried out around 1600 BC.

At East Kennet, one mile further east, there is a smaller and as yet unexcavated barrow which is covered in tall trees; then at Overton Hill, near the village of WEST OVERTON, there is another large monument known as The Sanctuary. This stands at the southeastern end of West Kennet Avenue, the standing-stone-lined pathway which connects with the main megalithic circles at Avebury. The Sanctuary dates from the early Bronze Age and is believed to have been built as a replacement for an earlier structure which consisted of six concentric circles of timber posts. Concrete blocks have been erected to mark the missing standing stones and concrete posts to mark their timber equivalents, so that the whole pattern of the monument can be discerned.

Overton Hill is also the starting point of the Ridgeway long distance footpath which runs for 85 miles through the North Wessex Downs to the Chiltern Hills. Although a little steep at first, the first four miles offers a dramatic walk to the top of the 892 foot Hackpen Hill, followed by a gentler stroll through a downland landscape littered with sarsen stones and Bronze Age round barrows. A short diversion from the Ridgeway leads to Fyfield Down, the section of the Marlborough Downs which is believed to have been a source of the great stones used to build Stonehenge. The area is now a nature reserve and walkers should keep to the marked footpaths. The spectacular Devil's Den long barrow lies within the reserve in a shallow hollow known as Flatford Bottom. Satan is said to appear here at midnight and attempt to pull down the stones with a team of white oxen.

Cross back onto the southern bank of the River Kennet and drive eastwards to LOCKERIDGE; a pleasant village with a good pub (the Who'da Thought It), a school, a shop, a number of attractive old houses, but curiously, no church.

A quiet corner of Lockeridge is the location of a first-class bed and breakfast establishment, The Taffrail. The owners of this impressive modern detached house, Julie and Les Spencer, are a truly cosmopolitan couple. Julie, the charming hostess, hails from California, and she and Les have travelled the world together. Their home is splendidly appointed; there is a two-thirds size snooker table in the guest lounge, and also a swimming pool in the terraced garden. The three bedrooms, which share the bathroom and WC, are well furnished with small American and Japanese touches adding to the establishment's unique character. Guests are assured of a warm welcome at Les and Julie's lovely home, an exceptional place which makes a refreshing change from more traditional bed and breakfast accommodation.

The Taffrail, Back Lane, Lockeridge, Marlborough
Tel: 01672 86266

Those preferring farmhouse-style accommodation should drive a mile or so further east to Sunrise Farm, a modern detached bungalow which is tucked away on the hillside behind the ancient village of MANTON. Here, Mrs Couzens provides excellent accommodation at her charming country home. She has one double and two twin rooms available, both furnished to three crown English Tourist Board standard, and there is also a half-size snooker table and hot drinks facilities in the guest lounge. The

98

south-facing conservatory adjoining the breakfast room provides a blaze of colour throughout the summer and is a favourite with guests for that last cup of coffee at breakfast time.

Sunrise Farm, Manton, Marlborough Tel: 01672 512878

A mile and a half further downstream, is the historic market town of **MARLBOROUGH**. The town is thought to have inherited its name from Maerl's Barrow, an ancient barrow which is now contained within the grounds of the famous Marlborough College public school. Many centuries later, the Normans built a castle on the site and a number of English kings are known to have come here to hunt in nearby Savernake Forest. In the 17th century, the castle was rebuilt as a house by Inigo Jones' pupil, John Webb, and became a regular haunt of Samuel Pepys. Then around 1700, it was converted into the Castle Inn and became one of the most popular stopping places on the busy coaching route between London and Bristol. Finally, it was incorporated into Marlborough College when the school was founded in 1843.

The best way to explore Marlborough is on foot (look out for the first-class leaflet, Marlborough, A Guided Walk, which is available from the information office at St Peter's Church). Despite having experienced three damaging fires in the late-17th-century, the town possesses one of the most beautiful (and widest) old high streets in the country. Amongst the buildings which can be seen here are two Perpendicular churches, some handsome Tudor houses, and a number of Georgian shops with colonnades. A narrow passageway behind St Mary's Church leads to the Green, once the site of a Saxon settlement and the place where Sheep Fairs were held until 1893. Each year in October, a 'Mop Fair' is held in commemoration of the old hiring market, the annual custom where tradespeople looking for work would stand in the marketplace carrying a tool of their trade.

Your walk around Marlborough may lead to the Parade, Marlborough's former main thoroughfare which once formed part of the busy London–Bristol coaching route. This is where you will find the **Lamb Inn**, a delightful former coaching inn which was built here in the 17th century to cater for passing travellers. Today, landlord Viv Scott serves an excellent pint of Wadworth's ale and a varied range of bar meals; he also has a number of charming en-suite letting bedrooms available.

The Lamb Inn, The Parade, Marlborough Tel: 01672 512668

From Marlborough drive southeastwards along the A338 Burbage road and after two miles stop in the village of CADLEY to call in at the marvellous bed and breakfast establishment run by Hugh and Charlotte Renwick.

Kingstones Farm, Cadley, Nr. Marlborough Tel: 01672 512039

Kingstones Farm stands in a magnificent position beside Savernake Forest, the only ancient forest in England left in private hands. With its orange-red brickwork, wisteria- and Virginia creeper-covered walls and old walled garden, this truly is an enchanting and quintessentially English place to stay.

100

To the east of the A338 lies the magnificent SAVERNAKE FOREST. A royal hunting ground since pre-Norman times, the 2000 acres which survive today are leased by the Marquess of Ailesbury to the Forestry Commission, making this the only forest in England not to be owned by the Crown. Once under the stewardship of Sir John Seymour, it was here that Henry VIII is said to have met his daughter, Jane. The present-day forest is a legacy from the great 18th-century landscaper, Capability Brown. He laid out the four-mile Grand Avenue which runs in a straight line southeastwards from a crenelated toll house on the A4. He also created a circus about halfway along from which eight forest walks radiate in line with the points of the compass. Savernake contains some massive oaks, beeches and Spanish chestnuts and has been designated a Site of Special Scientific Interest for its wide variety of flora and fauna.

St John's Church, Devizes

For a luxurious break away from it all, the Savernake Forest Hotel and Restaurant has everything you could wish for. Situated on the edge of Savernake Forest, this magnificent Victorian country house hotel provides first-class accommodation in tranquil and unspoilt surroundings. The hotel is run by actor

101

Richard Johnson who recently starred in the Camomile Lawn and is world famous for his interpretation of Anthony in Shakespeare's Anthony and Cleopatra. The Savernake Forest is an outstanding hotel; there are sixteen beautifully furnished en-suite bedrooms and a top class restaurant where an imaginative and varied menu is served, along with an extensive list of carefully-selected wines. Whether for a romantic weekend away or a holiday stopover, a stay here will leave you refreshed, relaxed and eager to return.

Savernake Forest Hotel, Burbage, Nr. Marlborough
Tel: 01672 810206

Two miles to the west of the A346, the village of **WOOTTON RIVERS** has a highly unusual church clock. It was built by a local man in 1911 from old prams, bicycles, farm implements and pieces of mechanical scrap for the villagers who wanted to mark the coronation of George V. Known as the Jack Spratt clock, it has 24 different chimes and a clock face bearing letters instead of numbers.

Visitors to the pretty village of **WEST GRAFTON** will find superb accommodation at **Mayfield**, the delightful home of Chris and Angie Orssich. Their charming thatched house dates from the 15th century and was originally a Wiltshire 'A'-frame longhouse. The timbered brickwork dates from Elizabethan times and inside, the beautifully furnished rooms are full of character with sloping ceilings and little nooks and crannies. Guests soon feel at home in this family house which is full of life and atmosphere; the focal point is the homely farmhouse kitchen where a ready supply of wine, peanuts and cakes is always available. Set in eight acres, the extensive grounds incorporate a heated swimming pool, a Victorian fruit cage and an all-weather tennis court. A wonderful base for exploring the lovely Kingdom of Wessex, Mayfield comes highly recommended.

Mayfield, West Grafton, Nr. Marlborough Tel: 01929 480216

North of here is the village of **CROFTON** and the next destination is the old engine house which stands at the highest point on the Kennet and Avon Canal. This handsome Georgian building contains some of the oldest and largest working beam engines in the world, one of which dates from 1812. At one time, these were capable of pumping water into the canal at a rate of eleven tons a minute. The working engines are demonstrated by the Kennet and Avon Canal Trust on a number of set days during the summer months.

The tomb of Sir John Seymour, the father Henry VIII's third wife, Jane Seymour, can be found in the chancel of the 11th-century Church of St Mary the Virgin in **GREAT BEDWYN**, two miles to the northeast. A Victorian lamp standard on a traffic island in the centre of The Square marks the centre of this sizable village. A walk along Church Street to the south of here leads to Lloyds' Stone Museum, an exhibition dedicated to the skills of the stonemason. The museum is run by the seventh generation of a family of stonemasons which can be traced back over 200 years. Items on show include a stone aeroplane with an eleven-foot wingspan, a number of brightly-coloured tombstones, and a well-presented display on the history and secret skills of stone-carving.

Two miles further northwest, the road running parallel to the Kennet and Avon Canal brings you back onto the A4 near **FROXFIELD**, an attractive village of brick and flint buildings which includes a 17th-century development of almshouses known as the Somerset Hospital. This consists of a chapel and fifty dwellings set around a quadrangle which is entered through an impressive early-19th-century archway.

Marlborough to the River Thames

The Great Western Railway Museum, Swindon

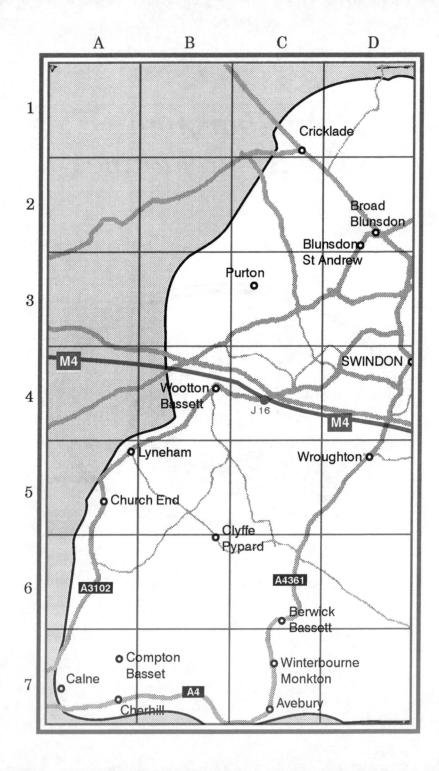

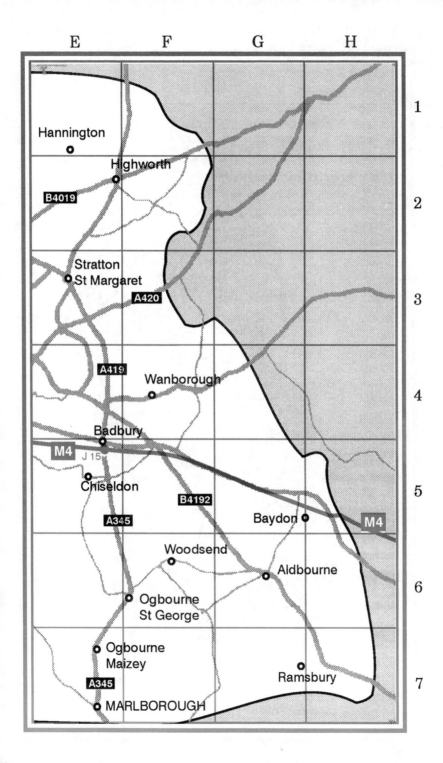

Lydiard Monument

CHAPTER FIVE

Marlborough to the River Thames

From the A4 at Froxfield turn north onto a minor country road to reach Littlecote House, our first port of call in northeast Wiltshire. This gabled Tudor country mansion was built between 1490 and 1520 on the site of a 13th-century manor and hamlet. Some of the earliest visitors to the house were Henry VIII and Jane Seymour whose entwined initials appear in a stained-glass window in the Great Hall, evidence that some of their early encounters took place here.

The most notorious occupant of the Littlecote, however, was 'Wild Darrell', the master of the house who was responsible for building the magnificent 110 foot-long Long Gallery. According to legend, he was also responsible for making one of the resident ladies-in-waiting pregnant, then after she had given birth, for taking the baby and throwing it onto a fire. The house is said to be haunted both by the spirit of a screaming infant and by the ghost of its mother who wanders the corridors looking for her lost child.

In 1589, the house was acquired by Sir John Popham who went on to become the Lord Chief Justice. An original set of the finger stocks he used to restrain offenders appearing before him can be seen in the Great Hall. During the English Civil War, his grandson, Alexander Popham, was a Roundhead colonel who commanded a force known as the Littlecote Garrison. A fine collection of Parliamentarian uniforms and arms from this period are on display in the Great Hall.

Littlecote House stands in a wonderful position on the banks of the River Kennet. The site has been occupied since Roman times, and indeed around 170 AD, a Roman villa was built here to which an elaborate floor mosaic was added around 360 AD. This was unearthed in the 18th century, although to prevent its destruction, it was reburied in situ where it lay undiscovered until 1977. The three-acre villa site has now been thoroughly excavated and forms one of Littlecote's main attractions. Others include a Puritan chapel, steam railway, children's adventure playground and regular demonstrations of medieval jousting and falconry. (Open daily, 10am to 6pm between March and end-September. Admission charge payable.)

The road to the northeast of Littlecote crosses the Kennet half a mile south of CHILTON FOLIAT. This pleasant community contains a 13th-century flint-and-stone church, some lovely old timbered cottages and a number of handsome Georgian residential buildings. Our next stop, RAMSBURY, is situated a mile or so from the B4192 Hungerford to Swindon road, three miles further west. Once an important ecclesiastical centre, the residence of the Bishops of Wiltshire was located here between 909 and 1058; the parish church was built in the 13th century on the foundations of a much-earlier Saxon building.

Present-day Ramsbury contains a number of attractive Jacobean and Georgian buildings, many of which have gardens stretching down to the River Kennet. The oak tree in the square was planted by a building society in 1986 to replace a mature oak which they had used as a logo. The action in removing the old tree caused certain amount of controversy however, for according to village lore, it was thought to be the home of Maud Toogood, a legendary local witch.

While in Ramsbury, call in at the historic Crown and Anchor public house in Crowood Street. Once a private house, in 1778 this lovely old building was acquired by James Mors, a local gunsmith who augmented his income by selling beer; then around 1840, it was bought by a brewer, Richard Hazell, who turned it into an alehouse and gave it its present name. Old maps show a building on the site in the late 1600s and the original beams in the main lounge bar would appear to date from around that time. The large longitudinal beam was hand-carved by a craftsman who must have spent days fashioning the centre joint.

At one time, the old Victorian beer engines on display were connected to a cellar which collapsed around the turn of the century. The entrance to this cellar was through a trap door which was situated at the entrance to what is now the dining room. The upper floor of the house is said to be haunted by an old woman who, it is claimed, once had an 'unpleasant experience' in the pub. What that experience was, no one knows, but she is supposed to appear at the top of the stairs at midnight when the moon is full, although the current proprietors, Kay and Paul Warner, admit to never having seen her.

As well as a first-class pint of beer, you can enjoy a very good and reasonably priced meal at the Crown and Anchor. The menu is varied and you will leave the table feeling well fed. There are always delicious homemade daily specials too, including a choice for vegetarians. If you care for a glass of wine you will find that the house wine is more than palatable. Food is available at lunchtimes and in the evenings seven days a week, and there is a pleasant beer garden which can be enjoyed on warmer days. An attractive craft and coffee shop have also been added to this already pleasant watering hole.

Crown and Anchor, 11 Crowood Lane, Ramsbury Tel: 01672 20335

Just outside Ramsbury, the River Kennet borders the grounds of the impressive Ramsbury Manor, a private house which was built in 1680 by Inigo Jones' son-in-law and pupil, John Webb.

Rejoining the B4192 to the north of Ramsbury after two miles you will arrive in the picturesque village of **ALDBOURNE**. Set 700 feet up in the Marlborough Downs, this attractive community has all the ingredients of a model English village: there's a charming village green with a duck pond and weathered stone cross, a 15th-century parish church containing a superbly-carved alabaster tomb of a priest, a 16th-century court house, and a square

surrounded by ancient cottages and Georgian houses. In the 17th-
and 18th-centuries, Aldbourne was renowned for its bell founding,
millinery and cloth-weaving; today, it is a more tranquil place and
is a regular winner of the best-kept village in Wiltshire award.

From Aldbourne, head due west along a minor road into the
heart of the Marlborough Downs. Our destination is the largest
and most northerly of the three villages known as the Ogbournes,
OGBOURNE ST GEORGE, an ancient settlement which lies just
to the west of the main A345 Marlborough to Swindon road. The
village has Saxon roots and is mentioned in the Domesday Book.
Its delightful 12th-century church stands just below the Ridgeway
long-distance footpath which at this point makes a dramatic curve
around the village, almost surrounding it on three sides.

The Old Crown, Ogbourne St George, Marlborough
Tel: 01672 841445

Within a few yards of the church can be found the splendid
traditional inn, the Old Crown. Run by Megan and Michael Shaw,
the cosy and traditionally-furnished bars offer a fine selection of
beers and first-class bar meals, including imaginative daily
specials, all of which can be enjoyed to a background of appropriate
music – there are no juke boxes here. The thirty-seater dining
room features a seventy foot wishing well and provides an excellent
à la carte menu which includes an extensive range of vegetarian
dishes. For those wishing to stay, there is also a beautifully
appointed en-suite guest room.

112

A truly exceptional place to stay or dine out in Ogbourne St George is the **Parklands Hotel and Restaurant**. This impressive establishment can be found in the centre of the village, just west of the A345 Marlborough to Swindon road and within easy reach of Junction 15 on the M4. Owners Peter and Faith Rostron have built Parklands into a truly outstanding hotel; all guest bedrooms have en-suite facilities, telephones, colour televisions and beverage-making facilities. Peter is also a renowned chef with an exquisite cosmopolitan touch who takes great pride in providing a top class food and drink. For the adventurous at heart, bicycles can be hired at Parklands for making the delightful journey down the old railway line (now a bike trail) to Marlborough and the Savernake Forest.

Parklands Hotel, Ogbourne St George, Marlborough
Tel: 01672 841555

Alternatively, those looking for guesthouse accommodation in this sheltered part of the Marlborough Downs should make a point of finding **Laurel Cottage**, a delightful thatched 16th-century cottage which is tucked away in the part of Ogbourne St George known as **SOUTHEND**.

Lying in a fold of the Marlborough Downs, Laurel Cottage is fully modernised and yet still retains its wonderful traditional charm. Your welcoming hostess, Adrienne Francis, is a superb cook who is happy to cater for any special tastes; she also makes a point of offering tempting alternatives to the traditional English breakfast. The three guest rooms offer first-class facilities and the

113

Ridgeway Suite adjoining the house provides luxury accommodation for two. Outside, the gardens are a positive delight and guests can enjoy their breakfast on the patio in fine weather. Walking, riding, touring and sight-seeing can all be catered for, making Laurel Cottage an ideal holiday location which provides everything guests could wish for.

Laurel Cottage, Southend, Ogbourne St George, Marlborough
Tel: 01672 841288

Leaving Ogbourne St George, pause a while to look at the dramatic remains of Liddington Castle. Lying to the east of the main road and just off the Ridgeway long-distance footpath, this impressive Iron Age hill fort occupies a seven-acre site on top of a 910 foot down. The structure consists of a series of wide ditches and earthwork defences, the northwestern ramparts of which provide some magnificent views over the Vale of the White Horse and the Cotswold Hills.

Nestling at the foot of the White Horse Downs and surrounded by breathtaking scenery, the picturesque village of **ASHBURY** lies three miles further northeast and just across the Oxfordshire border. The Ridgeway, one of Europe's oldest routes, runs close by the village, linking the Vale of Pewsey with Streatly-on-Thames.

In the heart of the village you will find the **Rose and Crown Hotel**, a delightful village inn which provides a marvellous touring base for exploring the surrounding countryside. The Rose and Crown has been refurbished to provide first-class accommodation in eleven well-equipped and attractively furnished guest rooms.

Guests can sample the fine real ales in the comfortable surroundings of the two bars, or enjoy the first-class cuisine in the elegant restaurant in an atmosphere of friendly hospitality. During the summer months, customers can relax on the patio and gaze out on a landscape of thatched cottages to the soothing sound of chiming church bells.

The Rose and Crown, Ashbury, Nr. Swindon Tel: 01793 710222

Retracing your steps, cross back onto the southern side of the M4 before turning west along the B4005 Wroughton road. After passing through the village of Chiseldon, turn south onto a minor road which led us up to the site of another Iron Age stronghold, Barbury Castle, one of the most spectacular and widely-visited hill forts in southern England. This clearly-defined twelve-acre site is surrounded by a double line of earthwork ramparts which are breached to the east and west by narrow entrances.

The view over the surrounding downland landscape from the perimeter rim of the castle is breathtaking; an Iron Age field system can just be made out to the east, and further on, a pleasant stroll leads along the Ridgeway Path to Burderop Down. An open hillside half a mile to the north of Barbury Castle was the scene of a bloody battle between the Britons and the Saxons in the 6th century. This ended in defeat for the Britons and established a Saxon kingdom of Wessex under King Ceawlin. The whole area has recently been designated the Barbury Castle Country Park.

After returning to the B4005, continue to **WROUGHTON**, home of the highly-regarded Science Museum which is housed in a number of refurbished aircraft hangers on Wroughton's disused airfield. Two of these buildings contain the national collection of civil and commercial aircraft, along with a display of historic space rockets, hovercraft, fire-fighting appliances and aero- and marine engines. Another contains a large collection of vintage buses, steam and motor lorries, cars, motorbikes and bicycles, and yet another, a collection of historic farm machinery and agricultural implements. The museum stages a number of specialist air shows and motor rallies throughout the year, and the nearby Butser Ancient Farm Project and Clauts Wood Nature Reserve are two further places of interest which are well worth a visit.

New Inn, Winterbourne Monkton, Swindon Tel: 01672 3240

Our next stop is WINTERBOURNE MONKTON, an attractive village which can be found on the A361 Devizes road, two miles north of Avebury. The tiny village church has an unusual shingled belfry which is supported on timbers sited within the church. If you want to break your journey here, seek out the New Inn, a lovely establishment run by Eric and Rachel Matthews. Inside, you will find a cosy, welcoming bar, an excellent restaurant and first-class en-suite accommodation. The restaurant overlooks ancient water meadows and features a fine old fireplace with an original studded iron 'soot catcher' door. The varied menu includes steak, rainbow trout and 'chicken breast in thyme and port sauce'; it is competitively priced and a children's menu is also available. To accompany your meal, choose a bottle from the extensive wine list which features some excellent Australian wines.

116

Not far away is the delightful small town of WOOTTON BASSETT. This bustling community contains a number of fine old buildings including the Old Town Hall, an unusual structure which was built on a series of tall stone piers. The open-sided ground-floor area once served as a covered market and today provides shelter for the old town stocks; the upper floor once contained the town chambers and now houses an interesting museum of local history.

Among the excellent shops and businesses in Wootton Bassett's High Street is the locally-renowned Cross Keys Inn. Once a busy coaching inn, the Cross Keys is a lively traditionally-run inn which is now a Grade II listed building. The proprietors, Paul and Jean Thomas, have worked hard to preserve the inn's character and appeal. (In fact, Paul was awarded the Gold Medal by the British Institute of Innkeepers in May 1992.) Take a drink in the Penny Bar where every surface is covered with pennies, or sample the excellent food accompanied by a bottle from the extensive wine list. With evening entertainment ranging from darts, pool and live music to Karaoke and outdoor barbecues, this truly is an inn in the finest tradition.

The Cross Keys, High Street, Wootton Bassett Tel: 01793 855476

Leaving Wootton Bassett, join the minor road which leads northwards over the M4 to the pleasant village of HOOK. Here is the School House Hotel and Restaurant, an exceptional establishment which stands at the gateway to the Cotswolds and just five minutes' drive from Swindon. Formerly a Victorian school,

117

it is now a Grade II listed building run by a charming and experienced couple, Mr and Mrs Ramselaar. The restaurant with its beautiful Victorian surroundings, is renowned for its creative menus using locally produced fish and poultry. You can sample such delights as 'pot-roasted boneless quail with chicken liver and apricot filling', 'king prawns with seaweed and shrimp sauce', or you can choose from the imaginative vegetarian menu. The bedrooms are all en-suite and excellently equipped, with charming period furnishings and delightful views over the rural downs. This is a very special place and a visit here will indeed be memorable.

School House Hotel, Hook, Nr. Swindon Tel: 01793 851198

Continuing northwards, the next stop is **PURTON**, a long sprawling community with a fine Norman church. St Mary's is one of the few churches in England that possess both a tower and a spire. According to local legend, this peculiar state of affairs came about when the two sisters who originally commissioned the church were unable to agree on its design; their answer was to build two towers. It turns out, however, that the structures were built 150 years apart: the central tower with its spire was constructed around 1325 and the western pinnacled tower around 1475.

Although much altered during the 14th and 15th centuries, evidence of the church's Norman origins can be seen in much of its architectural detail. The building also contains some wonderful fragments of medieval stained-glass and a number of striking painted murals, including a 17th-century interpretation of the Death Of The Virgin.

A bend in the road a mile to the north of Purton is known as Watkins' Corner after a man who was hanged here for a murder which turned out to have been committed by his father. According to local folklore, a sudden squall blew up as Watkins swung from the gallows' rope, causing the hangman's horse to bolt. The startled animal then proceeded to throw its rider to the ground, a fall which broke the hangman's neck . To this day, this lonely place is said to be haunted by the spirit of an unjustly condemned man.

Continue southeast towards the famous country house at **LYDIARD MILLICENT.** Now under the ownership of Thamesdown Borough Council, Lydiard Mansion was once the home of the St Johns. One 15th-century member of this distinguished family was grandmother to the House of Tudor; having married the Duke of Somerset in 1440, she gave birth to Margaret Countess of Richmond who went on to became the mother of Henry VII.

Lydiard Mansion

The original part-medieval manor house was rebuilt in 1745 with a neoclassical pedimented façade and a splendid rococo interior. The building has been extensively restored and is now furnished with fine paintings and elegant Georgian furniture. The mansion is the central attraction in the 260-acre Lydiard Park, an attractive area of open lawns and woodland which incorporates a visitor centre with an exhibition on local natural history and a children's adventure play area with a life-size western fort.

The settlement of **LYDIARD TREGOZE** was founded in Saxon times and once stood alongside the old manor house. However, the 18th-century fashion for 'emparking' large country houses required a landscape free from 'unnecessary' buildings and so the village was allowed to decline. The only building of note to survive is the lovely little Church of St Mary which is known for its exceptionally bright and colourful interior. Among its many remarkable features is the Golden Cavalier, a full-size gilded effigy of Edward St John who was killed in 1645 at the second Battle of Newbury. Other items of note are the early-17th-century pulpit, the St John family pew, a cabinet containing a brightly coloured triptych, and some striking 15th-century stained glass.

Great Western Railway Museum, Swindon

From here the A3102 will bring you straight into the heart of **SWINDON**, Wiltshire's largest town. Before the Great Western Railway's main London to Bristol line was built in 1835, Swindon was a sleepy community whose principal activity was agriculture.

120

A station was built here in that year, though it wasn't until some time later that the GWR's main engineer, Isambard Kingdom Brunel, made the decision which was to change the town beyond all recognition. According to legend, one day Brunel was walking along the Swindon stretch of line while wrestling with the question of where to locate the company's main railway workshops. Apparently, he found the problem so exasperating that he finally threw his half-finished sandwich into the air and shouted, 'wherever it lands, there shall I build'.

Construction soon got underway and during the golden age of steam, Swindon locomotive works grew to become one of the largest railway workshops in the world. At one time, 12000 workers were employed on the 320-acre site which incorporated a model Railway Village, a development of 300 artisan's homes which were built in Bath stone extracted from Box Tunnel (see chapter three). Today, this unique example of Victorian town planning is open to the public as a living museum; one of its most interesting features is a railway foreman's house which dates from 1842 and is furnished in period style. (Open daily, 10am to 1pm (not Sundays) and 2pm to 5pm, all year round.)

The Faringdon Road site also contains the world famous Railway Museum which is located in a former workers' hostel or 'navvies' barracks'. This houses a fascinating collection of steam locomotives, signalling equipment, railway signs and other GWR railwayana, and includes a special room devoted to the life and achievements of Isambard Kingdom Brunel. (Open daily, 10am (2pm Sundays) to 5pm, all year round.)

Present-day Swindon is a bustling commercial centre which at one time was the fastest growing town in Europe. Excellent shopping facilities are offered in Regent Street and the Brunel Centre, and the town is well catered for in the area of arts and entertainment. The Wyvern Theatre is a luxury 650-seat venue which stages everything from pop concerts to large-scale touring theatre and ballet productions, and both the Arts Centre and the Link Arts Studio have 200-seat auditoriums which provide a more intimate space for dance, drama and performance arts.

Swindon's renowned art gallery in Bath Road features work by such acclaimed modern artists as Ben Nicholson, Graham Sutherland and L S Lowry (open daily, 10am to 6pm (2pm to 5pm

Sundays), all year round), and the town also contains a number of beautifully-kept parks and open spaces, including Queen's Park, Penhill Park and Faringdon Road Park, part of the GWR's original Railway Village development.

The busy A419 Cirencester road follows the course of the Ermine Way, the great Roman road which linked the garrison towns of Glevum (Gloucester) and Calleva (Silchester) in Hampshire. The old road followed a virtually straight course for most of its sixty-mile length, a characteristic which is clearly demonstrated in the section which runs northwest from Swindon.

Three miles from the centre of Swindon, past the speedway stadium, is the pleasant community of **BLUNSDON ST ANDREW**. The ruins beside the tiny 13th-century village church are the remains of Blunsdon Abbey, a once-impressive monastic house which burnt to the ground many years ago. The abbey grounds now contain a caravan and camping park.

To the east is Blunsdon St Andrew's sister village of **BROAD BLUNSDON**, an ancient settlement which lies just to the north of the B4019. The village possesses a fine Early English church which is linked by a pathway to Castle Hill, the site of a pre-Roman earthwork fortification.

A little further to the west, the B4019 climbs a 400 foot incline at the summit of which is sited the aptly-named community of **HIGHWORTH**. This delightful small town contains some fine 17th- and 18th-century domestic architecture, several examples of which can be found around the old square in the centre of town; noteworthy buildings from this period include Highworth House and Jesmond House, now a hotel.

Highworth parish church was built in Perpendicular style during the 15th century; it was fortified during the English Civil War and shortly after, was attacked by Parliamentarian forces under Fairfax. A cannon ball which struck the building during the siege is on display inside. The church also contains a memorial to a Lieutenant Warneford who in 1915 was awarded the Victoria Cross for destroying the first enemy Zeppelin during World War I.

A pleasant walk can be taken to the top of the Highworth Hill; the views from here are spectacular and take in the three counties of Wiltshire, Gloucestershire and Oxfordshire. The land to the north of Highworth slopes gradually down into the valley of the

River Thames, a gentle landscape which is where we are now headed.

On the northern bank of the Thames is the charmingly-named community of MARSTON MEYSEY. This, the northernmost village in Wiltshire, has a long main street which is lined with handsome old houses and cottages. Just outside the village, we passed an unusual roundhouse, probably a former canal lock-keeper's cottage, and a bridge over the North Wiltshire branch of the Wiltshire & Berkshire Canal.

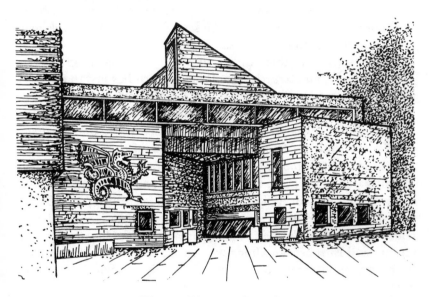

Wyvern Theatre, Swindon

The road to the west of Marston Meysey passes briefly into Gloucestershire before returning to Wiltshire near the junction with the A419. The lovely old village of LATTON lies a mile to the northwest of this junction. This pleasant community was originally part of an estate belonging to the Earl of St Germans, though in more recent times it has been brought under the ownership of the Cooperative Wholesale Society who use it for housing their agricultural workers, white collar staff and retired employees. Although relatively modest, the village possesses some delightful 17th-century Cotswold stone cottages, some rather more substantial Victorian houses, and a church founded in Norman times which was substantially rebuilt by the forthright Victorian architect, William Butterfield.

In the heyday of Britain's inland waterways, Latton stood at an important junction of the Wiltshire & Berkshire and Thames & Severn canals. Latton Basin, the holding area where barges used to manoeuvre and wait, can still be made out in the old canal bed, and a footpath along the course of the canal to the northwest leads to the remains of a lock and a lock-keeper's roundhouse similar to the one at Marston Meysey. Looking somewhat out of place, the impressive old wharf owner's (or wharfinger's) house with its imposing classical pediment can be seen from the A419 trunk road a little further to the southwest.

Continuing in this direction you will soon arrive at CRICKLADE, an attractive small town which lies just to the west of the main road. The town has a long history stretching back beyond the days of the Roman occupation; a mint was located here during Saxon times, then several centuries later, the Normans were responsible for founding the town's main church which they dedicated to St Sampson, a Breton saint born in 465. The main building was constructed between the 12th and 15th centuries, and magnificent cathedral-like tower was added during the Tudor period by the Duke of Northumberland in 1553. The interior features some fine Norman details, some rare heraldic carvings and an unusual Elizabethan altar table; each September, St Sampson's is the principal venue for Cricklade's widely-renowned festival of music.

The smaller St Mary's Church can be found at the other end of the High Street near the remains of a 13th-century priory and hospital; the priory has now been converted into small residential dwellings. The town also possesses a famous school which was founded by a London goldsmith, Robert Jenner, in 1651. Those keen to find out more about Cricklade's long and eventful history should make a point of finding the town's interesting small museum which is situated opposite the clock tower in Calcutt Street. (Open Wednesdays 2pm to 4pm and Saturdays 10am to 12 noon).

While in the centre of Cricklade, take the opportunity of calling in for some refreshment at the excellent White Hart Hotel, an impressive former coaching inn which is run by a charming couple,

Peter and Gillian Mortley. Once the meeting place of the local hunt, the townsfolk traditionally gathered here on Boxing Day to see the hunt off. (Although the hunt no longer meets, the tradition of meeting at the White Hart on Boxing Day continues.) An excellent pint of beer is served in the spacious bars, and there is also a beautifully appointed dining room where visitors can enjoy some of Gillian's mouthwatering and imaginative recipes. House specialities include game and fish, and all dishes are prepared using fresh locally-sourced produce wherever possible; customers can also choose from the extensive wine list. As well as providing excellent food and drink, the White Hart has fifteen attractively furnished and well-equipped guest bedrooms.

The White Hart Hotel, High Street, Cricklade Tel: 01793 750206

Those interested in industrial archeology should make a point of finding West Mill Wharf in West Mill Lane, a once-lively wharf which served the North Wiltshire branch of the Wiltshire & Berkshire Canal. Although now almost completely filled in, the site serves as a poignant reminder of the once-golden age of the narrowboat.

Cricklade is the only town in Wiltshire to lie on the River Thames (although at this point it could be better be described as a wide stream). At the northern end of the High Street, the river flows under a bridge, beyond which is a stile leading to a well-worn footpath. This leads to North Meadow, an ancient water meadow which was designated a nature reserve in 1973. This exceptional area of meadowlands contains some rare plants and flowers which are a delight to behold in late-spring and summer (though please respect the nature reserve and on no account remove any of the plantlife). The path upstream leads to a footbridge, allowing the return journey to be made on the opposite bank of the River Thames.

Northwest Wiltshire

The Unicorn Gallery, Castle Combe

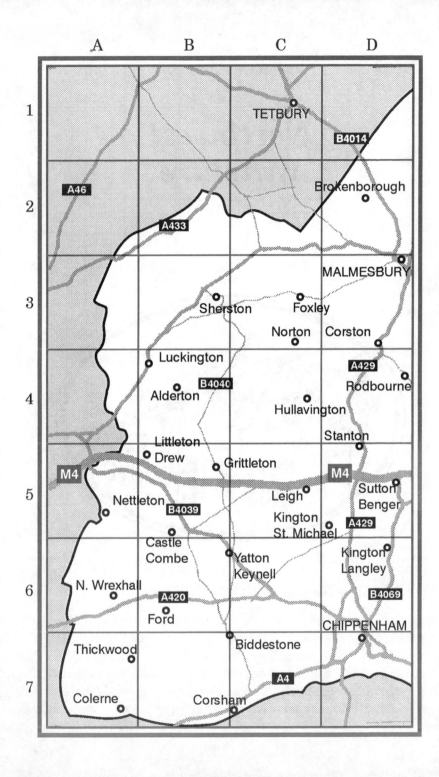

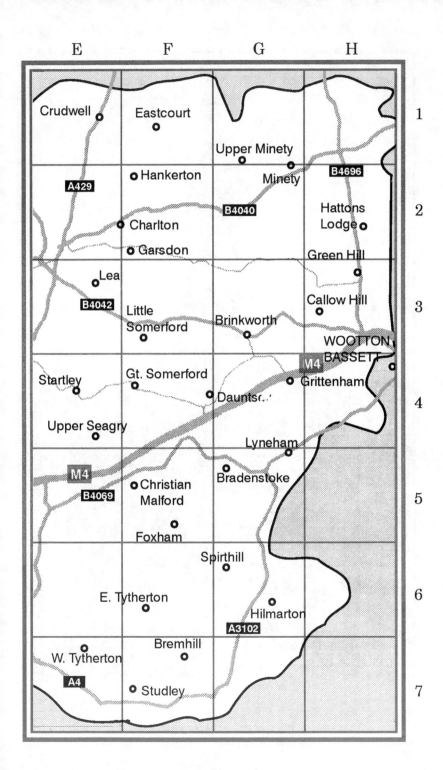

Market Cross, Malmesbury

CHAPTER SIX

Northwest Wiltshire

For lovers of ancient English churches, the villages in the upper reaches of the Thames to the west of Cricklade contain a couple of gems. The first can be found just to the north of the B4040 Malmesbury road near the village of LEIGH; now redundant, the Church of All Saints lies a quarter of a mile down a track from the Waterhay Bridge over the Thames. This lovely old building, which is also known as the Old Chancel, dates from the 12th century and was later altered during the 14th and 15th centuries.

A couple of miles to the northwest, the Church of the Holy Cross stands on the edge of the sprawling village of ASHTON KEYNES. Also founded in the 12th century, the church was extended in the 13th century and extensively restored during the 1870s under the direction of William Butterfield, the architect of Keble College, Oxford. The farmyard adjoining the church is the site of a monastic house which was founded in Saxon times, and both the church and the monastery are surrounded by the remnants of a double moat from this period.

An ancient cross stands in the centre of the churchyard; this is one of Ashton Keynes' four 'preaching' crosses, all of which were damaged during the English Civil War (this one was restored as a war memorial in 1917).

The churchyard also contains a number of table tombs belonging to the Richmond family, the local lords of the manor who lived at Cove House in the centre of the village. During the Civil War, the family's allegiances were seriously divided. Two sons chose to fight on opposing sides, and during a nighttime skirmish outside Ashton Keynes, one brother is reported to have unwittingly killed the other. When faced with the truth, the surviving brother was so full of remorse that he took off for America and subsequently founded a branch of the family there.

Once a manor belonging to King Alfred's sister, Ashton Keynes is crisscrossed by hidden walkways which connect with the village inn and the ancient church. The village contains a number of fine old Cotswold-stone residences, including Brook House and Ashton Mill. At the Ashton Mill end of the village, the infant Thames runs beside the main street and each house is reached by way of an attractive small footbridge.

Corner Cottage, Fore Street, Ashton Keynes Tel: 01285 861454

In Fore Street is the first-rate bed and breakfast establishment, Corner Cottage, which is run by Rosina and Jim Wiltshire. Rosina and Jim have lived in Ashton Keynes for more than twenty years and have welcomed guests into their delightful Cotswold cottage for almost as long. Set in a lovely part of the village, Corner Cottage offers excellent accommodation for which the Wiltshires have been awarded an English Tourist Board two-crown rating. All guest rooms have en-suite facilities, making this is an ideal base for hikers and motorists to explore the outstanding Cotswold countryside.

The country lanes to the southwest of Ashton Keynes lead through the pleasant rolling countryside of northwest Wiltshire. Just outside the village of UPPER MINETY is Flisteridge Cottage, a charming private residence which offers superb overnight accommodation. For a real taste of English heritage, a stay here is a must. This charming colour-washed cottage overlooks Flisteridge woods and is situated just outside Minety village, the professed home of the distinguished Quaker family, the

132

Penns, after whom Pennsylvania was named. Fay Toop-Rose loves sharing her home with her guests. Her house is beautifully decorated and offers a friendly and homely atmosphere, with the additional bonus of a delightful English garden in which guests are welcome to relax. Flisteridge Cottage provides a truly lovely and peaceful base for touring the Cotswold countryside.

Flisteridge Cottage, Upper Minety, Malmsbury Tel: 01666 860343

After passing over the B4040 continue southwards through the country lanes, crossing the B4042 and then the M4 near Callow Hill. Our next stop is the peaceful hamlet of LOWER GOATACRE, a pleasant community which is situated just off the A3102, one mile south of the town and military airport at Lyneham. Here you will discover Fenwick's, a small country house bed and breakfast establishment which is run by Margaret and Fen Fenwick.

Visitors to Fenwick's will find Margaret and Fen warm and welcoming hosts. Their non-smoking house provides high quality accommodation comprising one double room with en-suite shower, and one double room with en-suite bathroom and a single room adjoining (thus creating a family suite when required); all offer excellent facilities, including colour televisions. There is a choice of traditional English breakfast or a selection from Margaret's à la carte menu, either of which can be enjoyed on the beautiful patio overlooking the garden. One of the finest ways guests can relax is to take tea, either on the terrace in summer, or in front of a blazing log fire in the drawing room in winter.

133

Fenwick's, Lower Goatacre, Calne Tel: 01249 760645

From Goatacre, heading west into the country lanes, and after passing through the hamlet of Catcomb, continue southwest towards our next stopping place, the lovely old village of **BREMHILL**. The village stands at the eastern end of Maud Heath's Causeway, a remarkable raised footpath which runs for four and a half miles towards Chippenham. This surprising work of civil engineering was constructed in 1474 on the instructions of a local market trader, Maud Heath. Maud died owning property and land in Bremhill which not only provided funds for the building and upkeep of the causeway, but also for the construction of the village bridge.

A couple of miles to the northwest, the raised footpath runs over 64 brick and stone arches near the village of **KELLAWAYS**. In 1698, a ball and pillar was erected here in memory of the market pedlar who never forgot the many times she had to trudge, often wet through, with her basket of goods from Bremhill to Chippenham. A wonderful statue of Maud, her basket at her side, stands overlooking the flood plain at Wick Hill.

Not far away is **KINGTON LANGLEY**, a pleasant community which lies between the B4069 and the main A429 Chippenham to Cirencester road and where you will find the charmingly-named **Finnygook**, a delightful private home which also offers excellent overnight accommodation. A lovely secluded house set in delightful gardens, its tranquillity belies the fact that it is situated only a few minutes away from the M4. Run by Ena Weston and her husband, a lovely friendly couple, Finnygook is a very relaxed and welcoming establishment offering spacious, well furnished accommodation. Ena is an excellent cook and is happy to cater for special tastes given prior notice. As a touring base Finnygook is ideal; Bath, Bristol, Longleat and Castle Combe are all close by, and a warm welcome awaits you on your return. All in all, this is a truly delightful place to stay.

A short journey south leads to the centre of the charming old market town of **CHIPPENHAM** This historic settlement was founded on the banks of the Bristol Avon around 600 AD by the Saxon King Cyppa from whom the town gets its name. Within 250 years it had become an important administrative and hunting centre in King Alfred's Wessex. At the heart of present-day Chippenham is the ancient market place which still hosts a flourishing weekly market every Friday.

Finnygook, Days Lane, Kington Langley, Chippenham
Tel: 01249 750272

The streets of Chippenham contain number of fine old buildings, including the 15th-century twin-gabled town hall with its unusual wooden turret. The half-timbered Yelde Hall was used by the Bailiff and Burgesses of the Chippenham Hundred until 1841; having been extensively restored, the building was reopened as a museum of local history in 1963. The museum contains a number of interestingly arranged rooms, including one which has been

135

refurbished as the old town lock up. (Open Mondays to Saturdays, 10am to 12.30pm and 2pm to 4.30pm between mid-March and end-October. Admission free.)

Of the four churches in Chippenham, St Andrew's is the oldest. It was founded during Saxon times, and although little from this period now remains, it contains some fine monuments from the 13th and 15th centuries. There is also an exquisite stained-glass window and several references to the Hungerford family, the local lords of the manor. St Paul's Church in Malmesbury Road was built in Gothic revival style by architect Sir Giles Gilbert Scott in 1855.

Sheldon Manor

Other noteworthy buildings in Chippenham include the handsome early-19th-century structure, Ivy House and the Grove, the home of a short-lived spa during the 18th century. At Hardenhuish Hill (pronounced Harnish) on the edge of Chippenham, John Wood the Younger of Bath built the Georgian church of St Nicholas on the site of a ruined medieval church. Completed in 1779, it is noted for its elegant Venetian windows.

Leaving Chippenham along the A420 Bristol road, and turning south after a mile or so, brings you to the historic country house of Sheldon Manor in the village of **SHELDON**. A manor has existed

136

here since the late 12th century when the lands of the old Chippenham Manor were divided into three (the lordship of the Chippenham Hundred was awarded to Sheldon). With parts of the present-day house, including the porch, dating from the late-13th-century, the building has been continuously occupied since 1424, the year the Hungerford family first acquired the estate. After remaining in their family for over 250 years, the house changed hands several times before being bought by the current owning family in 1917. Sheldon Manor is open to the public on Thursdays, Sundays and Bank Holiday Mondays; garden 12.30pm to 6pm, house 2pm to 6pm. Admission charge payable.

Continuing west along the country lanes, you amy pass a sign to Starveal Farm, a delightful old farmhouse which has been converted into a working pottery. Situated between Biddestone Manor and Sheldon Manor, half a mile from the picturesque village of Biddestone, the Starfall Pottery will provide an afternoon of great interest. In the studio, you can see the beautiful and skilled work of Gordon and Dorothy Whittle, two delightful people who are always pleased to see visitors. As well as being able to admire their pottery making skills, you can also view a wide range of domestic stoneware and commemorative pottery for all occasions.

Starfall Pottery, Sheldon, Nr. Biddestone Tel: 01249 713292

Not only are the Whittles superbly clever with their hands, but they can also decorate the articles they have made with equal skill. As well as a display of pottery, there is a range of hand-woven and knitted items, including those from hand-spun, natural dyed wool.

137

All the articles on display are for sale at very affordable prices, or if you wish to order a special item, then all you have to do is ask. In addition they grow and sell a wide range of herb plants and are extremely knowledgeable on the subject. (The Starfall Pottery is open every day from 9am until dusk, all year round.)

A little further west is BIDDESTONE, an attractive community of stylish 17th- and 18th-century houses set around a village green with a large duck pond. Among the noteworthy buildings to be seen here is a handsome gabled farmhouse with a Georgian gazebo which can be found near the pond, and a grey stone manor house with a large walled garden which stands on the edge of the village.

The Bell Inn, Yatton Keynell, Nr. Chippenham Tel: 01249 782216

In the centre of the village of YATTON KEYNELL is its one and only pub, the Bell Inn. Not just a public house, the Bell has caravan and camping facilities for people touring the area or visiting the motor racing circuit at nearby Castle Combe.

The Bell overlooks the centre of the village and faces the 15th-century Church of St Margaret of Antioch. Part of the church was built as a shrine by local landowner Sir William Keynell who had it made to show God his gratitude for protecting him in battle and returning him safely to England from the Crusades.

The Bell was originally constructed as a farmhouse during the 15th century and only became a coaching inn some years later because of its proximity to what was then the main road between Bristol, Chippenham and London (the Bell lies 97 miles from Hyde

Park Corner). During renovation work, an unusual fertility stone was uncovered (evidently, this had not been in use for many years as the population of the village remains very small!). The interior is well preserved, with original oak-beamed ceilings and a 15th-century central fireplace. In winter, simulated log fires give off a surprisingly warm and cheering effect.

Landlords Don and Jan Milburn have been at the Bell for a number of years. When Don left the Royal Air Force he chose to join the licensed trade, something that was not new to him as his father had run a pub when Don was a lad. Jan has had many years experience working behind a bar and they both thoroughly enjoy the hectic pub life. One of Jan's hobbies is collecting owls and owl pictures, a large collection of which can be seen in the attractive lounge bar where there is also an interesting photograph of the village taken from a Hercules aircraft.

Castle Combe

The aromas coming from the kitchen are sure to make you feel like staying for a bite to eat. Pizzas, burgers, basket meals and omelettes, as well as the usual pub food, made up the menu and a choice of vegetarian and children's meals are also available.

Any inn more than five centuries old should have a ghost and the owners will confirm these suspicions. Although they have never seen one, a predecessor claims to have seen a young lady walk past him in the pub and straight through the far wall. Behind this wall, there is a spiral staircase which is no longer in use.

The Bell Inn is a friendly place where locals and visitors mix well and everybody is made to feel welcome. In summer there is a garden to enjoy with children's swings, a slide and a climbing frame.

From Yatton Keynell, it is only a short drive northwest to CASTLE COMBE, one of the loveliest villages in the whole of Wessex. Indeed in 1962, Castle Combe was named the prettiest village in England, one of the factors which led to it becoming a location for the film, Doctor Doolittle. Although this means the village is now well and truly on the tourist map, in the 15th and 16th centuries, it was a well-established cloth-weaving centre. Many of the present-day buildings date from this period of prosperity, including the Perpendicular St Andrew's Church with its fine fan vaulting, 13th-century font and memorial to Walter Dunstanville, the founder of the now-demolished castle from which the village takes its name.

Castle Combe lies in a deep, tree-lined valley and visitors are encouraged to park their cars at the top of the hill and walk down through the narrow streets. Once there, one of the finest views of the old village can be had from the picturesque three-arched bridge over the By Brook (this is also a good place for spotting trout). Castle Combe also contains a number of other impressive buildings, including a covered 15th-century market cross, the site of a once-regular wool market, and a lovely 16th-century manor house, now a hotel, which was much altered during the Victorian period.

Visitors to Castle Combe's main street will delight when they discover the Unicorn Gallery, a veritable 'treasure trove' where they can be sure to find a gift for that special occasion. The gallery's reputation has been built up and maintained by its owner, Jennifer Shepherd, and it has a regular clientele of local customers who come to seek out that special anniversary, birthday or wedding present; it is also a focal point for any Christmas shopping trip. Visitors can browse at their leisure, taking in the exquisite collection of gifts and antiques, and friendly and helpful advice always on hand, if required. Prices range across the board and there is something to suit everyone's taste and pocket. On your way out, you may well be tempted to take a photograph of the beautiful 'typical English cottage garden' which adjoins the gallery.

Unicorn Gallery, The Street, Castle Combe Tel: 01249 782291

On Castle Combe's old Market Place there is a delightful tearoom and bed and breakfast establishment called The Gates. The Gates is a delightful place, owned and run by Hilary Baker and her cheerful staff whose attention to detail is renowned.

The Gates, The Market Place, Castle Combe Tel: 01249 782111

Situated in the heart of this lovely Cotswold village, it was built in the 15th century and was formerly a bordello. It is the perfect place to relax and enjoy a tasty lunch or to while away an hour or two over a cup of coffee and a piece of one of the mouthwatering cakes on offer. Hilary also provides bed and breakfast accommodation in two rooms, one family and one double, both of which have low-beamed ceilings and are full of character.

In marked contrast with the rest of Castle Combe, a popular motor racing circuit is located a mile or so to the east of the village.

The quiet rural backwater of UPPER WRAXALL is one of several delightful communities which lie on the southwestern fringe of the Cotswold Hills; it is also the location of The Coach House, an impressive country guesthouse which is set within eight acres of beautiful secluded grounds.

If you are looking for somewhere to stay that combines peaceful seclusion with easy access to places of interest, then the Coach House is perfect. This tiny hamlet provides a tranquil setting for this beautifully converted barn. David and Helga Venables are friendly and welcoming hosts whose former guests often return as friends. Their lovely stone-built house offers first-class accommodation. The interior is elegant and spacious and has three beautifully furnished en-suite guest rooms which provide every modern comfort. Set in attractive landscaped grounds containing a full-sized croquet lawn and hard tennis court, the Coach House makes a perfect holiday hideaway.

The Coach House, Upper Wraxall, Nr. Chippenham
Tel: 01225 891026

A mile or so to the west, and just over the Avon border, why not make a short detour to visit the exceptional old coaching village of

MARSHFIELD. The village stands on a ridge which, in the 18th century, formed part of the main London to Bristol coaching route. At almost a mile long, the High Street is one of the longest in the country; in its heyday, it contained over a dozen coaching inns, including the famous Catherine Wheel, one of only three survivors. Another of Marshfield's relics from the era of the stagecoach is an 18th-century road sign with the inscription, '103 miles to London, 12 miles and 1 furlong to Bristol'.

Marshfield was also an important wool trading and malting centre, and many of the large stone-built houses which line the main street were built on the proceeds of these activities. Despite them having been constructed in two almost continuous rows, the buildings still manage to create an atmosphere of elegance and charm. Indeed, much of the old part of the village, between the early-17th-century Crispe almshouses at one end of the High Street and the imposing parish Church of St Mary at the other, is now a designated conversation area.

One of Marshfield's more eccentric businesses operated in the High Street until 1983. Bodman's grocery and drapery shop was opened by Mr Bodman Snr in 1860s, and when it passed to his son at the beginning of this century, Mr Bodman Jnr made so few alterations that the store gradually became a living museum. Young Mr Bodman refused to make any changes to the Edwardian fixtures and fittings, and if a long-standing item of stock took his fancy, he would often refuse to sell it. This situation persisted until his death at the age of ninety, after which the contents of the shop mostly fell into the hands of museum curators and antique dealers.

Retracing your steps back across the Wiltshire border, turn north into the country lanes before stopping for some refreshment in the charming Cotswold village of NETTLETON. Here you will find the Nettleton Arms, a traditional inn which also offers first-rate overnight accommodation.

For lovers of country pubs, a visit to the Nettleton Arms is a must. It has a well-deserved reputation for good food, fine beers (there is a guest cask-conditioned beer each week), and an excellent selection of wines. The landlords, Sheena and Chris Phizaklea, are charming hosts, and the wonderful culinary skill of Sandra House allows customers to savour such delicacies as stuffed local trout, pork Provençale and beef Wellington, as well as a tasty selection of vegetarian dishes, all at very affordable prices. For those wishing to stay there are four beautifully appointed rooms in the old coach house (two doubles, two singles), all with en-suite facilities.

The Nettleton Arms, Nettleton, Nr. Chippenham Tel: 01249 782783

The nearby hamlet of **NETTLETON SHRUB** is the location of an exceptional country hotel and restaurant which goes under the unassuming name of **Fosse Farmhouse**.

Fosse Farmhouse, Nettleton Shrub, Nr. Chippenham
Tel: 01249 782286

Located in the heart of the Beaufort Hunt on the historic Fosse Way, Fosse Farmhouse is a lovely Cotswold country house built in 1750 which is now a first-class hotel and restaurant. It is owned and run by Caron Cooper, a chef of international repute who has

144

built a substantial reputation in the area for outstanding food and stunning interior decoration. An orchard links the main house to the tea and breakfast rooms where guests can enjoy a light lunch or treat themselves to a luscious cream tea. In the evening, there are further temptations on the dinner menu, such as smoked duck breast with salad, followed by chicken with wild mushroom sauce. Before leaving, guests are advised to look around the outhouses which are filled with interesting relics from the past, as well as antiques, flowers, homemade jam and lovely country gifts, all of them for sale. Immediately opposite the farmhouse is the Castle Combe Golf and Country Club which guests are welcome to use.

The 15,000-acre Badminton Estate lies a mile or so to the east of the B4040 Malmesbury road. Famous for its annual three-day horse trials which take place eachyear, this has been the country seat of the Dukes of Beaufort since the 17th century. Badminton House, an imposing Palladian-style mansion, contains an impressive art collection, including paintings from the Italian, English and Dutch schools and some exquisite wood-carving by master-carver Grinling Gibbons.

Many of the buildings on the Badminton Estate, including the parish Church of St Michael and All Angels which stands adjacent to the main house, were designed by architect Thomas Wright in a romantic castellated style. Examples of his architectural influence can also be seen in the two estate villages of LITTLE BADMINTON and GREAT BADMINTON, the latter of which contains some substantial stone-built residences and a row of splendid 18th-century almshouses.

On one wet afternoon during the 1860s, guests to Badminton House are said to have come up with an idea for a novel new game. Having found some crude children's rackets and corks studded with feathers, they decided to attempt a game of indoor tennis and proceeded to stretch a string across the hall as a net. That afternoon, the game of badminton was born. A few years later, one of the guests is believed to have taken a version of the game to the Indian subcontinent where the first formal rules were drawn up in Karachi in 1877.

Returning to the B4040 turn north near the village of Luckington to reach the lovely old community of SOPWORTH. Those looking for top quality farmhouse bed and breakfast accommodation should look out here for Manor Farm, a charming Jacobean country farmhouse which stands in a wonderful position overlooking the village.

The farmhouse is run by a lovely lady, Diana Barker, who was born here and has provided bed and breakfast accommodation for many years. Many of her guests return time and time again to enjoy her warm friendly hospitality and excellent cooking. All the guest rooms are en-suite and have breathtaking views over the surrounding countryside. The farm is actually part of the Badminton Estate and home of many spirited and finely-bred horses. Set in this idyllic location on the Gloucestershire-Wiltshire border, Manor Farm is a simply enchanting place to relax and get away from it all.

Manor Farm, Sopworth, Nr. Chippenham Tel: 01454 238676

From Sopworth, it is only a short drive to SHERSTON, an attractive village lying beside the B4040, two miles to the east (the village is also known by its historic name, SHERSTON MAGNA). At the centre of this ancient settlementyou will find the charmingly named Rattlebone Inn and Restaurant, a first-rate hostelry with a long and interesting history. In 1016, Edmund Ironside defeated Canute near here in the Battle of Sherston and John Rattlebone, a local hero, sustained a mortal wound and expired, it is believed, on the site where the inn now stands.

Today, the Rattlebone Inn has a deserved reputation for fine cask-conditioned ales and excellent food, with such delicacies on the menu as smoked trout mousse, or deep-fried brie with redcurrant jelly, followed by the likes of mushroom and chestnut Stroganoff or lamb steak with Madeira, honey and tarragon. Customers can also enjoy playing traditional and modern pub games in the public bar, or wander out to the old stables for a game of skittles. Full of traditional atmosphere, this really is a fine example of a typical English inn.

The Rattlebone Inn, Church Street, Sherston Tel: 01666 840871

A delightful place to stay in this tranquil backwater can be found at **Widleys Farm**. Situated in the heart of the Wiltshire Cotswolds, Widleys Farm is a 300-acre working arable and dairy farm.

Widleys Farm, Sherston, Malmesbury Tel: 01666 840213

The 18th-century farmhouse is run by a lovely lady, Mary Hibbard, who provides three spacious family rooms all with washbasins, colour televisions and hot drinks facilities. Here, you can be sure of real countryside hospitality and Mary will readily provide a fabulous four-course dinner on request. The farmhouse is surrounded by beautiful gardens and stables, while among the farm buildings, there is an impressive Cotswold stone tithe barn. With the famous Westonbirt Arboretum close by and Slimbridge Wildfowl Trust within easy reach, Widleys Farm makes a very comfortable touring base for the Cotswolds.

From here, continuing northeast along the B4040 and passing through Sherston Magna's sister village of Sherston Parva you will soon arrive in the fine old community of EASTON GREY. Here, the Sherston branch of the River Avon is spanned by a 16th-century bridge consisting of five low stone arches. The village itself rises from the riverbank along a curved main street of densely-packed grey limestone houses, most with mullioned windows and steeply-pitched gabled roofs.

A manor house has looked down from the hill above Easton Grey since the 13th century. The present-day mansion dates from the early-18th-century and has a classical façade with an elegant covered portico. The building stands within beautiful landscaped grounds which also contain a small church with a Norman tower and font and an interior which was extensively renovated during the 1830s.

Once owned by his sister-in-law, the house was used a summer retreat by Herbert Asquith, Britain's prime minister from 1908-16, then in 1923, it was occupied by the Prince of Wales for the duration of the Duke of Beaufort's hunting season at Badminton.

The village of STANTON ST QUINTIN lies not far from here. This attractive community possesses an exceptionally fine village church, St Giles, which dates from the 11th to 15th centuries and was much altered by the Victorians. Outside under the west window, there is an unusual 12th-century carved figure of the enthroned Christ with a dragon at his feet.

Superb bed and breakfast accommodation is also available at Stanton St Quintin's elegant former rectory, Stanton Court Now the impressive country home of Anne Adams, Stanton Court lies just one mile northwest of junction 17 on the M4. Mrs Adams also has connections with the Whole Hog, a first-class food, ale and wine house which stands on Malmesbury's Market Cross.

Stanton Court, Stanton St Quintin Tel: 01666 825845/837007

From here, driving north towards Malmesbury and you will soon pass through CORSTON, a pleasant village which is the home to a very pleasant bed and breakfast establishment, Manor Farm.

Manor Farm, Corston, Nr. Malesbury Tel: 01666 822148

Corston's Manor Farm is one of those delightful old farmhouses which is steeped in the age-old tradition of agriculture. Wiltshire still has a very strong farming community and nowadays, more and more of these wonderful farmhouses are opening their doors to welcome guests into their homes. Situated beside the main Malmesbury to Chippenham road and surrounded by attractive open countryside, the farmhouse is set amongst 436 acres of farmland producing milk and cereals. The house is full of character and guests have use of a shared lounge which has a lovely large stone fireplace. In winter, log fires are a treat for guests to enjoy and there is also a colour television for those wishing to curl up in front of the fire. In the dining room there is an old inglenook fireplace and a beautiful antique dining table on which guests are served their meals.

Be warned that the traditional English breakfasts Ross serves are large enough to satisfy the hungriest of appetites. The bedrooms were well furnished and very comfortable, and many have wonderful views over the beautiful Wiltshire countryside. Ross and John add to the lovely tranquil atmosphere of Manor Farm by making all guests feel very welcome throughout their stay.

From Corston, it is only a short drive north to the old ecclesiastical centre of MALMESBURY, a gem of a town which thankfully is bypassed by the main A429 Chippenham to Cirencester road. One of the finest attractions in this part of northwest Wiltshire, this historic settlement stands between two branches of the Bristol Avon around the site of a Saxon hill fort. A Benedictine abbey was founded here in the 7th century by St Aldhelm, then in 880 Alfred the Great granted the town a charter and so created what is perhaps the oldest borough in England.

King Athelstan, Alfred's grandson and the first Saxon monarch to unite the whole of England, was buried in the abbey in 941, an event which was commemorated in the 15th century when an impressive monument was erected on the site. Some years before, King Athelstan granted 500 acres of land to the townspeople of Malmesbury who had helped him resist a Norse invasion. The area known as King's Heath still belongs to around 200 residents of the town who can trace their ancestry back to the men who fought for the Saxon king in the 10th century.

One of the first attempts at human-powered flight was made from the abbey tower by a monk of Malmesbury early in the 11th century. Brother Elmer (who is also known as Oliver) strapped a pair of homemade wings to his arms, and flapping wildly, flew for some 200 yards before returning to earth with a crash, breaking both of this legs and crippling himself for life. Despite this mishap, he lived on for another fifty years and is said to have predicted the

Norman invasion following a sighting of Halley's comet. Elmer's pioneering flight is commemorated in one of the present-day abbey's stained-glass windows.

Following Henry VIII's Dissolution of the Monasteries in 1539, the abbey was sold to a wealthy local wool merchant, William Stumpe, for the sum of £1517 15s 2d. He proceeded to set up cloth-weaving workshops in several of the old abbey buildings; however, the great church, much of which is Romanesque, survived this indignity and was presented to the town as a new parish church in 1541.

Malmesbury Abbey

The remains of Malmesbury Abbey contain some of the finest Norman features in the south of England, most notably the south porch with its ornately carved arch depicting scenes from the Bible. Other noteworthy features are the 'watching loft', the 15th-century church screen and the ornate roof bosses in the nave. The building is also believed to have once possessed the oldest church organ in the country.

The base of the old town of Malmesbury is virtually surrounded by the two branches of the Avon. To reach the centre of town, it is necessary to cross one of six bridges and then climb up the steep

151

slope leading to the Market Square. An elaborate covered Market Cross stands in the centre of the square; an unusual octagonal building, it has some fine faulting and was constructed in the late 15th century to provide shelter for the market traders. A few steps from here is the **Whole Hog**, a first-class food, ale and wine house which has connections with Stanton Court, the excellent bed and breakfast establishment we visited in the village of Stanton St Quintin.

The Smoking Dog, 62 High Street, Malmesbury Tel: 01666 825823

Other noteworthy buildings near Malmesbury's Market Square are the Old Stone House with its handsome colonnade and grotesque gargoyles, the arched Tolsey Gate whose two cells once served as the town gaol, and the Abbey House which was constructed by William Stumpe to replace the old abbot's residence. A stroll down the High Street leads past some lovely old buildings, most of which are constructed of locally-quarried stone. At No. 62 pause and call in at the **Smoking Dog**, a historic pub with a wonderful friendly atmosphere and an air of old-fashioned affability. The Bath stone walls and old black beams reflect the town's Anglo-Saxon roots and create a wonderful mellow atmosphere. It is apparent that this is a popular pub as soon as you enter the busy laughter-filled bars.

The proprietor, Susan Robson, has a well-deserved reputation for serving excellent food, wine and cask-conditioned ales. The meals are reasonably priced and the portions healthy; the house specialities such as Old English eggnog pie and farmhouse chicken are particularly recommended. A visit to the Smoking Dog is sure to leave you relaxed and refreshed.

The Old Bell Hotel is situated in the centre of town next to Malmesbury Abbey and is believed to be one of the oldest hostelries in England. Established by an early Abbot of Malmesbury, the Old Bell was mentioned in the Domesday Book and is now a Grade I listed building. Present-day visitors can feel the great sense of history as they walk through the door. A wonderful original fireplace remains in the reception hall and visitors can imagine being welcomed in the way King John's guests would have been received 750 years ago; at that time, large numbers of people came to Malmesbury to study in the Abbey's famous library.

Each of the present-day guest rooms has been individually designed to reflect a part of the building's fascinating history. All have their own style and character, with heavy beams and mullioned windows adding atmosphere to the elegance of the rooms. All bedrooms are centrally heated and have tea/coffee making facilities, colour televisions, telephones and private bathrooms. One suite, the Athelstan, is named after the Saxon King who, in 925 AD, made Malmesbury his capital.

The Old Bell Hotel, Malmesbury Tel: 01666 822344

Before dinner, visitors can enjoy a drink in the cocktail bar which, like the dining room, is Edwardian, having been added in 1908. The whole atmosphere is one of elegance and quiet grandeur in keeping with the hotel's history. The menu is imaginative and tempting, and the wine list extensive and well-chosen. Like the

Stonehouse Court Hotel mentioned in our next chapter, the Old Bell is a member of the Clipper Hotels Group. This small collection of first-class hotels offers a high standard of comfort, service and a great attention to detail.

Bremilham House, Bremilham Road, Malmesbury
Tel: 01666 822680

Those looking for more secluded guesthouse accommodation in Malmesbury should make a point of finding Bremilham House in Bremilham Road. This handsome residence is a true Edwardian country villa built in the golden days before the First World War. Run by Sue and Peter Ball, the guesthouse has a friendly, relaxed atmosphere and first-class service is always provided with a smile. The accommodation comprises two double, one twin and one single room, all furnished to a very high standard. Sue is an excellent cook and her breakfasts are a real treat. The gardens are delightful and on fine days guests can enjoy their tea or coffee outdoors, or take the pleasant walk into Malmesbury.

Alternatively, first-rate farmhouse bed and breakfast accommodation is available on the southern outskirts of Malmesbury at Arches Farm. This traditional 17th-century farmhouse stands at the heart of a 250-acre working farm to the south. Run by a lovely lady, Ruby Webb, her light and airy house provides visitors with spacious and comfortable accommodation. The charming dining room, with its panelled and shuttered alcove windows, makes the perfect setting for the à la carte breakfasts which Ruby prepares for all her guests. The south-facing windows offer lovely views over rolling farmland and fill the house with light and warmth, enhancing the welcoming atmosphere.

Arches Farm, Arches Lane, Malmesbury Tel: 01666 822367

A minor country road to the east of Malmesbury leads to GARSDON, a peaceful community whose village church is noted for containing the 'Stars and Stripes' monument. This unusual tomb belongs to Laurence Washington, a local lord of the manor who was buried here in 1640, many years before the Stars and Stripes became a symbol of America. Washington bought the manor from Richard Moody, a contemporary of Henry VIII who is reputed to have been given the estate as a reward for freeing the king from a deep mud-filled mire and helping him back onto his horse. Earlier this century, the Stars and Stripes monument was restored with the help of funds donated by a number of American benefactors including the Bishop of New York.

The narrow country lanes to the north of Garsdon lead through the villages of Hankerton and Eastcourt to our next destination, the sprawling settlement of OAKSEY. The village possesses some fine 17th-century cottages and a small 13th-century church which contains a number of rare medieval paintings. The south wall also features an unusual painting entitled Christ of Trades which shows Jesus surrounded by an array of hand tools, a vivid reminder to the congregation that moral salvation lies in hard labour. The local lord of the manor, Lord Oaksey, is perhaps better known as John Oaksey, the former jockey and TV racing commentator. The interesting remains of the Norman motte and bailey fortification known as Norwood Castle lie on private land near Dean Farm to the north of the village.

An excellent base for exploring the Cotswolds can be found in the ancient farming hamlet of WEST CRUDWELL. Here, Zandra Browning not only provides wonderful farmhouse bed and breakfast accommodation, but she also has two superbly-equipped four-bedroom holiday cottages available which, like the farmhouse, are beautifully appointed and decorated in striking contemporary style.

Jacks Cottage and Rabbit Cottage, West Crudwell
Tel: 01666 577205

From Tetbury to the River Severn

Chavenage Manor

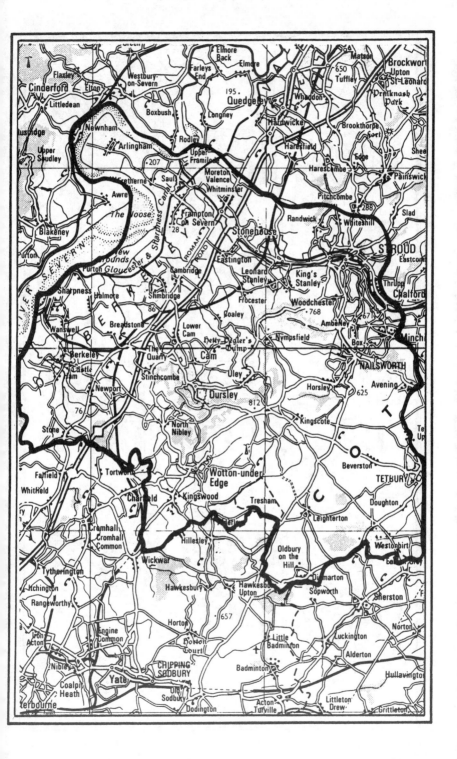

The Great Hall, Berkeley Castle

From Tetbury to the River Severn

We begin our tour around the minor roads of Gloucestershire in the delightful Elizabethan market town of TETBURY. Once an important centre for the wool trade, the now-restored 17th-century Market House can still be seen in the middle of the town. At one time, fleeces were weighed and sold amongst the stone pillars in the open colonnade. On Wednesdays, the building is filled with antique stalls and the exterior is surrounded by modern market stalls which sell an enormous variety of produce from fresh fruit and vegetables to handmade local crafts.

Chipping Lane connects the Market House to The Chipping (an Old English word meaning market) via the famous Chipping Steps. This ancient stairway descends past a collection of charming stepped houses which together give a marvellous impression of the town's historic past.

Also worth visiting in Tetbury is St Mary's Church. Restored in 1781 at the height of town's wool-trading prosperity, the interior is now considered an 18th-century period piece. It features pews with unusually high backs, vast windows made from recycled medieval glass, and slender timber columns which conceal iron supports, an innovative building system at the time. Look out also for stone tablet which carries the inscription:

> *"In a vault underneath*
> *lie several of the Saunderses,*
> *late of this parish; particulars*
> *the Last Day will disclose. Amen"*

The interesting Tetbury Police Bygones Museum is housed in the original cells of the Old Court House and police station and can be found adjacent to the tourist information office in Long Street. Admission is free to this unusual exhibition of historic artefacts, uniforms and memorabilia from the annals of the Gloucestershire

Constabulary. (Open Monday to Saturday, 10am to 4.15pm, Easter to the end-October.)

A point in the road outside the Crown Inn is the start and finish line of the Tetbury Woolsack races, held every year and in which the competitors run up and down nearby Gumstool Hill, one of the steepest in Gloucestershire. The name Gumstool derives from the 'ducking stools' which were used to inflict a damp and cruel torture on many an unfortunate inhabitant.

Those looking for top quality guesthouse accommodation in Tetbury should look out for Gordon House in Silver Street. This handsome Grade II listed residence is a fine example of an 18th-century merchant's house with a 19th-century frontage. Visitors receive a warm welcome from hosts Josie and Danny Drinkwater who provide good value and tasty home-cooked breakfasts; they are also happy to cater for vegetarian tastes. Weather permitting, guests can take coffee in the beautifully-kept walled garden, and indoors, there are two delightful dolls' houses on show. Indeed, Josie and Danny actually make one-twelfth scale reproduction 19th-century furniture and figures using pure silk, velvet and needlepoint for which exclusive commissions are undertaken. Gordon House is a non-smoking establishment.

Gordon House, 12 Silver Street, Tetbury Tel: 01666 503383

On the western side of the B4014 one-and-a-half miles northwest of Tetbury is Chavenage House, a fine Elizabethan mansion built of mellow grey Cotswold stone in the characteristic 'E' shape. The beautiful front aspect of Chavenage has remained

162

virtually unchanged since Edward Stephens added the wings and porch to the former manor house in 1576. At that time, the Stephens family were exceedingly wealthy but over the years they grew less so and Chavenage became heavily mortgaged. Despite this, it has always remained in the family, the present owners, the Lowsley-Williams, being connected to the Stephens by marriage.

Inside, there are some superb rooms containing rare 17th-century tapestries, period furniture, fine pictures and many relics of the Cromwellian era. In the main hall there is a contemporary screen which forms a delightful minstrels' gallery, and there are also two tapestry rooms where Cromwell is believed to have been accommodated. (Curiously, despite its Cromwellian connections the house is said to be haunted by King Charles I.)

Separated from the house by a narrow passage is the family chapel. The chapel tower was built as a folly in the early 1700s and the rest of the building was attached to it some 100 years later. Look out for the amusing gargoyles incorporated into the masonry. (Opening times are limited to 2pm to 5pm on Thursdays, Sundays and Bank Holiday Mondays between May and September. Admission charge payable.)

From Chavenage, head south onto the A4135 Tetbury to Dursley road to reach **BEVERSTONE**, a model village which was built by Victorian estate-owner R S Holford, a noted connoisseur of the Renaissance period. Conceived by consultant architect Lewis Vulliamy, the housing in the village combines careful design with improved standards of accommodation. The terraced cottages, lodges and model farms are built of golden Cotswold limestone and are positioned along the road which runs directly through the village. A side road leads to Beverstone Castle which was occupied by Earl Godwin, the father of King Harold, around 1051. The medieval village church has a tower containing a marvellous, though damaged, pre-Conquest sculpture of the Resurrection which is worth making the effort to find.

From Beverstone, head south again, this time towards Holford's sister project, Westonbirt House. The 22-acre Westonbirt Gardens contain magnificent lawns, trees and stonework and are a product of the once-fashionable practice of emparking, the process by which all village buildings standing within sight of the main house (except, in this case, the church) would be removed and rebuilt a discreet distance away. In this way, Holford and his landscape architect accomplice, W S Gilpin, were able to guarantee uninterrupted views over the country estate.

Westonbirt House is now a celebrated girls' boarding school and is only open to the public twice a year. The Gardens are open occasionally under the National Gardens Scheme. Admission charge payable.

Westonbirt Arboretum, Tetbury Tel: 01666 880220

Adjacent to Westonbirt Gardens and just a short distance further along the B4067 lies the world-famous Westonbirt Arboretum. Now incorporated into a 600-acre Forestry Commission estate, this unique place was founded in 1829 by Robert Stayner Holford of Westonbirt House, an amateur enthusiast who had a great love of trees and began planting for his own pleasure. In due course his son, Sir George Holford, acquired his father's passion for trees and continued the work with even greater zeal until 1926 when he died and was succeeded by his nephew, the fourth Earl of Morley. However, it was not until 1956 that Forest Enterprise acquired Westonbirt and opened it to the general public.

The grounds now contain some 18,000 listed specimens of trees and shrubs from all over the world, a collection which is considered to be one of the largest and most important in the world. Some plants are very rarely found in cultivation, others are extinct in the wild, their only sanctuary being collections such as this. Because Westonbirt Arboretum is primarily a research and conservation establishment there is always something going on at any time of the year. Perhaps the spring flowering shrubs in April and May and the autumn foliage colours in October are the most spectacular features of the Westonbirt, but whenever you come you will find the arboretum beautiful.

Visitors are able to wander wherever they like, however, for those who prefer a guided walk, there are several waymarked trails along selected sections of the seventeen miles of paths and glades. A trail guide can be bought at the visitor centre which also contains an interesting and informative exhibition area, a video presentation and a country gift shop. There is also a cafeteria which opens from 10am to 5pm each day from Easter until mid-November. Picnic tables are also provided adjacent to the car park.

Tavern House, Willesley, Nr Tetbury Tel: 01666 880444

A good place to stay within easy reach of Westonbirt Arboretum is Tavern House in WILLESLEY. This charming part 17th-century former coaching house is run as a first-rate guesthouse by a lovely couple, Tim and Janet Tremellen. The house enjoys a tranquil secluded setting opposite Silk Wood, a stretch of woodland which leads to the Arboretum. Inside, visitors will find superb accommodation in the form of three doubles and one twin room; all are exquisitely furnished with antique furniture and are equipped with en-suite bath- or shower-rooms (most also have a bidet). The full English breakfast menu is varied and includes freshly-cooked fillet of kipper or haddock. In fine weather, meals can be served outside in the beautiful walled garden. Despite its secluded

165

setting, Tavern House is situated within a thirty-minute drive of Bath and Bristol; it also lies only about three miles from Badminton, venue for the famous horse trials.

From here continue southwest on the A433 until you reach the charming village of **DIDMARTON**, site of the medieval church of St. Lawrence. Now disused but remaining open to visitors, this lovely little building stands bedside a towering Wellingtonia and, unlike most of its contemporaries which were remodelled by the Victorians, has remained unaltered since the 18th century. Inside, there are antique box pews painted in Georgian green, an unusual three-storey pulpit, and at the rear of the church, a row of hat pegs set sixteen feet above the floor, evidence that the church was either populated by a congregation of giants or that there was once an upper gallery.

Berkeley Castle

Set back from the church behind the Wellingtonia is a 17th-century manor house which has seen better days. On the other side of the road, look out for the semicircle of stones which marks the site of St Lawrence's Well. According to village legend, St Lawrence himself visited the spot in the 6th century, and after blessing the well, he assured the local inhabitants that it would never run dry.

In the centre of Didmarton, look out for Kingsmead House which stands out from the rest because of its unusual octagonal gazebo which was strategically built on the highway to allow the owner to get an early glimpse of the coaches from Bath. In the garden, there is also an interesting Gothic hermit's house made from yew wood.

From Didmarton, head north along a minor country road until you reach the secluded village of LEIGHTERTON. Here, why not stop to take a look at the church which is approached past a row of stone-built cottages and a pleasant-looking inn. This striking building has an ancient tower with a timber belfry and an oak spire and is surrounded by a churchyard containing characteristic dark-leafed yew trees.

From Leighterton, turn west across a narrow strip of Avon and descend into a wooded vale near the Gloucestershire village of ALDERLEY, another pleasant community with a castellated church and a handsome Elizabethan house which has been converted into a school. The gardens of Alderley Grange at Brackenbury contain some fine aromatic plants, herbs and old-fashioned roses. They are open under the National Gardens Scheme. Also of interest is the nearby Alderley Trout Farm.

A mile north of Alderley village make a point of stopping in WORTLEY to visit the site of a Roman villa which was discovered in 1981 when some local people were digging a hole for a fence post and unearthed a section of mosaic floor. Further excavation has taken place each year since then, and so far a bath house complex in two phases with over six rooms has been uncovered. Further Roman ruins have been discovered nearby, along with a 3rd-century paved courtyard and some enormous stone drain-blocks. A small museum on the site contains a selection of the many hundreds of historic items found here during excavations. (Open 2pm to 5pm, mid-June to end-September.)

Our next stop is the delightful small country town of WOTTON-UNDER-EDGE. For centuries, the town was involved in the wool and silk trade and at one time contained as many as thirteen textile mills. Several 17th- and 18th-century town houses remain, the top floors of which were once used as weaving rooms. These are built in a mix of styles from traditional stone-built Cotswold to the half-timbered brick more characteristic of the Severn Vale. Also constructed around this time (1632) were the Perry and Dawes

Almshouses which are set around a hidden cobbled quadrangle in Church Street. Look out also for Tolsey House on the corner of Market Street, an old brick building with a cone of Cotswold tiles, which was once the toll house for the market.

Going further back into the past, Wotton-under-Edge has a 14th-century school and a fine 13th- to 15th-century church dedicated to St Mary The Virgin. Subsequently refurbished on the wealth of wool and cloth trade, the room above the porch once contained a collection of rare books which are now housed at Christ Church, Oxford. The church also has a noteworthy organ which was removed from St Martin-in-the-Fields in London and is said to have been played by Handel.

During the time Isaac Pitman (1813-97) was a schoolmaster in Wotton he owned a house in Orchard Street where he devised his world-renowned system of shorthand. Another interesting building in the town is the imposing gabled woollen mill which has a clock tower and a large pond and dates from around 1800. The present-day complex still operates as a textile factory, though the old buildings are open to visitors by appointment. These contain a number of interesting industrial relics including a wool stove and a circular kiln in which washed wool was dried.

For those with a special interest in the local history of the district, Wotton-under-Edge Historical Society's Library and Museum is situated adjacent to the main library in Ludgate Hill. This contains a fascinating collection of books, documents, maps, photographs and historic ephemera. (Open Saturdays 10am to 12 noon; also Tuesdays (Easter to end-October), 2.30pm to 4.30pm. Admission free.)

Two miles east of Wotton-under-Edge, make a point of visiting OZLEWORTH for two reasons: firstly, the village Church of St Nicholas is one of the most noteworthy in Gloucestershire in that it stands within a circular churchyard, one of only two in England (the churchyard is thought to have been a holy place since pagan times). It also has an unusual six-sided Norman tower which is constructed in the middle of the church. Secondly, Ozleworth is the location of the National Trust-owned Newark Park, an impressive hunting lodge built close to a precipice by the Poyntz family in Elizabethan times. Major alterations were carried out by James Wyatt in 1790 to create a four-square castellated country house, and today, the house is undergoing a further course of renovation by the present tenant, R L Parsons, who is responsible for showing visitors around. (Open 2pm to 5pm, Wednesdays and Thursdays during April, May, August and September. Admission charge payable; free to National Trust members.)

There are also some fine walks around Ozleworth including one which takes in Midger Wood Nature Reserve (managed by the Gloucestershire Trust for Nature Conservation) and on up to Nan Tow's Tump, a huge round barrow which, being nine feet high and some 100 feet in diameter, is one of the largest and most mystical Bronze Age barrows in the west of England. It is thought to contain the remains of Nan Tow, a local witch who was buried in an upright position.

Jenner Museum, Berkeley

Marvellous views of the surrounding area can be enjoyed from the top of Coaley Peak in **NYMPSFIELD** where the Neolithic chambered Nympsfield Long Barrow can be found. Nympsfield Gardens are also worth a look, and for those interested in gliding, trial lessons and five-day holiday courses are offered by the locally-based Bristol and Gloucestershire Gliding Club (telephone 01453 860342).

Nearby you will come across Woodchester Park Mansion, an uncompleted Gothic country house which was designed by Benjamin Bucknall. This unfinished masterpiece is currently finding a new life as a centre for training stonemasons and building conservationists in traditional methods of construction. The site is open April to October on Bank Holiday weekends and the first weekend in every month. Admission charge payable. Unsuitable for children under twelve and dogs.

From here head south to the delightful old cloth-making village of ULEY. During the 17th and 18th centuries, Uley was a hive of economic activity, and as early as 1608, it was recorded that three local cloth-merchants earned a living from marketing the products of 29 local weavers, most of whom produced broadcloth.

Today, the village is a peaceful place which lies in the shadow of the massive Uley Bury Iron Age hill fort. Banked ditches mark the outer rim of this magnificent 32-acre construction which are mostly given over to the cultivation of arable crops and remain largely unexcavated. However in recent years, some evidence of the wealthy community who inhabited the fort in the first century BC has been unearthed. Items discovered include bronze, glass and shale jewellery, gold coins and iron ingots (a form of currency) which have been attributed to the Dobunni tribe within whose lands Uley Bury is situated.

About one mile north of the hill fort lies Uley Tumulus which is better known as Hetty Pegler's Tump, so-called after Hester Pegler, the wife of a landowner who lived nearby in the 17th century. This 180 foot long Neolithic long barrow contains four burial chambers, the keys to which can be obtained from Crawley Hill Farm, half a mile to the south on the B4066. Each of the chambers is reached by creeping along a short low passage. When inside, the torchlight reveals that the walls and ceilings were constructed of huge stone slabs filled with dry-stone material. In the last century, as many as 38 skeletons were discovered within these shadowy vaults.

Back in the car, drive west through DURSLEY, an undistinguished small town with an industrial feel. However, there are a couple of notable old buildings: the Market House dating from 1738 has overhanging upper floors supported by pillars and an interesting bell turret on the roof. It also contains a statue of Queen Anne and the coat of arms of the Estcourt family. The parish Church of St James was constructed in the 14th and 15th centuries and is also worth a look. William Shakespeare is rumoured to have spent some months staying with relatives at Dursley while laying low after being spotted poaching Thomas Lacy's deer at Charlecote. One legacy of his stay is the reference to a local bailiff in Henry IV.

One mile to the north is the village of CAM. Its modern urban appearance disguises the fact that it dates from the 11th century when its manor, known as Camma, formed part of the huge Berkeley estate. The village has been a cloth-making centre for centuries and today, Cam Mill continues the practice which began in 1522. Look out also for Hopton Manor School which was founded in 1730 making it one of the oldest primary schools in the country.

A short distance from Cam village is the small, uniformly-shaped hill known as Cam Long Down. This strange, isolated peak is steeped in local mythology. It is said that the Devil, thinking the landscape too much God's country, decided to cart the Cotswolds away in barrow loads to dam the Severn. After loading up, he set out on his journey and met a cobbler laden with shoes. 'How far is it to the river?' asked Satan. The cobbler showed him one of the shoes he was taking home to mend and replied, 'Do you see this sole? Well, I've worn it out walking from the Severn.' At this point, the Devil abandoned his task and tipped out his barrow, an act which is said to account for the unusual formation that can be seen today. Cam Long Down is also rumoured to be the site of King Arthur's final battle. Legend has it that he crossed the River Severn and confronted his enemies at an unknown place known as Camlann. Whatever its history, a strange mystical atmosphere persists here today.

To the west, heading along the B4060, is STINCHCOMBE, a charming village which stands beneath Stinchcombe Hill on the edge of the Vale of Berkeley. A couple of noteworthy buildings can be found in and around the village: Melksham House was built in the 17th century and was home to the Tyndale family for over 300 years; Piers Court, built during the 18th century, was once the home of Evelyn Waugh.

To the south of Stinchcombe lies Stancombe Park, a fine country residence rebuilt in 1880 on the site of a Roman villa whose original mosaic floor was removed and transported to Gloucester museum.

The surrounding gardens are open to the public under the National Gardens Scheme for a limited number of days each year.

Before crossing the M5, a slight detour south along the B4060 brings you to NORTH NIBLEY, the place where William Tyndale was born in 1484. He is thought to be one of the first scholars to translate the Scriptures into English, and it is upon his work that the authorised version of the Bible was subsequently based. For his trouble, he was unfortunately strangled and burned at the stake at Vilvorde near Brussels in 1536.

The Tyndale Monument was later constructed to commemorate the life and work of this early pioneer. Built in 1866 by public subscription, the monument stands 111 feet high on top of a 700 foot escarpment and forms a prominent landmark on the route of the Cotswold Way. North Nibley is also noted for being the site of the last 'private' battle in England which took place in 1471 between the rival barons William Lord Berkeley and the Viscount De Lisle.

The Bird in Hand, Mary Brook Street, Berkeley Tel: 01453 511192

From North Nibley, head northwest along a minor country road which, after crossing the M5, leads to the peaceful little town of BERKELEY. If you are in need of a refreshment stop, before setting out to explore the town call in at the Bird In Hand in Mary Brook Street.

Dating from the 17th century and containing original oak beams throughout, the Bird In Hand is a pub rich in character where customers come to enjoy an appetising bar meal or relax with a

172

drink in front of a welcoming open log fire. Its location makes it an ideal touring base, being close to Slimbridge Wildfowl Trust and within easy walking distance of Berkeley Castle and the Jenner Museum. Run by Keith Wood, this charming establishment has recently been modernised and extended and now includes a skittle alley, a luxurious guest lounge and a lovely restaurant with an extensive à la carte menu. Twelve comfortable en-suite bedrooms have also been available at the Bird In Hand since the spring of 1993, complementing the excellent facilities of this already first-rate establishment.

Although most of the buildings in Berkeley date from Georgian times, the town is dominated by its imposing castle, said to be the oldest inhabited castle in England. Built between 1117 and 1153 on the site of a pre-Norman fort, it has remained in the Berkeley family for over 800 years.

It was here that in 1215, the barons of the west congregated before setting out to witness the sealing of the Magna Carta by King John at Runnymede. Perhaps the event for which Berkeley Castle is most notorious, however, is the gruesome murder of King Edward II in 1327. Having been usurped from the throne by his wife and her lover because of his ineffectual rule and ill-judged choice of friends, Edward was imprisoned for months at the castle before meeting a literally terrible end, supposedly 'with a hoot brooche put into the secret place posteriale'.

Subsequent monarchs appear to have received rather better hospitality when visiting Berkeley: Richard II was well-entertained here and Elizabeth I is known to have stayed on several occasions.

The castle has been magnificently preserved and sumptuously furnished over the centuries by the various Lords and Earls of Berkeley. Today, members of the public are welcome to walk around this former military stronghold which is entered by a bridge over a moat. Visitors can view the circular keep, the 14th-century great hall, the state apartments with their fine tapestries and furniture, the medieval kitchens, the dungeons, and the actual cell where Edward II met his sticky end.

The castle is surrounded by a terraced Elizabethan garden which contains an example of an early bowling alley and a beautiful lily pond, formerly a swimming pool. Further afield, there is a free-flight butterfly house, gift shop, tearoom and a large well-populated deer park. (Berkeley Castle is open April to September, daily except Mondays (though open Bank Holidays) and on Sunday afternoons only during October. Admission charge payable.)

On leaving the castle, you may notice the famous Berkeley Arms Hotel. A focal point of the town, this imposing 16th-century coaching inn has an impressive coat of arms above its broad, arched entrance. Run by Chris and Annie Bryant, the hotel offers something for everyone. For a quiet dinner there is the Mallard and Claret Restaurant which offers fine food and an extensive wine list, or visitors can relax in the lounge atmosphere of the Boot and Bottle Bar with its good selection of bar meals. Morning coffee and afternoon teas are available each day, and in fine weather, guests can sit out in the courtyard and beer garden. The tastefully-decorated bedrooms all have en-suite facilities and are equipped with colour televisions, mini-bar, hot drinks facilities and direct-dial telephones.

Berkeley Arms Hotel, Berkeley Tel: 01453 810291

An easy walk around Berkeley leads to St Mary's parish church which has a Norman doorway and a detached tower built in 1783. Inside, there are memorials to several members of the Berkeley family and an impressive east window which has nine lights depicting scenes of Christ healing the sick. The churchyard contains the grave of pioneer immunologist Edward Jenner (1749-1823) who spent most of his life in the town.

The son of a local parson, Jenner became apprenticed to a surgeon in Chipping Sodbury in 1763 at the age of fourteen. Seven years later, he moved to London to become a student at St George's Hospital, studying under the great surgeon John Hunter. Some years after, he returned to Berkeley to practice as a country doctor and to continue his pioneering work in immunology.

While still an apprentice, Jenner had become aware of the link between cowpox and smallpox, noticing that one protected against infection from the other. His work over several decades resulted in his discovery of a vaccination against smallpox, a disease which is thought to have killed as many as 60 million people worldwide in the preceding century. Today, the disease has effectively been eradicated from the planet.

Jenner's former home in Church Lane is a splendid Georgian house known as The Chantry. A thatched rustic hut where he vaccinated the poor free of charge still stands in the grounds and was named by Jenner the Temple of Vaccinia. In the early 1980s, the building was purchased, thanks in part to a donation from the Japanese philanthropist Ryoichi Sasakawa, by a trust who converted it into The Jenner Museum and Immunology Conference Centre. (Open Tuesdays to Sundays between April and September. Small admission charge payable.)

On leaving Berkeley, head for the A38 Gloucester road. Our next port of call is SLIMBRIDGE, a long rambling village with a fine 13th-century church. (Look out for the large 18th-century windows which contain fragments of glass from the earlier medieval period.)

The main attraction here, however, is the world famous Slimbridge Wildfowl and Wetlands Centre which was founded in 1946 by Sir Peter Scott, the artist and naturalist son of Antarctic explorer, Captain Robert Falcon Scott. The centre is now a sanctuary for many thousands of wildfowl, some of which remain here all year round and others which drop in on their annual migrations each spring and autumn. Up to 3000 birds can be in residence at any one time making Slimbridge the largest collection of wildfowl in the world. (The Trust have now established seven other centres in the UK which together are home to over 200 different species of wetland birds.)

Slimbridge's 73 acres of landscaped pens, lakes and paddocks stretch down to the River Severn and are open to visitors all year round. Numerous species of ducks, geese, swans and other wildfowl can be viewed at close quarters (there are observation towers and hides for viewing the shyer birds). The collection also includes many rare and exotic species including the largest flock of flamingos in captivity. There is also a tropical house which simulates rain forest conditions and contains a variety of brilliantly-plumaged water birds and hummingbirds.

Black Swans at Slimbridge

Slimbridge is the headquarters of the Wildfowl and Wetlands Trust and provides an ideal day out for anyone with an interest in birds. The visitor centre includes indoor displays, a permanent exhibition area and a 100-seater cinema, as well as a restaurant and gift shop. (Open daily (except 24 and 25 December), 9.30am to 5pm. Admission charge payable.)

Our next stop is the delightful village of **FRAMPTON-ON-SEVERN** which lies just off the B4071, four miles north of Slimbridge. As you approach the village you should be able to make out the dim and distant Welsh mountains in the distance. Frampton-on-Severn is noted for having one of the largest village greens in England, the 22-acre Rosamund Green. It contains a cricket ground and three ponds, and was formed by draining the marshy ground outside the gates of Frampton Court in the 18th century. The Bell Inn is conveniently sited on the green for enthusiasts of cricket and good beer.

Frampton Court is an outstanding example of Georgian country house. Now Grade I listed, it was built in Palladian style in the early-1730s by architect John Strachan. Inside, there is a wonderful collection of antique porcelain, fine furniture, and the paintings from which the best-selling book Frampton Flora was comprised in 1985.

The house is screened from the green by trees, but it is still possible to catch a glimpse of the huge Vanbrugh-inspired chimneys and the Gothic-style orangery designed by William Halfpenny. (The orangery has since been converted into holiday accommodation.) The grounds are inhabited by strutting peacocks and contain a reflecting ornamental canal and a unique octagonal tower which was built in the 17th century as a dovecote. Frampton Court is the seat of the Clifford family and is open all year round by appointment only (telephone 01452 740267). Admission charge payable.

On the other side of the green is the Clifford family's former home, Frampton Manor, which was built between the 12th and 16th centuries. The part timber-framed manor house is thought to be the birthplace of Jane Clifford, Henry II's 'Fair Rosamund' who bore him two children and lived in a house surrounded by a maze at Woodstock. Legend has it that Queen Eleanor found her way through the labyrinth to Rosamund's bower by following a thread of the king's cloak and once there, she forced her rival to drink poison. (Rosamund was subsequently buried at Godstow nunnery.) Frampton Manor has a lovely old walled garden and is open all year round to parties of ten or more by written appointment only. (Admission charge payable.)

On the southern edge of the village, the charming 14th-century St Mary's church is reached via a footpath across a low meadow. The church stands beside the Sharpness Canal which joins Gloucester to the Severn estuary. Look out for the canal keeper's house built in mock-Doric style. The sight of sea-going ships passing along the canal within a few yards of the church is an occasional eye-opener.

The nine-mile long circumference of the Arlingham peninsula forms part of the Severn Way Shepperdine-Tewkesbury long distance walk. Along this stretch, the trail passes close to Wick Court, a 13th-century moated manor house which was extended three hundred years later, and the 200 foot Barrow Hill, which commands magnificent views of the Severn Bridge, the Forest of Dean, Gloucester and the Cotswolds.

The village of ARLINGHAM dates from the Iron Age, its name being derived from the Old English and meaning 'village by the running water'. The land on which it is built originally belonged to the Berkeley hundreds, though it was subsequently acquired by St Augustine's Abbey in Bristol. One reason for this is that a place further to the west marks the point where St Augustine is thought to have crossed the Severn on his way to convert the Welsh tribes to Christianity thirteen centuries ago. From the riverbank, there are fine views across to Newnham and Westbury-on-Severn.

Nearby St Augustine's Farm was built on the site of a monastic house in the 16th century, and indeed parts of the old building still survive today. However, the St Augustine's is now better-known as a fascinating open farm where visitors of all ages come to see a working 124-acre livestock farm in action. Activities include watching the cows being machine milked in a herringbone parlour, helping to feed the animals, following an interesting farm trail, and meeting the horses, sheep, goats, pigs, rabbits and other animals.

Owners Robert and Elaine Jewell and their staff promise a family day out with something for everyone, including a display of historic farm memorabilia, a children's playground, a picnic area, gift shop and refreshment area. (St Augustine's Farm is open daily 11am to 5pm, end-March to end-October. Admission charge payable.)

Following the river upstream brings you to EPNEY, a village which is perhaps better-known on the Continent than it is in the UK. Each year, thousands of three year-old elvers (baby eels) are exported from here to the Netherlands and other parts of Europe to replenish the stocks in the canals.

From Epney, turn east to reach the historic hamlet of MORETON VALANCE. Here, the ramparts of a 600 year-old castle which once belonged to the De Valence family can still be seen. The largely 15th-century church also remains. This features an earlier Norman doorway which incorporates a sculpture of the Archangel Michael thrusting a spear into a dragon's mouth.

Not far from Junction 13 of the M5 motorway is the renowned **Stonehouse Court Hotel**, an impressive establishment which offers exceptional food, service and accommodation. It provides a very convenient place for an overnight stopover. A visit for just one night, however, will not do justice to this wonderful 17th-century Grade II listed hotel which is set in six acres of parkland overlooking Stroud Water.

Stonehouse Court is somewhere to relax in true style and comfort. Just wandering around the beautifully kept gardens observing the abundance of rare shrubs and plants is totally therapeutic after a hectic time travelling; there is also the opportunity of some excellent fishing for those so inclined.

Stonehouse Court, Stonehouse Tel: 01453 825155

On entering the hotel, guests will immediately be struck by the style and warmth of the interior, with its mellow oak panelling, soft lighting and superb open stone fireplaces. The 37 guest bedrooms all have en-suite facilities and are furnished in a style more in keeping with a country house than a hotel. Each room has hospitality facilities, a colour television and telephone. The charming panelled dining rooms offer both table d'hôte and à la carte menus, complemented by an extensive and carefully selected wine list. As one might expect, standards are high. Lunch starts from 10.50am, and dinner from 5.50pm. We found the service excellent, and the staff throughout the hotel both efficient and friendly.

179

Stonehouse Court is a member of the Clipper Hotels Group, a small group of first-class hotels which are located in Jersey, Dorset, Hampshire and Wiltshire. Details about the other fine hotels in the group, including the Old Bell at Malmesbury, can be obtained at the reception desk.

The country lanes to the south of Stonehouse pass through some of the loveliest villages in the Severn Vale. The chapel in the centre of FROCESTER was built in 1680 using materials taken from the private chapel of nearby Frocester Court, the present owners of which will usually allow visitors to look round their 180 foot medieval tithe barn, one of the finest in the country.

Continuing east, our next stop is the village of LEONARD STANLEY. Here are the remains of a 12th-century priory and a largely-intact Saxon chapel. The latter contains an early clock and medieval carvings, despite having been used as a barn for many centuries. Henry VIII and Anne Boleyn are reputed to have visited Leonard Stanley in 1535 when the village would have been at the height of its wool-trading prosperity.

A further mile to the east is the larger community of KING'S STANLEY, a village with historic roots going back to Roman and medieval times. The parish church is Norman in origin though was comprehensively remodelled by the Victorians in 1876. The village also boasts one of the earliest nonconformist places of worship, the Baptist church constructed in 1640. Another architectural first, Stanley Mill, can be found on the outskirts of the village. Built as England's first fireproof industrial building, a measure of its success is that it is still used for the manufacture of cloth to this day.

Heading east once again and you will come to the village of SELSLEY which stands to one side of the B4066 Stroud to Dursley road. The village is associated with the Marling family, wealthy Stroud mill-owners who were responsible for building the local church. This is modelled on one Sir Samuel Marling spotted on his travels around Europe and features fine interior work by William Morris and Rossetti.

Nearby is the Selsley Herb and Goat Farm in Water Lane. Established in 1982 by Peter and Gillian Wimperis, this four-acre smallholding has been developed into a thriving enterprise. Here, visitors can learn how best to plant and cultivate herbs, whether in a wide herbaceous border or on a small urban patio. There is an attractive formal garden planted with 150 herb varieties, a traditional planted cartwheel, a herb ladder and a nursery selling a wide selection of herbs and aromatic plants.

Peter and Gillian also keep between ten and twelve goats and in spring and early summer, baby kids can often be seen (and sometimes bottle fed) by visitors. Goats' milk and soft cheese can be purchased at the farm shop, along with a wide range of items connected with herbs including chutneys, mustards, dried herbs and potpourri. (Open daily, April 1st to end-September. Small admission charge.)

Crowle Museum, Stroud

STROUD has for centuries been considered the capital of the Cotswold woollen industry. The town's geographical position on the River Frome at the point where five Cotswold valleys meet made it an ideal centre for the emerging cloth-manufacturing industry in the early 16th century; the area's hill farms provided the raw material and its fast-flowing streams the power. By the 1820s, there were over 150 textile mills in the immediate locality and the area became famous for producing broadloom fabrics and 'Stroudwater scarlet', a thick, brightly-coloured cloth used for military uniforms. Today, only six mills remain including one specialising in green baize for snooker tables.

For a town with such a history, Stroud makes an unexpectedly disappointing first impression. Its continual economic development has meant that few clothiers' houses and other old buildings can be found in the town centre. However, there are a number of interesting places which are best explored on foot. Before setting out, why not have a bite to eat at **Mills Café** at 8 Withy's Yard, just off the High Street.

Tucked away in a corner down a narrow 13th-century alley, Mill's Café is a European-style meeting place with a beautiful courtyard garden. Owned and run by John and Maggie Mills, the emphasis is on good wholesome food, freshly made from local produce including organic meat and vegetables. The café is renowned for its vast range of cakes, which are all baked on the premises, and for its delicious coffee, which is roasted and blended to a special house formula. Mill's Café is open Monday to Saturday from 8.30am to 6pm, and on Sunday mornings. It also offers a supper menu from 7pm to 11pm on Friday evenings for which early booking is advised.

Mill's Café, 8 Withy's Yard, High Street, Stroud Tel: 01453 752222

Also situated in the High Street is the excellent Inprint Bookshop, which specialises in secondhand and antiquarian books, and Stroud's Medieval Hall, a carefully restored civic hall which is believed to be the oldest building in the town. Dating from the Middle Ages, it contains a well and some fine stonework. (Some of

182

the ground floor area is now let as shops.) Perhaps the most famous part of Stroud, however, is The Shambles, the old commercial market which, together with the Tudor town hall built in 1597, forms a fascinating enclave which still plays host to a busy weekly market.

A short distance away in George Street, are the Stroud Subscription Rooms. The building has a splendid classical façade featuring a porte-cochére with Tuscan columns and a balustraded balcony above, and also incorporates the George Room art gallery where regular exhibitions are mounted.

Further afield, those interested in early industrial architecture should look for Lodgemoor and Ebley Mills. Similarly, Rooksmoor Mills on the Bath Road is a handsome 19th-century woollen mill which has been converted into a flourishing business offering a wide range of crafts and giftware.

Those interested in finding out more about the town's fascinating past should visit Stroud District (Cowle) Museum in Lansdown. Exhibits here include a twenty-foot dinosaur, fossils and information on local archaeology and the history of the textile industry. Nearby Lansdown Hall features a display of local crafts and industrial artefacts. Both open Mondays to Saturdays, all year round. Admission free.

Situated near the Paganhill Maypole on the western edge of Stroud is the Paganhill Arch, a Cotswold stone memorial erected to commemorate the 1833 Emancipation Act which ended slavery in the British colonies. The memorial once marked the entrance to Henry Wyatt's estate on Farmhill.

It is also worth making a trip into the beautiful Slad Valley which stretches northwards from Stroud, a magical place which was immortalised by Laurie Lee in his autobiographical novel, Cider With Rosie. Such a trip could perhaps be combined with a visit to Lypiat Hill Farm, a working livestock farm where visitors of all ages are encouraged to observe the animals being cared for in a natural environment. The farm is situated a mile and a half west of Stroud on the Bisley road. (Open daily 10.30am to 4pm, 1st April to 30th October. Closed Mondays except Bank Holidays.)

Leaving Stroud on the A46 Bath road and you will soon found yourself climbing upwards into the Cotswolds. After a couple of miles you will find WOODCHESTER, the location of a 26-acre

Roman Villa, one of the largest archeological sites of its kind in Britain. Originally excavated in 1796, it is kept covered in earth, only allowing an inspection on one of the rare occasions it is exhumed.

Continuing south on the A46 turn east off the main road following signs AMBERLEY which has a surprising amount to offer the casual visitor. There is a 13th-century privately-owned castle, a church dating from 1837 which was once described by a former Bishop of Gloucester as 'the ugliest in Gloucestershire', the grave in the churchyard of Beau Geste author P C Wren, and Rose Cottage where writer Mrs Craik worked on her novel John Halifax, Gentleman.

Amberley is also the home of the Chalk Pits Museum (open 11am to 5pm on Wednesdays to Sundays between June and October) and the Fine Arts Centre which holds exhibitions and offers courses in painting and photography. For those interesting in seeing the Cotswolds from the basket of a hot-air balloon, Cheryl Gillott offers expertly piloted flights from nearby Culver Hill (telephone 01453 873529).

One and a half miles further east, the small Cotswold town of MINCHINHAMPTON stands perched on the hill between the Golden and Nailsworth Valleys. At one time, it was owned by the nuns of Caen and its market charter is said to date back to 1213. Following the Dissolution of the Monasteries, Henry VIII presented Minchinhampton Manor to the first Baron Windsor in a forced exchange for their existing family estate near Windsor, a piece of land which Henry had apparently had his eye on for some time.

In 1651, the manor was acquired by Samuel Sheppard and one his descendants, Edward Sheppard, built Gatcombe Park, the current residence of the Princess Royal. Another member of the Sheppard family, Philip, was responsible for constructing the Market House in the centre of Minchinhampton which was once used for wool trading, but now is more commonly used as a theatre. (Visits by appointment only at weekends between 9am and 5.30pm.)

Cotswold stone has long been quarried around Minchinhampton and at BALL'S GREEN, freestone mines extend underground for over a mile. The material used for facing the inside of the Houses of Parliament was quarried here in the last century.

However, Minchinhampton is most widely known for the impressive ancient monuments which can be found on top of the nearby steep-sided plateau. Minchinhampton and Rodborough Commons are now under the ownership of the National Trust, the former having been donated in 1913 by Henry Ricardo so as to preserve one of the Cotswolds' last remaining commons. Together, they amount to almost 1000 acres of high woodland and open grassland which are rich in wild flora and fauna.

A number of important archeological sites can be found here including the remains of the Iron Age defences known as Minchinhampton Bulwarks, the Neolithic long barrow known as Whitefield's Tump from where the great methodist preacher George Whitefield is reported to have addressed a large audience in 1743, and the spot known as Tom Long's Post where six roads meet and where an notorious highwayman was hanged.

From Minchinhampton, head southwest to **NAILSWORTH**, a small commercial centre which, like many of its neighbours, was once an important clothiers' town. Despite its industrial feel, some fine Jacobean and Georgian merchants' houses can still be found in the centre. Stokescroft, a building known locally as 'the barracks', stands on Cossack Square. Originally constructed in the 17th century, graffiti uncovered during restoration work in 1972 suggests that local troops were billeted here in 1812 and 1815. It was also used to house Russian prisoners during the Crimean War, an occurrence which explains the name of the square. Several former woollen mills have been updated and continue in their manufacturing role. Others, such as Egypt Mill, have been given a new life. Formerly a grain and logging mill, this popular family pub retains two working water wheels and takes its name from the preindustrial site where gypsy merchants and 'travelling people from Egypt' once camped.

Another interesting place to visit in Nailsworth is **Ruskin Mill**. Originally a 19th-century wool mill, this recently renovated structure is now a thriving craft centre, the concept of which was inspired by the work of William Morris, John Ruskin and Rudolph Steiner. A vibrant place, the emphasis is on traditional crafts. There is an exhibition gallery showing a variety of arts and crafts, plus a working water wheel and an exhibition showing flow forms as a new type of water treatment. Workshops covering such skills as cobbling, woodworking, glass staining and environmental water design are available by prior arrangement. After touring the mill, visitors can relax in the vegetarian café which is open from 11am to 4pm on Tuesday to Saturday, and from 3pm to 6pm on Sundays and Bank Holidays.

Ruskin Mill, Old Bristol Road, Nailsworth Tel: 01453 832571

From Nailsworth, travelling east along the B4014 for two and a half miles, brings you to reach the ancient village of AVENING. The village church dates from 1070 and contains a memorial to the Hon. Henry Bridge, an infamous 17th-century highwayman who in his youth was reported to have carried out 'deeds of lawlessness and robbery almost unsurpassed'.

On the Sunday nearest to 14th September each year, Avening celebrates 'Pig Face Sunday'. This unusual festival originates from the time when wild boar roamed free throughout the area. One animal is said to have created so much havoc that when it was finally captured, it was 'hung from a sturdy oak before being roasted and eaten', a custom of which continues in an updated form to this day.

In Hampton Fields, just off the B4014 to the northeast of the village stands the Avening Long Stone, a massive prehistoric standing stone which is eight feet high and pierced with holes. According to local legend, it has been known to mysteriously move on Midsummer's Eve.

CHAPTER EIGHT

The
Cotswolds

Chastleton Manor, Moreton-in-Marsh

187

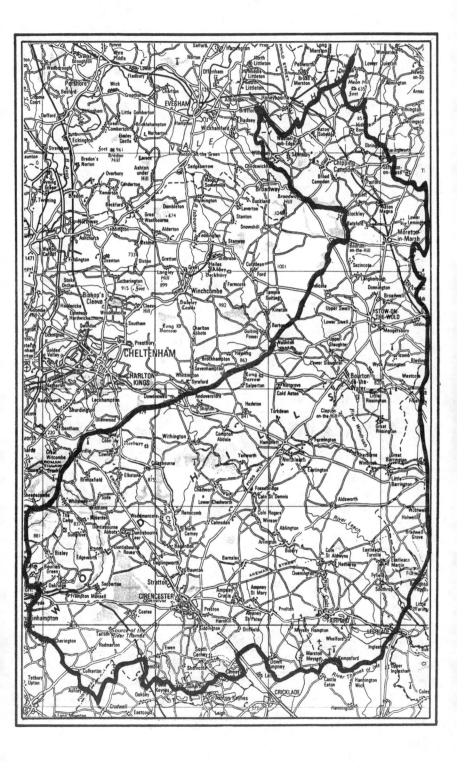

Fairford

CHAPTER EIGHT

The
Cotswolds

The first stop in our journey through the central Cotswolds is CHALFORD, a unique community consisting of a maze of narrow lanes which sprawl over the steep northern slope of the Golden Valley three miles southeast of Stroud. This is the centre of the area known as the 'Alpine Cotswolds', and at one time food and fuel had to be delivered up the steep gradient by donkey. Today, Chalford is best explored on foot, its tight thoroughfares being filled with interesting shops and pubs. Though not impressive architecturally, the church contains some interesting pieces of furniture made by craftsmen Peter Van Der Waals, Norman Jewson and W G Simmonds. The Round House, an unusual example of a former canal lengthman's house, stands opposite.

An easy walk from Chalford takes you to the isolated settlements of FRANCE LYNCH, AVENIS GREEN and BOURNES GREEN. Here there is an imposing Victorian parish church dating from 1856 and a disused 17th-century Congregational church whose decaying churchyard contains the graves of several old Puritan families.

Just outside Chalford there is a sign to Westley Farm Cottages. If you are looking for somewhere to stay in the lovely Cotswold countryside close to Cirencester, then Westley Farm is conveniently situated midway between Cirencester and Stroud. Set on the steep slopes of the beautiful Golden Valley, there are breathtaking views all around. This working family farm raises cattle, sheep, horses and domestic fowl. It also provides horse riding and pony trekking facilities and the land is crisscrossed by numerous well-maintained woodland paths and bridleways.

The farm's formerly-redundant stone outbuildings have been converted to provide four impressive self-catering cottages and two flats which each sleep from two to five. All well-equipped, the facilities include night storage heating, washing machines, telephones, televisions and open log fires, and there is also a farm shop. Whether on foot or on horseback, Westley Farm makes an ideal base for touring the beautiful Cotswold countryside.

Westley Farm Cottages, Chalford Tel: 01285 760262

From here, head north along the country lanes until you reach the historic village of **BISLEY**. The village stands 780 feet above sea level is known by local people as 'Bisley-God-Help-Us' because of the winter winds which sweep across the exposed hillside. The gabled Cotswold houses stand huddled together against the elements, and when approached from the southwest, they appear to form a semicircular amphitheatre.

In its time, the village has also been known as 'Beggarly Bisley' because of the hardship the inhabitants suffered during the decline of the local textile industry which was brought on by the Industrial Revolution.

Bisley's fine All Saints' Church dates from the 13th century and was restored during the early 19th century by Thomas Keble, the brother of poet and theologian John Keble after whom Keble College, Oxford was named. Thomas Keble was responsible for restoring the seven wells of Bisley which are set in an arc below the church. In 1863, he also founded the annual custom of 'dressing the wells' on Ascension Day, an event which continues to be witnessed by hundreds of spectators to this day. A decaying ornamental construction in the churchyard known as the 'Poor Souls' Light' dates from the 13th century and was used to hold candles lit for the souls languishing in purgatory. It is thought to be the only outdoor structure of its type in the country.

Perhaps the village's main claim to fame however, is the legend of the 'Bisley Boy'. In the days of its wool-based prosperity, Bisley possessed a royal manor, Over Court, where the young Princess Elizabeth (who went on to become Queen Elizabeth I) stayed on a number of occasions. Rumour has it that during one of these visits, the ten year-old princess caught the plague and, to the horror of her hosts, actually died. Fearing the wrath of her father Henry VIII, they hurriedly looked for a substitute and were fortunate enough to find a local child with red hair and remarkably similar physical characteristics. Similar, that is, except for one thing. Elizabeth's stand-in was a local lad called John Neville. Perhaps this would explain the Virgin Queen's reluctance to marry, her problem with hair loss and her 'heart that beats like a man's'?

Before leaving Bisley look at the 17th-century Bear Inn at the top of George Street, the frontage of which is supported by a row of external stone columns. Nearby FRAMPTON MANSELL is a pleasant village with some photogenic old buildings including the impressive Crown Inn and a manor farm which was built in the time of Charles II. The village church dates from a more recent period than its Norman appearance would suggest.

At SAPPERTON, a short distance to the east, the Thames-Severn Canal disappears into the two-mile long Sapperton Tunnel which, on its completion in 1798, was the longest in England's inland waterway system. Closed in 1911, the tunnel has a Gothic western portal at Daneway and a classical eastern portal at Coates, the latter having been restored as part of the plan to reopen the canal in the not-too-distant future. There are also interesting pubs at either end: the 18th-century Daneway Inn to the west and the Tunnel House at Coates to the east. These used to be the haunts of the bargees and professional leggers, the freelance artisans who used to 'walk' the narrowboats through the tunnel by lying on their backs and pushing against the walls and ceiling with their legs.

The village of Sapperton itself contains a number of fine old buildings, some dating from the 17th century and others built in sympathetic style during a short-lived renaissance which was ended by the outbreak of the First World War. It was during this fifteen-year period that Ernest and Sidney Barnsley and Ernest

Gimson founded a group of local artist-craftspeople known as the Sapperton Group. This had close links with William Morris and was centred around Daneway House, a nearby manor dating from the 14th and 17th centuries. The house containing the group's furniture workshops and showrooms can still be viewed (by appointment only) at any reasonable time between March and October. Small admission charge payable. The three group founders also designed and built distinctive houses for themselves in the village.

From Daneway House, continue northeast towards DAGLINGWORTH and the Duntisbournes, five delightful settlements which are sited along the exquisite valley of the River Dunt, or Duntbrook. Just to the east, the A417 diverts the speeding traffic along the undeviating course of the former Roman highway, Ermin Street. However, this charming little valley gives the impression of lying a million miles from the pressures of modern civilisation.

The church in Daglingworth contains a number of wonderfully-preserved Anglo-Saxon sculptures which are highly regarded for their simple artistry. The village also contains a handsome, if somewhat exposed, Georgian house, a large Victorian former-rectory, and a number of characteristic Cotswold cottages belonging to the Duchy of Cornwall. Further upstream, the road next passes through DUNTISBOURNE ROUSE. This also possesses a fine church, the tiny St Michael's, which has some fine features dating back to Saxon and Norman times. The 15th-century west tower has a rare saddleback roof and inside, there is a wonderful old Norman crypt and font.

The road fords Duntbrook in both MIDDLE DUNTISBOURNE and DUNTISBOURNE LEER, two sleepy hamlets, the latter of which once belonged to the abbey of Lire in France. In DUNTISBOURNE ABBOTS at the northern end of the valley, the old cobbled road actually follows the course of the stream as it flows through the village between two raised walls. This is a place where carters once cleaned their waggons and washed their horses hooves in the flowing water. Despite the risk of flooding, the present-day inhabitants continue to resist any plan to divert the course of the river. The mossy stone pool which was once the village water supply is also worth having a look at.

From Duntisbourne Abbots, zigzag through the minor country roads until you reach the village of **MISERDEN**, home of the renowned Miserden Park Gardens. The centre of this characteristic Cotswold village is marked by a large sycamore tree; this stands near a 17th-century barn which still contains a working forge. The famous gardens are situated on the northeastern side of the village and contain a wide variety of planting including spring bulbs, roses beds, herbaceous borders and topiary. (Open 10am to 4.30pm, Wednesdays and Thursdays between 1st April and 30th September. Admission charge payable (accompanied children free).)

Corinium Museum, Cirencester

Continue northwest for two miles and and you will soon find yourself in the unique community of **WHITEWAY**. At first sight, this windswept village set high up on a Cotswold ridge seems a hotchpotch of rather inhospitable buildings, many of which look homemade. Indeed, many of them were constructed by their owners, a group of Tolstoyan anarchists, who set up the village in 1898 following their resettlement from Surrey.

The inhabitants of Whiteway set up an economy based on horticulture and cottage industry and at first, refused all outside interference such as police, post office and public transport in their pursuit of self-sufficiency. This raised a few eyebrows amongst the surrounding inhabitants who spread rumours about their suspect moral code. (The villagers were said to walk around without clothes and to engage in partner-swapping.) However, unlike many similar utopian communities, the wooden shacks of Whiteway along with many of the principles they were founded upon, remain to this day (albeit in a much developed form) and the present-day village with its winding lanes, tall hedges and unconventional architecture is still the domain of creative, liberal-minded individuals.

From Whiteway, join the B4070 and drive northeast onto the A417 and then onto the A436. Our next stop is SEVEN SPRINGS near Coberley, one of several sites which claims to be the source of the River Thames. Despite there being an inscribed stone marker to back up this claim, a spring eleven miles to the south at THAMESHEAD seems a more likely contender. (This can be found by following a path across some fields behind the Thameshead Inn, a pub on the A433, three miles southwest of Cirencester.) Nevertheless, Seven Springs remains the undisputed source of the River Churn.

Colesbourne Inn, Colesbourne, Nr. Cheltenham Tel: 01242 870376

A short distance away is the pleasant village of COLESBOURNE. At the side of the main road is the impressive Colesbourne Inn. Run by Eric and Mary Bird, the welcome at this charming Cotswold inn is extended to all. The traditional bar offers excellent food and fine ales from the wood which you can enjoy while soaking up the atmosphere in front of a real log fire. The inn incorporates a first-class restaurant, Brambles, with a large patio which overlooks beautiful Cotswold countryside. Here, diners can choose from a selection of mouthwatering meals, with home-grown, freshly prepared produce being order of the day. Excellent accommodation is also offered in the recently converted stable block. This provides ten very comfortable en-suite bedrooms, all equipped to the English Tourist Board four crown standard.

Headed south once more along the A435 until you come to NORTH CERNEY, site of one of the most attractive and unusually decorated churches in the Cotswolds. 'Graffiti' thought to be the work of Tudor masons is etched into the internal and external walls of this fine 12th-century structure, much of it depicting the mythological animals which appeared in the medieval Bestiaries, the 'books of beasts' which contained descriptions of real and mythical animals, many of which had a wider moral significance. For example, a congregation-eating manticore (half man, half lion) with three rows of teeth is scored onto the church's outer south wall, and similarly a long-tailed leopard appears on the west wall. Other faces look down from gargoyles, roof-bosses and corbels, and four peer out from the Norman tympanum above the south doorway.

The ancient market town of CIRENCESTER, the capital of the Cotswolds, has a history dating back to the Roman occupation of Britain. In 47 AD, the Romans built the Fosse Way, one of the four royal roads of Britain, to link the prosperous wool-based centres of the South-West with Lincoln and the garrisons to the north. Along its length were constructed a number of defensive fortifications, one of which was sited at the junction with two other Roman highways, Ermin Street and Akeman Street. This fort quickly grew to become Corinium Dobunnorum, the second most important Roman settlement in England after Londinium. It was named after a conquered tribe of Britons, the Dobunni, who inhabited the southern Cotswolds.

Today, little evidence of Cirencester's Roman roots survives in situ. However, the award-winning Corinium Museum in Park Street houses one of the finest collections of ancient Roman antiquities in the country. Items on show include superb sculptures, domestic items and two remarkable floor mosaics, The Four Seasons and The Hunting Dogs. The museum also features life-size reconstructions of a Roman garden, dining room and kitchen, as well as a cut-away section of a surprisingly sophisticated central-heating system.

The Corinium Museum also covers the history of area from prehistoric to medieval times. (Open Mondays to Saturdays, 10am to 5.30pm and Sundays 2pm to 5.30pm between 1st April and 31st October; Tuesdays to Saturdays 10am to 5pm and Sundays 2pm to 5.30pm between 1st November and 31st March. Small admission charge payable.)

After a prolonged period of decline, Cirencester came under the domain of William FitzOsbern, the Earl of Hereford, following the Norman Invasion. In 1117, King Henry I founded the Augustinian Abbey of St Mary which was subsequently destroyed following Henry VIII's Dissolution of the Monasteries. Little of it now remains except for a single Norman arch which can be found in the northeastern corner of the Abbey Grounds. Today, the grounds form an attractive park containing a lake, trees and a population of wildfowl. An outline of the original abbey walls can be found here, along with the only remaining section of the old Roman fortifications.

Cirencester's Church of St John the Baptist was constructed in the 15th and 16th centuries and is perhaps the finest example of a Cotswold 'wool' church. Like many other similar structures in the area, the building of the church was financed by a wealthy wool merchant who prospered during that period. (Such churches are often characterised by the fact that they were built to a grander scale than befits the size of the community they now serve.) The funds for its pinnacled tower, however, came from a different source, the Earls of Salisbury and Kent who rebelled against Henry IV and who were arrested by the burghers of Cirencester as they passed through the town in 1399. After executing the rebellious pair, King Henry allowed the townspeople to keep the contents of the earls' strongboxes, a sum which covered the builder's charge.

St Johns is built of golden Cotswold stone and stands in a magnificent position in the Market Place. Inside, the pulpit is shaped like an enormous wineglass, beside which is placed a 17th-century hourglass which was used to keep a check on the duration

Cirencester

of the preacher's sermons. A statue of a blue-coated boy stands beside the door to the south aisle. This was used in the 18th century to collect funds for the church primary school which was founded in 1714 and still flourishes today.

The famous silver and gilt Boleyn Cup can also be found in the south aisle. This was made for Henry VIII's second wife in 1535, the year before she was executed for alleged adultery. Anne's personal insignia can be seen on the lid: a rose tree and a falcon holding a sceptre. Look out also for the cat chasing the mouse, a medieval craftsmen's joke which can be seen in the Lady Chapel.

Although no longer open at set hours, parties are welcome to climb the 120 foot West Tower by arrangement with the vicar. Visitors climb up past the peal of twelve church bells which were made by Rudhall of Gloucester and are thought to be the earliest of their type in the country. From the top, the birds-eye view of Cirencester's network of streets is breathtaking. These include Spitalgate, with its remains of the 12th-century Hospital of St John, and Coxwell Street with its row of original wool-merchants' houses and artisans' cottages. From the tower, there is also the chance to see over the 40 foot yew hedge which was planted in 1818 to conceal Cirencester House, the home of the Earl Bathurst.

Cirencester House stands on the western edge of town at the top of Cecily Hill and although not open to the public, its grounds are. Walkers and horse riders are permitted to roam freely over the 3000-acre Cirencester Park which has pathways stretching almost as far as Sapperton, five miles to the west. The park was laid out in the 18th century by the First Earl Bathurst with the assistance of his friend, Alexander Pope. Pope's Seat, a summerhouse standing at a point where ten pathways meet, was one of the poet's favourite places of contemplation.

Also to the west of the town are the remains of the Bull Ring, a once-glorious Roman amphitheatre which is perhaps one of the largest and best-preserved examples of its kind in Britain. Best approached from Querns Hill and Cotswold Avenue, the remains consist of an oval arena with twin entrances and a series of sloping earth banks which would have supported rows of timber seating.

Leaving Cirencester, make a short diversion northeast along the B4425 to visit the attractive Gloucestershire village of BARNSLEY, a conservation area which until a few years ago was owned by a single family. Almost all the buildings are constructed of the same locally-quarried golden limestone giving the community a unified yet unplanned character. At one time, all the houses in the village were lived in by local farmworkers; however, today, the estate is owned by a charitable trust which seems prepared to sell off vacant properties to outsiders.

In the centre of the village there is a pub, a village hall and a church with an Elizabethan tower. Also situated here is Barnsley House, a former rectory which is renowned for its beautiful gardens. These are usually open to the public on Wednesdays, and amongst other noteworthy features, contain two 18th-century summerhouses (one classical, one Gothic). Barnsley Park on the outskirts of the village is a baroque Georgian mansion which was probably designed by Hawksmoor. It is open to visitors by prior appointment only.

Glebe Farm Cottages, Barnsley, Cirencester Tel: 01285 659226

Glebe Farm Holiday Cottages are a collection of four outstanding barn conversions which are set in the heart of the peaceful Cotswold countryside just two miles outside Cirencester. These first-rate holiday cottages offer beautifully furnished and excellently equipped self-catering accommodation. Sleeping up to six (plus a cot), 'Calf Pens' is ideal for a large group or family, while accommodation in 'The Dairy' comprises one double and one twin bedroom. Both provide well furnished open plan kitchen, dining and sitting room areas, as well as a private patio. Additional shared facilities include a washing machine, tumble dryer and freezer. 'Granary One' and 'Granary Two' offer accommodation of the same high standard and, should you require it, there are babysitting and maid services available.

Heading south, the minor country roads lead to The Ampneys, three small villages which are connected by Ampney Brook. Furthest upstream is **AMPNEY CRUCIS**, a pleasant community with a large mansion (Ampney Park), an old mill, an attractive vicarage and a part-Saxon church with an unusual carved stone cross in its churchyard and medieval paintings on its interior walls.

The village of **AMPNEY ST MARY** was moved to its present position following the Black Death in the 1300s. All that remains of the original medieval settlement is its 12th-century church which stands on its own in the middle of a field half-a-mile away. **AMPNEY ST PETER** is perhaps the most attractive of the three villages. It has a small green, a Saxon church with a gabled tower, and some noteworthy buildings including a large Cotswolds residence designed by architect Sidney Gambier-Parry in the 1900s.

Poulton Fields Farms, Poulton, Cirencester Tel: 01285 851830

Before continuing your journey south, make a point of finding Poulton Fields Farms. Situated five miles east of Cirencester and one mile north of Poulton, Poulton Fields is an arable and sheep farm set in 811 acres of lovely Cotswold countryside. Owned by Major Andrew Wigram and his wife Gaby, this is also the home of the outstanding Poulton Chasers Course.

This impressive equestrian course was opened in May 1992 and is some eight miles long; it has a varied selection of 32 well-constructed jumps, including a water obstacle and bank. The jumps are all five to seven metres wide and range from one-and-a-half to three feet in height, which means both experienced and novice riders are able to attempt them all. Whether your penchant is hacking, jumping or carriage driving, the Poulton Chasers Course is ideal. It is open all year round by prior appointment subject to the condition of the course, and up-to-date information and bookings can be obtained by telephoning 01285 850851.

Poulton Fields Farms, Poulton, Cirencester Tel: 01285 851830

Riders register in a portacabin in the large parking area at the edge of the farm building complex. Here, they can use the facilities to wash, change, make telephone calls and purchase refreshments, while nearby there is a hitching rail, water and hose, mounting block, WC and short-term grazing facilities. Open to members of the UK Chasers, the course is also available to non-members on purchase of a day membership pass. In addition, lessons can be provided at the Poulton Chasers Riding School which can include the use of a mount and the Chasers Course if required.

Poulton Fields Cottages offer top class self-catering accommodation for visitors to the Wigrams' farm. Situated at the centre of the farm with attractive lawned gardens to the front, a patio to the back and enclosed by a Cotswold stone wall, this charming pair of cottages were extended and updated in early 1991. Both sleep up to six, with a communicating door enabling them to be let as a single twelve-bed unit if required. The facilities are excellent and include a fully equipped kitchen, colour television and convector/night storage heaters throughout. The quality of accommodation provided has earned Poulton Fields Cottages an English Tourist Board four-key commended rating.

To the south of Cirencester, the gentle slope of the Cotswolds creates a flat open landscape with river valleys so wide that they seem like gentle undulations in a rolling plain. This pleasant area of the upper Thames valley is also rich in valuable sand and gravel deposits which have been exploited by the building industry since the 1920s. The removal of the material has left a large number of hollows which have gradually filled with water to form shallow freshwater lakes. In recent years, the potential of this area as a leisure resource has been realised and today, the area is known as the Cotswold Water Park.

The Cotswold Water Park covers a total area of some 22 square miles and contains over 100 manmade lakes. As well as being an important centre for water-based sport, fishing and general recreational pursuits, it is also an internationally recognised nature conservation area. A large number of waterfowl breed and over-winter here, and several of the lakes and water meadows are designated Sites of Special Scientific Interest.

The water park lies to the west of the A419 Cirencester to Swindon road and is centred around the two villages of South Cerney and Cerney Wick. Though not a particularly pretty village, SOUTH CERNEY contains some pleasant old manor houses, a street called Bow Wow and a church with a carved Norman doorway which contains a noted work of art, the carved wooden head and foot of Christ taken from a crucifix in Compostela.

The Crown Inn, Cerney Wick, Nr. Cirencester Tel: 01793 750369

Lying two miles to the southwest, the village of CERNEY WICK is also a pleasant community. Those looking for first-rate refreshment or accommodation near the Cotswold Water Park should look out here for the celebrated 16th-century hostelry, the Crown Inn. Native Gloucestershireman, Colin Jackson, and his wife, Liz, take pride in serving the very best in beers, wine and food (try Liz's award-winning homemade steak and kidney pie). The

Crown also offers a number of comfortable, quiet and welcoming letting bedrooms.

Cerney Wick is also the location of the renowned South Cerney Riding School. This top-class riding centre is situated just to the west of the A419 Swindon to Cirencester road in the heart of the Cotswolds Water Park conservation area. Here, a high standard of tuition is offered to riders of all ages and levels of experience.

South Cerney Riding, Cerney Wick Tel: 01793 750151

A few miles further west, the Somerford Lakes Reserve near SOMERFORD KEYNES offers guided launch trips around a hundred-acre lake taking in an eel and trout farm and a variety of pens containing such exotic fauna as wallabies and ornamental pheasants. Open all year round to pre-booked parties of four or more. Admission charge payable.

From the Water Park, drive east across a narrow spur of Wiltshire before re-entering Gloucestershire near the village of DOWN AMPNEY, the birthplace of composer Ralph Vaughan Williams (1872-1958) who wrote the music to the hymn Come Down O Love Divine and named it Down Ampney. All Saints' Church, where Vaughan Williams' father was incumbent, dates from 1265 and can be seen for miles around across the flat surrounding farmland. Inside, a reclining effigy of the medieval soldier, Sir Nicholas de Valers (or Villiers), can be seen in the south transept.

During the Second World War, Down Ampney was the site of an important airfield and some years later, a modern stained-glass window was installed in the church in memory of the airmen based here. Each year in September, a service is held to commemorate those lost in the Battle of Arnhem. Not far from the church, a high yew hedge hides Down Ampney House, a handsome Tudor mansion which was remodelled in 1799.

Heading further eastwards along the minor country roads, you again cross a spur of Wiltshire before reaching KEMPSFORD, a Gloucestershire village with strong Lancastrian connections. The interior of the church is decorated with Lancastrian roses and the tower is said to have been commissioned by Blanche, the wife of John of Gaunt who was also an heir of the first Duke of Lancaster and mother of Henry IV. Look out for the horseshoe on the church door which is rumoured to have been shed by the Duke of Lancaster's horse with tragic consequences. Kempsford is also said to be populated by number of unusual ghosts including a silent monk, a youth in lace and breeches, a distraught mother and a repenting knight.

St Mary the Blessed Virgin, Fairford

From Kempsford, the road leads north to the large and bustling village of FAIRFORD, a stop on the old stagecoach route which stands on the gently-flowing River Colne. Of architectural merit in the village is the Church of St Mary the Blessed Virgin which contains a truly outstanding set of 15th-century stained-glass windows. At the time these were installed, Fairford was at the centre of a prosperous wool-producing area and a major church restoration was carried out by the wealthy wool merchant, John Tame. He is said to have commissioned the set of 28 windows which are thought to have been made by Henry VII's master glass painter, Barnard Flower, whose work appears in Westminster Abbey. St Mary's also contains some fine oak carving including Tame's original ceiling supports which are fashioned in the shape of angels. John Tame's memorial gravestone, along with those of his wife and son, are set into the floor of the church.

LECHLADE stands at the junction of the A417 and A361 and is consequently a rather busy place with wide streets and a bustling Market Place. It also stands at the point where the Rivers Leach (from which the town gets its name) and Coln join the River Thames; indeed Halfpenny Bridge, which is named after the halfpenny toll which was once payable, is the highest navigable point on the river. At one time, river barges used to line the wharves around St John's Bridge when they were being loaded with building stone bound for Oxford, London and beyond. Today, the barges have been replaced by pleasure craft which provide an enjoyable way to spend a few hours.

There are some fine Georgian buildings in Lechlade, many of them designed by an accomplished local architect called Pace. One of the characteristic architectural features of the town are its once highly-fashionable gazebos which were built at the bottom of every reputable garden. One such structure can be found in the garden of Church House and is said to be the place where in 1815 Shelley wrote his Stanzas in Lechlade Churchyard. The church itself has a tall spire which can be seen from miles away across the low surrounding water-meadows. Inside, there is an unusual carved roof boss above the nave depicting two wrestlers.

To the north Lechlade, a network of country lanes connect a number of interesting little villages. SOUTHROP is an attractive and beautifully-kept community with a small green and a fine manor house. The manor is set behind a pair of distinctive gateposts in grounds containing a restored riverside mill, ancient barns and a charming church with Norman features. John Keble lived in the Old Vicarage from 1823-25, the period he was laying the foundations of the Oxford Movement with William Wilberforce and others. Southrop is also noted for the distinctive stone ball-finials which adorn many of the older buildings in the village.

A little further north, the two hamlets of EASTLEACH MARTIN and EASTLEACH TURVILLE face each other across the River Leach. (Together they form the village known simply as EASTLEACH.) For many centuries, the two hamlets were owned by rival lords of the manor and so each contains its own church. Both date from Norman times and incorporate a number of fine architectural features. John Keble was appointed non-resident curate of both churches in 1815 and the ancient clapper footbridge across the River Leach which connects the two hamlets is known as Keble's Bridge.

A couple of miles to the west is HATHEROP, a model village of solid stone-built cottages which was built between the estates of Williamstrip Park and Hatherop Castle (now a girls' school) in the 1860s. The Victorian village church contains the chapel of Barbara, Lady de Maulay designed by William Burges. He was also jointly responsible for remodelling the castle in the 1850s.

On the banks of the River Coln a mile to the southwest, the village of QUENINGTON has a church with two exceptional Norman tympana. (Such is their importance that in the 1880s, two porches were added by the architect of Gloucester Cathedral, F S Waller, to protect them from the elements.) In the 12th century, the church became a preceptory of the Knights Hospitaller and their presence is reflected in several local place names including Knights' Mill and Knights' Gatehouse.

The wonderful village of BIBURY lies three miles to the north at the point where the B4425 bridges the River Coln. In the 19th century, it was described by William Morris as the most beautiful village in England. Thankfully, little has changed since then. At its centre, the delightful village square is overlooked by the ancient Church of St Mary, a much-altered building with parts dating back to Norman, medieval and Saxon times. In the churchyard, the lichen-speckled tombs and gravestones date from more recent times, their brilliant yellow mottle standing out in the moist Cotswold air.

The River Coln flows slowly past handsome stone-tiled buildings and under Bibury's late-18th-century road bridge. The river and its water meadows attract a wide variety of wildfowl and the National Trust-owned Rack Isle Water Meadow has been designated a bird sanctuary. Arlington Row, a short terrace of medieval stone-built cottages stands nearby and is also under the protection of the National Trust. Originally built in the 14th century to house sheep, the cottages were converted into cloth-weaving workshops in the early 17th century.

Arlington Mill

Fabric from here was supplied to nearby Arlington Mill, a water-powered fulling mill which was built on the site of a corn-mill mentioned in the Domesday Book. (Fulling was a process of cleansing and thickening woollen material by immersing it in water and beating it with mechanically-operated hammers.) Today, Arlington Mill is a museum which houses a fascinating collection of industrial artefacts, arts, crafts and furniture including items made in the William Morris workshops. There are seventeen display rooms in all, including a blacksmith's forge, a wheelwright's workshop and a number of machine rooms containing working equipment. (Open daily 10.30am to 7pm, mid-March to mid-November. (Weekends only during winter months.) Admission charge payable.)

The Bibury Trout Farm can be found adjacent to Arlington Mill. Originally established as a trout hatchery as long ago as 1906, it has grown into a flourishing working farm which welcomes visitors all year round. There is also a farm shop offering fresh and smoked fish, plants and gifts. (Open 9am to 6pm, Mondays to Saturdays and 11am to 6pm Sundays. Admission charge payable.)

In the 17th century, Bibury was famous as a horse racing centre and at one time was the home of a racing club which was founded during the reign of Charles II, the oldest such club in the country. Much of the racing activity centred around Bibury Court, a splendid country house which was built on the site of Roman, Saxon and Norman remains. Now a hotel, the building is still a focus for horse-riding activities. It was once owned by the influential Sackville family who were involved in a famous law suit involving a contested will. The case lasted several decades and is said to have provided the background for Charles Dickens' vicious inditement of the legal profession, Bleak House.

Upstream from Bibury, the villages lying along the course of the River Coln are both beautiful and unspoilt. The first of these gems is ABLINGTON, a community which was immortalised by J Arthur Gibbs in his chronicle of Victorian rural life 'A Cotswold Village'. A high stone wall surrounds the Elizabethan manor (and its extensive landscaped grounds) which was Gibbs' home. On the manor's main doorway there are five delicately carved heads, one of which is of Queen Elizabeth herself. Another interesting building in the village is the 17th-century gabled Ablington House which is also partly concealed behind a high dry-stone wall. Its iron gateway is guarded by two stone lions rampant brought from the Palace of Westminster.

From Ablington, continue northwest through the delightful communities of WINSON, COLN ROGERS and COLN ST DENNIS before crossing the A429 Fosse Way at FOSSEBRIDGE. Two miles further on is CHEDWORTH, a village which gives its name to one of the most impressive attractions in the area, the National Trust-owned Chedworth Roman Villa, the finest and most extensively excavated example of its kind in the UK.

The village is made up of a number of simple stone-built houses and farms which are huddled together in the shallow valley between Pancake Hill and Chedworth Beacon. As well as a handsome Norman church with a castellated tower, it possesses a number of fine gabled buildings including the Old Farm, Cromwell House and two rows of attractive 18th-century cottages known as Church Row and Ballingers Row.

The Roman villa is situated in the wooded valley of the River Coln one mile north of the village (it is more easily approached via Yanworth). It is thought to have been built between the mid-second century and the early-fourth century AD, and was accidentally rediscovered by a gamekeeper in 1864. This prompted a series of excavations organised by the owner of the land, Lord Elton, which revealed a complex layout of rooms and a remarkably sophisticated plumbing and heating system. This included separate steam and dry heat 'saunas', a pool for taking a cold plunge and a system for circulating warm air underfloor.

Chedworth Roman Villa

A number of beautiful and richly-patterned mosaic floors were also uncovered including a wonderfully patterned dining room floor. This consists of eight panels decorated with nymphs and satyrs set around a central octagon; another series of mosaics depicts the four seasons. A short distance away, there is a shrine above the villa's fresh water spring which is adorned with water nymphs.

In 1924, the site was acquired by the National Trust who have since erected a visitors' centre. An earlier museum building dating from the 1860s houses a display of some of the smaller objects unearthed on the site. A ten-minute video giving further background information on Chedworth Roman Villa can also be viewed here. (Site open daily 10am to 5.30pm, March to end-October (closed Mondays except Bank Holidays), plus restricted winter opening hours. Admission charge payable; free to National Trust members.)

Our next port of call is NORTHLEACH, a small country town situated near the junction of the A40 and the A429 Fosse Way, three miles to the northeast of the Roman villa. In common with many other Gloucestershire communities, this was once a major wool-trading centre which at one time rivalled in Cirencester in importance; as a consequence it possesses the disproportionately large 15th-century Church of St Peter and St Paul which is only outshone by those in Cirencester and Chipping Camden. The church is built in light Perpendicular style with pinnacled buttresses, high windows and a massive square castellated tower. The interior is noted for its ornately carved font and its unique collection of brasses, one of the finest in the country (permits for brass-rubbing can be obtained from Cotswold Pharmacy and the materials from the post office).

After a period of decline following the Dissolution of the Monasteries, Northleach reverted to a small market town before becoming an important stopping point on the Gloucester to Oxford coaching route in the mid-18th-century. In the 1780s, a House of Correction was built at the old crossroads where the main east-west and north-south routes met. This was a small prison which dealt out an early form of the 'short sharp shock' to offenders who had been found guilty of minor crimes. The 37 inmates were kept in relatively good conditions (for example, they were allowed washing facilities), but were subjected to hard labour including work on a treadmill.

Today, the building has been converted into a fascinating museum of rural life, the Cotswold Countryside Collection, which features a prison cell maintained in its original condition. The central theme of the museum, however, is its collection of historic agricultural implements which were originally gathered by Olive

Lloyd Baker, a local enthusiast with a special interest in the evolution of modern agriculture. Exhibits include a steam tractor, waggons, an early laundry and an interesting collection of below-the-stairs domestic items. (Open daily 10am (2pm Sundays) to 5.30pm between 1st April and 31st October. Small admission charge payable.)

Another highly entertaining museum, Harding's World Of Mechanical Music, is situated in a 17th-century merchant's house in Northleach High Street. This remarkable museum-with-a-difference houses a collection of antique music boxes, chiming clocks and an assortment of mechanically-driven musical instruments which are played to visitors during guided tours and demonstrations. Proprietor Keith Harding also restores clocks and music boxes and runs the on-site gift shop. Open daily, 10am to 6pm. Admission charge payable. Those interested in original works of art should also look for Fothergill's Gallery in the High Street.

An excellent place to stay in Northleach is Bank Villas Guest House, an attractive residence with white-framed leaded windows which is situated on the main village road leading to Northleach from the historic Fosse Way. This first-rate establishment makes an ideal base for exploring the beautiful Cotswold countryside and discovering the many local places of interest. The house is very well presented and deceptively spacious; the dining area is situated in a large double-glazed conservatory, and there is also a comfortable television lounge. Each bedroom has a washbasin and tea/coffee making facilities, while the family room also has en-suite facilities.

Bank Villas Guest House, West End, Northleach Tel: 01451 860464

SHERBORNE is a delightful village of characteristic stone-built houses which are strung out in twos and threes along the course of Sherborne Brook. In the centre of the village, a number of grander buildings surround Sherborne House, a classical country mansion rebuilt in 1830 which has been turned into private flats. The nearby Church of St Mary Magdalene is filled with monuments to the Duttons, the local landowning family. The village is surrounded by picturesque National Trust-owned parkland and woods which contain a number of lovely waymarked walks and scenic viewpoints.

Two miles further east are **THE BARRINGTONS**, two superb villages which at one time were an internationally-renowned source of Cotswold limestone. Several of the Oxford colleges and the interior of St Paul's Cathedral in London were constructed of stone quarried here. Indeed, Wren considered Thomas Strong, the owner of quarries at Little Barrington, to be the leading mason of his generation. (When Strong died, he left money to build the causeway across the River Windrush which can be seen today.)

For many years, river barges were loaded with stone at a wharf near the Fox Inn which were then floated down the Windrush and the Thames to London. Today, both Great and Little Barrington are quiet feudal villages built of indigenous Cotswold stone which together create an idyllic, though not altogether genuine, picture of English rural life.

From Great Barrington, a minor road follows the course of the River Windrush past Great Rissington to **BOURTON-ON-THE-WATER**

Rooftrees Guest House, Rissington Road, Bourton-on-the-Water
Tel: 01451 21943

This route into the small yet bustling Cotswold town takes you past **Rooftrees Guest House** in Rissington road. Situated in a quiet part of Bourton-on-the-Water just ten minutes walking distance from the centre, Rooftrees is a large, welcoming house built of Cotswold stone, with mullioned windows and a frontage adorned with attractive hanging baskets. The proprietors, Sylvia and Sean Farley, have gone to great lengths to provide top quality accommodation. This becomes immediately apparent on entering the master bedroom where a handmade four-poster bed with beautiful drapes and frills has been installed, a real showpiece. The same degree of care and thought has gone into the other rooms, an additional feature of which is the display of cuddly animals, all dressed in fine costumes and made by the proprietor. As well as a full English breakfast, first-rate evening meals are provided if requested; these are prepared from fresh local produce and are usually served with a complimentary drink.

The centre of Bourton-on-the-Water has a magical feel. The River Windrush flows through it under a unique series of low-arched pedestrian bridges, two of which date from the late 18th century. Narrow lanes run back from the willowed greens which line the river between small houses and cottages that are all constructed of the same golden Cotswold limestone. (In Sherborne Street, look out for the unusual dovecotes built into the walls.) The town possesses some fine buildings including St Lawrence's church with its 14th-century chancel and Georgian tower, and the Old Manse dating from 1784 which has since been converted into a hotel.

Coombe House, Rissington Road, Bourton-on-the-Water
Tel: 01451 821966

Also near the centre of the town is Coombe House, a charming family-run guesthouse which stands in its own attractive lawned garden and enjoys a peaceful location Proprietors Graham and Diana Ellis have seven guest bedrooms available, all of them excellently equipped with en-suite bath or shower; two are on the ground floor making them suitable for partially disabled guests. The sitting room and breakfast room are bright, fresh and airy, providing a comfortable and relaxing atmosphere. This is enhanced by the central heating and residential license. The quality of the establishment is reflected in its English Tourist Board two crown, highly commended rating. Graham and Diana are happy to provide their guests with information on places to visit and eat out. Please note, however, that there is a total non-smoking policy in the house, with a first floor balcony providing an ashtray for the desperate!

St Peter and St Paul, Northleach

Because of its attractiveness, Bourton-on-the-Water has become something of a lure for tourists, especially during the summer months, so don't expect to find a secluded gem. However, there are some unique attractions which are worth visiting, particularly if the weather is unreliable.

Birdland is a three and a half acre private zoological garden which is situated in the grounds of a Tudor manor. The zoo was

216

founded in 1956 by local builder, Leonard Hill, who set out to realise his dream of creating a living sanctuary for exotic birds of all descriptions. Today, the gardens are filled with aviaries, ponds and densely-treed groves which are home to over a thousand brightly-plumaged birds. Macaws and parrots fly freely in the open, sunbirds and hummingbirds flit about the tropical houses, toucans and flamingos inhabit the aviaries, and penguins swim in a glass-sided pool. (Open daily all year round. Admission charge payable.)

The gardens behind the enigmatically-named Old New Inn in the High Street are the location of another of Bourton-on-the-Water's attractions, its famous Model Village. During the 1930s, the present landlord's father and a team of skilled craftspeople built a one-ninth scale replica of the town complete with inn, church, shops, flowing River Windrush and working water wheel. All the buildings are made of Cotswold stone and there is even a miniature of the Model Village itself. (Open daily all year round. Small admission charge payable.)

The Lawns, Station Road, Bourton-on-the-Water Tel: 01451 821195

The Cotswold Motor Museum occupies an 18th-century corn-mill in Sherborne Street. In addition to the thirty or so cars and motorcycles on show, the museum contains a fascinating range of memorabilia including a collection of antique children's toys and the largest display of historic advertising signs in the country. (Open daily 10am to 6pm between February and November. Small admission charge payable.) Those interested in model railways

Birdland, Bourton-on-the-Water

Motor Museum, Bourton-on-the-Water

should also make a point of finding the Model Railway Exhibition in the High Street.

The Lawns in Station Road, one of the access routes leading from the historic Fosse Way, is another excellent guesthouse. Surrounded by lovely countryside, the Lawns is a modern, stone-built detached house which offers first-rate bed and breakfast accommodation. Beautifully constructed with a splendid solid wood staircase and balustrade, solid timber beams in the ground floor rooms, and first-class furnishings and decor throughout, the house oozes quality and charm. The accommodation comprises five letting bedrooms, some of which are en-suite family rooms; cot facilities are also available. For guests wishing to relax in these comfortable surroundings at the end of the day, an evening meal can be provided by prior arrangement.

Three miles outside Bourton-on-the-Water is the widely-renowned wildfowl and garden centre at Folly Farm. This interesting conservation farm has grown to become one of the largest private collections of domestic waterfowl and wildfowl in Europe.

The collection was started before World War II by Tom Bartlett, a recognised expert in his field who has written and broadcast on the subject throughout his life. The visitor area now covers over fifty acres and is home to over 160 breeds of birds and animals, many of them rare and exotic. (Open daily 10am to 6pm (3.30pm in winter), all year round. Admission charge payable.)

Situated only a couple of miles north of Bourton-on-the-Water yet entirely different in character are the twin villages known collectively as THE SLAUGHTERS. Despite the gruesome connotations, the villages actually take their name from the innocuous Anglo-Saxon word, slohtre, meaning 'muddy place'. Set a mile apart and joined by the River Eye, Upper and Lower Slaughter are both examples of the archetypal Cotswold village. Each consists of a cluster of honey-coloured limestone buildings set around a church and manor. Apart from the renovation of some cottages in Baghot's Square by Sir Edwin Lutyens in 1906, no new houses have been built in Upper Slaughter since 1904. Francis Edward Witts, whose Diary Of A Cotswold Parson was published in 1978, was the rector here from 1808 to 1854. The villages are both very photogenic and best explored on foot.

Those who wish to stay in this beautiful village setting should make a point of finding the Washbourne Court Hotel in LOWER SLAUGHTER. Lying just off the A429 Cirencester to Stow-on-the-Wold road a mile-and-a-half north of Bourton-on-the-Water, this must be one of the most picturesque locations in the Cotswolds. A truly outstanding place to stay, the Washbourne Court is a magnificent 17th-century country residence which stands within four acres of superb riverside grounds near the centre of the village. The hotel's interior retains much of its original character with stone-flagged floors, beamed ceilings and stone-mullioned windows. In winter, guests can relax in front of roaring log fires and in summer they can sit out on the charming riverside terrace, a natural habitat for birds and wildlife.

Washbourne Court Hotel, Lower Slaughter Tel: 01451 822143

The hotel is privately-owned and run by the Pender family. During a period of renovation, they took great care to harmonise the traditional character of the building with the luxuries expected of a modern first-class hotel. A choice of accommodation is now offered in the 17th-century main building, in the delightful beamed Barn, and in the recently-constructed cottage suites. All rooms have en-suite showers or bathrooms, colour televisions and the finest modern facilities. The hotel restaurant offers a high standard of cuisine which is prepared using fresh local produce wherever possible. Shortly after opening in March 1992, the AA awarded the restaurant their coveted rosette for food (the hotel was given a three-star rating), making this a truly exceptional place to

220

stay for exploring the Cotswolds and the many surrounding places of interest.

From Upper Slaughter, join the Cheltenham to Stow-on-the-Wold road making a short diversion west to visit NAUNTON. From the road running along the top of the ridge, Naunton looks like a village in miniature. It was founded in Saxon times and features a 14th-century church and string of characteristic stone cottages which congregate around the upper River Windrush. According to local legend, Naunton's first inhabitant was an imp who fell to the ground and broke a wing when flying over the Cotswolds with his satanic master. Finding himself unable to fly, he decided to build himself a cottage of local stone.

The area around CONDICOTE, to the west, contains some interesting ancient remains including the Roman Ryknild Street, the imposing Iron Age fortification known as Eubury Camp and the site of a prehistoric henge, an enclosure marked by stones dating from around 2500 BC.

At 800 feet above sea level, STOW-ON-THE-WOLD is the highest town in the Cotswolds. Eight roads converge near the town, although fortunately only one actually passes through its centre. Instead, Stow survives as an exceptional collection of 17th- and 18th-century stone houses clustered around a market cross.

Two of the Stow-on-the-Wold's main thoroughfares are called Sheep Street and Shepherds Way, reminders of the days when the town's main economic activity was wool trading. At one time, large twice-yearly sheep fairs (one of which was recorded by Daniel Defoe) were held on the open Market Square which was also the site of the stocks once used for punishing minor offenders. Narrow alleys known as 'tures' radiate from the Square and on market days, these were used for counting sheep in single file. The sheep fairs were eventually replaced by annual horse fairs which continued until 1985.

The Church of St Edward was named after the unfortunate King Edward the Martyr who was murdered at Corfe Castle by his wicked stepmother, Elfrida. It has been restored on a number of occasions throughout the centuries and is considered one of the outstanding Cotswold churches. It also contains a famous 17th-century painting of the Crucifixion by Gaspard de Craeyer of Antwerp. The town contains some other noteworthy old buildings,

221

including the 15th-century Crooked House (now an antique shop), the 16th-century Masonic Hall and the 18th-century Talbot which was once the local corn exchange.

During the English Civil War, forces of both sides regularly passed through Stow-on-the-Wold and the town was regarded to be of great strategic importance. On 21st March 1646, a hilltop to the northwest of the town was the site of the last open battle of the first Civil War. Following the battle, the defeated Royalist forces withdrew into the streets of Stow and some were fortunate enough to reach the relative safety of St Edward's Church. Others, however, were cut down in the Square and according to local reports, ducks were seen bathing in the blood which flowed through the streets. A Royalist officer, Captain Keyte, is buried beneath a slate slab in the chancel of the church.

From Stow-on-the-Wold, drive east along the A436 for four miles until you arrive in the delightful village of ADLESTROP. This is another Cotswold gem, filled with honey-gold cottages and boasting a Georgian mansion, a 13th-century church and a 17th-century rectory which Jane Austen regularly visited at the beginning of the last century. The mansion, Adlestrop Park, was built in Gothic style with grounds laid out by Humphry Repton. Sadly, neither are open to the public. The Church of St Mary Magdalene contains a number of memorials to the Leigh family who have lived at Adlestrop Park since 1553. Jane Austen's grandfather, Thomas Leigh, was incumbent here for many years. The rectory where he lived stands surrounded by mature cedar trees near a 19th-century school house and cottage.

Adlestrop is perhaps best-known, however, for being the title of a poem by Edward Thomas, a great lover of the English countryside who was killed in action during the First World War. The work was written following a brief halt at the now-demolished Adlestrop station which was actually situated some distance away from the village. The station nameplate which fired Thomas' imagination can now been seen in the village bus shelter along with a plaque inscribed with his famous poem.

From Adlestrop, a minor country road leads towards Moreton-in-Marsh, a journey which will take you through the quiet country village of EVENLODE. Here you will discover Portland House, a charming double fronted period residence which offers first-rate bed and breakfast accommodation. Surrounded by countryside, every window offers a view over the surrounding landscape, creating a wonderful sense of peace and tranquillity. Despite carrying out a thorough renovation, the proprietors, Mr and Mrs Dancer, have take care to ensure the property retains its original character and charm. This is enhanced by some fine period furniture, beautiful drapes and tasteful decor in each room, making Portland House a simply charming place to stay.

Portland House, Evenlode, Moreton-in-Marsh Tel: 01608 51653

A two-mile walk across the Oxfordshire border to the east of Evenlode leads to Chastleton House, a magnificent mansion which has remained virtually unchanged since it was constructed in 1603. The interior contains period furniture and a secret room where a Royalist family is said to have been concealed during the English Civil War. A nearby garden contains some amusing examples of box topiary.

Stow-on-the-Wold

MORETON-IN-MARSH is a bustling market town which stands at a busy junction on the A44 and the A429 Fosse Way. In its time, the town has been an important stopping place for stagecoaches and, unlike many of its Cotswold equivalents which were solely bound up in the wool trade, it was also a leading linen-weaving centre. The present-day centre is full of 18th- and 19th-century buildings which give it a great deal of period character. Some of the structures date from an earlier era such us the old town gaol and the unusual Curfew Tower with its bell dated 1633 which in its time has been used to summon the local fire brigade.

The Marshmallow, The High Street, Moreton-in-Marsh
Tel: 01608 51536

A walk down the High Street in Moreton-in-Marsh reveals a couple of other noteworthy stopping places. **The Marshmallow Licensed Restaurant** is one of four tea shops nominated for the 'Teashop of the Year' award; it is also highly praised in The Teapot Trail guidebook which lists the best tearooms in the country. This is a comfortable traditional tearoom with tastefully coordinated decor, exposed stone walls and old pine furnishings. Outside, there is a flagstoned patio surrounded by beautiful hanging baskets. The menu offers a selection of food to suit every palate. Lunchtime fare includes vegetable crumble, baked potatoes and daily specials, with Sunday lunches also being available. In the evening, the candlelit dinner menu offers such exotic-sounding dishes as 'coriander lamb with orange rice' or 'mushroom and nut fettucine', along with steaks and chef's specials. Table reservations advised at weekends.

At the northern end of Moreton-in-Marsh High Street, visitors will find the delightful **Townend Cottage and Coach House**, a first-rate bed and breakfast establishment and licensed restaurant which is run by Elizabeth Alderson and Stephanie Jenvey. Guests will particularly love the 'Tree House' which is like a lovers' hideaway; situated on the top floor of the coach house, this unique en-suite bedroom is accessed by a wooden stairway leading to a stable door. The room has a beautiful view of the garden with its many attractive hanging baskets and plants. On the ground floor of the cottage there is a beamed, licensed restaurant where food is available every day except Mondays and Wednesdays. Restaurant fare ranges from economically priced dishes for the 'pop-in' visitor to wonderfully presented home-baked dishes, all prepared using the finest local produce. Visitors can also purchase homemade cakes and crafts as a memento of their visit.

Townend Cottage, High Street, Moreton-in-Marsh Tel: 01608 50846

Moreton-in-Marsh also contains two specialist museums: the Bygones Museum at Aston Magna contains an interesting display of historic farm implements and folk memorabilia (open Wednesdays and Sundays between Easter and end-October), and the Wellington Aviation Art museum in Broadway Road contains a unique collection of World War II aircraft paintings, prints and models, together with details of the aircraft's historical background. (Open Tuesday to Sunday, 10am to 12.30pm and 2.30pm to 5.30pm; admission charge payable, profits to RAF Benevolent Fund.)

Like Stow-on-the-Wold, Moreton-in-Marsh was strategically important during the English Civil War and King Charles I himself is reported to have stayed at the White Hart Inn during one fleeting visit.

Those wishing to stay here a little longer will have no trouble finding Treetops in London Road. Treetops is a detached stone-built house with a private drive which is set in a delightful secluded position. Run by Liz and Brian Dean, this first-rate establishment offers spacious overnight accommodation. The beautifully presented en-suite bedrooms with their wide doors and easy access extend an obvious welcome to disabled guests. Only a few minutes' walk from the main street of this delightful market town, Treetops makes an ideal touring base for exploring the beautiful Cotswold countryside.

Treetops, London Road, Moreton-in-Marsh Tel: 01608 51036

From Moreton-in-Marsh, head west along the A44 and after a couple of miles you will find the road climbing a steep hill. At the top is BOURTON-ON-THE-HILL, a pleasant village with a fine part-Norman church and a mansion, Bourton House, which is surrounded by beautiful landscaped grounds containing a 16th-century tithe barn.

One mile south of Bourton-on-the-Hill is another impressive country house and garden, this time the highly eccentric Sezincote. In 1805, the house was rebuilt for a director of the East India Company, Sir Charles Cockerell, by his architect brother. He was assisted in his task by the noted Indian artist Thomas Daniell, hence its distinctive copper-covered onion-shaped dome; this was once burnished but is now coated in thick blue-green verdigris. Sezincote was visited in 1807 by the future Prince Regent and its design is said to have provided the inspiration for Brighton Pavilion which he built some years later. The grounds also contain a number of Indian-influenced features including a wonderful water-garden laid out by Repton and Daniell. (House open 2.30pm to 5.30pm on Thursdays and Fridays during May, June, July and September; gardens open 2pm to 6pm on Thursdays and Fridays all year round except December, plus Bank Holidays and selected Sundays. Admission charge payable.)

From here, retrace your steps to Bourton-on-the-Hill before joining the B4479 for the journey to BLOCKLEY, a mile and a half further north. The idyllic and unspoilt appearance of the present-day village hides an unexpectedly diverse industrial past. The fast-flowing Blockley Brook is fed by a large number of local springs giving it a constant head of water; as a consequence, the village became a popular site for water-powered mills and as many as a dozen were recorded in the Domesday Book back in the late 11th century. In the centuries which followed, the main industrial activity in the village was silk spinning, most of the output of which went to ribbon weavers in Coventry. At one time, however, the village also boasted a piano, a soap and a collar factory, as well as an iron foundry. Today, the picturesque silk mills have been made into desirable private homes and the village has an air of secluded wellbeing.

For a short period in the early 19th century, Blockley became famous as the home of Joanna Southcott, an eccentric who announced to the world that she would give birth to Shiloh, the second Messiah. Following a series of disturbances in the village, her house was eventually burnt to the ground. Today, the rebuilt Rock Cottage is marked with a commemorative plaque attached to two sturdy gateposts.

Lower Farm Cottages, Blockley, Moreton-in-Marsh
Tel: 01386 700237

Visitors seeking a truly idyllic country holiday need look no further than **Lower Farm Cottages**. Situated beside a brook in a quiet corner of Blockley, these exceptional self-catering cottages have been tastefully converted from period farm buildings to provide six luxury holiday homes. All are named after places and characters from Wind In The Willows: Ratty's Retreat is a tranquil hideaway for two people with a galleried bedroom and Victorian half-tester bed, Toad's Hall is the largest cottage which makes an ideal home for a large family or group, and Willow End, Mole's Cottage, Badger's Den and Otter's Abode are charming cottages which each accommodate either four or five people. Each cottage has a superb fitted kitchen, and visitors are welcomed with a pint of milk in the fridge and other essentials. (Guests can even arrange to have an order of groceries awaiting their arrival.) Outside, there are various slides, play equipment and even an immobilised tractor for children to play on, as well as a delightful little boat.

CHIPPING CAMPDEN is an ancient community of attractive gabled buildings which has remained largely unaltered for centuries. Chipping is a name which occurs several times in the Cotswolds and is derived the Old English word meaning 'market' or 'trading centre'. More a large village than a town, Chipping Campden was a regional capital of the wool-trade between the 13th- and 16th-centuries and many of the fine buildings that can be seen here today date from this era of prosperity. The Perpendicular 15th-century Church of St James with its 120 foot pinnacled tower is one of the finest wool churches in the Cotswolds (second only to Cirencester). Inside, there are several monumental brasses including one of William Grevel, which at eight feet by four feet, is thought to be the largest in the country. Presumably erected in an attempt to secure his immortality, its inscription (translated from Latin) reads 'the flower of the wool merchants of all England'. Also on view in the church is a glass display case containing a rare collection of embroidery including one example dating back to the time of Richard II.

Another noted 17th-century wool merchant and financier, Sir Baptist Hicks, was responsible for several of the finer Cotswold-stone buildings in the village including the unique Jacobean Market Hall with its open arcade and steeply-pitched gable ends which was completed around 1627. Fifteen years earlier, he endowed a group of attractive Almshouses built in the shape of the letter 'I' in honour of Kings James I (or Iacobus in the Latin of the day). Hicks was also responsible for building what was the largest residence in the village, Old Campden House. During the English

Almshouses, Chipping Campden

The Market Hall, Chipping Campden

Civil War, it was allegedly burned to the ground by Royalists to prevent it falling into the hands of the Parliamentarians. All that remains of it today are two unusual gatehouses near the church and the old stable block which was converted to a dower house some years after the end of the Civil War. Towards the end of his career, Hicks is said to have been so rich that even the King and members of his court asked to borrow from him.

Another unique character from Chipping Campden's past is William Harrison, an elderly rent collector who vanished in 1660. A woman and two of her sons were subsequently found guilty of his murder and hanged. Two years later, Harrison, the 'Campden Wonder', suddenly turned up in the village with an unconfirmable story of kidnapping, robbery and Turkish pirates.

Woolstaplers' Hall, Chipping Campden

Other points of interest in present-day Chipping Campden are the town hall, Grevel House and the Ernest Wilson memorial garden with its Chinese and Japanese botanical specimens. Also in the High Street is the Woolstaplers' Hall, a 14th-century former merchant's house which is now an interesting museum. Its eleven rooms contain a diverse collection of historic memorabilia including kitchen items, cameras, office equipment, clothing and an

230

apothecary's shop. (Open daily 11am to 6pm between 1st April to 31st October. Small admission charge payable.)

Those interested in the art of embroidery should make a point of finding the **Campden Needlecraft Centre** in Chipping Campden High Street. A true heaven for needlecraft enthusiasts, this attractive 17th-century building positively bulges with a vast array of materials of every conceivable type and colour. There are canvases from all over the world and every kind of thread, braid and fabric imaginable. Visitors can even purchase footstools ready to be worked on.

A nationally renowned business, the Campden Needlecraft Centre was originally opened by the mother of the current proprietor and has been established for over twenty years. Today, Helen Kirkup and her staff regularly dispatch orders abroad; they offer friendly, knowledgeable advice and can provide a fast and efficient postal service if required.

Campden Needlecraft Centre, High Street, Chipping Campden

Between 1612 and the mid-19th-century, a natural amphitheatre above Chipping Campden known as Dover's Hill was the venue for an annual series of organised games. These 'Olimpick Games' partly followed the traditions of Ancient Greece and partly involved more vernacular activities such as shin-kicking and bare-knuckle fighting. After having flourished for almost 250 years, the lawlessness and hooliganism which had grown up around the games led magistrates to close them down in 1852. However in 1951, they were revived in a modern form and each year on the

Friday following the spring Bank Holiday, a series of competitions takes place which ends in a spectacular torchlight procession.

Two miles east of Chipping Campden on the B4035 Banbury road is EBRINGTON , a quintessential Cotswold village of honey-coloured walls and neat thatched roofs. The village falls away to the north in irregular steps into a valley filled with apple and cherry orchards. There was a manor at Ebrington as early as the 13th century, although the present-day house dates from around 400 years later. The village church, St Eadburgha's, contains a number of ancient features including a Saxon stone coffin, a Norman nave and a medieval tower. It also contains an unusual 17th-century pulpit and a statue of Sir John Fortescue wearing the full regalia of a mid-15th-century Lord Chief Justice.

Lower Slaughter

From Ebrington, negotiating the network of country lanes will soon bring you to the National Trust-owned Hidcote Manor Garden at HIDCOTE BARTRIM . This exceptional garden is said by many to be one of the most beautiful built this century. In 1907, an American army officer, Major Lawrence Johnston, began a process which was to transform an exposed Cotswold escarpment into a series of delightful enclosed gardens. His only raw materials were a copse of mature beech trees, a lone cedar of Lebanon, a number of empty fields and a stream which flowed through a small valley. After creating several wide terraces, Johnston laid out a series of protective hedges which were deliberately made up of contrasting plant types (for example, yellow-leaved yew was interspersed with dark-leaved yew and copper beech with standard beech).

This created a series of sheltered compartments, each of which was planted with a carefully selected range of shrubs and plants which often followed to a recognisable theme (for example, some have flowers and foliage in a single colour). The water garden is less formal and consists of a rambling path overhung with trees which winds along the course of the stream between species shrubs and flourishing water-loving plants. There is also a large kitchen garden near the house with walls covered in clematis and old-fashioned climbing roses. (Open daily (except Tuesdays and Fridays), 11am to 7pm between April and the end October. Admission charge payable; free to National Trust Members.) In July, Hidcote Manor Garden also hosts outdoor performances of popular Shakespearean plays.

Brymbo, Honeybourne Lane, Mickleton Tel: 01386 438876

Another attractive garden, Kiftsgate Court, can be found adjacent to Hidcote. This also features a wide range of less well-known flora including tree peonies and old-fashioned roses. (Open Sundays, Wednesdays and Thursdays between 1st April and 30th September. Admission charge payable.)

A charming place to stay in this attractive northern tip of Gloucestershire can be found one mile to the northwest of Hidcote in the village of MICKLETON. 'Brymbo', the home of Gene and Barry Jeffrey, is a former farm building which has been tastefully converted into spacious, comfortable accommodation comprising one twin, one double and one family room. Two rooms have en-suite facilities, and all have television and tea/coffee making facilities. Gene and Barry go out of their way to ensure their guests are informed about the best attractions and eating places in the area. They even offer an evening tour in a four-wheel drive vehicle around places which might prove inaccessible in a normal car. Their helpfulness, keen prices and prodigious supply of maps and local information have made 'Brymbo' a highly popular place with overseas visitors. Advance booking is strongly advised.

The Vale of Gloucester

Tewkesbury Abbey

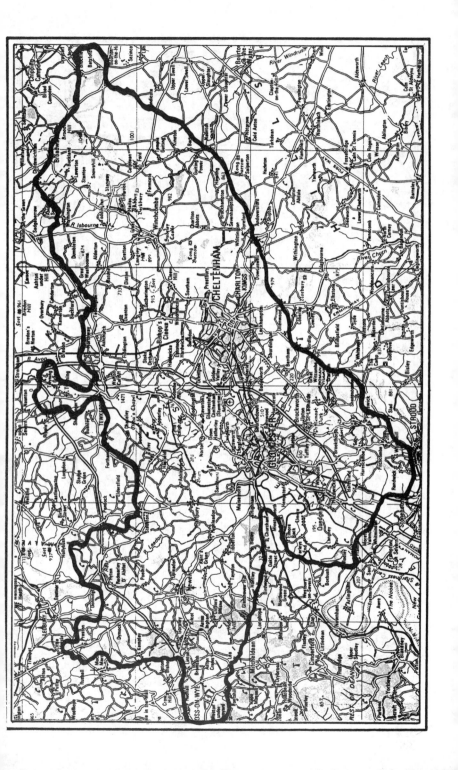

Gloucester Cathedral

CHAPTER NINE

The Vale
of Gloucester

BROADWAY is an exceptionally attractive Worcestershire village which has earned a reputation for being the 'show village of England'. Many of the honey-gold Cotswold stone buildings which line the unusually long and wide main street date back to Tudor and Jacobean times. In recent years, some have been converted into interesting antique shops and other retail premises designed to cater for passing visitors. The village has a broad green overlooked by St Michael's parish church and the Broadway Hotel. A short distance away, the 16th-century Lygon Arms Hotel, formerly a private residence, stands beside the famous furniture workshops belonging to Gordon Russell Ltd.

Should you wish to stay in this area, then adjacent to Broadway Golf Club, you will find Dormy House. Dormy in golfing terms means 'unbeatable' and that is a very fair description of this fine hotel which offers the visitor the opportunity to relax in superb surrounings. Everything about Dormy House is tasteful. The bedrooms are all en-suite and furnished attractively with a mixture of antique and traditional pieces that lend charm to the rooms. Each bedroom has tea and coffee making facilities, colour TV and telephones. For people with young families there is a baby listening service which is always a boon to parents.

The restaurant is broken up into a series of small intimate areas. The linen is in lovely pastels of beige and cream and every table has a single fresh rose. In such a relaxing atmosphere you feel absolutely right to enjoy the very best of English and French cuisine. Why not start your meal with an unusual terrine of Lobster and Asparagus with a basil sauce and followed it with Supreme of Guinea Fowl with wild rice and a creamed marsala sauce. These are just two from a range of nine starters and twelve main courses on the à la carte menu. There is also a table d'hôte menu which

239

changes daily. The choice is hard to make and care is taken to ensure that you can have simply grilled or steamed fish for example if your diet demands it. With every main course there is a selection of fresh seasonal vegetables which come to the table cooked perfectly. Follow this with one of the delectable sweets, or cheese from the wide choice available from the cheeseboard and you will leave the table replete and happy. The fine wine list reflects the quality of the food and includes some superb vintages.

Dormy House is an excellent place for visitors from abroad to stay at because it is just the sort of hotel that upholds all that is good about English hospitality.

Dormy House Hotel, Broadway Tel: 01386 852711

A mile and a half to the southeast of Broadway, Fish Hill rises to over 1000 feet and is topped by a highly conspicuous folly, the 55-foot Broadway Tower which was built in 1800 by the Earl of Coventry solely so that it could be seen from his home at Worcester nearly twenty miles away to the northwest. The tower contains an elegantly-proportioned observation room and an exhibition on the history of Broadway and its famous folly. (Open daily, April to early-October.) A further exhibition, this time on local natural history, is housed in nearby Tower Barn; this stands at the centre of the network of footpaths and nature trails which crisscross the attractive area known as the Broadway Tower Country Park. (Open daily, all year round.)

A couple of miles further south ,make a point of calling in at the National Trust-owned country house, Snowshill Manor. This small

240

yet elegant manor house dates from Tudor times and once belonged to Catherine Parr, the sixth wife of Henry VIII. The present-day building has an attractive 17th-century Cotswold stone façade and contains 21 rooms, most of which are open to the public.

These rooms contain a fascinating collection of historic artefacts assembled over several decades by the last private owner, Charles Paget Wade. Articles on display include clocks, toys, bicycles, sedan chairs, oriental furniture and nautical items such as compasses, telescopes and model ships. There are also a number of exhibits relating to Wade's special interest in the occult. Towards the end of his life, the collection became so large that Paget was forced to move in to one of the outbuildings. (Open Wednesdays to Sundays and Bank Holiday Mondays between May and September, and on Saturdays and Sundays only during April and October. Admission charge payable; free to National Trust members.)

From Snowshill, continue south on a small country lane, crossing the B4077 at Ford which will bring you to TEMPLE GUITING, an exceptionally attractive north Cotswolds hamlet on the banks of the Upper Windrush which has a fine church and a handsome Georgian mansion. In the 12th century, the Knights Templar founded a preceptory here. A couple of miles downstream, Temple Guiting's sister village, GUITING POWER, consists of a delightful collection of Cotswold stone cottages clustered around a triangular green. In the 1970s, Richard Cochrane, a local property-owner who had acquired about half the cottages in the village, set up a trust to ensure that the housing here would continue to be offered to local people at affordable rents. This arrangement has done much to preserve the rural character of the village with its steep gables, mullioned windows and neat blue doors. Other noteworthy features here are the part-Norman St Michael's Church which was extensively remodelled in 1903, the memorial cross which was erected after the First World War, and the old bakery in Well Lane which has an unusual columned frontage dating back to the early 17th century.

Midway between the Guitings, and approximately one mile to the east, stands the Cotswold Farm Park, a characteristic Cotswolds hill farm which contains one of the largest collections of rare farm animals in the country. Visitors are encouraged to meet the animals which include longhorn cattle, Gloucester Old Spot pigs and a local breed of thickly-fleeced sheep known as Cotswold Lions. Also on offer is a children's adventure park, pets corner, café and farm trail. (Open daily, 10.30am to 6pm between Good Friday and 1st October. Admission charge payable.)

Our journey westward from the Guitings crosses the Salt Way, an ancient packhorse path which runs along the ridge between the Windrush valley and the vale of Sudeley. Because of the lack of winter foodstuffs, it was a common medieval practice to slaughter livestock in the autumn and then preserve the meat in barrels of salt. The mineral became a valuable commodity and a network of routes grew up between its source (in this case Droitwich in Worcestershire) and the rest of the country. The most accessible section of the Cotswolds Salt Way runs for seven miles south from Hailes Abbey to a point on the A436 three miles east of Andoversford. Near its northern end, the route passes close to Salter's Hill, an impressive viewpoint lying two miles east of Winchcombe.

To the west is Sudeley Castle, the burial place of Catherine Parr. After outliving Henry VIII, Parr married her former lover, Sir Thomas Seymour of Sudeley, but sadly died in childbirth the following year. Not long after in 1549, her husband was executed for treason after unsuccessfully attempting to turn Edward VI against the Lord Protector, Seymour's own brother. The marble tomb of Catherine Parr can be seen in St Mary's Chapel. This, however, is not the original but a 19th-century substitute designed by Sir Gilbert Scott to replace the one destroyed during the English Civil War.

Sudeley Castle was a Royalist headquarters during that war and was twice besieged, once in 1643 and again in 1644. The conflict left the castle badly damaged by cannon fire and a large gap can still be seen in the wall of the Octagon Tower. During the following two centuries, Sudeley was badly neglected and much of the stone was carted away by locals for use as building material. By the 1820s, it had degenerated into a common alehouse, the Castle Arms, and it wasn't until 1837 that the castle and sixty acres of land were rescued by the Dent family. Emma Dent was responsible for completing the period restoration of the exterior and for refurbishing the interior in sumptuous Victorian style. She was also responsible for accumulating a a large number of priceless old

242

masters, including work by Constable, Turner, Van Dyck and Rubens, as well as a unique collection of tapestries, period furniture, costumes and one of the largest private collections of toys in Europe.

As well as being able to tour of the interior, visitors can walk around Sudeley's extensive grounds which contain a lake, a formal garden and a fifteen-foot double yew hedge. A more recent addition has been a large adventure playground complete with replica castle. (Castle open daily, 12 noon to 5pm between 1st April and 31st October. Admission charge payable.)

Sudeley Castle

The attractive small town of **WINCHCOMBE** was once a regional capital of Saxon Mercia. One of the town's more enduring legends concerns, Kenelm, a popular child king who is said to have been martyred here by his jealous sister, Quendrida, in the 8th century. As a way of calming a mob which had gathered to voice its disapproval at this murderous act, legend has it that she recited Psalm 109 backwards, an act which resulted in the divine loss of her sight. In medieval times, St Kenelm's shrine grew to rank second only to Thomas à Becket's as a destination for pilgrims, a factor which made the town one of the wealthiest tourist attractions in the country. Winchcombe grew to become a walled town with an abbot who presided over a Saxon parliament; however in 1539, the abbey was destroyed by Thomas Seymour of Sudeley following Henry VIII's Dissolution of the Monasteries. All that remains of it today is a section of a gallery which is on view at the George Inn.

In the centre of Winchcombe is a fine inn, the Plaisterers Arms. This impressive establishment dates from the 18th century and inside has oak-beamed ceilings and a wonderful traditional atmosphere. Landlord David Gould serves an excellent selection of hand-pulled ales and a range of bar meals including delicious homemade pies and a traditional roast lunch on Sundays. He also has three comfortable letting rooms available which are all pleasantly appointed and equipped with en-suite facilities. The land to the rear of the inn slopes away sharply to form a delightful beer garden. An attractive patio area has been created here and in spring and summer, the whole area overflows with spectacular floral displays. The garden enjoys fine views over the surrounding landscape and also contains a charming pets' corner and large children's play area. Children are also very welcome in the pub's pleasant cellar bar.

Plaisterers Arms, Abbey Terrace, Winchcombe Tel: 01242 602358

Following the destruction of the abbey, the local merchants were forced to find an alternative source of income. This they found in a new crop which had just been introduced from the New World, tobacco. Despite the vagaries of the English climate, for several

244

decades Winchcombe earned a healthy living growing this increasingly popular cash crop, a fact which is reflected in several present-day place names such as Tobacco Close and Tobacco Field. Unfortunately, this new-found prosperity was brought to an abrupt end in 1670 when an act of Parliament banned home-produced tobacco in favour of imports from the struggling colony of Virginia.

The long period of decline which followed this legislative interference has left the town with a great many unaltered buildings. These include the Tudor houses in Hailes Street and the splendid parish church with its forty leering gargoyles and alter cloth reputed to have been embroidered by Catherine of Aragon.

The Olde Bakery, High Street, Winchcombe Tel: 01242 602469

On the corner of Castle Street is the delightful Olde Bakery Tea Shoppe. This handsome stone building is believed to be between 200 and 300 years old, and earlier this century, operated as a working bakery (the old bakehouse can still be seen at the bottom of the tea garden when visiting the outside loo!). Proprietors Sally and Colin Snell maintain the tradition of home baking, with the vast majority of items being made on the premises (their special homemade carrot cake is renowned.)

Customers can sit in either of the two tea rooms, in the vine-covered conservatory or, weather permitting, in the delightful walled tea garden. On Sundays, an excellent traditional roast lunch is served for which booking is advised. Sally and Colin also have two charming en-suite letting bedrooms available - ring for details and availability.

Also in the High Street is the excellent **White Hart Hotel**, a splendid inn which is believed to be one of the oldest in Winchcombe. This impressive half-timbered building has a private car park at the rear and for much of the year is covered in wonderful hanging baskets of flowers. Inside, it has lost none of its original character and charm with oak-beamed ceilings, open fires and an interesting collection of horse racing memorabilia, including several antique saddles. Proprietors Alistair and Mari MacPherson and John Steele-Scott offer a fine selection of traditional hand-drawn ales and an extensive bar meals menu, with dishes ranging from sandwiches and jacket potatoes to steaks and chicken Kiev. The White Hart also has several letting bedrooms available which are all comfortable, well-appointed and provide a good base for exploring the Cotswolds. Residents are also able to make use of the inn's snooker cellar and games room, though they should keep an eye open for the friendly ghost which is said to pay a visit from time to time.

The White Hart, Winchcombe Tel: 01242 602359

Winchcombe also contains two interesting specialist museums. Winchcombe Folk and Police Museum is situated adjacent to the tourist information centre in the town hall. As well as information on the history of the town from neolithic times to the recent past, the museum also houses an intriguing collection of police equipment and uniforms, both from British and overseas forces. (Open Mondays to Saturdays, 10am to 5pm between 1st April and 31st October. Small admission charge payable.)

A half-acre garden behind an ordinary-looking Victorian house in Gloucester Street is the home of the Winchcombe Railway Museum, thought to be the oldest private railway museum in the country. All types of railway-related exhibits are on show with the exception of locomotives and rolling stock. There is even a working signal box, a booking office and a number of signals which visitors are encouraged to operate. Also on show is a collection of over 200 cast iron line-side signs and a large display of printed memorabilia, including tickets and posters. (Open daily, 1pm to 6pm. Admission charge payable; accompanied children free.)

Standing near the centre of you will find the first-rate bed and breakfast establishment which has been run since 1984 by Mrs Sally Simmonds. **Gower House** is an attractive stone-built residence with an atmosphere which is exceptionally friendly and welcoming. The oak-beamed bedrooms are comfortable and well-appointed and have access to two guest bathrooms. Mrs Simmonds provides her guests with the warmest of welcomes and a traditional Cotswold breakfast which is guaranteed to set them up for the day. She also has an interesting collection of antique weighing scales. To the rear of the house, there is a delightful garden with its own well, raised beds and an unusual sundial on the wall.

Gower House, 16 North Street, Winchcombe Tel: 01242 602616

Those preferring the relaxed atmosphere of farmhouse accommodation should make a point of finding **Ireley Farm**, a delightful bed and breakfast establishment which is run by Margaret and Ian Warmington. Situated just off the Broadway road on the edge of Winchcombe, Ireley Farm has a history going back to Roman and medieval times. It is centred around an elegant 18th-century residence built of golden Cotswold limestone which stands within 500 acres of beautiful rolling farmland. Inside, the house has a handsome panelled hallway, open fires and three spacious letting bedrooms, all oak-beamed and decorated in charming country style. Maggie and Ian provide the warmest of welcomes and a delicious farmhouse breakfast. Horse riding and rough shooting are also available nearby.

Ireley Farm, Winchcombe Tel: 01242 602445

Not far outside Winchcombe is Hailes Abbey, founded in 1246 by Richard, Earl of Cornwall, son of King John and youngest brother of Henry III, following his narrow escape from a shipwreck off the Scilly Isles. Unfortunately, it was built to such an ambitious scale that the Cistercian monks found it difficult to maintain financially; that is, until a wealthy patron donated of a phial which was said to contain the blood of Jesus Christ. Thanks to this holy relic, Hailes Abbey soon became one of Europe's most important pilgrimage destinations and was even referred to in Chaucer's 'The Canterbury Tales'.

This state of affairs lasted until the Dissolution of the Monasteries in 1539 when the authenticity of the relic was questioned and the phial destroyed. The abbey then fell into disrepair and today, the only significant structures still standing are seventeen arches of the monastic cloister. Because of its illustrious past, however, a large number of artefacts have been found on the site including medieval floor tiles and fragments of elaborate stone sculptures. These are now on display to the public in an interesting museum which is open daily, 10am to 6pm between 1st April and end-September. (Admission charge payable; free to National Trust and English Heritage members.)

The nearby parish church of Hailes was constructed around 1130 and predates the abbey. Many of the floor tiles belonging to the abbey were transferred here following the Dissolution, and there are also some fine 14th-century wall paintings and a canopied pulpit dating from the 1600s.

Our next stop is **STANWAY**, a charming village which lies tucked under the western ridge of the Cotswolds a couple of miles to the north. The view down to the village from the A4077 on the escarpment above is one of the loveliest in Gloucestershire. Stanway itself contains a number of interesting architectural features including a 14th-century medieval tithe barn, an unusual bronze of St George on the war memorial, and private cricket pavilion built on curious mushroom-shaped staddle-stones. An ornate Jacobean gatehouse guards the entrance to Stanway House, a fine Tudor mansion built of mellow honey-gold Cotswold limestone which is one of the most remarkable houses in the county.

Stanway House, Stanway, Cheltenham Tel: 01386 73469

Stanway House is an outstanding example of an English Jacobean manor house, built between 1580 and 1640 by the Tracys of Stanway, a landed family who owned property in Gloucestershire since pre-Norman times. Other than by inheritance, the estate has only changed hands once in the last 1200 years. Today, Stanway is the home of Lord Neidpath; he has personally written an excellent guide to the house which is on sale to visitors to help them enjoy a tour around the property. (It is also a pleasure to read the guide after a visit when it helps to refresh the memory of the many delights of the house.)

The gatehouse which is situated between the church and the main house was built around 1630, it was believed, by Inigo Jones, though more recently it has been ascribed to Timothy Strong of Barrington. Whoever the designer, it is one of the gems of Cotswold architecture.

Hailes Abbey

There is an interesting piece of history connected with the scallop shells which adorn the gatehouse. Sir William de Traci of Barnstaple was one of the four knights who murdered St Thomas à Becket in Canterbury Cathedral at the instigation of King Henry II. After the King repented of this horrendous crime, Sir William was obliged to go on pilgrimage to Jerusalem, and so, it is supposed, the Tracys adopted the scallop shell crest of St James of Compostella, the patron saint of pilgrims.

The shuffleboard table along the west wall of the hall was built about 1620. The game of shuffleboard, an early form of shove-halfpenny, was very popular in the 16th and 17th centuries. As there are only three known to be in full working order complete with their brass counters, this is a rare example indeed. It is particularly special because it has a single piece of oak as the playing surface. The table has a moulded frieze on the side which is visible from the hall, but none on the side nearest the west wall, suggesting that it has always stood in its present position.

In the bay window there is a Chippendale exercising chair; at one time, half-an-hour's vigorous bouncing each day on this was considered to be good for the health. There are also two fine Broadwood pianos which, until recently, lay neglected in an unheated, unlit, unventilated and uninhabited room. Despite hardly ever having been played, they have remained in excellent condition. Stanway is filled with fine paintings, many of them portraits of family ancestors, all of which add to the atmosphere and well-being of this lovely house.

Stanway House is also known for being the home of Thomas Dover, the sea captain who rescued Alexander Selkirk from a deserted island, an event which gave Daniel Defoe the inspiration to write Robinson Crusoe.

Stanway's sister village, STANTON, lies a mile further north. This exceptional Cotswold village consists almost entirely of steeply-gabled limestone cottages built during the 16th- and 17th-centuries. One of the reasons Stanton is so well-preserved is that it was owned by the architect Sir Philip Stott between 1906 and 1937. Stott's home, Stanton Court, is an elegant Jacobean residence which was built by the Chamberlain to Queen Elizabeth I when the original 16th-century manor, Warren Farm House, had become outmoded. The house is set within attractive landscaped grounds which are occasionally open to the public on summer Sundays.

Attached to Stanton Court are the superb Stanton Court Cottages, a collection of eight top-class self-catering holiday cottages which were constructed of local Cotswold limestone in the 16th and 17th centuries. Now luxuriously renovated, the cottages provide the ideal place to get away from the daily trials of life and completely unwind. The cottage buildings are set around a wonderful old courtyard and stand within five acres of impressive landscaped gardens containing orchards, sweeping lawns and beautifully-kept flower beds. The grounds also contain a heated outdoor swimming pool (open during the summer months), a tennis court (open weekdays) and a games room containing table tennis, table football and darts.

The eight holiday cottages sleep from two to seven people and are appointed to an extremely high standard. All have full gas central heating, direct-dial telephones, fully-equipped modern fitted kitchens, attractively decorated dining/sitting room areas with colour televisions, modern bathrooms with showers and plenty of hot water, and bedrooms with all linen and continental quilts provided. There are also excellent laundry facilities on site. The cottages are luxurious and stylish, yet comfortable and informal, and provide the ideal environment in which to relax and enjoy the beautiful surroundings and many nearby places of interest. Open all year round.

Stanton Court Cottages, Stanton, Nr. Broadway Tel: 01386 73551

Stanton's village Church of St Michael's and All Angels has a number of noteworthy features including a fine Perpendicular south aisle and porch, an east window containing stained glass from the ruined abbey at Hailes, and a number of medieval pews whose ends have been deeply scarred by the leashes of dogs said to belong to local shepherds. A number of early-20th-century additions were made to the church by the architect Sir Ninian Comper; these include the organ loft, the rood screen and a number of stained-glass windows which can be identified by the designer's signature, a wild strawberry.

Those looking for first-rate farmhouse accommodation in this delightful village should make a point of calling in at The Vine. Lying just to the east of the B4632 between Winchcombe and Broadway, this exceptional place to stay can also be reached on foot via the Cotswolds Way. The Vine is a friendly, family-run bed and breakfast establishment which is run by Jill Gabb. Her substantial 17th-century stone-built farmhouse stands within a beautiful low-walled garden and was once the home of the local bailiff. Inside, the atmosphere is warm and relaxing with open log fires, a superb dining room and three spacious letting bedrooms, each with a four-poster. Mrs Gabb is happy to offer accommodation to unaccompanied children who come to take advantage of the excellent riding facilities which are offered at the nearby stables.

The Vine, Stanton, Nr. Broadway Tel: 01386 73250

Before turning west, make a short detour to the northeast to visit the village which is believed to possess the oldest rectory in England. BUCKLAND is a quiet and picturesque settlement which is situated under the crest of Burhill, just to the east of the B4632 Broadway road. The ancient rectory dates from the Middle Ages and includes a 14th-century great hall which has unusual hammerbeams carved with angels. One of the rectory windows dates from the 15th century and has a design attributed to the Malvern Priory school of glass making. John Wesley is said to have preached at the rectory which is open to visitors 11am to 4pm on

Mondays only during May, June, July and September. Admission free.

There is also a fine Perpendicular church in Buckland with a 15th-century east window which was restored in the 19th century on the instructions of William Morris. The lovely little building is surrounding by an interesting churchyard containing an unusual table tomb and the graves of several local luminaries.

From Buckland, retrac your steps southwest along the B4632 for three miles before turning west onto the B4077. Toddington Station, the northern terminus of the privately-owned Gloucestershire-Warwickshire Railway, is situated close to this road junction. From here, it is possible to take a steam train for an enjoyable six-mile return trip through some of the loveliest countryside in Gloucestershire. The restored Great Western Railway station is open to the public all year round and includes a signal box and a goods shed. (Small admission charge payable.) Train trips at an extra charge depart between 12 noon and 5pm on Saturdays and Sundays between March and October.

Stanway Grounds, Toddington, Cheltenham Tel: 01242 620079

A mile or so further west, turne north off the B4077 Tewkesbury to Stow-in-the-Wold road to visit the delightful village of TODDINGTON. The village is home to the renowned bed and breakfast establishment which is run by Mrs Pratley at her spacious country home, Stanway Grounds. Set within beautiful open countryside, this handsome late-Victorian farmhouse can be found approximately one mile northeast of the village. (For accurate directions, telephone the owner on 01242 620079.) Mrs Pratley has three spacious and comfortable letting bedrooms available (either double or twin), all with tea/coffee making facilities and either en-suite facilities or a private bathroom. For those keen on horse-riding, a stables is attached to the building which offers riding lessons and accompanied pony trekking rides. Children and pets welcome.

Approximately three miles to the west of Toddington, is **LITTLE WISHBOURNE**, a charming village which lies in the broad valley which sweeps down from the Cotswolds to the River Severn.

The Hobnails, Little Washbourne, Nr. Tewkesbury
Tel: 01242 620237

Here you will find the **Hobnails Inn**, a renowned country pub which dates from 1474 and has been run by the same family since 1743. The present landlords, Stephen and Vanessa Farbrother, have built up an excellent reputation for good pub food, and in particular, for their range of Scottish baps which they serve with a huge variety of delicious fillings. They also offer an imaginative range of vegetarian dishes, homemade entrees and a mind-blowing selection of desserts. A good selection of traditional ales is served in the bar which, like the dining room, lounge and games room, is full of traditional atmosphere. Queen Elizabeth I is believed to have stopped at the here on her way to visit Catherine Parr, and Harry the friendly poltergeist is rumoured to be a regular visitor to this day!

One mile to the northwest of Little Washbourne, the village of **ALDERTON** is home to the impressive **Brooklands Farm Touring Caravan Park**. This small and attractive family-run caravan park stands within twenty acres of rolling farmland just six miles to the east of junction 9 on the M5. Set around a small lake, the site enjoys fine views over the surrounding countryside to Gretton Hill and beyond. It has been run since 1988 by Caravan Club members Sue and Simon Greener, a very friendly couple who have done much to improve the facilities on offer. There is now an excellent toilet block with showers, hair dryers and laundry facilities, a large games room with indoor bowls and table tennis, electric hook-ups and a small site shop selling, amongst other things, bottled butane and propane. Coarse fishing is also available in the lake during the season.

Brooklands Caravan Park, Alderton, Nr. Tewkesbury
Tel: 01242 620259

The upland area to the northwest of here, Bredon Hill, is a spur of the Cotswolds which extends from the main range across the Hereford and Worcester border. Following the country lanes to the northeast will bring you to the pleasant village of **ASHTON UNDER HILL**.

Some of the finest farmhouse accommodation in the area can be found at **Home Farm** in the historic village of **BREDONS**. Owned by Anne and Mick Meadows, Home Farm is a lovely brick-built farmhouse which forms part of a 150-acre family-run working livestock farm. Guests are assured of a warm welcome at this cosy

Village Cross, Stanton

friendly establishment, the central part of which dates from the late 17th century and was originally quite small, containing only a kitchen, sitting room and four bedrooms, two at attic level. Today, there are three comfortable letting rooms available, two with en-suite facilities and all tastefully furnished and centrally heated. Anne provides superb home-cooked food, much of which is prepared from her own produce (make a point of sampling her delicious homemade jams). Evening meals are also available by prior arrangement. For those preferring self-catering accommodation, the Meadows also have a well-equipped three-bedroom cottage which sleeps up to six people.

Home Farm, Bredons Norton, Tewkesbury Tel: 01684 72322

Heading towards Tewkesbury once more, our journey south takes us through the village of **BREDONS HARDWICK**, the location of the renowned **Croft Farm Leisure and Water Park**. Situated just to the north of the B4080, this impressive leisure facility is a mecca for enthusiastic windsurfers of all ages and levels of ability.

Formerly a market garden, the site was taken over in 1976 by a sand and gravel company whose excavations led to the formation of the lake which can be seen today. Proprietors Alan and Agneta Newell offer fully qualified instruction at their RYA recognised windsurfing school. They also offer excellent value caravanning and camping facilities between 1st March and 31st October at two attractive lakeside sites. For further information or to book in advance, telephone 01684 72321.

From Croft Farm, it is only a short journey across the Gloucestershire border to TEWKESBURY, a historic and strategically important town which stands at the confluence of the rivers Severn and Avon. Because its geographical position restricted outward development, Tewkesbury grew as a series of narrow streets packed with unusually tall buildings, many of which were constructed during the 15th- and 16th-centuries. Thanks to the period of relative decline which followed this late-medieval period of prosperity, a great many black and white half-timbered structures remain; these are best seen on foot.

Croft Farm, Bredons Hardwick, Tewkesbury Tel: 01684 72321

Tewkesbury's three main thoroughfares, the High Street, Church Street and Barton Street, form a 'Y' shape around the abbey. The area in between is filled with narrow alleyways and hidden courtyards which contain some wonderful old pubs and medieval cottages. At the centre of the 'Y' stands the spectacular Tewkesbury Abbey, a parish church of cathedral-like proportions which was originally founded in the 8th century and re-consecrated at the end of the 11th century. It was once the church of the mighty Benedictine Abbey of Tewkesbury and was one of the last monasteries to be dissolved by Henry VIII; in 1540, it was saved from destruction by the astute town burghers who bought it from the Crown for just £453.

Inside, one of its most striking features is the double row of massive Norman pillars; these support some fine early-14th-century roof vaulting which in recent years has been restored to its original colour.   In the central quire, there are seven superb stained-glass windows containing panes dating from the 14th century.   Two other outstanding features are the abbey's Milton organ, which has pipes dating from around 1620 that are thought to be some of the oldest in the country still to be in regular use, and the high alter which consists of a single massive slab of Purbeck marble over 13 feet in length.

At 132 feet high and 46 feet square, Tewkesbury Abbey's colossal main tower is believed to be the largest Norman church tower still in existence.   Those making the climb to the top will be rewarded with a breathtaking view of the town and the surrounding landscape.   Indeed, the tower was used as a lookout position during one of the bloodiest and most decisive confrontations of the Wars of the Roses, the Battle of Tewkesbury.

Tewkesbury

The battle took place on Saturday 4th May 1471 in a field to the south of the town which ever since has been known as Bloody Meadow.   Following the Lancastrian defeat, those who had not been slaughtered on the battlefield fled to the abbey where they were pursued by the victorious Yorkist troops.   A further massacre took place before it was halted by timely intervention of Abbot

Strensham; however, two days later the refugees, who included the Duke of Somerset, were handed over to the king and executed at the town's Market Cross. The seventeen year-old son of Henry VI, Edward Prince of Wales, was also killed during the conflict and a plaque marking his resting place can be seen in the abbey.

Almost two centuries later, Tewkesbury was again the scene of military action, this time during the English Civil War. It changed hands several times during the conflict and on one occasion, Charles I began his siege of Gloucester by requisitioning every pick, mattock, spade and shovel in the town.

Those keen on finding out more about the town's turbulent military history should follow Tewkesbury's Battle Trail, an informative guide for which is available at the Tourist Information Office. Alternatively, there is an interesting model of the battlefield in the Tewkesbury Town Museum. This fascinating museum is housed in a medieval timber-framed building in Barton Street and contains a number of displays on the social history and archeology of Tewkesbury and its surrounding district. (Open daily, 10am to 1pm and 2pm to 5pm between Easter and the end of October. Admission charge payable.)

Two other specialist museums can be found almost adjacent to each other in Church Street. The Little Museum is situated in a timber-framed merchant's house which dates from around 1450. The building was fully restored in 1971 and is laid out as a recreation of a typical Tewkesbury merchant's home and workplace during the late-Middle Ages. (Open Tuesdays to Saturdays and Bank Holiday Mondays, 10am to 5pm between Easter and October. Admission free.)

The nearby John Moore Countryside Museum contains a huge variety of artefacts relating to the Gloucestershire countryside, past and present. It was opened in 1980 in commemoration of the work of John Moore, a well-known local writer, broadcaster and natural history enthusiast who was born in Tewkesbury in 1907. Items on show include agricultural implements, domestic equipment and a wide range of unusual rural memorabilia; most of the exhibits are set out to be particularly appealing to children. The museum also concerns itself with nature conservation and the effects of human intervention on the natural environment. (Open Tuesdays to Saturdays and Bank Holiday Mondays, 10am to 1pm and 2pm to 5pm between Easter and October. Small admission charge payable.)

Another place in Tewkesbury well worth visiting is the Abbey Mill in Mill Street. Standing in a lovely position by the river, this charming restaurant can cater for up to 140 people. A mill began operating on the site in the 8th century which was run by a monk, most probably from the abbey. In the 17th century the building was rebuilt in Tewkesbury brick and, more recently, it was converted to a comfortable, modern restaurant. A large working waterwheel stands next to the attractive patio which is open throughout the summer. Customers can drop in at the Abbey Mill for morning coffee, lunch or afternoon tea, or book in advance to join one of their famous fun evenings; these include medieval banquets, Cockney nights and Bavarian evenings.

Abbey Mill, Mill Street, Tewkesbury Tel: 01684 292287

Tewkesbury is also known for its literary associations. Charles Dickens set part of 'The Pickwick Papers' in the town's Royal Hop Pole Hotel, and the Victorian romantic writer, Mrs Craik, based her novel 'John Halifax, Gentleman' on the people and places of the borough.

A three-mile detour across the River Severn to the west of Tewkesbury leads to FORTHAMPTON, an unspoilt Severn Vale village with a genuine historic character. The village consists of an assortment of 16th- and 17th-century timber-framed farmhouses and cottages which are loosely grouped around a knoll containing the part-13th-century Church of St Mary's. A series of narrow lanes cuts through the village offering a number of beautiful walks past some of the most delightful old buildings in Gloucestershire. These include the Sanctuary, with its 15th-century great hall, the imposing 18th-century Forthampton House, and the similarly-aged Southfield House with its handsome brick-built dovecote. The grounds of Southfield House are occasionally open to the public and contain the former country retreat of the abbots of Tewkesbury, Forthampton Court.

Southwest of Tewkesbury is the attractive Severn-side hamlet of DEERHURST. The tiny present-day village disguises the fact that in Saxon times, it was of much greater importance. Indeed, this was the site of the most powerful monastery of Hwicce, the Anglo-Saxon principality of the lower Severn. The village church is one of the oldest in Britain and has parts dating back as far as the 7th century, the period when the monastery would have been at the height of its influence. The building has a distinctive Celtic flavour; the elaborate double east window is unique to Deerhurst and is considered to bear more resemblance to a window in Ethiopia's Debra Damo monastery than it does to any equivalent construction in Britain. The interior of the church contains some unusual Saxon carvings, including an angel in the apse which probably dates from the 9th century and an exceptionally fine carved font which was found buried in a local farmyard. This also dates from the 9th century and is carved with a Celtic trumpet spiral, a vine scroll and an unusual Northumbrian motif. The present-day base has different origins and originally belonged to a carved Saxon cross.

St Alphege, who went on to become Archbishop of Canterbury and was subsequently martyred by the Danes, was a monk here during the 10th century, and some decades later, a nearby island in the Severn was the place where the Saxon king, Edmund Ironside, signed a treaty of cooperation with Canute, King of the Danes. The church also contains a number of memorial brasses dating from the late-14th-century commemorating the Cassey family, the owners of the estate one mile to the south which now encompasses the handsome 16th-century residence, Wightfield Manor.

The floor of nearby Abbots Court once concealed the remains Odda's Chapel, another Saxon treasure which was founded in 1056 by the Earl Odda, a trusted friend of Edward the Confessor. A stone inscribed with the date of consecration was discovered in 1675 and is now on view in the Ashmolean Museum in Oxford. A copy of this Odda Stone can be seen inside the chapel which is now administered by English Heritage.

One mile southwest of Deerhurst, is the attractive village of UPPER APPERLEY where you will find the impressive Tyms Holm Country Guest House. This fine establishment is owned and personally run by Ann Sabin and her husband, two extremely thoughtful people whose care and attention to detail make this delightful guesthouse really stand out. On booking their accommodation, guests are sent comprehensive details on how to find the place, along with a wonderful little guide, beautifully hand-drawn, showing all the places of interest which lie within easy reach. Produced and detailed by Richard Harrow, these little maps show, for example, Apperley to Bibury via the Coln Valley, or Apperley to Snowshill or Worcester.

Tyms Holm Guest House, Tyms Holm, Upper Apperley,
Gloucester Tel: 01452 780386

Situated in the ancient parish of Deerhurst, Tyms Holm lies midway between Tewkesbury, Cheltenham and Gloucester making it ideal for exploring the Malverns, Cotswolds and the Forest of Dean. The guesthouse is set within an acre of beautiful lawned and shrub-filled gardens which give it almost total seclusion, and is reached along a lovely tree-lined drive. The building is a very old cottage which has been restored and enlarged. In fact, the present dining room was originally called Hawkers Cottage; a charming place, it features lovely old Jacobean-style furniture, including an original monk's bench. Guests certainly eat well here on the fine home cooking. Delicious morning coffees, lunches and afternoon teas are served in the licensed restaurant, as well as first-rate breakfasts and evening meals. (Because the food is so tempting, diners can put on pounds if they are not careful!)

The accommodation comprises one single, two twin and two double rooms, with one double and one twin offering en-suite facilities. The Sabins take the business of running a successful guesthouse all in their stride and manage to create a wonderful relaxed atmosphere. Children are very welcome and the proprietors are happy to cater for any practical request during your stay. Tyms Holm has been awarded two crowns by the English Tourist Board and is open all year round except during Christmas week. In winter, roaring log fires supplement the central heating, making this a truly splendid place to stay.

Setting off from Upper Apperley in an easterly direction, make your way to CHELTENHAM via the B4213, A38 and A4019. Unlike most of the other settlements we have so far visited in Gloucestershire, Cheltenham's history is relatively short, really only beginning in the 18th century. Indeed, the only surviving medieval building here is the parish Church of St Mary's in Clarence Street which has parts dating back to the 12th century. This building is worth a visit, partly to make a comparison with the rest of the town and partly to view some of its exceptional features. The most noteworthy of these is the circular east window which is renowned for its delicate 14th-century tracery; there are also some fine Victorian stained-glass windows and an unusual 13th-century Sanctus bell in the chancel.

Until the beginning of the 18th century, Cheltenham was a small market town consisting of one main street. However in 1715, a local farmer accidentally uncovered a saline spring in one of his fields, an occurrence which would eventually change the character of Cheltenham out of all recognition. Twenty years later, his son-in-law, the retired privateer Captain Henry Skillicorne, saw the potential of the discovery and built an enclosure around the spring along with a meeting room, a ballroom and a network of walks and rides to provide access. (These grew to form the modern tree-lined

Promenade.) Later, he added a stylish Long Room to the complex of buildings.

As the reputation of Cheltenham Spa grew, a number of other springs were discovered locally, including one in the High Street around which the first Assembly Rooms were constructed. In 1788, the prosperity of the town was assured following a visit from George III who, along with his queen, daughters and assorted members of the court, spent five weeks in Cheltenham taking the waters. This royal endorsement made the town into highly fashionable resort and a period of spectacular development followed. The local luminaries of the day commissioned a team of eminent architects to plan an entirely new town which would incorporate the best features of neoclassical Regency architecture. The scheme turned out to be so successful that it attracted many prominent figures of the day, including the Duke of Wellington who spent several weeks in Cheltenham in 1816 treating a liver complaint he had contracted in the tropics.

Today, Cheltenham continues to attract visitors to its splendid Regency streets which are best explored on foot. These include Suffolk Place, Lansdown Place and Montpellier Walk. Montpellier Walk is modelled on the Athenian Temple of Erechtheion, though the Rotunda at its southwestern end has more in common with the Pantheon in Rome. One of the common features of Cheltenham's Regency architecture is the delicate ironwork which is built into many of the upstairs balconies and verandas.

This golden era of architecture reached its high point with the completion of two unique structures in the late-1820s. The Promenade is noted for its superb fountain of Neptune, and the Pittville Pump Room is an extravagant masterpiece which stands within spacious parkland to the north of the town centre. The latter was designed by John Forbes and features a great hall fronted by a colonnade of Ionic columns and topped by a domed gallery. It was built for Joseph Pitt MP as a place to entertain his circle of friends, though by the time of his death in 1842, its construction had left him heavily in debt. Cheltenham's famous spa water can still be sampled here today (it is also available at the Town Hall). Said to be the only naturally occurring alkaline spring water in the country, it is believed to be instilled with beneficial medicinal properties. It is certainly an acquired taste.

Today, the building also houses the Pittville Pump Room Museum, an imaginative museum which brings to life Cheltenham's past from its Regency renaissance to the 1960s using the medium of original period costumes. There is also an interesting display of historic jewellery and tiaras which charts the changes in fashion that occurred between the Regency and Art Nouveau periods. (Open Tuesday to Sundays (also summer Sundays and Bank Holiday Mondays), 10am to 4.20pm between February and November. Admission charge payable.)

The Promenade, Cheltenham

Two other worthwhile museums are situated nearer the centre of Cheltenham. The Gustav Holst Birthplace Museum in Clarence Road is housed in the terraced Regency house where the famous composer (of among other things, the 'Planets Suite') was born in 1874. Among the items on show in the music room are Holst's original concert piano and an interesting display giving the background to the composer and his music. The house has been refurbished in keeping with the 'upstairs-downstairs' way of life which would have prevailed in the late-Victorian era and includes a gracious Regency drawing room, a children's nursery filled with period memorabilia, and a working kitchen with a housekeeper's room, pantry, scullery and laundry. (Open Tuesdays to Saturdays, 10am to 4.20pm, all year round. Admission free.)

The Cheltenham Art Gallery and Museum in Clarence Street is also worth a visit, especially by those interested in furniture and silver. The museum possesses a fine collection of Cotswold-made pieces inspired by William Morris, the founder of the much-respected Arts and Crafts Movement in the 19th century. Other work on show includes an impressive display of oriental porcelain, English ceramics, pewter, glassware and a permanent collection of paintings by Dutch and British masters. Information on the social and archeological history of Cheltenham is also available here, along with a fascinating collection of personal items belonging to Edward Wilson, one of the members of Captain Scott's ill-fated team of Antarctic explorers. (Open Mondays to Saturdays, 10am to 5.20pm, all year round and on Sunday afternoons between June and August (closed Bank Holidays). Admission free.)

Each year, Cheltenham hosts a number of top class arts' festivals. In May, a two-week Festival of Music, Speech, Drama and Dance is held; this is followed in July by the International Festival of Music, again lasting two weeks and featuring a wide variety of classical concerts, opera and recitals; then in October, the Festival of Literature features readings, exhibitions and a range of literary events. The Everyman Theatre, Cheltenham's former opera house, provides an excellent venue for performed work of all kinds.

A Cricket Festival has been held in Cheltenham each August since 1877, and the town is also the home of one of the nation's premier horse racing events, the Cheltenham Gold Cup, which takes place each year in March. Cheltenham Racecourse, Britain's top-rated steeplechasing venue, is situated at Prestbury Park, two miles north of the town centre and just to the west of the A435. The nearby village of PRESTBURY contains an abundance of thatched, timber-framed buildings, a couple of welcoming pubs and the lost remains of a medieval bishop's palace. Its largest claim to fame, however, relates to the unusually large number of ghosts which are said to inhabit the village. These include Old Moses the groom, a young woman playing a spinet, a lone strangler, a black abbot and a man on a bicycle.

A spectacular view of Cheltenham and the surrounding landscape can be obtained from Cleeve Cloud, which at 1083 feet above sea level is the highest point in the Cotswolds. The summit is situated four miles northeast of Cheltenham and can be reached by walking southeast along the Cotswold Way for one and a quarter miles from the village of CLEEVE HILL. The view from the Cotswold ridge is spectacular; Tewkesbury Abbey, Herefordshire Beacon and the distant Brecon Beacons can all be seen on a clear day.

One of the finest examples of a neolithic long barrow can be found two miles east of Cleeve Cloud (it can either be approached from Cleeve Hill or in the opposite direction from the village of Charlton Abbots). Known as Belas Knap, the grass-covered 180 foot by 60 foot barrow was constructed by New Stone Age people around 5000 years ago. Excavations discovered four burial chambers which together contained the remains of thirty people. One of the most remarkable features of Belas Knap is its false entrance at the broader northern end which was probably installed to discourage grave robbers and unwanted spirits. The burial chamber hidden nearby was found to contain the remains of a man and five children who had possibly been buried as part of some ancient sacrificial rite.

Another dramatic hilltop site can be found two and a half miles south of Cheltenham and just to the east of the B4070 Birdlip road. Leckhampton Hill is an imposing limestone crag with a bare cliff face and a grassy crest on which an Iron Age fortification once stood (evidence of more recent Roman and Saxon occupation has also been found here). Just below the summit stands the fragile rock column known as the Devil's Chimney which is rumoured to have been 'sent straight from hell'.

The hill is best approached from the north along a path which rises sharply from the B4070. After some distance this divides, offering the choice of a direct route to the top or a circular route around the summit to the west which allows a spectacular view of the Devil's Chimney.

Much of the fine limestone which was used to face Cheltenham's splendid Regency buildings was quarried at or around Leckhampton Hill and the old quarry workings add to the rugged character of the landscape. LECKHAMPTON village has a 14th-

Painswick

Rococo Gardens, Painswick

century manor house and a church of a similar age which contains some unusual brass monuments.

The exposed ridge of the Cotswolds escarpment winds southwest from Leckhampton Hill, taking with it the course of the Cotswolds Way. This impressive long-distance footpath offers spectacular views across the Severn Vale to the Severn Bridge and Brecon Beacons to the southwest, and across the Vale of Gloucester to Bredon Hill and the Malverns to the north. This superb three-mile stretch also takes in a number of dramatic promontories. The first of these is Cooper's Hill, a nature reserve covering 137 acres of common land which is now owned by Gloucestershire County Council. This was once the site of some of the most extensive Iron Age fortifications in the area, though since the early Middle Ages, it has been set aside as common agricultural land. Owners of local farms are still entitled to special commoners' rights including estover, the right to collect wood for fuel, and pannage, the right to allow pigs to feed freely.

Each year at Whitsun, Cooper's Hill is the site of the famous and highly risky cheese rolling ceremony where participants chase a whole cheese down the steep slope from a maypole on the ridge above. The event is thought to have formerly taken place on Midsummer's Day as part of a prehistoric sun-worshipping ceremony. Sheltering in a coombe half-a-mile from Cooper's Hill are the remains of Great Witcombe Villa, a once-grand Roman villa with a bath wing and some fine mosaic floors.

A little further to the southwest, evidence of occupation by neolithic people has been found at Crickley Hill. (This was also the location of an Iron Age fort some centuries later.) Today, this magnificent National Trust-owned site is run as a country park in conjunction with a neighbouring tract of land owned by Gloucestershire County Council. The area is filled with unusual geological and archeological feature, and a number of interesting walks are described in the leaflets which are available at the information point.

Those interested in geology should look out for the nearby memorial to the young geologist, Peter Hopkins. This is constructed of five different rock types, all of which can be found within the Cotswold and Malvern Hills. The third viewpoint on this stretch of the Cotswold ridge, Birdlip Hill, is approached from the A417 through attractive private mixed woodland. The famous bronze Birdlip Mirror, now in Gloucester City Museum, was found in an Iron Age burial mound known as Barrow Wake which lies just to the north of the Birdlip village.

The pleasant community of BIRDLIP stands near the junction of the B4070 and the A417 Ermin Way, close to the point where the old Roman road descends into the Vale of Gloucester. One of the highest villages in Gloucestershire, this is where we discovered the renowned Kingshead House, a restaurant with a national reputation for owner Judy Knock's distinctive and imaginative cooking. Customers entering this 16th-century former coaching inn are welcomed into a relaxing oak-beamed bar which is presided over by Warren Knock. A varied lunchtime menu is available on weekdays, with a more traditional three-course lunch being served on Sundays. For those who can't tear themselves away, Kingshead House also offers a large and attractive letting bedroom equipped with en-suite bathroom.

Kingshead House, Birdlip Tel: 01452 862299

Those preferring first-rate guesthouse accommodation in Birdlip should look for the family-run Beechmount Guest House. An extremely friendly place to stay, Beechmount has been owned and run since 1978 by Pauline and Mike Carter. Originally built as a temperance hotel, this imposing stone-built residence stands within easy reach of the Cotswolds Way. Inside, there is a large lounge, an impressive dining room and seven spacious guest bedrooms, two of which have en-suite facilities. The rooms to the

272

rear look out over attractive gardens to open fields beyond. Pauline and Mike offer an excellent choice of breakfast dishes and also provide first-rate evening meals by prior arrangement. With most of the Cotswolds lying within 45 minutes drive, this English Tourist Board two-crown commended guesthouse provides an ideal base for exploring the area.

Beechmount, Birdlip, Nr. Cheltenham Tel: 01452 862262

Leaving Birdlip, join the B4070 Stroud road for a couple of miles before turning north to reach the village of CRANHAM, home of the famous Prinknash Abbey and the neighbouring Prinknash Bird Park.

The Abbey at Prinknash (pronounced Prinnage) consists of two separate buildings set on opposite sides of a beautiful wooded estate. The old abbey was built between the 14th and 16th centuries for the Benedictine monks of Gloucester Abbey. For a short period following the Dissolution of the Monasteries it became the country retreat of the Bishops of Gloucester before passing into private hands for over 400 years. The most recent private owner, Thomas Dyer-Edwardes, became a devout Roman Catholic in his declining years and gifted the property to a community of Benedictine monks who were struggling to eke out a living on Caldey Island off the south Wales' coast.

When the white-robed monks returned to Prinknash in 1928, they found a cluster of attractive honey-gold buildings, including a fine medieval chapel with some elaborate carved woodwork and stained glass. They soon realised, however, that the old buildings were unsuitable for the needs of their expanding brotherhood, and in 1939 the foundation stone for a modern abbey was laid. The new Cotswold stone structure was designed with practical simplicity in mind and was eventually completed in 1972.

Today, the monks of Prinknash are involved in a number of home-based economic activities including the production of world-renowned Prinknash Pottery. Members of the public are welcome to visit the pottery workshops which were established on the site following the discovery of clay deposits during construction work. (Viewing gallery open daily, 10.30am to 4.30pm (2pm to 5pm Sundays), all year round.) Although the brightly-coloured earthenware is not to everyone's taste, a range of other hand-crafted items are available in the abbey's gift shop including carved woodwork, stained glass, incense, wrought-ironwork and fresh produce from the home farm.

A nine-acre section of the abbey grounds is run as a separately-managed establishment, the Prinknash Bird Park. As well as being the home to a wide variety of free-roaming peacocks (including white, black-shouldered and Indian blue) and waterfowl (including mute swans, black swans and snow geese), the bird park contains a number of interesting animals including African pygmy goats and fallow deer. A lovely woodland path leads though the Golden Wood to a haunted 16th-century Monk's fish pond which was built before the Reformation and is still stocked with large trout. (Open daily, 10am to 5pm between Easter and October. Admission charge payable.)

From Prinknash, stay on the small country lanes and headed south for approximately two miles towards SHEEPSCOMBE, a pleasant unspoilt community of gabled Cotswold stone farmhouses and small cottages. One of the first Sunday schools in the country was opened here by a local weaver in 1780 and is thought to have provided Gloucester's Robert Raikes with the inspiration for founding the national Sunday School Movement shortly after. Not far from Sheepscombe, the National Trust-owned Ebworth Estate offers some fine walks through three attractive woodland areas: Workman's Wood, Lord's and Lady's Woods and Blackstable Wood. Access is via public rights of way, however, parking is limited.

Two miles to the west of Sheepscombe, a minor country road will bring you to the beautiful small town of PAINSWICK. This attractive community had been dubbed 'The Queen of the Cotswolds' and is full of characteristic pale grey limestone cottages built of stone quarried at Painswick Hill, a mile to the north. Between the 15th and 18th centuries, Painswick was a prosperous wool trading and cloth manufacturing centre, and a number of substantial merchants' houses dating from this period can be found in and around Bisley Street. The churchyard, too, is filled with elaborate table-top graves, many of which are inscribed 'clothier'.

Painswick churchyard also contains a large quantity of carefully-manicured yew trees. Local legend has it that only 99 yew trees will ever grow here, the Devil having pledged to do away with any more. Some of the trees were planted as long ago as 1714 and together they form a series of skillfully-clipped arches, cones and hedges, creating the atmosphere of a living sculpture garden.

Each year on the Sunday following September 8th, St Mary's Churchyard is the venue for the annual Clipping (or Clypping) ceremony. Here, garlanded children join hands to encircle the church before dancing around it singing hymns. Afterwards, each child receives a silver coin, a traditional Painswick bun and a slice of 'puppy dog pie', a traditional pie whose ingredients include a china dog. The church itself dates from around 1378 and contains some unusual corbels thought to represent Richard II and his queen. Its colossal 172 foot spire contains a peal of twelve bells and can seen for many miles around. (One of the finest views of Painswick is from the top of Bulls Cross to the southeast, a mystical place referred to by Laurie Lee in 'Cider With Rosie'.)

St Mary's Church was the site of a skirmish during the English Civil war when a party of Parliamentarian soldiers came under fire while sheltering here, resulting in considerable damage to the building. Earlier in the conflict, Charles I is said to have stood at the top of nearby Painswick Beacon and enquired as to the name of woodland below. On hearing it had none, he replied, 'let it be called Paradise', a name which has stuck to this day. A month after confidently supervising the campaign to take Gloucester, he passed this way again, defeated.

The streets of Painswick village contain a number of interesting features including a set of unusual 19th-century 'spectacle' stocks in St Mary's street, the Tudor Byfield House with its elegant 18th-century façade, Dennis French's renowned Painswick Woodcrafts in

New Street, and the fine half-timbered Post Office dating from 1428 which is said to be the oldest functioning post office in the country. There are also two impressive manor houses in Painswick, Court House, which was built in 1604 for a local cloth merchant, and Castle Godwyn, a small 18th-century manor owned by the Milne family which is open to visitors all year round by written appointment only.

Tucked away off Edge Road on the southern side of Painswick is the charming bed and breakfast establishment, Dryknapps House, which is run by Hamish McLean and his family. This Grade II listed residence was built around 250 years ago and at one time was believed to have been used as the local police station. Inside, it has oak-beamed ceilings and a wonderful warm and friendly atmosphere. The guest rooms are comfortable and spacious and enjoy wonderful views across the valley to Edge village and beyond.

Dryknapps House, Edge Road, Painswick Tel: 01452 813652

Painswick House is located on the northern edge of the village, and although the interior of this splendid Palladian mansion is not open to the public, its six-acres of grounds are. Painswick Rococo Garden is hidden in a broad coombe and contains a number of old gardeners' outbuildings and some delightful woodland walks. (Open Wednesdays to Sundays and Bank Holiday Mondays, 11am to 5pm between February 1st and mid-December. Admission charge payable.)

Those looking for top quality farmhouse accommodation in this idyllic part of the Cotswold should seek out Damsels Farm on the edge of Painswick. This is charming Grade II listed farmhouse dates back to the 14th century and was originally the Dower House for Painswick Manor; later, it was used by Henry VIII as a hunting lodge. Proprietors Michelle and Peter Burdett have 100 acres on which they rear sheep and cattle. They also offer cosy accommodation in the farmhouse in three twin/family rooms, and have a first-rate self-catering cottage available which sleeps up to four. Children are welcome at Damsels Farm and can delight in feeding the ducks, geese, calves and orphaned lambs. Michelle is chairman of 'Stay On A Farm' in Gloucester and can put visitors in touch with other members of the organisation within the area; she can be contacted on 01452 812148.

Damsels Farm, Painswick Tel: 01452 812148

The upland area to the west of Painswick offers some magnificent views of the Severn Vale and the Forest of Dean. The National Trust-owned Haresfield Beacon overlooks the River Severn as it bends around the Arlingham peninsula and is the site of a once strategically-important Roman hill-fort. A short distance away, the outline of an early-British encampment known as Broadbarrow Green can also be detected. At 700 feet above sea level, it is possible to see for over fifty miles from here on a clear day.

The village of HARESFIELD lies tucked below the headland and is the home of the widely-renowned Countryside Centre. These attractive wildlife gardens contain a large walk-through aviary, a collection of owls and other birds of prey, a pets' and small animals' corner, and a number of interesting nature trails. A wildlife rescue unit and sanctuary is also based here. (Open daily, 10am to 4.30pm, all year round. Admission charge payable.)

Gilberts, Brookthorpe, Gloucester Tel: 01452 812364

The country lanes to the northeast of Haresfield led us to **BROOKTHORPE**, a pleasant village containing a 13th-century church with an unusual saddleback tower. This is where you will discover Gilbert's, a truly charming country house built around 400 years ago using stone from the Cotswold Hills and timber from the Forest of Dean. Originally Whaddon Manor and later a farmhouse, it was subsequently divided into cottages. Restored in 1939, it is now a Grade II listed building which is run as a charming bed and breakfast guesthouse by Jenny Beer. The house has been upgraded through the addition of central heating and double glazing, while still retaining the charm and character of its 16th-century origins. There is still a 1930's Aga (fondly referred to by Jenny as 'Agatha') which helps to provide the English part of the delicious wholefood breakfast. The Aga is the focal point of the attractive kitchen where guests breakfast around the large table. At Gilbert's, the emphasis is on wholesome, home-cooked food, and the owners even have a smallholding which ensures a plentiful supply of delicious organic produce, vegetables and fruit.

At Gilbert's, there are four en-suite letting bedrooms available (one single, one double, one twin and one honeymoon room), all

278

with excellent facilities, including colour televisions. Downstairs, there is a lovely, cosy sitting room where guests can relax in front of the wood-burning stove or browse through the plentiful supply of books listing local places of interest. With an English Tourist Board two crown, highly-commended rating the standard of comfort can be relied upon to be high, so if you are looking for first-rate bed and breakfast accommodation with a difference, Gilbert's is the place to stay.

Gloucester Cathedral

The city of GLOUCESTER has a surprising amount to offer the visitor, partly because of its long and distinguished history, and partly because of the revitalisation that has taken place in recent years around the old docks area. Although there was a settlement here in the days of the Iron Age, it was the Roman legions who made an indelible impression on this strategically important site following their invasion of southern England in the first century AD. Their first undertaking was to build a fort to guard what was then the lowest crossing point on the Severn; this was followed about twenty years later by the construction of a much larger fortress on higher ground. The central point of these later fortifications can still be seen in the modern street plan of the city at the place now known as Gloucester Cross where the four streets of Westgate, Northgate, Eastgate and Southgate converge. Within a few years, the new Roman settlement of Glevum had become an important military base which was to play a vital strategic role in confining the rebellious Celts and Britons to the bleak uplands of Wales.

Following the founding of a Saxon monastery in the 7th century, a number of other ecclesiastical buildings were constructed in Gloucester during the following four centuries. The next important influence on the town, however, came with the Norman invasion. William the Conqueror followed the Saxon tradition of holding a Christmas Court at Gloucester and it was here in 1085 that he took the decision to commission the Domesday Book. Four years later, he instructed the Norman monk, Serlo, to restore the Saxon abbey, a task which took 33 years to complete and which resulted in the construction of the great church which went on to become Gloucester Cathedral. The following centuries led to a series of renovations resulting in a structure which skillfully combines the Norman, early English, Decorated and Perpendicular styles of architecture.

Two rows of colossal Norman pillars dominate the cathedral's 174 foot long nave, the original timber roof of which was replaced in 1242 by stone vaulting in early English style. The Norman presbytery and choir were replaced in the 14th century, and the west end of the nave was rebuilt in Perpendicular style during the 15th century. At 72 feet by 38 feet, the great east window is largest surviving medieval stained-glass window in the country. It was built to celebrate the victory at the Battle of Crécy in 1346 and depicts the coronation of the Virgin surrounded by a colourful entourage of saints, popes and monarchs.

The exquisite cathedral cloisters were constructed around an attractive garden in the 14th century and contain some of the finest fan tracery still in existence. From here, an excellent view of the 225 foot cathedral tower can be enjoyed; this was rebuilt in the 15th century is estimated to weigh over 600 tons. Several interesting monuments can be seen in the cathedral, most notably the wooden effigy of Robert Duke of Normandy dating from 1134 and the elaborate carved tomb of Edward II, murdered at Berkeley Castle in 1327 by his queen and her lover. The cathedral also houses a recently-opened exhibition of Anglican church plate from the Cathedral Treasury. (Open Mondays to Saturdays, 10.30am to 4pm between Easter and November. Admission free.)

The old part of the city centred around Gloucester Cross contains a number of interesting old buildings. Among them is the fine late-19th-century Guildhall in Eastgate Street, the ancient church of St Mary de Crypt in Southgate Street, St Johns Church in Northgate Street, and the home of Robert Raikes, founder of the Sunday School Movement, in Ladybellegate Street. A good way to explore the city is to join one of the guided walks which leave the tourist information centre at St Michael's Tower at 2.30pm on Wednesdays and Sundays (daily during August). A map of the Via Sacra, a self-guided tour around old Gloucester, is also available here.

National Waterways Museum

Three great inns were established in Gloucester during the 14th and 15th centuries to cater for pilgrims who came here to visit the tomb of Edward II. Two these remain today: the magnificent galleried New Inn was founded by a monk from the abbey in 1450 and can be found close to Gloucester Cross in Northgate Street, and the Fleece Hotel, which has a stone-vaulted undercroft dating from the 12th century, can be found in Westgate Street.

Another building well worth finding is Maverdine House, a luxurious four-storey residence which was occupied by the commander of the Parliamentarian forces during the infamous Civil War siege of 1643. Despite most of Wessex being in Royalist hands, the strategically-important city of Gloucester held out for Cromwell and survived a month-long attack which was personally commanded by Charles I. Colonel Massey's headquarters can be reached via a passageway adjacent to No. 26 Westgate Street.

Gloucester's City Museum and Art Gallery is situated opposite the Gloucestershire College of Art in Brunswick Road, near the city's main shopping centre. The honey-coloured stone façade hides a treasure of rare and beautiful artefacts originating from both the city and county of Gloucester. A three-ton column in the entrance hall is a relic of the Roman city; this provides a foretaste of the exhibits which gleam in the darkened interior of the archaeology gallery. The Birdlip Mirror, made in bronze for a Celtic chief just before the Roman conquest, is a superbly engraved abstract ornament. Two tombstones depict Romans involved in the conquest: one a horseman spearing a British foe, the other a merchant muffled in a thick cloak. Several altars and votive tablets are carved with simple images of the Roman gods. The gallery floor is cut away to reveal the Roman city wall which passes under the building.

There is also a Norman backgammon (or tables) set here, dating from about AD 1100 which is unique in Europe; the bone counters are carved with zodiac signs and the board is engraved with a hunting scene and covered in a bone veneer. Also, be sure not to miss the closing ring from St. Nicholas' Church which was made about AD 1300 and has an escutcheon in the form of two grotesque human heads. Upstairs under the elegant plaster ceiling, is a magnificent set of walnut furniture from the Queen Anne period. On the hour, the gallery echoes with the chimes of grandfather clocks made by Gloucester and London makers of the 18th century, including a fine Gloucester-made clock which only needs to be wound once a year. The early walnut barometers on display are amongst the finest in the country, and include three examples by the doyen of barometer makers, Daniel Quare (1649-1724).

Visitors should also look out for the collection of Cromwellian silver spoons, which were found under the floorboards of a shop in

Cirencester's Market Place, and the apostle spoons made by a silversmith who was Sheriff of Gloucester in 1675. Several English landscape paintings of the 18th- and 19th-centuries are on display, including works by Gainsborough, Richard Wilson and Turner. (The gallery stages a varied programme of special exhibitions throughout the year.) A small aquarium and a beehive, ever popular with children, stand at the entrance to a gallery dedicated to the natural history and geology of Gloucestershire. A sixty foot dinosaur and plesiosaur 'sea-dragon' were recently found in the north Cotswolds and their massive bones are on display here. (Open Mondays to Saturdays, 10am to 5pm, all year round. Admission free.)

City Museum, Gloucester Tel: 01452 24131

The 16th-century timber-framed house known as Bishop Hooper's Lodging can be found in Westgate Street. This is said to be the place where the martyred Protestant Bishop spent his last night before being burnt at the stake in 1555. Today, the building and its immediate neighbours house one of the most highly regarded folk museums in the country, the Gloucester Folk Museum. Here, the social history of Gloucester and its county are brought to life in a series of beautifully laid-out displays. These include a reconstruction of an 18th-century pin making factory, a cobbler's workshop, a dairy, and a 19th-century schoolroom. Artefacts on show include historic farm implements, tools, kitchen equipment, toys, dolls and a number of relics from the Civil War siege. A series of special exhibitions are held at regular intervals, and outside there is a lovely secluded courtyard with its own herb garden. (Open Mondays to Saturdays, 10am to 5pm, all year round. Admission free.)

Within 200 hundred yards of the Folk Museum, a small collection of historic vehicles has been assembled at the Gloucester Transport Museum in Bearland. Exhibits on show include a horse-drawn tram from around 1880, a fire engine from around 1895, and an early-19th-century baby carriage.

Children of all ages will be interested in the World of Beatrix Potter at 9 College Court. The shop was used as the model for her much-loved story, The Tailor Of Gloucester, which was based on a local folk tale. Today, this commercially-run gift shop displays a number of interesting features relating to the life and work of Beatrix Potter, including a working model of the mice stitching the Mayor of Gloucester's waistcoat. (Admission free.)

For centuries, Gloucester has been an important river port on the busy route between the Midlands and the Bristol Channel, a state of affairs which was recognised by Queen Elizabeth I when she granted the city formal port status in 1580. However, the introduction of larger vessels during the 18th century necessitated the building of a canal which would directly link Gloucester with the deep water of the Severn estuary. After once being abandoned due to lack of finance, the canal project was finally completed in 1827, resulting in a greatly increased level of commercial activity which continued for several decades.

From the 1860s onwards, however, the area around Gloucester Docks began to suffer a steady decline due to competition from more efficient rail and road transport. By the end of the 1970s, the docks were virtually derelict and a radical solution was needed to secure the area's future.

After much consideration, an ambitious project of renovation was initiated which was to transform the 23-acre site into a vibrant cultural centre which today should be included on every visitor's itinerary. The handsome old warehouse buildings have been brought back into use as flats and commercial units, and a stylish new shopping area, Merchants' Quay, has been constructed on the waterfront. A converted barge, the Semington, now operates as an arts centre and café, and there is also a bustling antique centre containing a large number of retail units where anything from a small item of bric-a-brac to an expensive piece of antique furniture can be found.

Three floors of the recently converted Llanthony Warehouse are taken up by the National Waterways Museum, a fascinating establishment devoted to the 200-year period when Britain's inland waterways carried the goods of the nation. The warehouse building forms part of the museum and is named after Llanthony Priory, a ruined monastery on the eastern edge of the Welsh Black Mountains which in its heyday was one of the wealthiest and most influential in the country. The museum features working engines and models, live craft demonstrations, archive film presentations and hands-on computer simulations of canal navigation. A number of barges and narrowboats are moored outside on the quayside, one of which, the Queen Boadicea II, takes visitors on short cruises around the docklands area. The site also contains a working forge, a massive 'No. 4' steam dredger, a stable with a shire horse, an activity room for younger children and a number of canal-related workshops. (Open daily, 10am to 6pm (5pm in winter), all year round. Admission charge payable.)

Gloucester's Victoria Dock is now a thriving marina. This is where you will find the Albert Warehouse, a converted storehouse which houses another specialist museum, Robert Opie's Museum of Advertising and Packaging. Robert Opie is an enthusiastic collector of commercial ephemera who, in the last twenty years, has assembled around 30,000 packaging and advertising items. The result is a fascinating exhibition which offers a real insight into the presentation of consumer products since the mid-1800s. As well as consumer packaging, the museum contains a interesting collection of posters, enamel signs and point-of-sale promotions which together map the changing trends in popular taste. A continuous screening of vintage television commercials is also featured. (Open daily, 10am to 6pm between May and September and Bank Holidays; Tuesdays to Sundays, 10am to 5pm between October and April. Admission charge payable.)

Gloucester's old custom house in the Docks is the home of the recently-modernised Regiments of Gloucestershire Museum. Winner of the prestigious 1991 Museum of the Year Award for the best small museum, this absorbing exhibition gives an animated account of the county's two army regiments, the 'Glorious Glosters' and the Royal Gloucestershire Hussars, over their distinguished 300-year history. (Open Tuesdays to Sundays, 10am to 5pm, all year round. Small admission charge payable.)

Our visit to Gloucester almost over, why not make a short detour north along the A38 Tewkesbury road to visit **TWIGWORTH**, home of the internationally-renowned museum of wildlife art, **Nature in Art**.

Nature In Art is housed in a fine Georgian mansion, Wallsworth Hall, which dates from the 1740s and set in its own grounds on the northern outskirts of Gloucester. The building is owned and managed by the Society for Wildlife Art of the Nations, an organisation which sets out to fill an important gap in the collections of art which are available to the public. The Society strives to give honour where honour is due by encouraging the pursuit and appreciation of wildlife art and the conservation of wildlife through the stimulation of fresh insights which only truly fine art can generate.

Nature in Art, Wallsworth Hall, Twigworth Tel: 01452 731422

Nature in Art is a museum with a growing and ever-changing collection. At the time of writing there were 600 items by 350 artists from 40 countries spanning 1400 years. In its scope, appeal and stature, the collection is unrivalled. Although paintings in every medium make up the bulk of the items on display, visitors are also able to see sculptures (both inside and outside), tapestries, ceramics, glass engravings, prints and many other items such as Japanese netsuke and Chinese painted bottles. Each provides an exciting way of depicting nature and, in its own way, is a fine example of its artistic type. Between February and November, there is a full programme of artists in residence which gives visitors the opportunity to see international artists working in a wide variety of media. The museum is fully accessible to wheelchair users and is open Tuesdays to Sundays (and Bank Holiday Mondays), 10am to 5pm, all year round. Admission charge payable.

Without returning to the centre of Gloucester, drive across the eastern channel of the River Severn to the northwest of the city before turning north onto the A417. Shortly after crossing the river's western channel, you will come to the lovely village of MAISEMORE where there is a very pleasant inn, the White Hart.

The White Hart is a delightful 400 year-old inn which is full of character and warmth. The front of the inn is adorned with a beautiful array of hanging baskets and window boxes, and inside, there are original beams in the lounge and an open fire during the winter months. Run by Christine and Ralph Creed, the inn is renowned for its excellent home-cooked food. The extensive menu includes a variety of ploughman's platters, 'designer toasties' in a variety of fillings, and the particularly popular 'sizzle platters', succulent pieces of steak or gammon served on a hot plate. Visitors to the White Hart can also admire Christine's unique collection of chamber pots which adorn the ceiling of the bar.

The White Hart, Maisemore Village, Gloucester Tel: 01452 526349

Those looking for first-rate farmhouse bed and breakfast accommodation within easy reach of Gloucester and the Forest of

Dean, should look out for Linton Farm bed and breakfast at HIGHNAM, two miles southwest of Maisemore. Linton Farm is a large traditional farmhouse run by keen vegetable and arable farmers, Caroline and Richard Keene. They offer three simply-furnished letting rooms (two large, one small) and welcome guests into their comfortable lounge and dining room. Just three-quarters of a mile further down the road, their son Robert runs Over Farm Market, a marvellous fruit and vegetable shop offering a vast selection of homegrown produce, local cheeses and homemade pickles, chutneys and jams, all of which make ideal holiday gifts. (For those staying at Linton Farm there is a 10% discount here provided you remember the magic password, 'Hidden Places'!) Outside, visitors will find an assortment of livestock, including donkeys, goats and even ostriches.

Linton Farm, Highnam, Gloucester Tel: 01452 306456

Just north of Hartpury, turn east off the main road to reach the delightful Severn-side settlement of ASHLEWORTH. The focal point of the village is the 12th-century Church of St Andrew and Bartholomew which has some unusual herringbone masonry and a 14th-century spire. The church stands surrounded by attractive medieval buildings, including an enormous 15th-century Tithe Barn which features two projecting stone porches and an elaborate system of interlocking roof timbers with queenposts. The barn is owned by the National Trust and open daily, 9am to 6pm between April and the end of October. (Small admission charge payable; free to National Trust members.)

The surrounding estate, which once belonged to the Abbey of St Augustine in Bristol, contains two splendid 15th-century manor houses: the handsome stone-built Ashleworth Court and the timber-framed Ashleworth Manor. The latter was originally built as the abbot's summer residence and has since been enlarged. (Both are open to the public by written arrangement only. For information, telephone 01452 70241 and 70350 respectively.) The village pub, the Boat Inn, has been in the hands of the Jelf family for over a hundred years. During the English Civil War, one of their ancestors is said to have rowed Charles I across the Severn and as a reward was granted a monopoly to ferry passengers at this point. Foscombe, an elaborate 19th-century Gothic mansion standing on a low hill overlooking the river, was once owned by the Rolling Stones' drummer, Charlie Watts.

A little further up the A417, is the charmingly-named village of SNIG'S END. The nucleus of the settlement is a crescent of attractive sturdily-built stone cottages which date from the days when the village was at the centre of a Chartist land colony. Founded in 1847 by Feargus O'Connor, the movement placed great importance on education and constructed a sizable school building to serve the few dozen resident families who formed the community of self-supporting smallholdings. However, thanks to a combination of inadequate financing, confused aims, poor soil, inaccessible markets and a population of townspeople ill-suited to rural life, the project failed within six years. Today, all that remains of the Chartist utopia is a collection of well-built cottages and the old schoolhouse which now functions as the Prince of Wales Inn.

A couple of miles northwest of Staunton, the A417 passes to the east of Pauntley Court. Although today you will find a private country residence dating from more recent times, in the 14th century, this was the birthplace of Dick Whittington, three times mayor of London between 1397 and 1419. Whittington was no poor boy who made his fortune with the assistance of a quick-witted cat; rather, he was the offspring of a wealthy landed family who went on to grow even richer as a mercer in the City of London. (The only other fact that is consistent with the original folk tale was that he married Alice Fitzwarren, the daughter of a wealthy Dorset knight.)

Why the famous pantomime legend grew up around Sir Richard Whittington of Pauntley is unknown, although similar rags-to-riches stories are said to exist in countries all over the world. One event which helped to create the myth was the discovery of a carving in the foundations of a medieval house in Gloucester in 1862. This carved figure of a youth holding some kind of animal became widely known as 'Dick and his Cat' and was responsible for establishing the legend in the British Isles. Today, the carving can be seen in Gloucester's Folk Museum.

Continuing west, and you will soon arrive in the small hilltop village of DYMOCK, a delightful collection of cottages loosely arranged around the early-Norman Church of St Mary. The church contains some unusual artefacts, including Dymock's last railway ticket dated September 1959, and stands beside the pleasantly shaded Wintour's Green. The old buildings in northeast Gloucestershire differ from those in the east of country in that they are often built of red brick instead of Cotswold stone. Dymock contains some fine examples of early redbrick building including the White House and the Old Rectory near the church, and the Old Grange which is situated three-quarters of a mile to the northwest and incorporates the remains of the Cistercian abbey of Flaxley.

In the years immediately prior to World War I, a group known as the Dymock Poets based itself in the area, causing the village to become something of literary centre. The group, which included Rupert Brooke, sent their quarterly poetry magazine 'New Numbers' to addresses throughout the world from Dymock post office.

Run by Ken Thomson and Jackie Julier, the Horseshoe Inn at Broom's Green is a small friendly pub well favoured by local people who go out of their way to make visitors feel welcome. Outside, there is a large garden with a children's play area, while inside, the traditional beamed bars are cosy and welcoming, with horseshoes, brasses and harnesses on the walls adding to the character of the establishment. A free house, the Horseshoe offers a selection of fine real ales, and there is also a charming restaurant where diners can enjoy such excellent local fare as 'pork in Hereford cider sauce', prepared using fresh, local produce. Ken and Jackie are always keen to know if visitors have discovered the Horseshoe through the pages of Hidden Places.

A couple of miles to the west of Dymock, make a point of visiting the famous Church of St Mary in KEMPLEY. This unlikely gem was built between 1090 and 1100 and stands a short distance to the south of the present-day village. Inside, the chancel contains a virtually complete set of 12th-century frescoes, some of the most widely regarded in the region. It is believed that these fine works of art were created to assist the local priest in conveying the rudiments of the scriptures to his uneducated congregation. A series of 14th-century tempera paintings can also be found in the nave. In the mid-16th-century, both sets of paintings were concealed behind a whitewash coating and weren't rediscovered until 1872. Then during the 1950s, a major renovation successfully restored these exquisite frescoes to their former glory.

The Horseshoe Inn, Broom's Green, Dymock Tel: 01531 890385

The village of Kempley contains another interesting church, the red sandstone Church of St Edward the Confessor which was built in 1903 in line with the finest traditions of the Arts and Crafts Movement. Most of the fabric was made by local craftspeople using readily-available materials; look out for the imposing scissor beams which were fashioned from green oak taken from the nearby Beauchamp estate.

The Granary is a charming farmhouse situated at Lower House Farm in Kempley. Situated close to the Forest of Dean and Dymock Woods, it offers delightful nature walks including the 'Daffodil Way', an eight mile stretch of countryside where wild daffodils grow in profusion. As well as excellent farmhouse bed and breakfast accommodation, owners Jill and Glyn Bennett offer self-catering accommodation in an adjoining wing. They also have their own horses and ponies on the farm and provide first-rate riding holidays. Being central to the Cotswolds, the Wye Valley and the Malvern Hills, the beautiful location of the Granary makes it a walkers' paradise. Visitors can contact the Bennetts on 01531 890301.

The Granary, Lower House Farm, Kempley, Dymock
Tel: 01531 890301

From Kempley, make your way southeast towards the old market town of **NEWENT**, the capital of the area of northwest Gloucestershire known as the Ryelands. The route into the town from the north passes the Three Choirs Vineyard, a working vineyard producing good quality English wines which members of the public are welcome to sample and buy. (Open daily, 9am to 5pm, all year round.)

Newent stands at the centre of the broad triangle of land known as 'Daffodil Crescent' where in spring, the delicate small flower known as the Lent lily grows freely in the wild. The rich, brightly-coloured soil of the Leadon Valley was traditionally used for the growing of rye and the raising of Ryeland sheep, an ancient breed which produced wool of such quality that it sold for twice the price of its Cotswold equivalent. As a result, the town grew to become one of Gloucestershire's principal wool-trading centres, a factor which accounts for the large number of 18th-century merchants' houses that can still be seen today.

292

The nave of Newent's medieval church had to be completely rebuilt after Royalist troops removed the lead from the roof to make bullets, causing it to collapse during a heavy snowfall in 1674. (Reconstruction only went ahead after Charles II agreed to donate sixty tons of timber from the Forest of Dean.) Newent's most distinctive building, however, can be found on the old Market Square – the splendid timber-framed Market House. Originally constructed as a butter market in 1668, its upper floors are supported on sixteen oak pillars which form a unique open colonnade.

Those interested in finding out more about the history of Newent should make a point of visiting The Shambles Museum of Victorian Life in Church Street. This impressive museum is laid out as a Victorian town complete with cobbled streets, gas-fired street lamps, shops and workrooms. The core of the museum a four-storey house which has been furnished throughout as a Victorian draper's home. (The house in fact belonged to a butcher, the name 'shambles' coming from the Old English word for slaughterhouse.) To the rear, the narrow streets and alleyways contain over thirty shops and workshops, including a chemist's, a dairy, a pawnbroker's, an ironmongers' and a blacksmith's, each of which is stocked with its own unique collection of historic artefacts. The museum also contains a modern gift shop and tearoom. (Open Tuesdays to Sundays and Bank Holiday Mondays, 10am to 6pm between mid-March and December. Admission charge payable.)

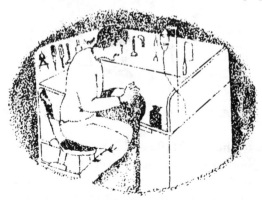

Newent Silver and Gold, 15 Broad Street, Newent
Tel: 01531 822055

A fine collection of original handcrafted silver and gold pieces can be found at **Newent Silver and Gold** in Broad Street. This unique establishment was founded upon the design skills, talent and craftsmanship of gold- and silversmith, Ken Vowles. Ken has a particular feeling for the materials and techniques of his craft, and it is quite amazing to watch him take a dull piece of metal and transform it into an article of beauty. Ken designs all his own work and many of his hand-crafted creations are on sale at the studio. A very welcoming place, Ken does not seem to be disturbed at all by visitors browsing around. He accepts commissions and is especially delighted when someone asks him to design an item as a special gift.

A tradition of glass making was established in Newent by French Huguenot refugees in the 17th century. In recent years, this highly-skilled practice has been revived at the Glassbarn in Culver Street. Here, visitors can view the delicate process of glass-blowing and examine the items of finished glassware in the gallery. (Open Mondays to Fridays, 10am to 5pm, all year round. Small charge payable for tours of the workshop.)

The Kings Arms, Ross Road, Newent Tel: 01531 820307

Adjacent to the B4221 Ross Road on the western outskirts of Newent, is the first-rate pub and eating house, **The Kings Arms**. This attractive family-run inn stands next to a handsome redbrick building which was formerly a Victorian workhouse. Landlord Martin Young provides a warm welcome for both visitors and regulars alike. Inside, there is a charming atmosphere with an

294

open log fire and a collection of traditional pub pastimes such as skittles and shove halfpenny. There is also a good selection of hand-drawn beers and an imaginative bar meals menu. (Booking is advised for evening meals.) Martin also has four comfortable letting bedrooms available which are all spacious and well-appointed.

Another of Newent's attractions is the Butterfly Centre in Birches Lane, just to the north of the town centre. As well as being able to see exotic butterflies flying freely in the tropical house, members of the public can visit the menagerie, aquarium, natural history exhibition and garden centre. (Open daily, 10am to 5pm between Easter and October. Admission charge payable.)

Newent's famous National Bird of Prey Centre can be found on the western side of the B4216, one mile south of the town. The centre boasts the largest private collection of birds of prey in Europe, including eagles, hawks, owls, falcons, condors and vultures. There are also a number of aviaries which have been set aside for breeding purposes. The site incorporates the widely-renowned Falconry Centre where visitors are offered the exhilarating experience of observing trained birds in free-flight. Up to four flying demonstrations take place each day, weather permitting. (Open daily, 10.30am to 5.30pm between February and November. Admission charge payable.)

A couple of miles further south, is TAYNTON, an attractive hamlet which in spring is filled with daffodils. The village church is unusual in that it was constructed during Oliver Cromwell's Commonwealth government; it was the view of the Puritans that the presence of God had no geographical limitations, and so it was built along a north-south axis rather than along the conventional east-west. Nearby, Taynton House has three impressive barns, one of which dates from 1695.

Hown Hall in Taynton is the home of the widely-renowned Taynton Farm Centre, a wonderful open farm run by Priscilla and John House. The farm has been in their family for four generations, and the 16th-century renovated farmhouse now has an attractive tearoom and farm shop where visitors can purchase delicious homemade produce. All cakes are baked by Priscilla, and cream teas are a speciality, with clotted cream supplied by the farm's Jersey cows. As well as specialising in duck breeding, the

Houses keep a variety of other livestock, including rare breed cattle; pony rides are also available on most weekends. (The farm centre is open daily, 9am to 7pm between 1st March and 31st October; between 1st November and the end of February, the shop and tearoom are open from 10am to 6pm.)

Taynton Farm Centre, Hown Hall, Taynton Tel: 01452 790220

Two miles west of Taynton stands the National Trust-owned May Hill, a dramatic and mystical place which is crowned by an unusual copse of trees planted in 1887 to mark Queen Victoria's golden jubilee. This was once the scene of the annual 'May Games', an event in which the children of the area would meet in mock battle to celebrate the coming of summer. Today, walkers taking the pleasant stroll to the 969 foot summit are rewarded with magnificent views of the Forest of Dean and the Severn's distinctive horseshoe bend around the Arlingham peninsula.

CHAPTER TEN

Southwest Gloucestershire

Westbury Court

297

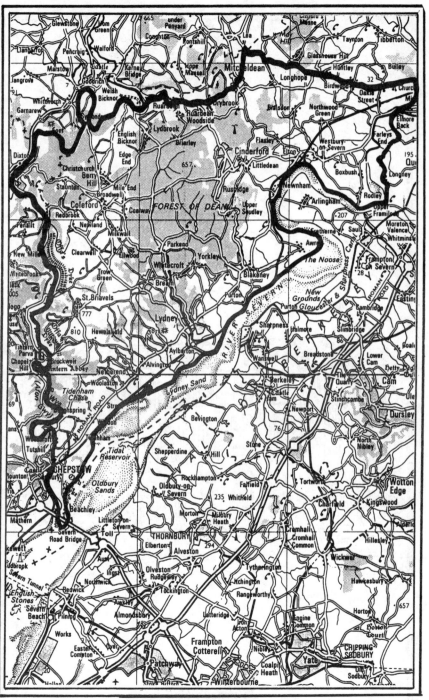

Please turn to Reference Section for further information

Littledean Hall

CHAPTER TEN

Southwest Gloucestershire

Our journey into Southwest Gloucestershire begins along the A4136 Gloucester-Monmouth road. Turn north off this road in the hamlet of Nailbridge to reach our first stopping place, the lovely old village of RUARDEAN. The village church is known for its stone plaque on which two highly-unusual fish are carved. These are thought to have been sculpted by craftsmen from the Herefordshire School of Norman Architecture during the Romanesque period around 1150. The carving is thought to have once belonged to a frieze which was set in one of the church's exterior walls. However around 100 years later, it was removed, most probably by local people looking for readily available building materials, and was considered lost until 700 years later, an inspection of a bread oven in a nearby cottage revealed the two fish set into the lining. Today, these have been returned to the church and can be seen on one of the inside walls near the font.

From Ruardean, follow the narrow country lanes in a southwesterly direction towards the two sister villages of UPPER and LOWER LYDBROOK. For many centuries, the Forest of Dean was an important iron ore and coal mining area, and the position of these two communities on its northwest fringe made them ideally suited for the processing of ore into metal. Indeed, the first commercially-viable blast furnace in the area was sited here at the beginning of the 17th century and, despite it being hard to imagine today, at one time Lydbrook rivalled Sheffield as a producer of pig iron.

Lower Lydbrook also stands at the point where the River Wye comes closest to the mineral extracting areas of the Forest of Dean and for several centuries, flat-bottomed barges were loaded with coal here before being hauled upstream to Hereford. (Before the completion of a tow-path suitable for horses in 1811, this was done by manpower alone.) This river trade continued until the 1840s when it was superseded, first by the Gloucester-Hereford Canal, and then the Severn and Wye Railway.

Today, the two villages are relatively quiet and secluded, and reveal little of their energetic industrial past. The house where tragedian actress Sarah Siddons lived as a child can be seen here, and there are also a number of excellent places to stay.

Among these is Lydbrook House, a charming 18th-century Georgian building set in large, neatly laid out gardens, with outstanding views over the River Wye. Guests receive a warm welcome at this informal, friendly household. The proprietor, Anne Hayes, provides three letting bedrooms, one of which is en-suite, all tastefully furnished in character with the house. In addition to bed and breakfast, Anne is happy to supply an evening meal by prior arrangement. The house is surrounded by many local beauty spots, and guests can enjoy lovely walks, canoeing and even fishing if they so wish. Guests should not be surprised to see rabbits hopping around the gardens of Lydbrook House, since Anne's daughter Holly owns several which roam around quite freely.

Lydbrook House, Lydbrook Tel: 01594 861267

SYMONDS YAT is an imposing outcrop of rock which forms part of Huntsham Hill, the promontory which juts out into the Wye Valley forcing the river to make a spectacular horseshoe deviation to the north. Though strictly in Hereford and Worcester, make a point of visiting this popular place either to enjoy the magnificent views of the Wye Valley or in the hope of catching a glimpse of the

302

wild peregrine falcons which inhabit the barren slopes of Yat Rock. This dramatic 500 foot rock is reached along a quarter mile forest trail which can be joined at the Symonds Yat car park. (Parking fee payable; refreshments and toilet facilities available here during summer months.)

On the riverbank below Yat Rock there is an usual man-powered rope ferry which takes passengers across to SYMONDS YAT WEST. Here, there are some first-rate visitor attractions including the widely-known Jubilee Park Museum of Mazes which is run by the Heyes brothers, two keen maze-building enthusiasts. As well as containing a great deal of interesting background information on the art of maze design, the museum has an internationally-renowned centrepiece, the Jubilee Puzzle hedge maze, which visitors are encouraged to tackle. (Open daily throughout the year except during January. Admission charge payable.)

There is a useful visitor centre at Symonds Yat West, as well as a heritage centre on the nearby Doward hillside. This stretch of the River Wye is also renowned for its leisure and watersports activities. As well as a wonderful series of walks and trails, there are excellent facilities here for canoeing, rock climbing, abseiling, and even hot-air ballooning.

Crossing back to SYMONDS YAT EAST retrace your steps onto the A4136 before turning west to reach the village of STAUNTON. This pleasant community has a Norman church and a row of charming almshouses which were built in the 1600s with funds donated by Benedict Hall.

The church has been twice altered, first during the early English period and again in the 15th century, episodes which have left the east window oddly offset from the nave. Look out also for the two stone fonts, one of which is claimed to be a converted Roman altar, and the unusual corkscrew staircase which leads up past the pulpit to the belfry door.

Two enormous mystical stones, the Buck Stone and the Suck Stone, lie a short walk from the centre of Staunton. The famous twelve-foot high sandstone monolith known as the Buck Stone can be reached along a path leading up onto Staunton Meend Common from the White Horse Inn. From here, the views in all directions are breathtaking. The Suck Stone can be reached by following a track from the village across Highmeadow Woods. Look out also for the Bronze Age standing stone which can be seen beside the A4136 at Marion's Cross, just to the east of the village.

Two and a half miles southeast of Staunton, is COLEFORD, a lively and aptly-named former mining centre on the western edge of the Forest of Dean. In the 17th century, the town received a royal charter from Charles I in recognition of its loyalty to the crown. By then, it had already grown to be an important iron processing centre, partly because of the availability of local ore deposits and partly because of the easily obtainable forest timber which was used to fuel the smelting process. (In order to generate the high temperatures this process required, the timber had first to be converted into charcoal.)

As the industry began to grow towards its peak in the 13th century, an ever-increasing amount of wood was required to sustain it (it is said 5000 cubic feet of timber were needed for every iron bar produced). At this time, as many as 72 furnaces were operating in and around the Forest of Dean, resulting in deforestation on a massive scale. This began to worry the nation's naval commanders who also required large numbers of mature oaks for shipbuilding.

In the end, the navy was given priority and severe restrictions were placed on the felling of trees for conversion into charcoal. This sent the local iron industry into decline, a trend which continued until the beginning of last century when coke was introduced to replace charcoal in the smelting process. Within a few decades, however, the iron industry in the Forest of Dean had been driven to the brink of extinction by a series of technological advances and competition from other UK iron producing areas.

Nevertheless, Coleford has a special place in metallurgical history for it was here that the Mushets, a father and son team of local free miners, made many discoveries which were to revolutionise the iron and steel industry. Indeed, it was here that the son, Robert Forester Mushet, discovered the importance of Spiegeleisen (an alloy of iron, manganese, silicon and carbon) in the reprocessing of 'burnt iron'. This led him to develop a system for turning molten pig iron directly into steel, a system which predated the now-familiar process developed by Sir Henry Bessemer. Tragically however, Robert Mushet failed to pay stamp duty on his patents and allowed them to lapse, an oversight which must have resulted in untold financial consequences for him.

Puzzle Wood, Coleford

Today, Coleford continues to be regarded as the capital of the Royal Forest of Dean and is a busy commercial centre with an interesting church and a number of unusual industrial relics. It is also the home of the Great Western Railway Museum, an old GWR goods station dating from 1883 which contains a number of large-scale model steam locomotives and an interesting display of railway photographs and memorabilia. (Open Tuesdays to Sundays and Bank Holiday Mondays, 2.30pm to 5.30pm between Easter and end-October; also Saturdays only during the winter months. Admission charge payable.)

From the centre of Coleford, drive south for a mile along the B4228 to reach Lower Perrygrove Farm, the site of the ancient woodland mine workings which were imaginatively landscaped during the last century to form Puzzle Wood. This historic place first became a centre for open-cast iron ore mining during the early Iron Age over 2700 years ago. One of its most active periods was during the Roman era when the site formed part of the famous Lambsquay mine workings; indeed in 1848, workmen discovered a small cave containing three spherical earthenware jars which turned out to be filled with over 3000 Roman coins from the third century AD.

For much of the site's history, the mining of iron ore was carried out using hand tools only and initially, most of it was recovered from the high quality deposits which lay near the surface. However, as these were gradually exhausted, the miners were forced to look for fresh deposits which often lay trapped between layers of solid rock. Before the invention of explosives, the tightly-compressed ore had to be loosened using the 'fire-setting' method of mining; this involved lighting fires against the exposed rock face, and then dowsing the hot stone with water, causing it to crack.

By the late-19th-century, the fourteen acre site was virtually exhausted. It was then that it was bought as a private woodland estate by the Turner family who decided to build a network of trails between the steep moss-covered outcrops and mine workings. However, instead of laying out the paths according to a logical plan, they constructed a series of confusing maze-like circles, a deed which accounts for the wood's unusual present-day name. This unique and historic place has now been open to the public for over fifty years. In 1981, both Puzzle Wood and Perrygrove Farm were acquired by their present owner, Ray Prosser, who installed an attractive tea garden and souvenir shop. (Open Tuesdays to Sundays and Bank Holiday Mondays, 11am to 6pm between Easter and end-October. Admission charge payable.)

Carvings, Ruardean Church

Before continuing south to Clearwell, make a short diversion west to visit the charming village of NEWLAND, home of the so-called 'Cathedral of the Forest'. This is the nickname given to the vast local Church of All Saints which has an aisle almost as wide as its nave and a huge pinnacled tower which needs the support of flying buttresses. Like many other churches in Gloucestershire, it was built during the 13th and 14th centuries and later remodelled by the Victorians. Inside, it has a number of noteworthy features, including a 17th-century effigy of a reclining archer and an unusual monumental brass featuring a medieval miner holding a pick and a hod and with a candle in his mouth. This is thought to depict Sir John Greyndour, a former Sheriff of Gloucester who, along with a company of miners from the Forest of Dean, accompanied Henry V's forces to France where they went on to capture and hold the town of Harfleur.

The sturdily-bred artisans of the Forest have a long history of assisting in military campaigns and were often called on by the monarch of the day to operate as an early form of special task force. Indeed, the 'Free Miners of Dean' were given their title by King Edward I after he had successfully put their demolition skills to use undermining the Scottish fortifications around Berwick-on-Tweed.

Newland contains an unusual number of large and well-maintained buildings reflecting a stable and prosperous past which seems to have endured into the present. Among the most distinctive of these are the almshouses near the church which were built for eight men and eight women in 1615 and then thoughtfully updated during the 1950s. There is also a charming 16th-century pub, the Ostrich, and an excellent farmhouse bed and breakfast establishment, Tan House Farm.

Tan House Farm, Newland, Coleford Tel: 01594 832222

Tan House Farm is an immaculate Queen Anne period house which stands within fourteen acres of lush green fields. (According to architectural historian Nikolaus Pevsner, it resembles an '18th-century dolls' house'.) Throughout the year, it is used as a medieval field study centre offering courses covering such topics as Gothic architecture and stained glass. When courses are not being run, the proprietors Peter and Christie Chamberlain provide members of the public with first-rate bed and breakfast accommodation. They have several tastefully furnished twin-bedded rooms available, all with washbasins, and four with additional en-suite shower and toilet. An informal relaxed air pervades the house giving it a comfortable and homely feel. If you are looking for peace and quiet, then Tan House Farm at Newland is an ideal place to stay.

A two-mile journey through the lanes to the southeast of Newland leads to the famous Clearwell Caves, the site of ancient iron mines which were worked for over 2500 years from the dawn of the Iron Age until 1945. The mines were originally a natural cave system which over a long period became filled with rich deposits of iron ore. These deposits were gradually removed to form a labyrinth of interconnecting passages and chambers which in recent years have been renovated and opened as a fascinating museum.

Eight large caverns (or 'churns') are now open to the public, most of which contain special displays showing the primitive techniques that were employed (and atrocious working conditions that had to be endured) by mine workers throughout the ages. (For example, it was common practice for the ore to be manhandled to the surface by youths who were expected to carry over half a hundredweight at a time.) The deepest point normally open to the public is 100 feet below the surface, although the ancient mine workings extend into the hillside for another 500 feet; tours into these deeper levels can be made by special arrangement.

The last stop on the tour, the Engine Room, contains a marvellous collection of vintage mining equipment and mine engines which on the day we visited included a compressor built by Ingersol Rand in 1915, a 30-horsepower horizontal engine built by Fielding in 1924, and a 20-horsepower horizontal engine built by Crossley in 1925. The site also contains a tearoom and an interesting shop stocked with souvenirs, mineral samples, geological maps and books relating to the world of mining and geology. (Open daily 10am to 5pm between 1st March and 31st October and also during December for special Christmas attraction. Admission charge payable.)

Nearby CLEARWELL village contains a number of interesting features, including a 14th-century sandstone standing cross, the Wyndham Arms inn, which is believed to date from the same century, and the extravagantly decorated 19th-century Church of St Peter. The church was built by Caroline Wyndham, Countess of Dunraven, to replace an earlier building which once stood at the other end of the village. She was the last member of her family to

live at Clearwell Castle, the ornate neo-Gothic mansion which was
built in the 1720s by her ancestor, Thomas Wyndham. The house
was constructed around an Elizabethan great hall and was used as
a base by the notorious Judge Jeffries when he travelled around
Wessex trying and sentencing (usually to death or transportation)
the supporters of the Duke of Monmouth's ill-fated rebellion of
1685.

Clearwell Caves

The building was practically destroyed by fire in 1929, and
despite being rebuilt, by the 1950s it was again in desperate need
of major structural repairs. An unlikely rescuer came in the form
of the son of a castle gardener, Frank Yeates, who had been brought
up in Clearwell and gone on to earn his fortune as a baker in the
North. Yeates bought the neglected estate and proceeded to spend
the last years of his life in a labour of love, restoring it to its former
glory. The castle and grounds now operate as a hotel, although they
are open to the public on Sundays only between Easter and
October.

Two miles south of Clearwell, and just to the west of the B4228,
lies the impressive village of **ST BRIAVELS**. The community was
named after a 5th-century Welsh bishop whose name appears in

various forms throughout Celtic Wales, Cornwall and Brittany, but at no other place in England. In the Middle Ages, this was an important administrative centre for the Forest of Dean; it was also a major armaments manufacturing centre supplying weapons and ammunition to the Crown. (In 1223, Henry III is believed to have ordered 6000 crossbow bolts (or quarrels) from workshops in St Briavels.)

The somewhat oversized village church was built in Norman times to replace a Celtic chapel on the same site. It was significantly enlarged in the 12th and 13th centuries, and further remodelled by the Victorians who, perhaps rashly, demolished and rebuilt the original chancel. Each year on Whit Sunday, the Pound Wall outside the church is the site of a unique custom, the St Briavels Bread and Cheese Ceremony. Following the evensong service, a local forester stands on the wall and throws small pieces of bread and cheese to the assembled villagers below. This action is accompanied by the chant, 'St Briavels water and Whyrl's wheat, are the best bread and water King John can ever eat.'

The ceremony is thought to have originated over 700 years ago when the inhabitants of St Briavels successfully defended their rights of estover (the right to collect wood from common land) in nearby Hudnalls Wood. As a gesture of gratitude, each villager agreed to pay one penny to the church warden towards feeding the poor, an act which in turn led to the founding of the bread and cheese ceremony. At one time, this annual charitable event took place inside the church; however, by the middle of last century, the festivities had become so rowdy that the whole procedure was banished to the wall outside. Local legend has it that the small pieces of bread and cheese bring good luck; they were traditionally cherished by Forest of Dean miners who believed, being like the bread of holy communion which was said never to perish, they would keep them from harm.

St Briavels also possesses an impressive castle which, perhaps due to its unassailable position on a 900 foot promontory above the River Wye, never saw any military action. It was founded in the early-1100s by Henry I and was considerably enlarged during King John's reign in the 13th century when it was used as a hunting lodge. Much of the original structure, including the keep, collapsed during the 18th century; however, the two fortress-like gatehouse towers survived along with a number of 13th-century castle buildings, most of which now function as a youth hostel. Some other parts of the castle are open to the public, including the court and jury rooms and the castle dungeon with its poignant graffiti. The structure is bordered by a grassy flower-filled moat, creating an atmosphere more characteristic of a fortified country house than an important military stronghold.

From St Briavels, drive northwest along the narrow lane which eventually leads down to Bigsweir Bridge across the River Wye. This 160 foot single-span structure carries the main A466 Chepstow to Monmouth road and is thought to have been designed either by Thomas Telford or Charles Hollis, the engineer of Windsor Bridge. An unusual toll house stands at its eastern end, while near the other end, Bigsweir House can be seen at the foot of Hudnalls Wood.

Church Farm Guest House, Mitchel Troy, Monmouth
Tel: 01600 712176

The Wye forms the border between England and Wales along most of the fifteen-mile stretch between Monmouth and the sea, so if you follow the A466 south you are, in fact, driving through Gwent. If you are planning to explore this area, then why not stay at the Church Farm Guest House in the quiet village of MITCHEL TROY, the charming home of Derek and Rosemary Ringer. The couple also run Wysk Walks, a business which provides walking weeks and short break holidays within the superb surrounding countryside. A 16th-century former farmhouse,

312

Church Farm features magnificent timbered ceilings and inglenook fireplaces and is tastefully furnished throughout. Accommodation is provided for non-smokers in eight attractive and well-equipped bedrooms, most are en-suite and all meals can be provided. Outside in the acre of woodland gardens with stream, you can see many varieties of birds while in an outbuilding Rosemary has a small pottery where you may be able to purchase samples of her work which includes vases, jugs and tableware.

The idyllic little village of **LLANDOGO** is situated on the banks of the River Wye in a landscape latticed with former horse and donkey tracks which once were the only means of access to the pretty cottages dotted across the hillside.

Yallup Gallery, Wye Valley Road, Llandogo, Monmouth
Tel: 01594 530940

Llandogo makes a perfect location for the Yallup Gallery, a fascinating establishment which is run by South African-born Pat Yallup, herself an accomplished artist. Formerly the village school, the gallery now holds regular monthly exhibitions of work by reputable artists, as well as permanent displays of sculpture, pottery and jewellery. It is open every day (including all day Sunday), and visitors are encouraged to call in and browse. Pat also runs painting courses and workshops for budding artists, whether beginners or more experienced. Set in an idyllic location, the Yallup Gallery is a true artists' haven.

Continuing south along the western bank of the River Wye you will soon come to the open water meadow which is the site of the superb remains of Tintern Abbey. Though now sadly roofless and beyond repair, this is one of the finest legacies of the late-medieval monastic period. Originally founded in 1131 by Cistercian monks from Citeau in France, the buildings which remain date mostly from the 13th to 15th centuries. The walls are still largely intact and feature some fine Gothic architecture, including a delicate traceried rose window at the eastern end of the great church which measures over sixty feet in diameter. As well as some impressive arches, windows and doorways, the abbey site also contains the remains of several ancillary buildings, including the chapter house, refectory and kitchens. (Open daily, 9.30am (2pm Sundays) to 6.30pm (4pm in winter), all year round.)

The Cistercians were known for their austere and diligent lifestyle. They intensively farmed the surrounding monastic estate, using lay brothers to carry out some of the more arduous tasks. Some light relief, however, may have been provided by a predecessor of the present-day Anchor Inn which can be found on the nearby riverbank. The route from the inn to the water's edge passes under a 13th-century archway which was probably the abbey's water gate. On the other side of the river, a natural rock platform can be made out which is known locally as the Devil's Pulpit. Legend has it that Satan would stand here and scream insults at the Cistercian monks. Having survived this verbal barrage for several centuries, Tintern instead fell prey to Henry VIII's Dissolution of the Monasteries in 1539, and despite being concealed amongst the steep tree-covered slopes of the Wye Valley, it was abandoned soon after.

The Old Station at Tintern now functions as a delightful visitor centre. Built during the Victorian era as a halt on the picturesque Wye Valley line, it is surrounded by an attractive picnic area and also houses a small exhibition on the history of the local railways. The recently-published Wye Valley Walk map pack is also available here at a special discounted price. Open between April and end-October. Small car parking charge payable.

Retracing your steps along the A466 for half a mile, cross back into Gloucestershire near the village of BROCKWEIR. Before the present bridge was built in 1904, this pleasant settlement of white-painted buildings was reached from the west bank by ferry. Some of the houses in the village date back to Tudor times, and there is also an unusual Moravian chapel which incorporates an assortment of architectural styles from Gothic to art nouveau.

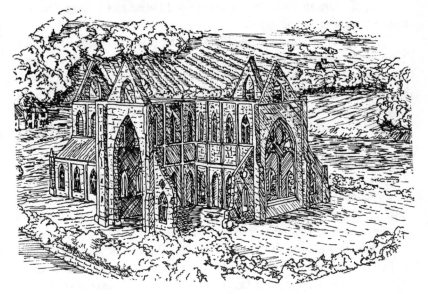

Tintern Abbey

Brockweir was once an important river port and boat-building centre. For centuries, small vessels of up to 100 tons were constructed along the quay, then in 1824 an improved facility was built which could handle craft of up to 500 tons. This was also a place where river barges bound for Monmouth, Hereford and even Hay, were filled with coal and iron ore from the Forest of Dean. These were then hauled upstream by gangs of men harnessed together in teams of eight. Working in relays, it took four such teams to cover the gruelling eight-mile stretch of river between Brockweir and Monmouth. It must have been thirsty work for during its heyday, as many as sixteen pubs were open in the village to serve the combined workforce from the wharves and boatyards. Both boat-building and the river-barge trade were brought to an abrupt end by the arrival of the railways in the second half of the 19th century.

The River Wye continues to be a well-stocked salmon river thanks almost entirely to the efforts of a lone Brockweir campaigner, Frank Buckland. Until the 1920s, salmon netting was allowed along the river's entire length, causing an alarming decline in numbers. However, due to Buckland's successful campaign, the netting of salmon was strictly controlled below the village and was banned altogether above it.

The course of the famous Offa's Dyke passes through Brockweir. This great earthwork ditch and rampart was built by Offa, King of Mercia, between 757 and 795 AD to define the western boundary of his kingdom. The original construction ran for nearly 170 miles from the River Severn in the south to the River Dee in the north, with gaps occurring only in areas of dense forest. The dyke was also used to defend Mercia from parties of marauding Welsh raiders, a role which continued throughout the medieval era. During this period, a line of motte and bailey castles was built to strengthen the border defences; many of these can be seen today, and although some are now in ruins, those in a suitable state of preservation are generally open to visitors.

Offa's Dyke long-distance footpath follows the course of King Offa's 8th-century ramparts. The eight-mile stretch between St Briavels and the sea contains a number of spectacular vantage points which look out across the Wye Valley to the Welsh mountains in the west and the Severn estuary in the south. In particular, there are two outstanding viewpoints, both of which lie within easy reach of the B4228 St Briavels to Chepstow road. The first is from the northern edge of the Ban-y-gor rocks where the road runs along a ridge above the River Wye. There are two dramatic vistas from here: straight down the almost vertical rock face to the river, or westwards across the Severn towards the Vale of Berkeley and the Cotswolds.

The second vantage point can be found three-quarters of a mile further south at Wintour's Leap, the massive rocky outcrop which towers 200 feet above the Wye.

At this point, the river is forced to make a hairpin turn after completing its circuit around the Lancaut peninsula and the abrasive action of the water has created a pronounced hook in the solid rock riverbank. The crag gets its name from Sir John Wintour (or Winter), a royalist officer who, while being chased by Parliamentarian forces during the English Civil War, is alleged to have ridden his horse over the edge of the precipice and swum across the river to safety.

The triangle of land lying between the B4228 and the A48 to the east of here is known as Tidenham Chase. This 1000-acre area once belonged to the lords of Chepstow who set it aside for the hunting of deer. In places, the underlying limestone breaks through the surface to form a series of rocky outcrops which make excellent standpoints for surveying the surrounding landscape.

The River Wye reaches the mouth of the Severn near the ancient Gwent market town of CHEPSTOW. This strategically-important place was the location of the Normans' first stone-built fortress in Wales. Chepstow Castle was extended several times over the centuries and it now occupies a large site on a limestone ridge above the River Wye which in turn forms a natural moat along its eastern side. Visitors to this colossal structure will find four courtyards, a lofty keep and a series of massive castle walls interspersed with defensive towers. During the 13th century, the tower which later became known as Martens Tower was added; this was where Henry Marten, a co-signatory of Charles I's death warrant, was confined until his death in 1680. (Chepstow Castle is open daily, 9.30am (2pm Sundays) to 6.30pm (4pm in winter), all year round.)

A short distance away, Chepstow Museum houses a permanent exhibition on the history of this important port and military stronghold. Here, the working life of the town, which once included wine shipping, shipbuilding and salmon fishing, is brought to life in a series of imaginatively devised settings. Also on display is an interesting collection of 18th- and 19th-century prints featuring Chepstow, its castle and the countryside of the Wye Valley.

From Chepstow, join the main A48 and drive northeast along the southern edge of Tidenham Chase. After about seven miles, you will come to the pleasant village of ALVINGTON, the centre of which is located to the north of the main road. The village churchyard contains the Victorian graves of the Wintours, one of the area's most illustrious families who in the 16th century, played an important role in the defeat of the Spanish Armada. Just over half a century later, Sir John Wintour was involved in his remarkable escape from Cromwell's forces following the Battle of Lancaut (see Wintour's Leap).

Continuing northeastwards along the A48 takes you past the entrance to the famous Lydney Park Gardens. Nowadays, this beautiful valley garden is filled with rhododendrons, azaleas, magnolias and other flowering shrubs which are at their best during May and early-June. During the Second World War, however, this eight-acre site was used for growing potatoes, and it wasn't until the second Lord Bledisloe and his head gardener, 'Mac' Stracey, set to work that the present-day woodland paradise was created. These breathtaking lakeside gardens are only open to the public for a short season each year, namely on Sundays, Wednesdays and Bank Holidays between Easter and early-June, also every day during the week of the Whitsun Bank Holiday. (To confirm opening times, telephone 01594 842844.)

The grounds of Lydney Park also contain herd of fallow deer and a number of unusual features which together form a fascinating record of human occupation in this part of the country. As well as the site of an Iron Age hill fort, the park contains the remains of a late-Roman temple dating from the 4th century AD which was excavated by Sir Mortimer Wheeler in the 1920s. It is likely that the builders of this unusual temple complex were wealthy Romanised Celts, similar to those occupying Chedworth or Great Witcombe. The temple had a mosaic floor (now destroyed) depicting fish and sea monsters and was dedicated to the god Nodens, a Roman-Celtic god of healing, whose emblem, in common with other early symbols of curing, was a reclining dog.

A unique collection of Roman artefacts from the site, including the famous 'Lydney Dog', are now housed in the nearby Lydney Park Museum. The museum also contains a number of interesting items which were brought back from New Zealand in the 1930s by the first Viscount Bledisloe following his term there as the Governor General. (Museum opening times similar to gardens. Admission charge payable.) Lydney Park also contains evidence of Roman iron-mine workings and a line of earth fortifications of a similar age which were later reinforced by the Saxons.

The sprawling town of LYDNEY occupies a site midway between the River Severn and the Forest of Dean. The largest settlement between Chepstow and Gloucester, it has the locality's only remaining railway station.

Lovers of Chinese food will appreciate Jimmy Wong's excellent restaurant in the centre of Lydney. With its attractive decor and cosy, relaxing atmosphere, Wong's Cuisine makes the ideal venue,

318

whether for that intimate dinner or a party booking. With eighty covers, Wong's can also cater for banquets and receptions. Open seven days a week, Jimmy provides an extensive, quality menu, and is happy to cater for any special tastes by prior arrangement. In the summer, the restaurant is air conditioned for the comfort of customers. The popularity of Wong's Cuisine is self-evident judging by the number of visitors who return time and again to sample Jimmy's outstanding cooking.

Wong's Cuisine, 11 Hill Street, Lydney Tel: 01594 844555

Those interested in the evocative world of steam railways should make a point of visiting the Norchard Steam Centre on the northern outskirts of Lydney. This is the headquarters of the Dean Forest Railway which was originally built in 1809 to haul coal and iron ore from Parkend in the Forest of Dean to the docks on the Severn.

The line operated as a horse-drawn tramway until 1868 when it was updated to a broad gauge railway. Despite regular passenger services ceasing in 1929, British Rail continued to utilise the line for transporting coal and ballast until 1976.

In the early 1980s, members of the Dean Forest Railway Society acquired the decaying line and began the first major stage of restoration. This was completed in 1991 when a short stretch of track was reopened between Norchard and a new station at Lydney Lakeside, four miles to the south. Further work is currently in progress to reinstate the entire line between Lydney and Parkend, a project which will take several years to complete.

Today, visitors to the Norchard Centre can see a unique collection of steam locomotives and rolling stock, many of which are still undergoing restoration; they can also visit the Society's railway museum with its huge display of signs, nameplates, posters, photographs, number plates and other railwayana including many from the local Severn and Wye line. There is also an on-site picnic area and a sizable shop offering a wide variety of gifts and souvenirs.

On certain designated 'steam days', a number of locomotives are made ready and excursions are offered along the restored stretch of line. The eight-mile return trip takes 35 minutes and includes a fifteen-minute stop at Lydney Lakeside. Steam days: all Sundays and Bank Holidays between April and September, plus Wednesdays in June and July, and Tuesdays, Wednesdays and Thursdays in August. Admission charge payable (lower on non-steam days), plus additional charge for train rides.

Rejoining the A48, drive northeast for four miles to reach the attractive small village of BLAKENEY. At this point you can join the Forestry Commission's designated Scenic Drive through the central area of the Forest of Dean. (The suggested entry point for this 25-mile circular route is at its most northwesternmost point at Cannop, near Coleford)

The first stage of this journey takes you up the twisting route of the Soudley Valley. Here, the road follows the course of the steep-sided river valley, resulting in a series of challenging gradients and bends. At Blackpool Bridge, the scenic drive crosses a recognisable section of the old Roman road which once ran between Lydney and Ariconium, near Ross-on-Wye. The bridge itself dates from the same period and was constructed to replace a ford which crossed Blackpool Brook at this point.

By now you are getting close to the heart of the ROYAL FOREST OF DEAN, a place with a long and fascinating past. Throughout its history, this ancient forest has been a wildwood, a royal hunting ground, an important mining and industrial area and a naval timber reserve, and because its geographical location effectively isolated it from the rest of England and Wales, it has developed its own unique character which endures to this day.

As the trees gradually returned to western Britain at the end of the last Ice Age, 53 species established themselves as our native trees. During this period, the Forest of Dean became established and grew to cover an area of some 120,000 acres between the Rivers Wye, Severn and Leadon. Around 4000 BC, the farmers of the New Stone Age began a process of field clearance and crop cultivation and gradually, large numbers of trees were cleared using highly-prized flint axes. The cut timber was used for many purposes including building materials and fuel, and it was also around this time that the process of coppicing was devised where the new shoots growing from the bases of felled trees were cultivated for periodical cutting.

Norchard Steam Centre

Many species of animals and birds continued to inhabit the forest, and indeed the presence of deer led to it being designated a royal hunting forest by King Edmund Ironside early in the 11th century. Later that century, King Canute established the Court of Verderers, an ancient council which had overall responsibility for everything that grew or lived in the forest. The court still meets ten times a year at the Speech House near Cannop Ponds, a unique building, now part of a hotel, which was built as a courtroom to settle disputes between the foresters and the new wave of 17th-century iron-founders.

Iron ore deposits were first discovered in the forest over 2500 years ago along an irregular arc which runs between Staunton and Lydney in the west and south, and Ruspidge and Wigpool in the east and north. Although these were widely exploited by the Romans, it wasn't until the Crown allowed areas of the forest to be leased to commercially-motivated entrepreneurs in the 1600s that mineral extraction began to take place on a grand scale. Far more devastating, however, was the demand for timber to fuel the iron-smelting process; such was the scale of the requirement that by the 1660s, the once-magnificent forest had been reduced to a few hundred trees.

Seriously concerned about the shortage of mature oaks for naval shipbuilding, the government finally acted in 1668 by passing the Dean Forest (Reforestation) Act, one of the earliest examples of conservation legislation, and by cancelling all the mineral leases. This led to an extensive replanting programme which eventually restored the forest to something approaching its original state. The Napoleonic Wars prompted further restocking and by 1840, nearly 20,000 acres had been replanted, mostly with young oaks. However, by the time these trees had reached maturity, steel had replaced timber as the principal shipbuilding material and they were never required. (Some examples of the early-19th-century replanting can still be seen in the Cannop Valley Nature Reserve.)

During the Victorian era, coal began to be extracted in large quantities from the Forest of Dean and at one time, up to a million tons were removed each year, mostly from open cast workings. Large-scale coal extraction came to an end during the 1930s, although a few seams are still being worked today by groups of 'free miners', the individuals who exercise their traditional right to extract minerals from the forest. Although centuries of outcrop mining has left large areas scarred and unfit for agriculture, the forest has gradually reclaimed these 'scowles', or surface workings, often concealing them in a dense covering of moss, trees and lime-loving plants.

Today, the wooded area of the Royal Forest of Dean covers some 27,000 acres and although still under the ownership of the Crown, it has has been vested in the Forestry Commission since 1924. The forest is known to be one of the organisation's most successfully managed areas; it has opened up a large number of waymarked woodland walks, most of which are fully described in an excellent series of leaflets and guides, and has also been responsible for laying out a number of tastefully-landscaped picnic areas and car parks. Its principal task, however, has been to manage the commercial woodlands, half of which are planted with broad-leaved deciduous trees, predominantly oak with beech, ash and sweet chestnut, and the balance being non-native conifers such as larch, fir and spruce.

Further information on the background and history of the forest and its inhabitants can be obtained at the Dean Heritage Centre. Standing in a cleft in the wooded hills, this fascinating place lies on the B4227 at Camp Mill on the edge of LOWER SOUDLEY.

Situated deep in the very heart of the forest, the Dean Heritage Centre is a real gem. It is a tranquil spot where time slows to a leisurely place and where a new face of the Forest unfolds to entrance the visitor with every changing season: the fresh greens of spring, the dark leafy greens of high summer, the russets of autumn and the brown greys of winter. In this unique haven, you can catch a glimpse of the unique heritage of the Forest of Dean and understand its very essence. Visitors are welcomed here every day of the year, with the exception of Christmas Day and Boxing Day.

The Dean Heritage Centre is housed at Camp Mill, an old corn mill standing on a site with a varied industrial history stretching back over the four hundred years. During the 17th century there was a foundry here; then some years later, the buildings were modified to form a leatherboard mill where heel stiffeners and shoe insoles were manufactured. More recently, Camp Mill has been a saw mill and a piggery, then in 1981, it was presented to the Dean Heritage Museum Trust as as a prospective home for a Forest of Dean Museum. (At that time, its most eye-catching feature was the rusty remains of a car dump and scrap-yard.) However, within just two years, the first specialised displays of the new Dean Heritage Centre were opened to the public.

Since then, the displays have been extended and improved following the Trust's aim 'to preserve the heritage, information, objects, culture and sites of the Forest of Dean in perpetuity for the community, by the provision of museum services'. There is now a reconstructed miner's cottage within the mill complex with a living room, bedroom and wash house which was built around 1900. (The contrast between modern homes with their many labour saving devices and the basic living conditions which existed at the turn of the century is all too apparent.) An example of the miner's workplace can be found near the cottage where one can imagine the rigours of life underground. The absence of explosive gases within the Forest of Dean coalfield enabled the miners to work with naked flames, candles at first, then later, carbide lamps. However, the mines here were subject to flooding and many of the deeper pits periodically filled with water, sometimes with disastrous consequences.

The social history of the Forest people is shown through domestic artefacts and documents which have been given to the museum by the local inhabitants. The importance of the close community spirit is felt; the Forest folk are fiercely independent, a result of their geographical isolation from both Wales and England. (Before the advent of the car and the Severn Bridge, this plateau area of closely wooded hills and deep valleys was relatively impenetrable.) The Forest folk developed their own customs, rights and even law courts, as well as a deep suspicion of outsiders.

The Centre houses a beam engine which was built by Samuel Hewlett around the turn of the 18th century on this very site when it operated as a foundry. Recently, a twelve foot overshot water wheel was constructed within the original wheel pit of the mill to emphasise the importance of water power in the industrial development of the area.

Outside, there is a typical Forest smallholding, complete with an orchard and some Gloucester Old Spot pigs, and nearby there are some old agricultural carts and a reconstructed cider press. Charcoal burning was a traditional Forest occupation, and a charcoal burner's hut and demonstration charcoal stacks have been constructed at the Centre. Each year, several batches of charcoal are made by this traditional method which requires them to be tended day and night over several days until the burning process has been completed. Excellent for barbecues, the end product is on sale to the public.

Several nature trails radiate from the Centre. Visitors can stroll through ancient oak and beech woods, past old stone quarries, and on through fir plantations along waymarked paths. There is also a level, all-weather footpath leading for about half-a-mile around the beautiful Soudley Pond, a Site of Special Scientific Interest for its aquatic insect life, in particular, dragonflies.

Local craftspeople carry out a variety of crafts at the Dean Heritage Centre. These include pottery, wood painting, stone sculpture, iron-working, and glass and wood engraving. Unusual hand-crafted gifts, ideal as extra-special presents, can be found in the shop and gallery. You can also enjoy the home-baking in the Heritage Kitchen where the menu offers a wide choice from snacks to three-course meals; they also serve an excellent pot of tea. (Parties are welcome if booked in advance).

The facilities on site include ample coach and car parks, toilets (including a mother and babies room), and good access and facilities for disabled visitors. A large and much praised adventure play area is situated near the car park. Picnic tables can be found both under the trees on the slope of Bradley Hill and beside the car park on the mossy banks of Soudley Brook. There are also several barbecue hearths which can be booked in advance. Throughout the year, special events, displays and art exhibitions are regularly staged. Guided tours of the Dean Heritage Centre and the surrounding woodlands are also available, making this the ideal place to take your family and friends for a day of interest, fun and education, whatever the weather.

Dean Heritage Centre, Camp House, Soudley Tel: 01594 822170

Leaving the Heritage Centre, return to the scenic drive and you will soon passed the attractive small lakes known as Soudley Ponds. Then, just past the White Horse pub, we turned north onto the Littledean road to make the short diversion to visit the Blaize Bailey viewpoint; this can be reached by turning east after a mile or so onto a forest track. Once there, visitors are rewarded with breathtaking views over the village of Newnham and the Vale of Gloucester to the Cotswold Hills beyond. Another wonderful view, this time of Soudley village, can be obtained from a lay-by which is passed on the return to the scenic drive.

Our next stop is the famous Dean Sculpture Trail, a unique collection of eleven outdoor sculptures which are spaced along a delightful woodland walk. The artists have all used the forest setting as their theme, for example, the final piece on the trail is an impressive stained-glass window known as The Cathedral which depicts the forest trees and wildlife. The Sculpture Trail is accessible either from the picnic area adjacent to the stained-glass window, or from the award-winning Beechenhurst picnic site a mile or so further west; both are sited on the northern side of the B4226.

Situated on the southern side at this point is the Speech House Arboretum, a fascinating place for those interested in finding out more about the world of trees. Visitors are welcome to inspect the large collection of native and imported specimen trees which are laid out along a pleasant woodland trail. A little further west is the historic Speech House Hotel, the official meeting place of the ancient Verderers' Court. At Cannop Crossroads a sign will direct you east to the Cannop Ponds picnic area. These picturesque pools were originally hollowed out in the 1820s to provide a regular water supply for the local iron smelting works.

Continuing south, our next stop was the wildlife reserve at NAGSHEAD near Parkend. The Forest of Dean has long been a haven for a huge variety of animals and birds, including deer, badgers, woodpeckers and the famous forest sheep which have been permitted to range freely in the forest for centuries. The Nagshead reserve is particularly noted for its resident population of pied flycatchers and its visiting peregrine falcons. The attractive former mineral extracting community of PARKEND stands at the northern terminus of the still to be reopened Dean Forest Railway. Those looking to break their journey should look out here for the first-rate Parkend House Hotel.

Situated within three acres of parkland containing a private croquet lawn, the Parkend House Hotel offers guests total seclusion. Run by Mrs Bobby Poole and Andrew Lee, it is a small country house hotel, over 200 years old, which provides excellent facilities while still retaining its original character and charm. The bedrooms are all en-suite with colour televisions, hot drinks facilities and direct-dial telephones. Three of the rooms are on the ground floor, offering easy access to disabled guests. Children are also welcome and several family rooms are available. The restaurant offers a varied menu and Bobby is happy to cater for vegetarian and special diets. All meals are prepared using fresh produce, including unusual and exotic vegetables; Andrew and Bobby also make their own chutney and marmalade, the latter of which is served at breakfast.

Parkend House, Parkend, Nr. Lydney Tel: 01594 563666

Not far from the hotel is the charmingly-named New Fancy View, a delightfully landscaped picnic area which was once the site the New Fancy Colliery. It's worth making the effort to climb to the top of the nearby hill for the breathtaking views over the surrounding landscape.

Half a mile after returning to the main circuit, another detour to the north takes you to the beautiful Mallards Pike Lake. This is another good place for a short walk; however, for those wishing to press on, the track follows a circular route back onto the main scenic drive.

The final place worth mentioning on our tour around the forest is the Wenchford picnic site. This is situated a mile further east and can be reached by turning north onto the Soudley road, and then immediately east onto an old railway track which leads the parking area (toilets available here).

Rejoined the A48, drive northeast for three miles to reach the pleasant village of NEWNHAM. This is said to be one of the best places for viewing the famous Severn Bore, the natural wave formation which is created when the incoming tide from the Bristol Channel meets the water flowing seawards from the Severn. Although small-scale bores occur throughout the year, during certain tidal conditions, a wave of some nine feet in height can be generated, usually on the spring tides of early spring or late autumn. The phenomenon is popular with surfers and canoeists who like to 'catch the wave'. Information on times and the best viewing points can be obtained from local retailers.

At Newnham, turn away from the river and drive west up a steep lane towards Littledean Hall. This remarkable country house is surrounded by sweeping informal grounds and occupies a dramatic position overlooking the great horseshoe bend on the Severn. (It lies only a short distance from Blaize Bailey viewpoint, visited on the scenic drive around the Forest of Dean). Littledean Hall has a rich history and claims to be one of the oldest continuously occupied country residences in England. In 1984, the remains of one of the largest rural Roman shrines, Springhead Temple, were discovered in the foundations, and there is also evidence here of a great hall dating from Saxon times. The Norman core of the present-day house dates from the 11th century when it was built for the Dene family. This was later replaced in 1612 by a new Jacobean building, carved wood panelling from which is still much in evidence throughout the interior. However, the new hall did not escape further alterations and was itself remodelled on a number of occasions between 1664 and 1896.

Perhaps Littledean Hall's main claim to fame, however, are its many ghosts, most of which seem to have their origins in the period since the 17th century. One of the earliest apparitions dates from the English Civil War when the royalist garrison based here was surprised by a Parliamentarian attack. Following the royalists' surrender, one of their troops unfortunately killed one of the Roundhead soldiers, an act which resulted in the entire garrison being massacred. Royalist colonels Congreve and Wigmore were standing next to the main fireplace when they were put to the sword and today, phantom bloodstains are said to appear at this spot which no amount of cleaning can remove.

Another event which is said to account for some of the present-day poltergeist activity took place a century later. According to legend, the owner of the house, Charles Pyrke, was murdered by his black manservant in 1744, despite them having been friends since childhood; Pyrke was alleged to have been responsible for making his servant's sister pregnant and for subsequently murdering the baby. Today, the ghostly butler is said to haunt the landing outside his garret bedroom high in the east wing.

Some years later, the Pyrke family were involved in another incident when two brothers in love with the same woman ended up killing each other during an argument at the dining table. Their spirits are still said to inhabit the dining room. One unfortunate result of all this poltergeist activity is that one of the best guest rooms, the Blue Room, is alleged to be so disturbed by the sound of footsteps and the clashing of swords that no one has dared to spent the night there for over forty years. (Littledean Hall is open daily, 10.30am to 6pm between April and October. Admission charge payable.)

Leaving the secret passageways and haunted garrets behind, we turned east onto the A4151 and drove on through LITTLEDEAN village towards our final stopping, WESTBURY-UPON-SEVERN. This is the home of the unique National Trust-owned Westbury Court Garden which, having been built between 1696 and 1705, is the earliest surviving example of a formal Dutch water garden in the country. When the Trust acquired the property in the 1960s, it was in a state of extreme dilapidation. The house had been demolished, the lawns were like hayfields, the canals were silted up, and garden walls and yew hedges were in a serious state of disrepair. However, with the help of an engraving of the original garden plan, the records of the initial plantings and a series of special grants, the Trust were able to begin a programme of restoration which was finally completed in 1971.

Today, these most attractive and unusual gardens stand as a unique example of the style of formal landscaping which existed before the onset of emparking later in the 18th century. The only surviving building, the pavilion, is an elegant two-storey redbrick structure with a tower and weather vane which stands overlooking the garden's delightful waterlily-filled canals. Another particularly appealing feature of Westbury Court Garden is that it was exclusively replanted with species known to have been available in this part of England before 1700. (Open Wednesdays to Sundays and Bank Holiday Mondays, 11am to 6pm between April and end-October. Admission charge payable; free to National Trust members).

CHAPTER ELEVEN

Bristol to the Southwolds

Bristol Harbour

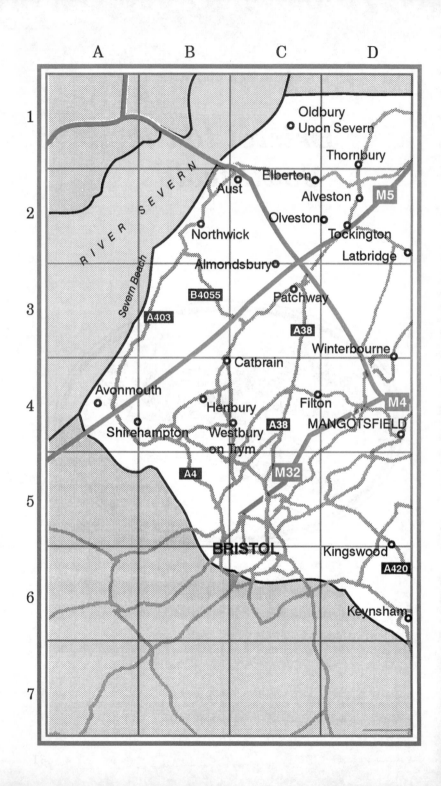

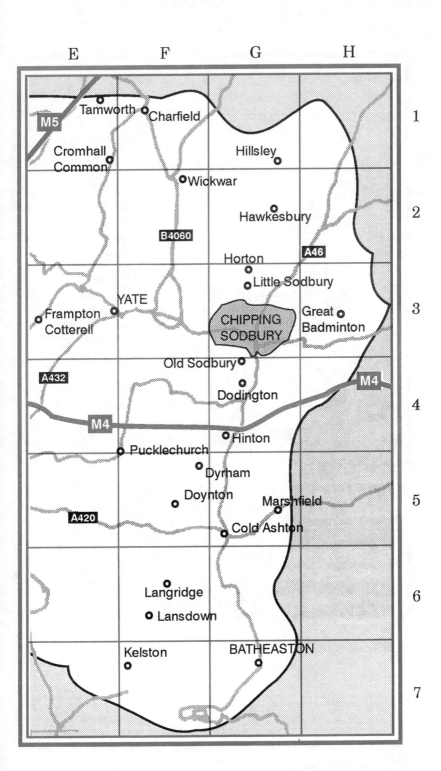

Blaise Hamlet

Bristol to the Southwolds

With a current population of over 400,000 and a history dating back to the time of the Saxons, BRISTOL is a diverse regional capital which takes time to get to know. A good way for the visitor to begin is to climb to the top of the Cabot Tower on Brandon Hill, an area of open ground near the city centre which can be found to the west of the Park Street shopping area. The 100 foot tower stands near the site of a chapel dedicated to St Brendan the Navigator and was erected in memory of another maritime pioneer, John Cabot, the first non-Scandinavian European to set foot on Newfoundland; his expedition of 1497 was financed by Bristol merchants.

For centuries, the city was a major commercial seaport, and the magnificent view from the top reveals the complex series of docks and wharves known as the floating harbour which were created when the course of the River Avon was diverted to the south early in the 19th century. This massive feat of engineering took over five years to complete and was largely carried out by Napoleonic prisoners using only picks and shovels. Today, the docks have moved downstream to Avonmouth and the floating harbour has become the haunt of recreational craft.

Bristol was founded during Saxon times at the point where the River Frome curved to join the River Avon. This strategically-important bridging point at the head of the Avon gorge soon became a prominent port and market centre, and by the early 11th century it had its own mint and was trading with other ports throughout western England, Wales and Ireland. In 1067, the Normans began work on a massive stone keep which stood between the present-day floating harbour and Newgate, a site which is still known as Castle Park despite the almost total demolition of the structure at the end of the English Civil War. The heart of the old city lies to the west of here around the point where Corn, Broad, Wine and High Streets converge.

A third of a mile further west, Bristol's Anglican cathedral stands on College Green. Founded in the 12th century as the great church of an Augustinian abbey, several original Norman features remain, including the southeast transept walls, the chapter house, the gatehouse, and the eastern side of the delightful enclosed cloisters. Elsewhere there is some good 14th-century stained glass and a series of striking roof bosses in the north transept. Following the Dissolution of the Monasteries in 1539, Henry VIII took the unusual step of elevating the church to the status of a cathedral, and soon after, the richly-carved choir stalls were added; the superb organ case was carved by Grinling Gibbons over a century later. The building wasn't fully completed until the 19th century when a nave was built to match the choir in sympathetic style. This area contains some exceptional monuments and tombs, as well as a pair of unusual candlesticks which were donated in 1712 by the rescuers of Alexander Selkirk, the actual castaway on whom Daniel Defoe's character, Robinson Crusoe, was modelled.

Bristol expanded enormously as a trading centre during the medieval period, and at one time it was second only to London as a seaport. Its trade was based largely on the export of raw wool and woollen cloth from the Mendip and Cotswold hills, and the import of wines from Spain and southwest France. The city's first major wharf development was carried out during this period: the diverting of the River Frome from its original course into the wide artificial channel now known as St Augustine's Reach. A remarkable engineering feat for its day, the excavation created over 500 yards of new berthing space and was crucial for Bristol's developing economy. The city's increasingly wealthy merchants also founded one of the most impressive parish churches in the west of England at around this time. Originally standing in a suburb to the east of the main channel, the Church of St Mary Redcliffe is a wonderful concoction of pinnacles, flying buttresses and immense stained-glass windows. The soaring 290 foot spire was added to the original 13th-century tower in the 19th century, and the ornately decorated north porch was built to an unusual hexagonal design which is thought to have been influenced by the Chinese architecture of the period. Look out also for the unusual roof boss in the shape of a circular maze in the north aisle, a giant replica of which has been built in Victoria Park with water channels and raised walkways. The local sandstone contains a network of natural underground passages known as the Redcliffe Caves, guided tours around which are conducted from time to time by the City Engineer's Department.

A stroll around Bristol city centre reveals an unusual number of interesting historic buildings. Queen Square, to the northwest of Redcliffe Bridge, is lined with handsome early 18th-century buildings, although two sides had to be rebuilt following their destruction in a riot in 1831. The Theatre Royal in King Street is the home of the Bristol Old Vic theatre company and is said to be the oldest theatre in the country still in regular use; it was built in the 1760s with a semicircular auditorium, a rare feature for the time. At the end of the street stands a timber-framed merchant's house of 1669 known as Llandoger Trow, and continuing northwards into the area once contained within the city walls, the Exchange in Corn Street was built in the 1740s by the neoclassical architect, John Wood the Elder, whose work is much in evidence at Bath. Symbolic heads depicting Asia, Africa and America can be seen above the doorways leading off the entrance hall, and outside, there are four bronze 'nails', low flat-topped pillars which were used by local merchants to transact their business and gave rise to the saying, 'to pay on the nail'.

Other noteworthy buildings in Bristol include The Red Lodge in Park Row, a house containing the only remaining 16th-century domestic interior in Bristol (open Tuesdays to Saturdays, 10am to 5pm, all year round).

Part of the Bristol Museums and Art Gallery, The Red Lodge was built for a wealthy gentleman, Sir John Younge, together with a similar building called the White Lodge. With few alterations made during its lifetime, today it boasts one of the finest Tudor oak-panelled rooms in the whole of the West Country. Admission £1 for adults, 50p concessions and children and students free of charge.

The Red Lodge, Park Row, Bristol Tel: 01179 211360

The elegant Georgian House in Great George Street (open as above) was originally a merchant's town house and was built in

1791. Furnished in the style of the period, the contents have been selected from the permanent collections of the City Museum and Art Gallery and include purchases made specifically for the house. Admission charge £1 adults, 50p concessions, children and students free of charge.

The Georgian House, 7 Great George Street, Bristol
Tel: 01179 211362

The City Museum and Art Gallery in Queen's Road contains an exceptional collection of Chinese glass (open daily, 10am to 5pm, all year round), and the Trinity Almshouses to the east of the city centre in Old Market Street (grounds open daily except Sundays, 10am to 4pm, all year round).

City Museum and Art Gallery, Queen's Road, Bristol
Tel: 01179 223571

In Park Street, not far from the City Museum and Art Gallery you will find Melbournes Restaurant, and as you would guess from the name, it offers the best in Australian style cooking. This former Wimpey Bar has come a long way in the few years since Tony and Nick took it over and most days it is busy and lively. It is beautifully decorated with Australiana everywhere you look, and if you ever wanted a change from the usual run of the mill restaurant - this is it! There is seating for up to 100 diners, and while you are waiting for your meal you could try a Red Back Beer - brewed in and shipped directly from Freemantle, Western Australia. You may have thought a redback was a spider, but in any event it packs quite a punch.

Just a quick glance at the menu will start your taste buds tingling and you will quickly see this is no 'shrimps on the barbie' affair. The choice is superb, with unusual starters like Warm Tartlet of Broccoli, Leeks and Vegetarian Cheese; or the House-style Gravadlax, which is salmon marinated with fresh lime juice and fennel fern. Main courses include a fine range of lamb, pork and chicken dishes, and mouthwatering desserts such as profiteroles with cream and hot chocolate sauce will have you going back for more. This is an excellent opportunity to taste fine national cooking without the obvious stereotypes. Fabulous! Melbournes is open every lunch time and evening except Sunday night and Monday lunch.

Melbournes, 74 Park Street, Bristol Tel: 01179 226996

Much of Bristol's waterfront has been now redeveloped for recreational use. The Watershed Media Centre on the western side of St Augustine's Reach is a modern arts complex with its own cinemas, galleries and harbourside café; the adjacent buildings have been converted to a first-rate exhibition centre. On the opposite bank, the excellent Arnolfini Gallery specialises in exhibitions of contemporary art. It also has its own cinema, bookshop and café-bar, and is open daily, 10am to 7pm, all year round; admission free. Two impressive attractions lie across the swing bridge to the south: the Lifeboat Museum and the Bristol Industrial Museum. The latter houses a fascinating record of the

339

achievements of the city's industrial pioneers, including those with such familiar names as Harvey (wines and sherries), Fry (chocolate), Wills (tobacco) and McAdam (road building). (Open on Tuesdays to Sundays, 10am to 5pm, all year round.)

Bristol Industrial Museum displays part of the rich and varied history of the city's manufacturing past and present. Based in the heart of the historic harbour, you can find out about Bristol's history as a port, see aero engines and aircraft made here since 1910 and inspect road vehicles of all types dating back to Victorian times. At weekends during the summer, the Museum always has something extra - it runs a steam railway, two historic ships, a giant crane and a printing workship. Telephone for further details.

Bristol Industrial Museum, Princes Wharf, Wapping Road,
Bristol Tel: 01179 251470

Another excellent museum dedicated to the pioneering Victorian engineer, Isambard Kingdom Brunel, is located in the Great Train Shed at old Temple Meads station; the nearby Exploratory is a hands-on educational facility designed to put fun into everyday science. Among the increasing number historic vessels which line Bristol's wharves is Brunel's SS Great Britain, the world's first iron-hulled, propeller-driven, ocean-going ship which was built in Bristol in 1843. After a working life of 43 years, it was retired to the Falkland Islands where it lay as a storage hulk for over seventy years before being rescued in 1970 and brought back to the dry dock of its birth where it is nearing the end of a long and painstaking process of restoration. (Open daily, 10am to 6pm, all year round.)

The Maritime Heritage Centre is not far from the city centre, and can be found on the south side of the city docks. The centre illustrates the history of shipbuilding in Bristol. A fascinating day out for all. Open daily, 10am to 6pm in summer and 10am to 5pm in Winter.

The Maritime Heritage Centre, Wapping Wharf,
Gasferry Road, Bristol Tel: 01179 260680

If at this stage of your journey you wish to find somewhere to relax then make your way to The Ginger Gallery and Café in

Hotwell Road, which overlooks the Marina. The two adjoining buildings were built between 1750 and 1780 and started life as boat builders' cottages, a tangible part of the sea-faring heritage of the city. Indeed, from the Mardyke Steps just beyond the Gallery, it is possible to take the ferry to the S.S. Great Britain.

The Gallery specialises in a wide variety of contemporary art including paintings; etchings; screenprints; monotypes; sculpture; ceramics; enamels; jewellery; turned wood; and photographic art. There is also an excellent selection of artists' cards, original clocks, wall sconces and mirrors.

The Ginger Gallery is the sole agent for watercolours by Arthur Elliott, whose work is also in print worldwide. The fine selection of work by local and international artists includes watercolours, etchings and monotypes by Simon Bull, David Bowyer, Wendy French and Brenda Hartill; paintings on hand-made paper by Elaine Cooper, whose work is receiving great acclaim in Japan. Three-dimensional work includes sculpture by Helen Sinclair and Vanessa Marston; ceramics by Jack Doherty, Bridget Drakeford, Deborah Prosser, Catherine Finch, Hilary LaForce and Hannah Turner; jewellery by Jane Adam, Julie Arkell, Mitsue Maeda, Marlene McKibben, Diana Porter and many more.

A finalist in The Fine Art Trade Guild 'Retailer of the Year Award', the Ginger Gallery has a reputation for excellent customer service. Exhibitions are held on a regular basis.

The Ginger Gallery has been operating for nine years and goes from strength to strength. The stylish café on the first floor has outstanding views over the Marina and the S.S. Great Britain. Here you can relax over morning coffee, lunch or afternoon tea in very pleasant surroundings. All the food is home-made to a very high standard and moderately priced.

The Ginger Gallery and Café, 84-86 Hotwell Road,
Bristol Tel: 0117 929 2527

Brunel was also responsible for designing one of Bristol's most graceful landmarks, the Clifton Suspension Bridge, which spans the Avon gorge a mile and a half to the west of the city centre. Opened in 1864, five years after its designer's death, the roadway is suspended over 200 feet above the river and offers a magnificent view of the city and surrounding landscape. The National Trust-owned Avon Gorge Nature Reserve on the western side on the bridge offers some delightful walking through Leigh Woods to an Iron Age hill fort. A former snuff mill on the Clifton side has been converted to an Observatory containing a rare example of a camera obscura. A nearby passage leads to the Giant's Cave, a subterranean chamber which opens out onto a ledge high above the Avon.

Once a genteel suburb, modern CLIFTON is an attractive residential area whose elegant Georgian terraces are interspersed with stylish shops and restaurants. Clifton's Goldney House, now a university hall, is the location of a unique subterranean folly, Goldney Grotto, which dates from the 1730s. This fantastic labyrinth is filled with spectacular rock formations, foaming cascades and a marble statue of Neptune, and its walls are covered with thousands of seashells and 'Bristol diamonds', fragments of a rare quartz found in the nearby Avon Gorge. A conservation programme is restoring the chamber to its former glory. (Open most weekends between Easter and September.) Bristol Zoo Gardens are located on the northwestern edge of Clifton in Clifton Down. (Open daily, 9am to 6pm, all year round.)

Pizza Provencale, 29 Regent Street, Clifton, Bristol
Tel: 01179 741175

The appeal of pizza seems to have really taken hold of the British public, and in Regent Street you will find the ultimate pizza restaurant - the Pizza Provençale. Reminiscent of a typical

342

French pizza house, the decor has a true continental feel to it, with wooden tables, chairs and casks providing a warm, cosy atmosphere. The variety of bygone memorabilia which adorns the walls, adds to the rural air. The menu offers an excellent range of pizzas to suit every taste, and a variety of other items - baked potatoes, Provencale pancakes, bar-b-que meat dishes and pasta. All the portions are generous, and the owner, Mr Richard Geleit, assures customers that his pizzas are large, two can share a 'regular' and come away well fed! Desserts such as the Chocolate Cream Pie are gorgeous and if you want to tackle Banoffie Pie then you are in for a real treat. There is live music and singing to accompany your meal. At the time of writing, the restaurant is being extended to the rear, to accommodate a further 20 diners. The new section will have a glass roof, making the most of any British sunshine, and the decor will be in keeping with the original building. All in all, this is a great place to relax with friends.

Continuing northwestwards out of Bristol city centre, the modern suburb of HENBURY contains the remarkable early-19th-century oasis of Blaise Hamlet, a collection of nine detached stone cottages which was designed in romantic rustic style by John Nash in 1809. Each was built to a different design for the retired estate workers of the nearby Blaise Estate. (Free access to village green; cottages not open to the public.) Bristol's museum of everyday life is housed in nearby Blaise Castle House, a late-18th-century country mansion which is set within 400 acres of parkland; the exhibits include toys, costumes and household equipment. (Open Tuesdays to Sundays, 10am to 5pm, all year round; admission free.)

Blaise Castle House Museum, Henbury, Bristol Tel: 01179 506789

Also in Henbury is Vine House, a two-acre landscaped garden with a water garden and an impressive collection of trees and flowering shrubs. (Open at selected times under the National Gardens Scheme.) Nearby WESTBURY-ON-TRYM is the location of the National Trust-owned Westbury College Gatehouse, the 15th-century gatehouse of a now-demolished ecclesiastical college. (Open by arrangement with the local vicar.)

In the centre of the village you will find the unusually named Post Office Tavern. Surprisingly, the building is not a former Post

Office, but was once a coaching inn where the Royal Mail coach stopped to change horses on the London to Glasgow route. Not surprising is the decor which incorporates much Post Office related memorabilia, with prints, photographs and a red telephone box on display.

A wooden bar area with stained glass murals above is where the secret really lies. Here you will find a vast selection of real ales, reputedly the best range that you will find in the surrounding area - there are at least 12 at any one time, enough to satisfy the most dedicated of real ales fans. Traditional pub fare is available each lunch time, but in the evening everything changes. Between 5pm and 10pm it becomes a Pizzeria Inn where Pizza is the only option, although there are plenty of toppings to choose from or you could take one away!

Post Office Tavern, The Post Office, 17 Westbury Hill,
Westbury-on-Trym. Bristol Tel: 01179 401233

In a peaceful tree-lined avenue is the beautiful Victorian Mayfair Hotel, owned and personally run by Kay Heaney. The house is delightful and on you're arrival you can't help but notice the warm and welcoming atmosphere. Starting downstairs, there is a luxurious guests' sitting room furnished with antiques and adjacent to it is the cosy dining area, where evening meals can be provided by prior arrangement. There are nine spacious bedrooms and three are en-suite. To the rear of the property there is parking space for nine cars. The Mayfair is open all year round except Christmas week.

Mayfair Hotel, 5 Henleaze Road, Westbury-on-Trym, Bristol
Tel: 01179 622008

Most of today's ocean-going cargo ships are too gigantic to make it through the narrow Avon gorge to Bristol and instead, modern dock facilities have been built downstream at Avonmouth, a place of heavy industrial activity which should generally be avoided by the casual visitor. The A403 to the north of Avonmouth runs along the flat margin of the Severn estuary to SEVERN BEACH, a small resort and dormitory town which developed in the 1920s as a destination for day-trippers from Bristol. The Severn rail tunnel passes under the estuary at this point, and this is also the site of the second Severn crossing. The original Severn suspension bridge lies three miles to the north at AUST. Completed in 1966 at a cost of £8 million, this elegant toll bridge replaced the treacherous ferry crossing which had crossed this turbulent stretch of water since Roman times. The bridge carries the busy M4 across the mouth of Britain's longest river to South Wales; however, it is susceptible to high winds and is already incapable of carrying peak volumes of traffic.

On The Street in the village of OLVESTON, you will find the charming establishment, The White Hart Inn. Dating back over 300 years, The White Hart oozes character, style and class. The bar and lounge area are very 'olde worlde' and the real beams and original fireplaces give the pub a cosy, intimate air. Present owners,

345

Nigel and Sharon Wight, have been here for just a year and have great plans for development. The first is for an upstairs restaurant area, seating 35 people (opening Spring 1995). Other plans include opening up the courtyard area for drinking and dining, so this will be something to look forward to later in the year. They serve real ales here and bar food is available all the time.

The White Hart Inn, The Street, Olveston, Bristol
Tel: 01454 612175

Approximately four miles inland, the sprawling village of **ALMONDSBURY** stands beside the old ridgeway route from Bristol to Gloucester, now the A38. Despite some heavy-handed 'restoration' by the Victorians, the parish Church of St Mary retains a couple of its original Norman features: the font and the doorway in the north porch. It also has a rare lead-covered broach spire which is one of only three in southern England. One of the church windows stands as a memorial to Charles Richardson, the 19th-century engineer who designed and built the Severn tunnel. The parish is said to be frequented by a number of ghosts: the ruins of the Elizabethan mansion, Over Court, are said to be haunted by a white lady, and the local inn, the Blue Bowl, is inhabited by the spirit of a six-year-old French girl, Elizabeth Maronne, who sometimes can be heard reciting nursery rhymes in her mother tongue.

The most curious event in Almondsbury's history took place in 1817 at nearby Knole Park when a young woman turned up at the local squire's door purporting to be a kidnapped oriental princess

Goldney Grotto, Bristol

who had escaped from her captors by jumping overboard from their ship as it sailed up the Bristol Channel. Pretending to be incapable of speaking English, and abetted by a Portuguese sailor who claimed to understand her, she managed to convince the squire and his family that she was the Princess Caraboo. She was taken in, and within weeks, she was being wined and dined by fashionable Bath society. Sadly, her notoriety eventually came to the attention of her former Bristol landlady who exposed her as Mary Baker, a penniless woman from Devon. Her embarrassed hosts raised enough money to buy her a one-way ticket to Philadelphia, but she returned to Bristol some years later and continued to live there until her death in 1865.

The attractive former salmon-fishing village of OLDBURY-UPON-SEVERN lies to the north of the M4 between two great monuments to 1960's technology: the Severn bridge and the Oldbury nuclear power station. Despite its name, the settlement lies over half-a-mile from the bank of the river, an indication that the flat strip of land beside the estuary was once subject to severe flooding. The parish church stands in a superb position on top of a small hill some distance from the centre. According to local legend, repeated attempts to build the church in the village were foiled by a mysterious force which demolished the newly constructed walls during the night. A local sage then suggested that two maiden heifers should be released in the parish, and the church built on the spot they chose to graze; as a result, the building now stands on Cowhill. The church is dedicated to the martyred St Arilda, a virgin who was beheaded at nearby Kington because she refused to surrender her honour to an evil local baron. The original Norman spire collapsed in a storm in 1703, and much of the rest of the building was destroyed by fire in 1897. As a result, the present-day church is largely late-Victorian, although it contains some interesting 17th- and 18th-century monuments and table tombs. From the churchyard, there is a magnificent view across the Severn estuary to Chepstow and the Forest of Dean.

The local inn in the hamlet of SHEPPERDINE, two miles to the north, is named the Windbound after a traditional mariners' excuse. Severn bargees having one too many in the pub formed the habit of blaming their reluctance to put to sea on the local weather conditions. The practice of telling their employers they were 'windbound' eventually became so rife that the pub's name was changed from the New Inn. Despite its close proximity to a high sea wall, the combined of effects of strong winds and an exceptionally high tide can occasionally cause seawater to blow onto the roof and down the chimneys.

The Windbound Inn, Shepperdine, Bristol Tel: 01454 414343

Dating back to the 16th century, The Windbound has lost none of its original character and charm and is liberally decked out with fishing and sailing memorabilia, including a stained glass window depicting a boat in full sail. It has recently been taken over by Stan and Marj Bradburn who work hard to make all their customers feel right at home. The restaurant has an excellent menu which includes Garlic and Herb King Prawns, which is just for starters, Thai Style Chicken from the International section of the menu and trout fillets. The menu includes much, much more, with a further specials board too. Behind the bar, there is a fine selection of ales, with three real ales available, and is itself beamed and pillared, with saddleback chairs and wooden tables.

Outside you will find a children's play area, ample parking space and wonderful views of the river. Stan and Marj and their regulars pride themselves on the many charitable events they have undertaken over the years, and as a result they have raised a great deal of money for many causes. This is an establishment where you will feel very welcome, and with good food, good ale and the sight of Stan's cheery face behind the bar, what more could you want from a pub?

The bustling market town of THORNBURY lies midway between the Severn and the M5, two-and-a-half miles southeast of Oldbury. Now a prosperous dormitory settlement with many recent housing developments, its old centre still contains an unusual number of Georgian and earlier buildings. The main streets retain their medieval 'Y' pattern and converge on the old market place, a modern bottleneck standing at the junction of High Street, Castle Street and the Plane. Not far away, two giant 18th-century creatures, a lion and a swan, stare out at each other across the High Street from their positions above the doorways of the White Lion and Swan hotels, two former coaching inns which have similar front porches. Elsewhere, several prominent Victorian buildings are constructed in curious revival styles, including the registry office of 1839 with its Egyptian doorway, Doric pilasters and Georgian pediment. (There is also a neo-Renaissance bank, a neo-Gothic Methodist chapel, and a neo-Gothic street fountain.)

Thornbury was an important producer of woollen cloth in medieval times and its surprisingly large parish church reflects this early period of prosperity. It is set away from the centre in an older part of the town which was also occupied by the manor house and is a largely 14th-century Perpendicular building which incorporates parts of an earlier Norman structure. It has an impressive tower and contains a chapel dedicated to the Stafford family, the local lords-of-the-manor whose family emblem, the Stafford Knot, is much in evidence. Edward Stafford, the third Duke of Buckingham, was responsible for starting work on the adjacent Thornbury Castle in 1511. Sadly, however, he never had the chance to see it through to completion for in 1522, he was charged with high treason by Henry VIII and beheaded on London's Tower Hill. Part-castle, part-country mansion, the construction work was eventually completed in the 1850s by Anthony Salvin. The building is now run as a first-class restaurant and is not open to the general public; however a good view of it can be had from the north side of the churchyard.

The roads to the northeast of Thornbury lead over the M5 (junction 14) to the former estate village of TORTWORTH. The settlement is arranged around a broad green which is overlooked by St Leonard's Church, a part-14th-century building which was substantially remodelled by the Victorians; inside, there are some fine 15th-century stained-glass windows and a pair of canopied tombs to the Throckmorton family, former owners of the Tortworth Park estate. The famous Tortworth Chestnut can be seen in a field near the church. This massive Spanish chestnut tree was described by the 17th-century diarist, John Evelyn, as 'the great chestnut of King Stephen's time', and it was already believed to be over 600 years old when a fence was put up to protect it in 1800. At the same time, a brass plaque was erected which was inscribed with the verse:

"May man still guard thy venerable form
From the rude blasts and tempestuous storms.
Still mayest thou flourish through succeeding time
And last long last the wonder of the clime."

The tree still manages to do well, and over the centuries, its twisted lower limbs have bent to the ground and rooted (or layered) themselves, creating the impression of a small copse. Its appearance is particularly enchanting in early spring when the ground beneath is carpeted with wild snowdrops.

One-and-a-half miles to the southeast of Tortworth, the village of **CHARFIELD** lies beside the main Bristol to Birmingham railway line. The old parish churchyard lies to the south of the village at Churchend, and here can be found the common grave of fourteen unfortunate victims of a railway accident which took place early one morning in 1928. The disaster happened in thick fog when a freight train failed to clear the main line in time to allow a passenger express to pass. The express train was travelling at full speed at the time of the collision, and the force of the impact piled the carriages against the road bridge in Charfield. To make things worse, a second freight train travelling in the opposite direction crashed into the wreckage which was then set alight by exploding gas canisters. Of the fourteen victims, two who were thought to be children were never claimed by their relatives. It has been suggested that they may have been jockeys, as some were known to have been on the train, but even then, it remains a puzzle why no one made enquiries about them. For years after, however, a mysterious woman dressed in black was seen from time to time kneeling by their memorial in the churchyard.

A couple of miles to the south, the B4060 passes through **WICKWAR,** another tranquil backwater which was once an important medieval wool centre. Despite the fact that its population rarely exceeded 1000, Wickwar was once a market town with its own mayor and corporation. At one time, it could boast two breweries, and it was one of the first towns in the west of England to install electric street lighting in the 1890s, earlier even than Bristol. The curious round tower near the church stands above a vertical shaft which was built in 1841 to ventilate a half-mile-long railway tunnel which runs beneath the village. The church itself is a Victorian rebuild, except for the tower which survives from the original 15th-century structure; inside, there is a rare medieval sculpture of St John the Baptist which came from Pool House, the now-demolished Tudor manor house which once stood in parkland to the southwest. Elsewhere in Wickwar, there are an unusual number of elegant Georgian buildings, including the late 18th-century Town Hall with its distinctive bell tower and arches. The old grammar school and schoolmaster's house in the main street were built in the 1680s by Alexander Hosea, a wealthy Dick Whittington-like character who, at the age of fourteen, ran away to London to make his fortune.

A minor road to the east of Wickwar leads across the delightfully-named South Moon Ridings and on up to the crest of the Cotswold escarpment. The Hawkesbury Monument stands in a dramatic position on the brow of the hill; designed by Vulliamy in appealing Chinese style, it was erected in 1846 as a memorial to Lord Robert Somerset of nearby Badminton, an army general who fought at Waterloo. Those climbing the 145 steps to the top are rewarded with a magnificent view along the Cotswold ridge to the north and south, and across the Severn to Wales to the west.

The village of HAWKESBURY is divided into two parts; the surprisingly grand parish Church of St Mary the Virgin stands at the foot of the escarpment surrounded only by the old parsonage and a small collection of farm buildings. The scale of the church reflects the time when this large rural parish was a prosperous medieval producer of woollen cloth. Visitors entering the church through the Norman south doorway pass the charming announcement: 'It is desired that all persons that come to this church would be careful to leave their dogs at home, and that the women would not walk in with their pattens on.' (Pattens were a type of wooden clog with a raised metal under-sole which kept the wearer's feet clear of the mud.) An example of the antique footwear hangs nearby. The building is constructed in a succession of Norman and Gothic styles, and contains a number of impressive monuments to the Jenkins family, the earls of Liverpool. Nearby Hawkesbury Manor, their now-demolished family home, was the setting for a tragic 17th-century story of forbidden love when the daughter of Protestant Sir Robert Jenkins' fell in love with a member of the Catholic Paston family of Horton Manor. The couple were forced to part, and as her lover rode away, the young Miss Jenkins waved her final farewell from a top floor window and toppled to her death. The other part of the village, Hawkesbury Upton, stands high above on the ridge and is a fine example of a Cotswold village, grey and windswept in bad weather, yet transformed into an idyllic community of stone-built cottages and country inns when the sun shines.

Back at the foot of the escarpment, the long ribbon-like village of HORTON lies a mile-and-a-half to the south of Hawkesbury church. The National Trust-owned Horton Court lies on the northeastern edge of the village. This graceful Cotswold-stone manor house is largely Tudor and was built for William Knight, the royal ambassador who was given the task of presenting Henry VIII's case to the Pope when the King was attempting to divorce Catherine of Aragon. The building contains many quirky Renaissance features which were inspired by the ambassador's travels in Europe. One of the finest is a covered walkway, or ambulatory, which is detached from the main house and is thought to have been modelled on a Roman cloister. Prior to its Tudor rebuilding, Horton Court had been the official residence of a prosperous ecclesiastical estate which was founded in Norman times. The remarkable early-12th-century great hall survives from this period, although a number of alterations, including the insertion of windows and a dividing floor, were made throughout the centuries. In 1884, the hall was restored to something resembling its original state, and it and the ambulatory are open to the public on Wednesdays and Saturdays, 2pm to 6pm between late March and end of October. The attractive little Church of St James stands next to Horton Court; heavily restored in 1865, it was built between the 14th and 16th centuries and still retains many of its original features. Inside, there's a remodelled Norman font and a number of memorials to the Paston family, the local lords of the manor during Jacobean times. The church, along with the manor house and nearby farmstead, create an archetypal English scene.

A mile-and-a-half to the south of Horton, the pleasant hamlet of LITTLE SODBURY stands on a slope below the great Iron Age hill fort from which the settlement takes its name. The church, the only one in Britain dedicated to St Adeline, was built in Victorian times to replace one which stood further up the hill near Little Sodbury Manor. This privately-owned manor house was built in Tudor times for Sir John Walsh, and Henry VIII and Anne Boleyn are reputed to have stayed here whilst en route to Bristol in 1535. Despite being extensively remodelled in 1919, the early 15th-century great hall with its impressive open-timbered roof remains, along with a number of other features from an earlier Elizabethan renovation. William Tyndale, the first translator of the New Testament into English, served as a chaplain and tutor to the Walshe family during the 1520s. Tyndale chose to bypass the approved Latin texts and use original Greek and Hebrew sources, a choice which eventually led to his death at the stake in 1535. In a presumably unrelated incident, the house was struck by a massive lighting strike in 1556; the bolt killed one boy outright, and seven other people died from shock within two months.

On the opposite side of the Iron Age hill fort, one mile to the south, the village of OLD SODBURY stands on a loop off the busy A432. Despite some intrusive modern residential development, it has a good part-Norman church which contains three exceptional monuments: one is a carved stone effigy of a 13th-century knight who is almost covered by his shield; the second is a wooden effigy of another knight which was carved at Bristol in the late-14th-century and is one of only five of its type still in existence; and the third is to David Harley, the Georgian diplomat who negotiated the treaty which ended the American War of Independence. The churchyard stands on a mound above the village and offers some dramatic views of the surrounding landscape. The castellated tower to the east stands over a vertical shaft and is one of a series built to ventilate a two-and-a-half mile long tunnel which carries the main London-South Wales line through the Cotswold escarpment. Opened in 1903, the tunnel required its own brick-making works and took over five years to complete.

The famous Badminton Park estate lies within a couple of miles of the eastern end of the tunnel, and indeed a railway station known as Badminton once stood near the village of Acton Turville. The estate was founded by Edward Somerset, the wily son of the unfortunate Marquis of Worcester who spent most of his vast family fortune supporting the Royalist cause of Charles I. After denouncing Catholicism and allying himself to Oliver Cromwell, Edward later championed the restoration of Charles II and was created the Duke of Beaufort for his pains. A striking 25 foot monument to the first Duke can be seen in the little church which adjoins the main house; it was originally installed in St George's chapel, Windsor, but was removed to make space for a memorial to Queen Victoria's father.

The central section of Badminton House dates from the 1680s and contains some exceptional lime-wood carving by Grinling Gibbons. The remainder is largely mid-18th-century and was designed by William Kent, an architect of the Palladian school who was also responsible for landscaping the grounds and erecting the many impressive gateways and follies which litter the estate. Each year in April, the park is the venue for the famous Badminton Horse Trials, an international three-day event which attracts participants and spectators from all over the world.

A former duke and his guests are reputed to have devised the game of badminton in the entrance hall of the house during a weekend party in the 1860s. Having decided to play indoor tennis, they wanted to avoid damaging the paintings on the walls, and so came up with the idea of using a cork studded with feathers in place of a ball. Badminton Park stands between the twin estate villages of Great and Little Badminton; the former contains and a handsome row of early-18th-century almshouses which carry the brand of their benefactors, the Beauforts, and the latter is set around an attractive village green which has a medieval dovecote at its centre and is overlooked by a small part-13th-century church.

The former market town of CHIPPING SODBURY lies on the A432, a couple of miles to the west of Old Sodbury. One of the earliest examples of town planning in Britain, the settlement was laid out in the 12th-century in narrow strips on either side of the broad main street. Although the market has long since disappeared, the main street, which is wide enough for cars to park end-on, remains a pleasant concoction of 17th- to 19th-century buildings which display a variety of architectural styles and building materials. The part-13th-century church is unusually large and reflects the town's early prosperity as a medieval weaving and market centre. After a century-long period of decline, the second half of the 20th-century has seen some rapid development, both in Chipping Sodbury and nearby Yate, communities which are now virtually joined together by a series of modern housing estates which have been thrown up to cope with the population overspill from Bristol and Bath.

Le Rendezvous Restaurant, 1 Horse Street, Chipping Sodbury, Bristol Tel: 01454 312186

In a book entitled 'The Hidden Places', **Le Rendezvous Restaurant** seems an appropriate setting for a romantic dinner. The owners, Anna and Ken Hutchings, have made this a very special restaurant, with much attention to detail and a real knowledge of how to please people. Anna should know, as she has been involved with Le Rendezvous for over ten years. She started out working in the restaurant, and then she and Ken bought it in 1990. Credit must go to them for providing excellent service in a very relaxed atmosphere.

The restaurant is lovely, with the building dating back to the 16th century. Once a set of cottages, it has served as a tea room and an antique shop in its time. The menu and wine list is superb, and Anna will happily cater for parties and other functions. Dishes range from Frog's Legs for a starter, to a variety of classic meat and fish dishes, so even the heartiest appetite can be whetted. Only the freshest produce is used and for those of you on a slightly tighter budget, Bistro-style meals are available on Wednesdays, Thursdays and Fridays, when Anna likes to experiment and go Continental! Even if you are not staying in the immediate vicinity, we can definitely recommend this as a place worth making a detour for.

A lane to the south of Old Sodbury leads to Dodington House, another in the string of country mansions which lie along the base of the Cotswolds escarpment. The 700 acre estate was acquired in the 16t -century by the Codrington family when the previous owner exhausted all his funds building himself an extravagant stately home. A century and a half later, Capability Brown was brought in to landscape the grounds, and he is responsible for the bold vistas, lakes and the small castellated Gothic structure now known as the Cascade Building. The present house was built between 1796 and 1816 on the site of its Elizabethan predecessor and was intended to be one of the great houses of its day. It was designed with three fronts in lavish neo-Roman style by the celebrated classical architect, James Wyatt. Its exterior is a satisfying mixture of pilasters, pediments and porticos, although the interior, with its overabundance of gilt, marble and brass, may be considered a little over-the-top by present-day standards. An elegant curved conservatory connects the house to the little private Church of St Mary, another Wyatt creation designed in the shape of a Greek cross. (Sadly, the architect never saw his work through to fruition as he was killed in a carriage accident in 1813, three years before the house was completed.) Dodington now offers a variety of ancillary attractions, including a carriage collection in the stables, an adventure playground, and an exhibition of early maps, deeds and architectural plans. (Open daily, 11am to 6pm between Easter and end-September.)

In the village of CODRINGTON, only 4 miles from Chipping Sodbury, is another hidden gem - The Codrington Arms. Judging by the custom this pub receives, and its recent award from the Bristol Evening News, Pub Food of the Year 1994, it has already been discovered by some. Built in 1722 the pub was built for, and owned by the Codrington family who were wealthy landowners of the time. Although much has changed over the years it has retained its wonderful character, style and charm. André and Liz,

Bristol Harbour

your hosts, came here 4 years ago and through much hard work have turned the place into a first class establishment. The Codrington Arms is renowned for its varied menu and delicious home-cooked food and in addition there are numerous daily specials. The inn can seat about 100 people, and with its low, beamed ceilings and bygone memorabilia, wherever you sit you'll feel cosy and at home. Behind the bar, there are always 4 or 5 real ales one tap, of which one will be a local brew! You'll go a long way to equal the sheer delight of this establishment.

The Codrington Arms, Codrington, Bristol Tel: 01454 313145

After crossing the M4, the A46 to the south of Dodington passes close to the site of a momentous battle which took place between the Saxons and the Britons in the 6th-century. According to the Anglo-Saxon Chronicle, three British kings were killed in the encounter which paved the way for the Saxon occupation of Bath, Cirencester, Gloucester and much of rural West England. On the slope of the Cotswold ridge, one mile to the southwest, the National Trust-owned property of Dyrham Park will be recognisable to some as the setting for the film starring Anthony Hopkins and Emma Thompson, The Remains Of The Day. This striking baroque mansion was built at the turn of the 18th century for William Blathwayt, a career civil servant and diplomat who rose to become the Secretary of State to William III. The building was in fact constructed in two lateral 'slices': the first, which includes the west front and faces down the valley, was designed by the Huguenot Samuel Hauduroy and completed around 1696, and the second, which includes the stable-block, orangery and elegant many-windowed east front, was designed by William Talman, a deputy of Sir Christopher Wren, and completed around 1710. The remarkably unaltered interior contains many fixtures and artefacts which the original owner accumulated during his postings to Holland and North America, including an assortment of rare Dutch paintings and a magnificent collection of blue and white Delft pottery. Indeed, the Netherlands connection continues with the recent naming of a Dutch flame tulip, 'Dyrham Park'. (Open daily except Thursdays and Fridays, 12 noon to 5pm between late-March and end-October.)

The west front looks out across a charming terrace to the lawned gardens which at one time were laid out in formal Dutch style. These were in place until the end of the 18th century when the fashion for sweeping tracts of parkland came in and encroached upon the earlier formality. Much of the 263 acre estate is now stocked with fallow deer, an apparent reversion to its ancient use (the name Dyrham is the Saxon term for 'deer enclosure'). A charming little church stands on a terrace overlooking the garden a few yards from the house. A largely 15th-century structure with 13th-century parts, it contains a Norman font, a fine 15th-century monumental brass, and a number of impressive memorials to members of the Wynter and Blathwayt families.

Situated in the tiny, sleepy village of HINTON, The Bull Inn was built as a farm in 1544 and did not become a pub until 1650. Although the inn has been brought up to date regarding its facilities, it still retains its old character, with beamed ceilings, inglenook fireplaces and stone floors. The pub is conveniently located only 2 miles from the M4, but because of its great situation you feel like you are miles from anywhere.

The old milking parlour and creamery have been tastefully converted into the Bull Ring restaurant, seating up to 50 people. An à la carte menu is available each day with a carvery on Sundays. The food is delicious, and in addition to the set menus, there are daily blackboard specials. The restaurant can get busy, so booking is advisable at weekends. To the rear of the pub is another room, called The Pantry, where small meetings and functions can be held. The bar and lounge areas are cosy and are decorated with lots of bygone memorabilia. There are always at least three real ales on offer - Wadworths 6X, Bass and Henry's IPA are permanent fixtures - with regular guests ales. The excellent standard of the ales is such that The Bull Inn features in the Good Beer Guide. Set in 4 acres of its own land, the pub also has an attractive beer garden and plenty of off-road parking. A warm welcome awaits you in this traditional English pub, and it is a real hidden gem.

The Bull Inn, Hinton, Dyrham, Nr. Chippenham
Tel: 01179 372332

Three miles to the southeast, the A420 skirts around the old market town of MARSHFIELD. Although it's hard to imagine today, during the 14th-century this was the fourth wealthiest town in Gloucestershire after Bristol, Gloucester and Cirencester, thanks to its thriving malt and wool industries. Now, it is little more than a village, although it possesses a long and interesting main street which is lined with handsome buildings of the 17th- and 18th-centuries, an era when Marshfield was an important stop on the old coaching route between Bristol and London. Of particular note are the almshouses of 1619 founded by Elias Crispe, the Tolzey market hall of 1690 which was rebuilt in 1793, and the two early-18th-century coaching inns, both of which have shell-hooded doorways. The handsome part-Norman parish church was substantially rebuilt in the 15th-century; inside there is a fine Jacobean pulpit and some good 17th- and 18th-century monuments.

Each year on Boxing Day, the main street is taken over by the Marshfield Mummers, a troupe of seven players who perform a unique piece of street theatre with origins going back to pagan times. This unique celebration was revived in the 1930s by the local vicar after an interval of over fifty years and is based on the ancient themes of fertility and good versus evil. The characters go by such wonderful names as 'Doctor Phoenix', 'Saucy Jack' and 'King William, a man of courage and bold', and the action includes such set pieces as the death of winter and the rebirth of spring. The performers wear wonderful shaggy costumes made from strips of newspaper and are accompanied around the streets by a town crier wearing a top hat with a bright yellow band. An interesting folk museum can be found approximately one mile to the north at Castle Farm, a working farm which is open to the public during the summer months.

A twisting lane to the south of Marshfield leads through a delightful Southwolds valley to the scattered hamlet of ST CATHERINE'S. A surprisingly tranquil place without any real centre, it was once a monastic village and still retains a classic trio of medieval buildings: church, tithe barn and manor house. The church is largely late-15th-century and contains an impressive stained-glass window of that date, the four lights of which depict the Virgin Mary, the Crucifixion, St John and St Peter. The privately-owned great manor house, St Catherine's Court, is a former grange which once belonged to the Benedictine priory at Bath; although predominantly 19th-century mock-Tudor, the entire north front is genuine 16th-century. The landscape around St Catherine is exceptionally pleasant and provides some excellent walking.

On the opposite side of the A46, two miles to the west, a lane leads up from the village of LANGRIDGE onto the top of Lansdown, the site of the famous English Civil War battle of 1643. Despite the encounter ending in a Parliamentarian withdrawal, the Royalist commander, Sir Bevil Grenville, was mortally wounded and died later at the rectory in nearby Cold Ashton. A monument erected in 1720 stands at the place he is believed to have fallen. Throughout the summer season, flat races are held at Bath racecourse on the southern edge of Lansdown, approximately one mile to the south.

Without doubt, one of the most evocative smells for many is the distinctive combination of coal dust and steam, and if the chugging of an engine and the clanking of carriage wheels puts you in an reminiscent mood, then the place to go is Bitton Station at WILLSBRIDGE, between Bristol and Bath. The Avon Valley Railway provides a fascinating day out that the whole family are sure to enjoy.

Avon Valley Railway

The original railway, which ran from Mangotsfield to Bath, opened in 1869 as part of the Midland Railway. The line saw healthy traffic until the 1950's when the widespread use of the motor car led to declining passenger figures - it was finally closed down in 1972. Attempts were made to reopen the line for weekend tourist traffic, but the track was removed in 1973 which appeared to spell the end of the line. From the early preservation attempts came the Bristol Suburban Railway Society, the forerunner of the Avon Valley Railway. They took over Bitton Station, which was in very poor condition, and with a volunteer workforce rebuilt the station, re-laid the track and restored locomotives and rolling stock enabling a train service to be operated once again to the next station to the North, Oldland Common.

Today, the hard work of these volunteers continues, and at the same time brings pleasure to the many visitors to the railway but their work goes on. In August 1994 the first stage of a southern extension was opened, part of a grand plan to 'Return Steam to the Avon Valley'. This three stage plan has the aim of extending the railway firstly as far as the River Avon, and eventually to the outskirts of Bath. This would give the Avon Valley Railway a total length of five and a half miles, allowing passengers to enjoy a respectable train ride. Car parks would enable the railway to offer people a pleasant way to reach the recreational facilities of the Avon Valley without the need to bring more cars into the area.

These plans require considerable amounts of money - the volunteers may give their service free of charge, but the track materials for the second stage alone will cost in excess of £40,000. All the entrance fees, and profits from the sale of souvenirs are re-invested in the railway, so why not bring the family for a fun day out, and help to recreate history.

Avon Valley Railway, Bitton Railway Station, Willsbridge,
Bristol Tel: 01179 327296

Bath to Weston-Super-Mare

Roman Baths, Bath

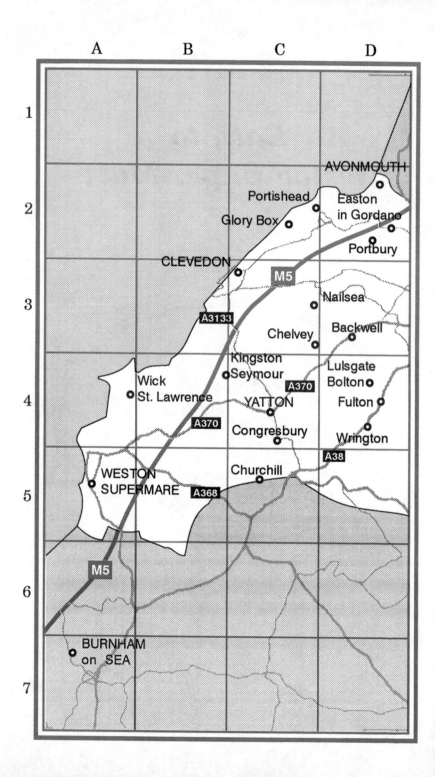

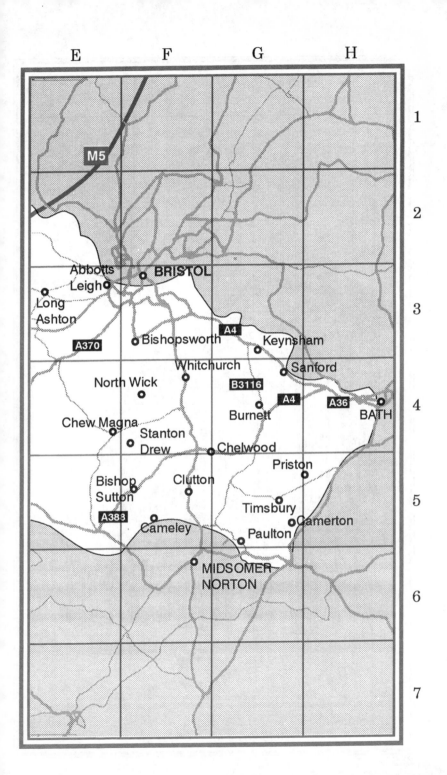

Holbourne Museum, Bath

CHAPTER TWELVE

Bath to Weston-Super-Mare

BATH is one of the most remarkable cities in Britain. It is a glorious assembly of architectural set-pieces and less spectacular buildings which have been constructed since the time of the ancient Romans around the only thermal springs in the country. Since time immemorial, over half a million gallons of water a day have bubbled to the surface here at a constant temperature of 46°C.

The Celts believed that the mysterious steaming spring which emerged from within a great curve of the River Avon was the domain of the goddess Sulis, and it is likely that they were aware of its healing properties long before the arrival of the Romans in 43AD. However, it was the new arrivals who first enclosed the spring and created the spectacular health resort known as Aquae Sulis, a name coined as a diplomatic gesture to the local population they now controlled; indeed the temple adjoining the baths was dedicated to the joint goddess, Sulis-Minerva, to embody both the Celtic and Roman ideologies.

With the possible exception of Hadrian's Wall, the great Roman baths are the most outstanding monument to the Roman Empire to survive in Britain. After remaining buried under seven feet of mud for centuries, they were only rediscovered in the late 19th century and indeed, their full extent didn't become apparent until the 1920s. (Ironically, they had remained hidden throughout the whole of Bath's 18th-century renaissance as a spa town.)

The complex of buildings which can be visited today is centred around the Great Bath, a lead-lined rectangular pool which is surrounded by steps and the truncated remains of a colonnaded quadrangle.

Five separate phases were constructed over a 200-year period which began in the middle of the 1st century and included the building of swimming pools, mineral baths and a series of chambers heated by underfloor air ducts which would have functioned as saunas and Turkish baths.

By the 3rd century, Bath had become so renowned that high-ranking soldiers and officials were coming here from all over the Roman Empire; public buildings, such as a temple and forum, were added, and the whole city enclosed behind a stone wall. However, by the year 410, the Empire was crumbling and the last remaining legions were forced to return to Rome. Bath was abandoned, and within a few decades the drainage systems failed, the marsh returned, and the bath complex was engulfed by alluvial mud below which it lay entombed until the 1870s. The excavated remains of the Roman baths are now open to the public, along with a fascinating museum of Roman coins, artefacts, jewellery, and perhaps the finest exhibit of all, a bronze head of the goddess Sulis Minerva. (Open daily, 9am to 6pm, all year round.)

The population of Bath fell away during the dark ages, and it wasn't until the 8th century that the Saxons founded a nunnery here which put the settlement back on the map. This was later elevated to monastic status when King Edgar of Wessex (he claimed to be 'king of all England') chose to be crowned here in 973. The present great church of Bath abbey was begun in 1499 after its Norman predecessor had been destroyed by fire. However, the new building wasn't finished before Henry VIII's Dissolution of the Monasteries of 1539 halted work. The building then remained without a roof for three-quarters of a century and indeed, it wasn't fully completed until 1901.

With its soaring buttresses, spiky ramparts and vast windows of clear glass, the present-day abbey is considered the ultimate example of English Perpendicular church architecture.

Its delicate stone fan-vaulting hangs 70 feet above the nave, and its curious castellated tower is rectangular rather than square because it was built using the pillar-foundations of the previous building. Inside, there is an unusual 18th-century oak font which can be moved from one place to another, and an astonishing number of monuments and tablets, more than in any church outside Westminster abbey. Many of these were erected in memory of the wealthy invalids who flocked here in the 18th- and early-19th-centuries and who sadly found themselves unable to flock away again.

Tucked away on North Passage in the heart of Bath not far from the Abbey, is real gem called **Tilleys Bistro**. The Bistro is housed in a building that dates back to the 15th century and has four floors. Run by a team of four, Dave Mott and Pete Goswell are the chefs while Dawn Mott and Will Baber look after the front of house. The building was derelict when they took it over three years ago, but they have managed to turn it into an elegant and stylish establishment that is one of the best in the city. The basement is full of character retaining many original features like the exposed brickwork, slab stone floors and two huge inglenook fireplaces. Food is served here, and on the ground floor where the door to the kitchen is always open. The menu offers plenty of variety, and there is a completely separate vegan and vegetarian menu, which is worth looking over even if you aren't vegetarian or vegan, as it sounds so delicious. The first floor comprises a comfortable lounge bar for a drink before or after your meal. The restaurant is open Monday to Saturday, 12pm - 3pm and 6.30pm - 11pm, and Sunday 6.30pm - 10.30pm. It can get busy so booking ahead is advisable.

Tilleys Bistro, 3 North Parade Passage, Bath Tel: 01225 484200

One tablet in the abbey stands as a memorial to Richard 'Beau' Nash, a legendary Bath figure who was one of the three people generally considered to be responsible for creating the fashionable Georgian spa town. Prior to Nash's arrival in the first decade of the 1700s, Bath had been a squalid community of around two thousand inhabitants whose former prosperity as a medieval wool town had all but disappeared. Historical accounts tell of domestic animals roaming freely within the confines of the old Roman town and sewage running down the streets. Notwithstanding, small numbers of the rich and aristocratic continued to be attracted to Bath for its curative hot spring, and in the mid 17th century, the corporation finally took action to improve sanitary conditions, an initiative which was rewarded in 1702 by a visit from Queen Anne.

Nash, a man of great elegance and style, took on the job of cleaning up the city. Despite having been something of a reprobate himself – he had been a modest failure at Oxford, in the Guards and as a lawyer, and only came to Bath in an attempt to earn his living as a gambler – he rose to become Bath's Master of Ceremonies, an unpaid, yet highly influential position to which he ascended when the previous MC was killed in a duel. He pressurised the authorities into paving, cleaning and lighting the streets, he outlawed duelling and the wearing of swords, and he set about creating a relaxed social atmosphere in which the gentry (the landed middle-class) could mix on equal terms with their social superiors (the aristocracy). Under his guidance, Bath became elegant and fashionable, and soon began to attract significant numbers of the 'right people', not only patrons, but also the architects and entrepreneurs who shared Nash's grand vision for the city.

Among them were the architect John Wood who, along with his son (also called John), was responsible for designing most of the city's finest neoclassical squares and terraces. These include North and South Parades, Queen Square, The Circus, and most notably, Royal Crescent, John Wood the Younger's Palladian masterpiece which was the first terrace in Britain to be built to an elliptical design. Bath's third 18th-century founding father was Ralph Allen, an entrepreneur who made his first fortune developing an efficient postal system for the provinces and who then went on to make a second one as the owner of the local quarries which supplied most of the honey-coloured Bath-stone to the city's Georgian building sites.

One of Chaucer's most colourful characters in his Canterbury Tales was the Wife of Bath, and here in the city you can discover her namesake! The Wife of Bath can be found on Pierrepont Street, but you will have to keep a sharp eye out for this restaurant, which is at No.12 down in the basement. It was converted from the three cellars of a building that was built around 1740 on the site of the Abbey Orchard. Mr and Mrs Ensom have been here for the past 24 years in the same type of business, but the restaurant only took its present name three years ago.

The Wife of Bath has certainly lost none of her charm and character over the years! It is beautifully decorated, with a magnificent feature mirror which immediately draws your attention. In addition to the seating inside there is a small patio area, perfect for sitting out on a sunny day or warm summer's evening. The restaurant can cater for up to 80 people, and is very popular with locals and visitors who are just passing through. The menu offers a large variety of dishes with a good range of vegetarian food. You could try the Shellfish au Gratin containing fresh prawns, cockles and mussels or perhaps the Madeira and Mushroom Pasta, a vegetarian option that will appeal to all! There is plenty to choose from by way of drinks to accompany your meal, including wines, cocktails, draught beers, Elderflower Pressé and Malvern Spring Water. This is definitely a restaurant to seek out when you are visiting the city.

The Wife of Bath, 12 Pierrepont Street, Bath Tel: 01225 461745

The best way to explore central Bath is on foot, and good place to start is at the Roman baths, whose adjoining Pump Room looks much as it did when it was completed in 1796. The internal fittings include two sedan chairs, one of which was used as a public taxi by the idle or infirm. The room is filled with tables and chairs, and here a restorative cup of tea, coffee or spa water can still be enjoyed

373

to the soothing accompaniment of live chamber music. To the northeast lies the abbey and beyond it, the magnificent Pulteney Bridge, the only example of the work of Robert Adam in Bath. Inspired by Florence's Ponte Vecchio, it is the only bridge in Britain to incorporate a terrace of buildings.

The Moon and Sixpence, 6a Broad Street, Bath Tel: 01225 469062

In the heart of the city, just off Broad Street, you will find a very pleasant restaurant called The Moon and Sixpence, where diners can sit and eat inside or out from 12 to 2.30pm daily. The interior is a wine bar with the dining area in the conservatory, a lovely bright room with plenty of cane furniture and marble tables which lends an almost Parisian atmosphere. Outside, the secluded courtyard is lavishly decorated with tubs and flowering shrubs and a little dancing fountain - quite enchanting! The restaurant is also open in the evening from 5.30 to 10.30 (last orders) and until 11pm on Friday and Saturday. Upstairs there is a lovely room, with wood panelled walls to one side and exposed brickwork to the other. The staircase and lighting upstairs are remarkable too, but rather than going into detail, why not discover it for yourself! Having said all this, don't let the atmosphere of this exceptional restaurant carry you away from your main purpose, because the food is excellent. With such delights as Salmon wrapped in filo pastry with ginger in a butter, shallot and tomato sauce, you will really enjoy choosing your meal. Despite the elegance of the surroundings and the extensive menu, the Moon and Sixpence is very reasonably priced and should suit most pockets.

Straying further from the area once enclosed by Roman walls, Gay Street to the north leads (appropriately) through Queen Square to the Circus, a superb neoclassical set piece divided into three blocks of eleven houses. The street leading off to the northeast leads to the National Trust-owned Assembly Rooms, one of the places where a polite 18th-century society congregated to dance, play cards, or just be seen. After having been severely damaged by World War II bombs, the building was reopened in 1963 and now incorporates an interesting Museum of Costume. (Open daily, 9.30am to 6pm, all year round.)

Friendly informality and good food make the perfect combination for an enjoyable meal, and this is just what you will find at the Beaujolais Restaurant in Chapel Row. This five storey Georgian building is conveniently situated close to the Theatre Royal, and offers the best of French cuisine in a suitably continental atmosphere. The restaurant area features wooden floors and the decor and lighting make it bright and airy during the day, and warm and intimate in the evening. Small functions can be catered for upstairs, in a beautiful candlelit room which seems to have changed little since it was built, with wooden panelled walls and an original fireplace. You can also dine in the small rear garden during the day or on a warm summer's evening.

Beaujolais Restaurant, 5 Chapel Row, Bath Tel: 01225 423417

The menu changes daily, depending on what's in season at the time, and all the produce is fresh. Picking just a couple of item from the menu at random, how about chilled asparagus salad with quails

375

eggs and a sweet onion mustard? Or in true French style, a Bouillabaisse, which is crammed full of John Dory, cod and bream, and cooked in crab and fish soup - absolutely superb! Quite apart from the menu itself, there is plenty to catch the eye. The front window is engulfed with wine corks, and saucy postcards and erotic drawings and lamp stands adorn the walls. Everything at The Beaujolais seems larger than life, including owner-chefs Philippe Wall and Jean-Pierre Auge, who have devoted the past 22 years to making this a wonderful place to eat, chat, relax, and most of all, have a good time. Open for lunch 12 to 2, Monday to Saturday, and Friday, Saturday and Sunday evenings from 7pm.

The street leading west from the Circus leads to Royal Crescent where No. 1 has been acquired by the Bath Preservation Trust and restored to its original Georgian splendour. Now designated a World Heritage Building, it is open on Tuesdays to Sundays, 10.30am to 5pm between 1 March and mid-December.

The Royal Crescent is popularly regarded as the climax of the Palladian achievement in this most classical of English cities. It is the culmination of a grand plan which takes you from Queen Square, designed by John the Elder in the 1730s up Gay Street to The Circus and then along Brock Street to the Royal Crescent itself. The Circus was begun by John Wood the Elder but completed after his death by his son, John Wood the Younger, who went on to design the Royal Crescent.

The Royal Crescent was built between 1767 and 1774 in a style which is both majestic and conservative. The huge sweep of the Crescent comprises 30 houses of three or four bays, each of which are divided by a giant Ionic half column. Although Wood made it clear that there should be no variation in the external treatment of the Royal Crescent, there is an enormous variety in the internal arrangement and decoration of the individual houses.

The Crescent when first built looked out over unspoilt countryside which was later developed as part of the expanding 19th century city. At the beginning of the last century many of the windows in the Crescent were enlarged and glazing bars replaced by plate glass windows.

Number One, however, provides you with the opportunity to see how the correctly proportioned windows would have been before these changes. It was scrupulously restored by the Bath

Royal Crescent, Bath

Preservation Trust in the late 1960s, both outside and in, and subsequently opened to the public in 1970.

A flight of steps leads you over a bridge, which crosses the basement area and into the house through the main door. Rooms of the ground floor and first floor have been decorated and furnished to show you as accurately as possible how a late 18th century Bath house might have appeared.

No.1 Royal Crescent, 1 Royal Crescent, Bath
Tel: 01225 428126 Fax: 01225 481850

The dining room, on the left as you enter, has a mid-Georgian table laid for dessert and on the walls hang an interesting selection of 18th century portraits.

After dinner the gentlemen of the house might have retired to the Study - found on the right of the entrance hall - and here a decanter of port, playing cards on the card table, and a clay pipe and twist of tobacco, set the scene in the room, which also has some particularly fine Chippendale furniture.

In contrast to the masculinity of the Study, upstairs on the left, is the Bedroom. Here, femininity takes over, from the pretty floral hangings of the four poster bed to the gathered muslin dressing table. The room also has a secret door - the jib door - leading to the back stairs, for the maid to bring hot water, coals or her mistress's dresses or refreshments. Opposite is the drawing room, the most elaborately decorated room in the House with elegant furniture including a fine English fortepiano. Music can be heard in the room giving extra pleasure as one looks out at the superb view of the

378

Crescent. The basement houses the kitchen and a highly popular museum shop. There is an admission charge and special tours are available by arrangement.

Although the façades of Bath's Georgian houses were strictly controlled, the designs of the rear portions were left to the discretion of their owners, many of whom had their own very individual ideas. An inspection of this half-hidden world reveals a fascinating network of narrow alleys, tradespeople's entrances and eccentric guttering. The streets and buildings of the city are said to be inhabited by an unusual number of ghosts, the most renowned of which are the Grey Lady, whose characteristic jasmine scent has been detected around the Theatre Royal and nearby Garrick's Head inn, and the Black-hatted Man, who is said to appear in and around the Assembly Rooms. A guided 'ghost walk' departs from the Garrick's Head each evening at 8pm throughout the summer months.

Bath also contains an unusual number of specialist museums and galleries. The Victoria Art Gallery near Pulteney Bridge is the city's principal venue for major touring exhibitions; there is also a permanent collection of classic paintings and a smaller gallery displaying work from the area. (Open Mondays to Saturdays, 10am to 5.30pm, all year round; admission free.) The British Folk Art Collection, formerly the Museum of English Naive Art, in the Paragon is an exceptional collection of 18th- and 19th-century paintings which show 'a direct simplicity'. (Open Tuesdays to Sundays, 10.30am (2pm Sundays) to 5pm between 1 April and 31 October.) On the same site is the Building of Bath Museum, a fascinating display of models and illustrations which bring to life the city's unique architectural evolution. (Open Tuesday to Sundays, 10.30am to 5pm, between 1 March and mid-December.)

Bath seems particularly well favoured with unusual museums and one other that can be recommended is the Holburne Museum and Crafts Study Centre. Historic collections of fine and decorative art and 20th century craft collections are displayed together in a lovely 18th century house and garden at the end of Great Pulteney Street.

The nucleus of the original collection was formed in Bath by Sir Thomas William Holburne, a Victorian collector of some note and a lender to the great mid-19th century exhibitions at London and

Leeds. First opened in 1893, the Museum owes its foundation to Holburne's sister, Mary Anne Barbara, who wished to establish a memorial to the family name. The Crafts Study Centre opened at the Museum in 1977, the result of discussions among a group of craftsmen and educationalists who wanted to establish a centre where work of some of the best British makers could be seen.

Today, the superb collections consist chiefly of 17th and 18th century silver, paintings by Grand Masters, including Turner, Gainsborough and Stubbs, miniatures, porcelain, maiolica, bronzes and furniture. 20th century collections contain ceramics, woven and printed textiles, calligraphy and furniture. These are complemented by a lively programme of temporary exhibitions, special events and lectures. Nobody with a love of arts and fine craftsmanship should miss the opportunity of visiting this fascinating place.

Holburne Museum and Crafts Study Centre, Great Pulteney Street, Bath Tel: 01225 466669

The first known mailing of a Penny Black postage stamp was made in 1840 at No. 8 Broad Street, now the site of the Bath Postal Museum; exhibits include a reconstruction of a Victorian sorting office and a children's activity room. (Open Mondays to Saturdays (also Sunday afternoons in summer), 11am to 5pm, all year round.) Sally Lunn's House in North Parade Passage claims to be the oldest house in Bath; the cellar museum contains the ancient kitchen used by the celebrated 17th-century cook who invented the bun which carries her name. (Open daily, 10am to 6pm, all year round.)

The Bath Industrial Heritage Centre in Julian Road is a re-creation of an aerated water manufactory which provides an insight into the city's traditional industries. (Open daily, 10am to 5pm between Easter and 31 October, plus weekends in winter.)

Just a few minutes walk from the city centre, you will find The Bear - a hearty pub with friendly hosts and a good line in local chat. The regulars and visitors alike are obviously quite at home, sampling one or two of the ales from the vast range available, all of which are kept in superb condition by your hosts, Gordon and Julie Wright. The pub is open all day, six days a week with normal Sunday opening hours. Food is served lunch time and evening and there is an excellent range of dishes on offer. Whatever you choose, the food is delicious with good sized portions, and all very reasonably priced. You can take your meal in either the cosy and comfortable restaurant area where there is a non-smoking section, or in the public bar.

The public bar is alive with local characters and without doubt you will soon be drawn into the conversation. In this area you can also play pool, darts, listen to the latest music and at weekends enjoy live bands. A welcome is assured and with that going hand in hand with excellent ale and delicious food, what else could you wish for?

The Bear, 6 Wellsway, Bath Tel: 01225 425795

On the northern edge of the city, Lansdown Road leads up to the summit of Lansdown, the location of one the most remarkable follies in Britain. Beckford's Tower was built in the 1820s for the wealthy and eccentric scholar, William Beckford, to house his extensive collection of works of art. The pavilion and bell tower are a wonderful mixture of Tuscan, Roman, Greek and Byzantine influences, and the lantern at the top is an adaptation of the Lysicrates monument in Athens. Visitors climbing the 156 steps to the belvedere are rewarded with a magnificent view stretching from the Black Mountains of Wales to the Wiltshire Downs. There is also a small museum charting Beckford's extraordinary life through pictures, prints and models. (Open Saturdays, Sundays and Bank Holiday Mondays, 2pm to 5pm between early-April and end-October.)

Bloomfield House, 146 Bloomfield Road, Bath Tel: 01225 420105

The outskirts of the city of Bath is the location of the impressive Bloomfield House. The house dates back to the early 1800s. It is now a Grade II listed building of special Architectural and Historical interest and has been fully restored, retaining most of the original features yet providing every modern luxury. The decor is impressive, with many beautiful murals and the furnishings have been carefully chosen to complement their surroundings. The bedrooms, of which there are 8, are equally luxurious. All feature canopied or four poster beds, antique furniture, and the views across the city are wonderful too. Even the en-suite bathrooms are appropriate to the period with mahogany panelling and polished brass fittings. Your hosts are Bridget and Malcolm Cox, and they have created an exceedingly high quality establishment which also features in many other guides - Johansens, The Best Good Bed and

Breakfast Guide and others. Treat yourself to a touch of luxury and give this one a try.

Another curious folly, Sham Castle, was built on a hill to the east of the city by the quarry-owner Ralph Allen to be seen from his town house. As its name suggests, it is merely a romantic façade which is made even more picturesque by nighttime illumination. Later in his career, Allen moved out to an ostentatious country mansion on the southeastern edge of town. Designed in classic Palladian style by John Wood the Elder, Prior Park stands within impressive landscaped grounds whose artificial lakes and superb neoclassical bridge were created with the assistance of Capability Brown. (Grounds and chapel open daily, 9am to 5pm by arrangement.) The National Trust owns 560 acres of countryside and woodland which together form the Bath Skyline Walk. Described in a leaflet obtainable from the NT shop in the abbey churchyard, the eight-mile-long path begins to the east of the city above Bathwick, passes beside an Iron Age field system, and offers some spectacular views of the Georgian city.

The A4 to the northeast of Bath leads to BATHEASTON, a suburban village above and to the west of which lies Little Solsbury Hill, a 625 foot flat-topped knoll which is topped by a three-sided Iron Age hill fort, one of the simplest and earliest examples of its kind in the country. Excavations have shown that it was once encircled by a palisade, a sturdy fence made of stakes driven into the ground which was built onto a low bank faced with dry stone walling.

Another residential community which once belonged to Bath abbey, BATHFORD, lies near the Wiltshire border, a mile to the southeast of Batheaston.

The village retains some fine 18th-century residences, including Eagle House. which takes its name from the great stone eagle which stands with outstretched wings on the low-pitched gable facing the road. At one time, special paper for bank notes was produced at the old redbrick paper-mill by the river. On a hill above Bathford stands Brown's Folly, a tall Italianate tower built in the 1830s to provide local craftspeople with employment during the economic depression which followed the Napoleonic Wars. A steep path from the village climbs towards it through Mountain Wood and turns into an attractive nature trail.

Those travelling between Batheaston and BATHAMPTON on the opposite bank of the Avon have to pay a small toll to cross the bridge over the river. Although only a couple of miles from the centre of Bath, Bathampton's attractive grouping of canal, bridge, church and pub create their own distinct atmosphere. The last-named, the George, is a part-17th-century canalside inn which can be entered from the towpath or the road. Viscount du Barry, the unfortunate loser of the last legal duel to be fought in England (many illegal ones followed) was brought here following an ill-fated contest on nearby Bathampton Down. The viscount died soon after and was buried in the nearby churchyard, although his ghost has yet to be laid to rest and still haunts the inn.

The church is also the final resting place of Admiral Arthur Phillip, the first governor of New South Wales, who took the first shipload of convicts to the colony and established the settlement of Sydney. Considered by some to be the founder of modern Australia (though I suspect the aboriginal population might not agree), a chapel in the south aisle, which already contained memorials to Ralph Allen's family, was rechristened the Australian Chapel in the 1970s. Bathampton Down, above the village, is crowned by an ancient hill fort which, according to some historians, was the site of the 6th-century Battle of Badon in which the forces of King Arthur inflicted a crushing defeat on the Saxons.

The ostentatious tomb of Ralph Allen, Bath's 18th-century quarry-owning entrepreneur, lies in the churchyard at CLAVERTON, a pleasant linear village lying on a loop off the A36, a mile to the southeast of Bathampton. The church itself is an unremarkable Victorian reconstruction whose most notable feature is a panel of 14th-century stained glass in the north transept. Six years before his death in 1764, Allen bought Claverton Manor, a 16th-century country mansion which was later demolished leaving only a series of overgrown terraces with impressive stonework balustrades. Some of the stone from the ruined house was used to construct the present manor on the hill above the village. The building was designed in elegant neoclassical style by Sir Jeffrey Wyatville, whose work is much in evidence at Windsor Castle, and is set in superb landscaped grounds.

Sir Winston Churchill is recorded as having made his first political speech at Claverton Manor in 1897; however, it is as a remarkable museum that the building is now best known. In 1961, Americans Dallas Pratt and John Judkyn founded the only museum of American history outside the United States, and over the years the rooms have been furnished to show the gradual changes in American living styles, from the arrival of the Pilgrim Fathers in 17th-century New England, to the Philadelphia and New York of the 18th- and 19th-centuries. The New Orleans room is like a set from Gone With The Wind, and there are scenes from the days of the Mississippi steamboats and the early Spanish colonisers of New Mexico. There is also a large section dedicated to the history of the North American Indian and a display covering the religious sect, the Shakers. (Open Tuesdays to Sundays, 2pm to 5pm between late-March and early-November.)

The narrow river valley between Bath and Bradford-on-Avon is shared by the A36, the main railway line, and the Kennet and Avon Canal. At Claverton pumping station, water is mechanically transferred from the river to the canal which, a mile further south, makes a spectacular diversion over both river and railway by way of the Dundas Aqueduct, an impressive Bath-stone structure which is finished in characteristic neoclassical style. Designed by the great engineer, John Rennie, the canal was constructed between 1794 and 1810 to link the Thames with the Bristol Avon via Newbury and Devizes. A costly and ambitious project, much of its 75-mile length had to be cut through permeable rock which required a clay lining; however, the enterprise succeeded in paying its investors a small dividend before the Great Western Railway arrived in 1841 to poach all its business. In recent years, the Kennet and Avon Canal Trust has done much to restore the waterway, and it is now fully navigable from Bath to Caen Hill, near Devizes. For those interested in taking a canal journey, guided narrowboat trips can be joined at Bath's Top Lock and Sydney Wharf; alternatively, electrically-driven self-drive boats are available from various places, including the Dundas Aqueduct.

One of the newest ventures on the Kennet and Avon Canal is The Boathouse which can be found on the banks of the canal by the old bridge leading out of Bath on the Bristol Road. Opened by Christopher Patten MP on 1st March 1991, The Boathouse is super and has been designed to look just like - a boathouse! Wooden floors rather like decks, and wood-panelled walls featuring numerous photographs all connected with rowing, give this restaurant real character. Rowing colours, megaphones, caps and scarves; all this together with the beautiful views make The Boathouse a very striking and popular place.

As you climb the staircase to the dining area upstairs, you will no doubt be impressed with the large picture which hangs on the wall, of Bristol City Docks as it looked in 1865. You will be even more impressed by the range of meals and quite spectacular desserts on offer, including Amaretti Amaretto & Peach Yoghurt Ice Cream, Pistachio Delight, and 'River Surprise', a delicious blend of Cassis Sorbet, Strawberry Sorbet and Cream Vanilla Ice Cream. A lot of attention has gone into the design of this restaurant - the menu for the desserts is almost reminiscent of a Victorian greetings cars, which is a nice touch. Enthusiasts will also find a good selection of ales, including the infamous Brains Real Ale, which is referred to here as an 'S.A.'. Apparently this stands for 'Skull Attack', not 'Scull Attack' as you may think!

The Boathouse, Newbridge, Bath Tel: 01225 482584

Two-and-a-half miles south of the Dundas Aqueduct, the A36 passes close to the atmospheric ruins of Hinton Priory. This was only the second Carthusian monastery to be established in England when it was founded by Ela, Countess of Salisbury in 1232. As in other Carthusian houses, it was the practice here for the monks to occupy their own small dwellings, often with tiny gardens attached, which were set around a main cloister. Although the community was known for its passive tranquillity, one outspoken monk,

Nicholas Hopkins, achieved notoriety in Tudor times as the confessor and spiritual adviser to 3rd Duke of Buckingham. As is recorded in Shakespeare's Henry VIII, the so-called 'devil monk' prophesied that Buckingham would accede to the throne of England, and for his trouble, the Duke was executed and he was imprisoned in the Tower of London. The chapter house, with library and dovecote above, the undercroft of the refectory, and parts of the guest quarters survive and are open on Wednesdays and Saturdays, 2pm to 6pm between early-April and end-October. The Church of St John the Baptist at Hinton Charterhouse, one mile to the southwest, predates the priory by a century or so; although much altered, the font, south doorway and lower section of the tower survive intact from the original Norman structure.

To the west of Hinton Charterhouse, an undulating lane leads to the attractive village of WELLOW. The main street contains some fine old houses, a raised walkway, and a charming circular dovecote which is believed to have been built the 13th century. The part-14th-century Church of St Julian contain a unique series of wall paintings dating from around 1500 depicting Christ and the twelve Apostles. For those interesting in horse riding, Wellow is the location of a first-rate trekking centre which offers a selection of rides for enthusiasts of all ages and abilities. On the southern edge of the village, the road descends steeply to a ford on the Wellow Brook, beside which stands a striking medieval packhorse bridge and an old mill, now a private residence.

The Wheatsheaf can be found in the tiny, hidden hamlet of COMBE HAY and is, quite genuinely, one of the finest inns you will ever come across. It is one of those places which you could toy with keeping to yourself, but one can't be so selfish! Mike and Maria's 400-year old pub overlooks the village, with marvellous views of the surrounding countryside. The garden is absolutely delightful, and would not look out of place in a stately home. Here visitors can relax on seats hewn from fallen tree trunks and enjoy the colour and fragrance of the many shrubs and flowers which make this a lovely spot a real little 'Eden'. Inside, the low beamed ceilings and feature fireplaces give the inn plenty of character, and even the menu is superb. Aberdeen Angus steaks, pigeon, monkfish, game in season and a home-made sweet trolley - these are just some of the mouth-watering dishes on offer. Real ale is stored in barrels lined up behind the stone built bar, just waiting to be sampled. The service is exceptional, and full credit must go to Mike and Maria for providing everyone who is lucky enough to find it, a real gem of a an inn.

The Wheatsheaf, Combe Hay, Bath Tel: 01225 833504

One of the finest examples of a Neolithic long barrow in the west of England can be found beside the road to Shoscombe, three-quarters-of-a-mile to the southwest of Wellow. The multi-chambered tomb at STONEY LITTLETON was constructed around 4000 years ago and has since been restored. The interior can be seen by obtaining a key from nearby Stoney Littleton Farm, though it is advisable to take a torch.

Continuing westwards across the A3062, the area incorporating PEASEDOWN ST JOHN and RADSTOCK once stood at the heart of now almost-forgotten Somerset coalfield. Although Mendip coal had been extracted since the 1300s, it was during the 19th century that mining activities got underway in earnest. (Prior to 1817, the only building in Peasedown St John had been the Red Post Inn, still a pleasant pub.) The Braysdown colliery opened nearby in the 1820s and soon after, the deepest mine in the coalfield was sunk at Camerton, a couple of miles away to the west. Work underground was exceptionally hard; miners had to operate in seams which were often only a couple of feet thick, and were equipped only with a pick and a low sledge onto which the coal had to be shovelled for removal. The coalfield began to decline after the

388

First World War and the last colliery closed at Kilmersdon in the early 1970s.

Visitors now have to look hard to find evidence of the once-thriving industry which at one time employed over 6000 people and produced over a million tons of coal a year. A number of landscaped spoil heaps can still be recognised as such, and there are also traces of the succession of transport systems (coal canal, then tramway, then two rival railways) which were built to take the newly-mined coal to market. To save themselves from extinction, the former mining communities have had to reinvent themselves as dormitory settlements for Bath and Bristol. These include Paulton, Timsbury and Midsomer Norton, and together they have little to offer the casual visitor, except for those with an interest in industrial archeology. A memorial to twelve miners killed in an accident at Wellsway Coal Works in 1839 can be found on the western edge of the St John the Baptist's churchyard in Midsomer Norton. According to the inscription, the men plummeted to their deaths as they were being lowered down the mine shaft when the rope holding the cage 'was generally supposed to have been maliciously cut.' The excellent Radstock, Midsomer Norton and District Museum is housed in a converted 18th-century barn at Haydon, on the southern outskirts of Radstock. Devoted to the people of the North Somerset coalfield, it is open on Saturdays, Sundays and Bank Holiday Mondays, 2pm to 5pm, between January and November.

Situated in the sleepy village of HALLATROW, just half a mile off the main A37 is the Old Station Inn. Purpose-built as a hotel back in 1910, it stands adjacent to the disused Midsommer Norton - Bristol railway line. Although not as old as many of the other establishments we feature, it has traditional English values at heart. Once inside, you will immediately notice the walls and ceilings are adorned with items of all shapes, sizes and description, from old gramophone records to a light with an old petrol pump head as a shade! There are flags hanging from the ceiling, radios, typewriters, lamps, boxing gloves, gas masks, helmets, pots, shells, stuffed animals... - you name it, and you are sure to find one here! The most outstanding feature though, is probably the front end of an original 1954 Citroen 2CV that hangs over the fireplace. However, there is much more than just the unusual decor to enjoy here. Owner, Miles, who has been in the catering business all his life, always has 4 or 5 real ales on tap, and they are always kept in tip-top condition.

The inn is open throughout the year, and food is always available. The bar snack menu is varied, and there is also a blackboard to choose from too. All meals are fresh and reasonably priced. To one side of the inn, there are three en-suite letting rooms which offer first class facilities, and make this an ideal spot to use as a base for touring.

To the rear of the inn is a large car park and adjacent to this is a smashing, picturesque beer garden and children's play area. The atmosphere here, like the decorations, is very special. This pub is worth seeking out - another hidden gem to discover for yourself.

The Old Station Inn, Wells Road, Hallatrow
Tel: 01761 452228

As well as containing the deepest mine in the area, the ancient community of **CAMERTON** has some other interesting claims to fame. The village stands beside the Fosse Way, the great Roman highway which linked the Channel coast near Exeter with the North Sea near Lincoln, and during the 400-year Roman occupation, the settlement became an important metal-working centre producing pewter, bronze and iron. The site of the Roman settlement lay to the southwest of the present-day village, but has now completely returned to the earth. In the early 19th century, the rector of Camerton was the well-meaning but tormented John Skinner, a man whose life was made a living hell by the conflicting demands of his children, his congregation, the local gentry, miners, mine owners, farmers and rival denominations. In his personal journal, he wrote that 'he would bear testimony that Camerton folk were as bad as the inhabitants of Sodom and Gomorrah'. Unable to stand it any longer, he took his own life in the woods beside the rectory; his journal, all 98 volumes of it, is now in the British Museum. During the 1950s, the local branch line, now long gone, was used as a location for the classic Ealing film comedy, The Titfield Thunderbolt. Lying in the lanes to the west of Camerton is the Radford Farm and Shire Horse Stable, an open farm retaining the traditional methods of the 1940s and 50s.

The church tower at PRISTON, two miles to the north, is crowned with a disproportionately-large weathercock which was presented by the local lord of the manor in 1813 as a flamboyant gift to the parish. Priston Mill, on the northern edge of the village, was given to the monks of Bath Abbey in 931 and has supplied flour to the people of the city ever since. Powered by a spectacular 25 foot overshot water wheel, the millstones still produce stoneground flour for retail sale. Visitors can learn about the history and workings of the mill, or take a trailer ride around the working farm. There is also an award-winning nature trail and adventure play area. (Open daily, 2.15pm (11am at weekends) to 5pm between 1 April and 30 September.)

KEYNSHAM, five miles to the northwest of Priston, is an ancient settlement turned dormitory town which is thankfully now bypassed by the main A4 Bath to Bristol road. The remains of two Roman villas were discovered here which have been incorporated into a small museum at the entrance to a chocolate factory. An abbey was established in the late 12th century on the sloping ground between the parish church and the River Chew. Not always known for its high standards of piousness, the medieval canons had to be banned from keeping sporting dogs, employing private washer-women, going out at night, and inviting female guests into the abbey. Long since disappeared, some of the monastery's outbuildings now lie under the bypass. The part-13th-century parish church is a good example of Somerset Gothic; inside, there are two sizable monuments to members of the Bridges family. Two large brass mills were opened at Keynsham in the early 18th century, one on the Avon and the other on the Chew. The former ceased production in the 1890s, and the latter in 1927, leaving behind some impressive industrial remains.

The line of the ancient Wansdyke runs in a roughly east-west direction around the southern edge of Keynsham and Bristol. This great earthwork bank was built in the dark ages as a boundary line and defensive barrier against the Saxons. Although for most of its length it has long since disappeared, short sections can still be identified, for example along the ridge adjoining the Iron Age hill fort on Stantonbury Hill, east of Compton Dando, and at Maes Knoll, four miles further west.

Even earlier remains can be found around STANTON DREW, two miles to the south of Maes Knoll. The village stands beside a series of stone circles over half-a-mile across which together form a prehistoric site of major importance. Constructed by the Bronze Age Beaker People between 2000 and 1600 BC, the complex of standing stones consists of three stone circles, a lone stone known as Hauteville's Quoit, and a large chambered burial tomb known as the Cove. The stones are composed of three different rock types (limestone, sandstone and conglomerate) and were probably erected for religious, or perhaps astronomical, purposes.

In common with many of west Britain's stone circles, the origin of those at Stanton Drew are steeped in legend. The most widespread account tells of a foolhardy wedding party who wanted to dance on into the Sabbath. At midnight, the piper refused to carry on, and the infuriated bride screamed that if she had to, she'd get a piper from hell. Fortunately, another piper came forward and volunteered his services, but when the party began to dance, the music grew louder and louder and the tempo got faster and faster, and they found themselves in a furious jig they were powerless to stop. They realised too late that the good-natured piper was the Devil himself, and when the music stopped, he turned them all to stone.

To this day, one curious group of standing stones is known as 'The Wedding'. As well as the stone circles, Stanton Drew contains a number of noteworthy buildings, many of which are listed; these include the include several handsome 17th- and 18th-century private residences, the 15th-century stone bridge over the River Chew, and an unusual hexagonal thatched dwelling of the 15th century which later served as a turnpike toll-house.

CHEW MAGNA, one and a half miles to the west, is a former wool village which contains some handsome Georgian houses, most of which are now owned by well-to-do Bristol commuters. The nucleus of the village is a three-sided green whose shops and pubs are linked by an unusual raised stone pavement. At the top of the green stands a striking early-16th-century church house which once served the village as a meeting house, and beyond it, the impressive Church of St Andrew stands as a testimony to Chew Magna's former wool-based prosperity. The church contains a number of exceptional monuments, the most remarkable of which is reclining wooden effigy of a knight, reputed to be Sir John Hauteville, which shows him leaning on one elbow and resting his foot on a rather perplexed-looking lion. Others of note are the 15th-century double effigy of the 7 foot squire, Sir John Loe and his wife, and another of the Elizabethan sergeant-at-arms, Edward Baber and his wife, both of whom are sporting unusual double ruffs. Lying behind a high wall adjacent to the churchyard is Chew Court, a former summer palace of the bishops of Bath and Wells.

The Pony and Trap, Newton, Chew Magna, Bristol
Tel: 01275 332627

Situated just half a mile off the A368 and a mile outside of Chew Magna, in the village of NEWTON, is the 200 year old village pub, The Pony and Trap. Until only 20 years ago, it was called the Rising Sun, and around this time, it nearly closed down. The building really is typical of an olde worlde village inn, and features part exposed brickwork and lots of old prints and memorabilia decorating the walls. John Dobbs took over just two years ago, and through shear hard work has turned this little gem into a very popular and well patronised establishment. John also introduced food and is now able to offer and very varied and well-priced menu which changes regularly. The emphasis is on freshness of food and ample portions, which is successfully achieved. The inn overall is very comfortable and cosy, with a warm welcoming atmosphere. The panoramic views from the rear of the pub are outstanding and can be enjoyed from the delightful terraced area that has been created here.

Ring O' Bells, Compton Martin, Nr. Bristol Tel: 01761 221284

Another surprising church can be found in the village of **CAMELEY**, four miles to the southeast of Chew Magna. The building was referred to by John Betjeman as 'Rip Van Winkle's Church' because of the astonishing series of wall paintings which were discovered here behind several centuries of whitewash. The plain Georgian interior had remained unaltered since a side gallery had been installed in 1819, and indeed the church was closed for a period in the 1950s. However, restoration work in the 60s uncovered the murals which are believed to have been painted between the 11th- and 17th-centuries. The images include a rare coat of arms of Charles I, a charming 14th-century jester complete with harlequin costume and belled cap, and the foot of a giant St Christopher who is stepping through a fish and crab-infested river.

To the west of Cameley lie a pair of sizable artificial lakes which were constructed to meet Bristol's growing demand for fresh water.

Lying on the northern foothills of the Mendips, they form the region's 'lake district' and provide the area with a first-rate recreational amenity. The smaller Blagdon Lake was completed in 1899 and Chew Valley Lake in 1956; together they have around fifteen miles of shoreline and attract visitors from a wide area who come to fish, take part in watersports activities, or study the wide variety of waterfowl and other birdlife which are attracted to the habitat. Arguably, the two reservoirs make a picturesque landscape even more appealing, and many people come simply to enjoy the scenery.

On the A368, in the village of COMPTON MARTIN, you will find The Ring O' Bells. This is an Olde Worlde Inn of real character where you will find real ale too. Some barrels are kept behind to the bar to tempt the visitor, and there are always at least four to choose from. Bar meals are available each day at lunch time and in the evening. The menus offer an interesting selection of dishes alongside the usual sandwiches, jacket potatoes and ploughmans, and is very good value for money. Children are made very welcome and there is a family room in an adjacent converted barn. Outside, there is a large and well-kept beer garden, a children's play area and off-road parking.

The Plume of Feathers, Rickford, Nr. Burrington
Tel: 01761 462682

Tucked away, in the delightful village of RICKFORD, off the main A368, is the very impressive Plume of Feathers. A narrow road leads to the inn with a pretty stream flowing alongside it.

Dating back to the late 18th-century the premises were formerly a blacksmiths with stables. The present owners, Graham and Julie Stuckey took over the establishment just a year ago and they have developed a good reputation for their food. Meals are available every lunch and dinner time, right up until 10pm if required. The blackboard lists the dishes that are on offer, with a choice of up to twelve main dishes each day. Behind the bar there are four real ales on tap and they are all kept in tip top condition. Special features of the bar area are the impressive collection of foreign currency that is pinned to the beams, the inglenook fireplaces and feature log burner. To the rear of the inn is a safe and secluded beer garden.

Prior to the building of Blagdon lake, Bristol's fresh water came from the three small reservoirs at BARROW GURNEY, five miles to the north. The first of these opened in 1852, but had to be drained two years later when it developed a leak, causing a serious disruption to the city's water supply. The villages to the southwest of Bristol have undergone considerable changes since the Second World War, many having become dormitory settlements for the city's commuters. The village of CONGRESBURY, at the junction of the A370 and B3133, five miles to the west of Blagdon Lake, is no exception; however, it has had a long and eventful history which goes back to the time of the ancient Romans. At that time, the settlement stood at the end of a spur of the Somerset marshes, and fragments of Roman and pre-Saxon pottery have been found on the site of a hill fort which overlooks the present village.

The Bell Inn and Restaurant, (on the A370), Congresbury,
Nr. Bristol Tel: 01934 833110

In the village you will find The Bell Inn and Restaurant. Parts of the inn date back to the early 1800s with the main part added in the 1950s when the main road through the village was rebuilt. Steve, the proprietor, is a fully qualified chef, and keeps his hand in by helping out in the kitchen from time to time. The restaurant area itself is a delightful place to have a meal, as it appears to have once been a pitched roof barn. Lots of exposed ceiling beams remain, with bells and bygone memorabilia as decoration. The food that is served is freshly prepared and delicious with a reasonably priced menu and daily specials on offer. The restaurant can get busy so it is advisable to book ahead at weekends. The inn areas are also attractively decorated and furnished and real ale is served behind the bar. Elsewhere, there is a games rooms, an activity centre, a pets corner and an aviary.

The White Hart, Wrington Road, Congresbury
Tel: 01934 833303

The Celtic missionary, St Congar, is believed to have founded an early wattle chapel at Congresbury in the 6th century; according to local legend, one day he thrust his staff in the ground and the next day, it was seen to develop leaves. A tree bound by an iron hoop on the eastern side of the present-day church is reputed to have grown from the original sprouting and is still referred to as, 'St Congar's Walking Stick'. Several centuries later, the Saxon King Ine heard of the miraculous occurrence and granted land for the founding of a stone church and monastery here; however, no trace of it remains today. Congresbury's present church is a spacious, part-13th-

Cheddar Gorge

century structure with a soaring spire and a Norman font which incorporates some fine cable-carving. The handsome ecclesiastical-looking building which can be glimpsed through the trees from the churchyard is the part-15th-century vicarage. It was extended during Regency times, and its two distinctive architectural styles now appear side by side, the newer wing serving as the vicarage and the medieval part as the church function room.

Hidden away on Wrington Road is The White Hart. This delightful timber-framed inn dates back to the late 18th century and today still stands in its own grounds. The interior retains many original features including three fireplaces, floor to ceiling and ceiling beams and is decorated and furnished to complement the style. The modern conservatory serves as a dining area and overlooks the attractive rear beer garden. The menus are extensive and there are additional daily specials, and all the food is freshly prepared and home-cooked. Food is available every lunch time and evening, and booking is advisable for Friday and Saturday evenings and Sunday lunch. Sue and Ken Taylor, the managers, have created a very welcoming atmosphere, so once discovered, you are sure to return.

Cadbury Garden Centre, Smallway, Congresbury, Bristol
Tel: 01934 876464

On the B3133, half a mile from the main A370 Bristol to Weston Road, you will come across the Cadbury Garden Centre. Owners Ken and Jackie Lloyd and their son Richard have transformed what was a run down salad nursery eleven years ago, into a thriving garden centre. The culmination of their efforts was almost certainly winning the title of Garden Centre of the Year for 1993/4. The site extends to over 15 acres with 80,000 square feet under cover, and has everything the amateur and professional gardener could need. You may also be interested to learn that many of the plants are propagated here as well. Even if you have no interest in gardening there are plenty non-gardening items to look at too and the displays even extend to local crafts and pottery. If exploring the site tires you out, and you feel in need of refreshment there is the Orangery Coffee Shop. Beautifully decorated, it offers a good variety of beverages and food items, from just a snack to full meals. All the food is of good quality, is freshly prepared and very reasonably priced.

The Full Quart, Hewish, near Weston-super-Mare
Tel: 01934 833077

In HEWISH you will find a delightful inn called The Full Quart. It was built around 1750 and has been traditionally decorated, with oak beams and a feature fireplace in the bar area giving it a wonderfully cosy atmosphere. Pam and Alec Roud are your hosts, and besides always having a friendly word to say to their customers, the whole place is kept spotlessly clean - something which is often overlooked in busy establishments.

The restaurant here is first class and if you experience any delay while waiting for your meal, please be patient - only the freshest local produce is used, and this takes a little while to prepare. The extensive range of meals on the set menu is most impressive, but this is more than equalled by the choice of 'specials' which are chalked up on the blackboard every day. The comprehensive menu has its emphasis on wholesome food, home-cooked at a reasonable price. Pam works in the kitchen preparing home-made soup, paté, Mendip chicken casserole and Somerset pork steak, among other delicacies, as well as mouth-watering desserts. The choice would be difficult to beat. The wide range of beers includes Bass, Butcombe, Eldridge Pope, Whitbread's and Flowers. Also, each month they promote a particular wine.

Outside there is a lovely paved area where you can sit and enjoy the views of the surrounding countryside. There is also an extensive children's play area which any child would love.

Doubleton Farm Cottages, Hewish, Weston-super-Mare
Tel: 01934 520225

Also in the village of Hewish are Doubleton Farm Cottages. These are an attractive group of 13 character cottages set in and around the original Farmhouse. Run by David and Frances Peatling, they are acknowledged as the premier self-catering establishment in the area. The original Farm dates back to at least 1720, and the Peatlings have converted the original hay lofts, stables and barns into character holiday cottages. When one of the outbuildings was being converted, a diary dated 1891 was found in the eaves. Beautifully written, the diary is now treasured. With guest's comfort in mind, each holiday cottage is well equipped with all the facilities you would need on a self-catering holiday. On site there are many other features to help you enjoy your stay to the full

- patios, large lawns, a barbeque, children's adventure play area and a pets corner. The personal touches are what make Doubleton Farm Cottages extra special, so you can expect a fun pack for the kids, and a tea tray laid out, awaiting you on your arrival. You even get free Sunday papers too! For shopping and other essentials, there is an out of town shopping centre only a mile away, with supermarket, post office, chemist and newsagent. For the more energetic, there are also many sporting facilities nearby, including golf courses, horse riding, swimming, tennis, squash courts and even a dry ski slope! You are sure to have a great time here.

Lying in the lanes to the southeast of Hewish, the church at PUXTON has to be seen to be believed. Its low sturdy tower leans at such an angle, it looks as if it might topple over at any minute causing its precarious-looking weathercock to nose dive into the churchyard. The church interior appears to have little changed since the main body of the building was rebuilt in the 1530s, a wonderful assemblage of high box pews, old wooden benches, and later Jacobean fittings which include the pulpit, reading desk and altar rails.

Continuing southwards, a narrow lane leads to BANWELL, a pleasant village which once contained a Saxon monastery. The church has a striking tower with a single turret, and inside, there's a fine rood screen and a Norman stone font with later carvings which is crowned by a curious pointed font-cover belonging to a different era. In 1821, a remarkable series of caverns were discovered on Banwell Hill, above and to the west of the village. Known as the Bone Caves, they were found to discover the remains of prehistoric mammals, including bison, bear and reindeer. A few years later, the local bishop created a romantic park around the cave entrance which he filled with assorted pyramids, monk's cells, fairy cottages and other fanciful buildings. The village also contains a substantial Victorian mansion known as Banwell Castle. On the northern edge of Banwell, Court Farm is a country park and working farm with its own dairy herd and collection of shire and thoroughbred horses; a couple of miles to the east, the Avon Ski Centre and Mendip Riding Centre are located on the same site between the villages of Sandford and Churchill.

To the west of Banwell, the A371 skirts around the northern edge of the Bleadon Hills towards Weston-Super-Mare. A couple of miles after crossing the M5, the road passes Weston Airport, home of the renowned International Helicopter Museum, the world's largest collection of rotary wing aircraft. The only museum in Britain dedicated to helicopters and autogyros, this friendly volunteer-run establishment has over forty exhibits ranging from single-seater autogyros to giant multi-seater helicopters. There are also displays on the history and development of these remarkable flying machines, a flight simulator, and a conservation hangar where old aircraft are restored. (Open daily, 10am to 6pm, all year round.)

Moorlands, Hutton, Weston-super-Mare
Tel: 01934 812283

Situated in the picturesque village of HUTTON, overlooking the church, is Moorlands, a magnificent Georgian country guest house. This is the home of Margaret and David Holt who offer excellent accommodation in their beautiful home. The property stands in almost two acres of well-maintained landscaped gardens with extensive views to the rear. There are 8 guest rooms available and four of these have en-suite facilities. Throughout the whole house, the furnishings and decor are of the highest quality. All guests also have the use of a large and spacious lounge and the dining room is also delightful. The food served is excellent and fresh local produce is used as much as possible. Full English breakfast is served in the morning and four-course evening meals can be provided by arrangement. Moorlands is ideally placed for touring the Mendip Hills.

WESTON-SUPER-MARE is a popular resort which in recent years has developed as a centre of light industry. The town developed relatively late as a seaside resort: in 1811 it was still a fishing hamlet with a population of only 170; however, within the following 100 years it had grown to become the second largest town in Somerset, the most rapid development having taken place after the arrival of the railway in 1841. It now has a population of well over 50,000. The wooded promontory at the northern end of Weston Bay was the site of a sizable Iron Age hill settlement known as Worlebury Camp which in the 1st century AD was attacked and captured by the ancient Romans with great loss of life. (A number skeletons showing the effects of sword damage were unearthed during recent excavations.) Today, this ancient wooded site offers some delightful walking, with those making it to the top being rewarded with a magnificent view over the Severn Channel to Wales.

In the village of Weston, opposite the Marina, you may be lucky enough to discover a fabulous establishment called The Major from Glengarry. This pub is a real treat, and will come as a pleasant surprise to real ale fans, and will certainly be a place you will want to return to again. The place has quite a history to it - many years ago it was a casino called Fannies, and Diana Dors was a frequent visitor and close acquaintance of the then owner, it is quite possible you will come across some of the older locals who remember her! The establishment was later renamed the Glengarry, and permission was obtained to put the coat of arms of the Marines on its sign. A later owner was from a military background, and added his own title of Major to the name of the pub - hence The Major from Glengarry.

The decor of the pub is very traditional, and features wood panelled walls and partitions, old-fashioned wooden tables and chairs - not to mention the memorabilia and old photographs and prints that decorate the walls and ceilings. The inn is renowned in the area for its friendly welcome, its delicious food and excellent ales. Owners Terry and Nora usually have seven ales on tap - Wadworth 6X, Henrys IPA, Farmers Glory, Beetcombe and Bass are permanent and two others change fortnightly. The menu offers traditional pub fare at lunch time and in the evenings. Sunday lunches, when roast dinners are served, get very popular, so it is advisable to book. All the food is reasonably priced, and Senior Citizens get further special deals. The patio outside is very enticing, and in warm weather it is great to be able to sit out surrounded by the tubs of flowers and old-fashioned inn signs which are displayed on the walls. The patio is set below the level of the road so you do not have to stare at the traffic that goes by, but simply enjoy the delightful surroundings.

The Major from Glengarry, 10-14 Upper Church Street,
Weston-super-Mare, Tel: 01934 629260

Weston-Super-Mare has little of the grandiose architecture which characterises earlier seaside resorts such as Brighton or Torquay. Instead, it developed on a small comfortable scale with plenty of wide boulevards, leafy parks and open spaces. The town's greatest resource is its long sandy beach which at high tide is ideal for paddling, sunbathing and ball games; however, swimmers have to wade out long way to find water deep enough to take the plunge.

Good food is naturally the main consideration when looking for somewhere to eat on your travels, but it is an added bonus if the restaurant has something else to offer by way of interest. You will undoubtably be delighted to discover **The Old Thatched Cottage Restaurant** in Knightstone Road.

Although only part of the building is still thatched, it is most unusual to find this style right on the sea front. Built in 1774, the cottage is full of character and old world charm, with original beams and attractive honeycomb leaded windows, giving it a welcoming and stylish appeal.

This is very much a family-run restaurant, Peter and Maria Demetriou have been in charge for the past 20 years and it had been in the family for a further 15 years prior to that! The restaurant can seat up to 100 diners, with seating for 60 more outside. There is a newly created bar/lounge room where diners can partake of that welcome pre-meal or after-meal drink. The room is very cosy, full of character and very relaxing. The lunchtime menu features everything from roasts to beefburgers, with plenty of daily specials available. If you want to be more adventurous the full menu has continental theme to it with many speciality dishes. Why not try a delicious home-made Moussaka, or perhaps Kleftiko (beef cooked in a clay oven) à la Cypriot and served with potatoes and salads. Or maybe an Italian, French or traditional English dish may be to your liking, but whichever you choose, you will not be disappointed.

There is a good range of familiar wines, together with several unusual vintages from Italy and Cyprus, so do ask your hosts for advice before you choose. Don't be shy about taking your children with you either - they are most welcome here and the menus are extensive, with something for everyone.

The Old Thatched Cottage Restaurant, 14 Knightstone Road.
Weston-super-Mare, Tel: 01934 621313

In the centre of Weston-super-Mare, in an elevated position overlooking the bay, is the Queenswood Hotel. Run by David and Margaret Horler for the past 26 years, the hotel has developed a reputation for being the best in the area. The delightful building has been carefully modernised to provide a high standard of amenities to ensure guests enjoy their stay to the full. There are 17 bedrooms, all tastefully decorated, and all with en-suite bathrooms, colour TV and drinks facilities. Children are welcome in the family rooms, and are well provided for, with cots, high chairs and baby listening service. The air-conditioned dining room is designed to provide an elegant and relaxing atmosphere in which to appreciate the high quality of cuisine prepared by the hotel chefs. The menus have a good selection of meals to suit every palate and an extensive wine list is available to complement your food. All food is freshly prepared and careful attention is given to special diet requirements. The restaurant is open to non-residents, and is very popular, so booking is advisable. There are three lounges in the hotel where visitors and guests can enjoy a chat around the fire or over a drink from the well-stocked bar. You are sure to enjoy your stay in this friendly and luxurious hotel.

Queenswood Hotel, Victoria Park, Weston-super-Mare
Tel: 01934 416141 Fax: 01934 621759

Weston's early tourist development took place in the 1830s around the Knightstone, an islet now joined to the shore at the northern end of Weston Bay onto which eventually was built a large theatre and swimming baths. In 1867, a pier was built further to the north which connected offshore Birnbeck Island to the headland below Worlebury fort. Intended mainly for steamer traffic, it was slightly off the tourist track and so a new Grand Pier was built nearer the town centre which, prior to serious fires in the

1930s and World War II, was approximately twice its present length. Then, as now, the pier stood at the centre of an area crammed with souvenir shops, ice cream parlours, cafés and assorted attractions designed to appeal to holiday-makers from Bristol, Bath and beyond. Today's indoor attractions include the Tropicana Leisure Complex and the Winter Gardens and Pavilion, both on the seafront, and the Heritage Centre in Wadham Street which is run by the Weston-Super-Mare Civic Society and offers free admission.

Woodspring Museum, Burlington Street, Weston-super-Mare
Tel: 01934 621028

Woodspring Museum in Burlington Street is definitely worth going out of your way to visit. The exhibits to be seen here include The Victorian Seaside Holiday (where you can marvel at the bathing suits of our forebears!), Royal Potteries, Natural History, Early Bicycles, Costume and Period Settings and an Art Gallery with a constantly changing programme of exhibitions. Visitors can enjoy refreshments in the stylish cobbled courtyard and if you feel energetic, you can set off on a Woodspring Museum walk available on certain days between April and September. There is a nominal charge for this but it does include a guide. A telephone call in advance will advise you on what days the walks take place.

Next door to the museum is Clara's Cottage, a typical Victorian dwelling furnished in the style of 1900. Here you can see the range around which family life would have centred, and the 'best' parlour with its tasteful (and invariably uncomfortable) furniture which a proud housewife of the early 20th century would choose to set off her home.

In the entrance foyer is the Museum Shop where you can purchase souvenirs, museum publications and postcards. The Museum is open from Tuesday to Sunday, 10am to 5pm, and also on Bank Holiday Mondays.

Self-Catering accommodation is at a premium in Weston-Super-Mare, but one of the best you will find is **Daclare Holiday Flats**. Situated on the edge of the town centre, Daclare can be found in a quiet residential area within a few minutes walk of the sea front. Owners Sylvia and Rob Ford came here 11 years ago after running a hotel in Weston for five years and through much hard work have created ten high quality holiday flats. The flats accommodate either two or four people and are very well equipped. They are electric throughout and include colour TV, electric fires, modern sprung beds and everything including bed linen is supplied. Furthermore, three flats are on the ground floor and are ideal for those who cannot manage stairs. The Holiday Flats are available from April to mid-October.

Daclare Holiday Flats, 1 Beaconsfield Road, Weston-super-Mare
Tel: 01934 621865

Just a few minutes from Weston-super-Mare's main centre and sea front, is the very impressive **Regency public house**. This super establishment is run by brothers Mark and David Short who took over just a year ago. Formerly two Victorian houses, the inn has had many names during its lifetime - the Top Hat, the Silver

Jubilee, and for the past ten years, the Regency. The owners have successfully turned this pub into a place of real character, somewhere to enjoy good food and ale, and a place to relax. The decoration and furnishings are excellent and of the two original houses, one houses the bar and eating area while the other has a fine games room. Food is served every lunch-time except Sunday and the menus offer a wide choice. Real ales are served and there are usually four different varieties available. The pub is open all day, every day.

The Regency, 22/24 Lower Church Road, Weston-super-Mare
Tel: 01934 633406

A spectacular view can be had from the clifftop site of the semi-ruined part-Norman church at Uphill, at the southern end of Weston Bay, two miles to the south. Here you will also find Old Hall.

This very impressive early-19th-century property is as delightful inside as it looks from the outside. The front patio area, which is full of flowers, is a real sun trap and an ideal place to enjoy food and drink on a hot, sunny day. On the ground floor of Old Hall is a cosy Coffee Shop and outstanding dining room. The beautifully furnished and decorated coffee shop is open every day and offers a selection of snacks, salads, a roast dinner and a choice of fresh fish dishes. The dining room is only open on Saturday evenings when it serves a first class à la carte menu. The room is delightful with the wood panelling adding to the stately, grand appearance. The dining room is also available for hire for dinners and functions. For those who need somewhere to stay, Old Hall can offer 5 outstanding en-suite bedrooms all with a homely and cosy atmosphere. This establishment is a credit to its owners Tony and Joe - a real hidden gem.

Old Hall, 88 Uphill Way, Uphill, Weston-super-Mare
Tel: 01934 629970

The Ship Inn dates back to the 17th century and is reputedly the oldest pub in Weston-super-Mare. It has been completely modernised, but in such a way that it has not lost its charm and character.

The Ship Inn, Uphill Way, Uphill, Weston-super-Mare
Tel: 01934 621470

Clevedon Court

At street level you will find a cosy lounge bar and up a few steps, The Captain's Lounge where meals are served. A comprehensive set menu gives choices of starters, main courses, salads and much more. In addition, there are also several daily specials. The food is delicious, although you may have to wait a few minutes for your order as it is all freshly cooked. There is a wide selection of real ales with Flowers, Boddingtons and Bass on offer. The decor is attractive, with exposed brick and wooden beams, and the walls are covered with quality prints and pictures of ships. Downstairs, there is a comfortable family room and adjacent to it, a skittle alley. Owner, Martin, has created a great atmosphere here, and a warm welcome awaits all visitors. Once you have sampled The Ship's hospitality, food and ale, you're sure to be back!

To the north of Weston-Super-Mare, the narrow coast road bends sharply down to skirt Sand Bay before terminating at Middle Hope, a high ridge which juts out into the Severn Channel to form Sand Point. The ridge overlooks a lonely salt marsh which is inhabited by a variety of wading birds, including shelduck and oystercatchers. To the east, a path leads down to the Landmark Trust-owned Woodspring Priory, a surprisingly-intact medieval monastery which was founded around 1220 by William de Courtenay, a grandson of one of Thomas á Becket's murderers. The priory fell into disrepair following the Dissolution of the Monasteries and its buildings were used for agricultural purposed for many years. However, the church, tower, refectory and tithe barn have all survived, and the outline of the cloister can also be made out. (Open daily, 10am to 7pm (dusk in winter), all year round.)

In order to continue northwards along the Severn estuary from Weston-Super-Mare, it is best to join the M5 at junction 21 and leave it once again at junction 20, the Clevedon exit. Close to the motorway lies the National Trust-owned Clevedon Court, one of the earliest surviving country houses in Britain. Although the building is much altered, the major part dates from the early 14th century, with the great hall dating back to the 13th century, and the tower back as far as the 12th. This imposing part-medieval mansion has been the home of the Elton family since 1709, and during the early 19th century it became a mecca for the finest poets and writers of the day, including Coleridge, Thackeray and Tennyson. A later member of the family invented the technique for making a special type of brightly-coloured pottery known as Eltonware which was particularly popular in the United State. Many fine examples are on display, along with a collection of rare glass from the works at Nailsea. Clevedon Court is set within a delightful terraced garden which is renowned for its unusual shrubs and plants. (Open Wednesdays, Thursdays, Sundays and Bank Holiday Mondays, 2.30pm to 5.30pm between late-March and end-September.) An attractive footpath leads up through nearby Clevedon Court Woods onto the ridge overlooking the Gordano valley.

The genteel seaside town of **CLEVEDON** lies on the edge of the Severn Channel, a couple of miles to the west. As much a residential centre as a holiday resort, it now has a population of around 20,000, although prior to the arrival of the railway, it was larger and more popular than Weston-Super-Mare. The seafront is lined with bright stucco-fronted Regency and mid-Victorian houses in marked contrast to the grey limestone and brick of those further inland.

Walton Park Hotel, Wellington Terrace, Clevedon
Tel: 01275 874253 Fax: 01275 343577

On the coast road you will find **Walton Park Hotel**. Formerly three Victorian houses, it became a hotel at the turn of century. Completely refurbished by its present owners, it can now be regarded as one of the premier hotels in the area, as is evident from its English Tourist Board 4 Crown rating. The facilities are excellent, from the bars and restaurant through to the 37 spacious bedrooms. All rooms have en-suite facilities and are well-appointed to meet the needs of business guests and the holiday visitor. Many rooms also offer superb views over the Bristol Channel. The comfortable Somerset Restaurant also overlooks the channel and Welsh hills beyond, and is an ideal place to relax and enjoy the fine cuisine and wines of the hotel. Alternatively, comprehensive menus are also available in the Walton and Wessex bars. Other practical features of the hotel are lifts for disabled guests, comprehensive off-road parking and conference and function facilities. Despite its size, this is a hotel where you will feel right at home.

Although there are few of the popular attractions one would normally associate with a holiday resort, the exception is Clevedon pier, a remarkably slim and elegant structure which was built in the 1860s from iron rails which were intended for Brunel's ill-considered South Wales railway. When part of the pier collapsed in the 1970s, its long-term future was left in jeopardy; however, at the end of the 80s, a trust was formed to effect a full restoration which was expected to take around ten years to complete. The pier is now open to the public once again, and during the summer months, it is used as a landing stage by large pleasure steamers, including the Balmoral and the Waverley, the only surviving seagoing paddle steamer in the world.

The Little Harp, Elton Road, Clevedon Tel: 01275 343739

On the coast road in Clevedon, you will come across **The Little Harp**, the unusual name arising from Little Harp Bay which the pub overlooks. It was only as recently and 1988 that this became a pub, prior to that it had been many things, including a private house, tea rooms and a restaurant. It has been wonderfully refurbished by the present owners, The Churchill Group, who own five others in the area. The conservatory to the rear of the building and overlooking the Bristol Channel, is the dining area and can seat up to 200 people. The menu offers a good choice with additional daily specials. All in all, a great place to stop for a drink and a bit to eat.

Among Clevedon's noteworthy old buildings is the Market Hall of 1869 which was built to provide local market gardeners with a place to sell their produce. The parish Church of St Andrew is Norman at heart, although the nave was demolished and rebuilt in 1291, and the sturdy Norman tower was given another layer in the 17th century. The interior contains a number of poignant memorials to local parishioners who died young. A flower-lined footpath said to be popular with Victorian poets, and now aptly named the Poet's Walk, begins at Clevedon promenade and leads up around Wain's and Church hills. The former is topped by the remains of an Iron Age coastal hill fort and offers magnificent views over the Severn estuary, the Levels, and the town itself. Clevedon's appeal is still romantic rather than dramatic. Its geographical position has prevented the large-scale development which has plagued the larger seaside resorts, and through its modest landscape, fine scenery, winding paths and elegant Regency houses, it retains an atmosphere which is drowsy and refined.

High up, overlooking the Bristol Channel with unbeatable views, is **The Highcliffe Hotel**. This was originally two magnificent Victorian town houses which have been linked together by an attractive foyer area decorated with hanging baskets and plenty of pot plants. Behind the foyer is an outdoor balcony where guests can sit on sunny days and enjoy the views. On the ground floor is the dining room which is very well decorated and furnished with additional personal touches to each table. An à la carte menu is available every night as well as the chef's imaginative daily specials. Adjacent to the dining room is a characterful lounge bar which is cosy and homely. Here you can enjoy the excellent range of beers and wines on offer. There are 20 first class bedrooms, most of which have en-suite facilities, and all with remote-control, colour TV. For the young, and the young at heart, there is also a games room with pool table and Sky television. You are bound to enjoy a stay here, and owners Steve and Marilyn Bigland will go out of their way to make sure that you do.

The Highcliffe Hotel, Wellington Terrace, Clevedon
Tel: 01275 873250

To the northeast of Clevedon, two hill ridges diverge like a great 'V', and between them lies the low Gordano valley. This area of former marshland is edged with settlements which incorporate the valley's name, among them **WALTON-IN-GORDANO**, a small village containing an exceptionally beautiful four-acre garden, the Manor House, which is planted with rare shrubs, trees and herbaceous plants. (Open Wednesdays, Thursdays and occasional Sundays, 10am to 4pm between mid-April and mid-September.) Across the valley to the southeast, the land rises towards the dramatic site of Cadbury Camp, and Iron Age hill fort above the village of Tickenham from which there are fine views over the Levels to the Mendip hills.

Back on the Severn estuary, the early development of **PORTISHEAD** had much in common with that of Clevedon. The pier, a bath house (now the Saltings), and a number of elegant villas and hotels began to appear in the 1820s and 30s; however, the arrival of the railway in 1867 transformed the town into a port and industrial centre whose seaside attractions were soon redirected towards the cheaper end of the market. Now a flourishing residential centre, its finest features are Portishead Point, an impressive wooded viewpoint overlooking the Channel, and the part-14th-century parish church beside which stands the Court, a handsome Tudor residence with an unusual polygonal tower.

On the edge of Portishead town centre is The Albion Inn. The pub had been closed for many years, and the building had fallen into complete disrepair when it was purchased by The Churchill Group. Now completely refurbished, this has become a lively and popular pub that will appeal to all ages. A comprehensive set menu is available each lunch time and evening, plus daily specials. To the rear is a smashing skittle alley which can be easily converted to provide a function room. A warm welcome is assured, and along with delicious food and a variety of well-kept ales, who could wish for anything more!

The Albion Inn, Bristol Road, Portishead Tel: 01275 817906

North Somerset and the Mendips

Wells Cathedral

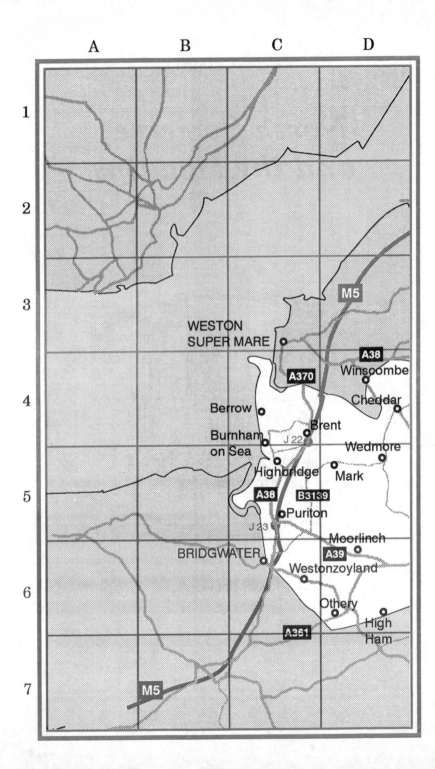

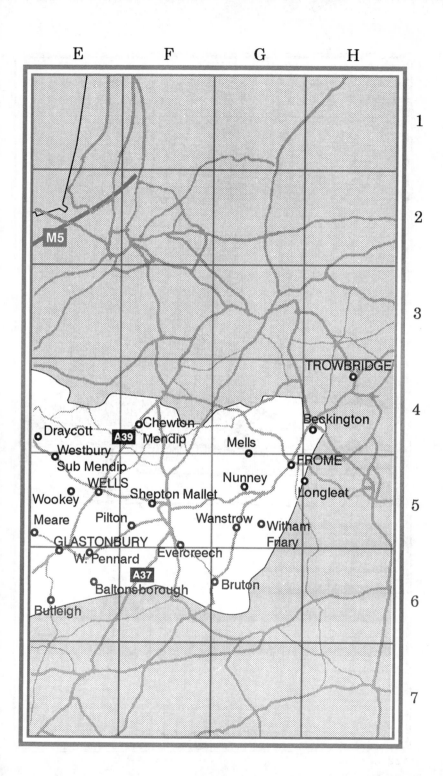

Glastonbury Tor

CHAPTER THIRTEEN

North Somerset and the Mendips

Standing beside the river from which it takes its name, the ancient settlement of FROME is the largest centre of population in northeast Somerset. The parish Church of St John the Baptist was founded as a Saxon monastic house by St Aldhelm in the 7th century, and by the time of the Norman invasion, Frome was already a sizable market town which stretched up the hill from the river to the church (markets continue to be held on Wednesdays and Saturdays). The Frome valley became an important centre of the wool industry during the Middle Ages when a series of weirs was constructed to channel water to the many water-powered weaving and fulling mills which lined the riverbank (fulling was a process which increased the volume of woven cloth by feeding it through a series of mechanical rollers). Despite the decline of the industry in the 18th century, one mill, A H Tucker's, continued in production until the 1960s.

The collapse of the textile industry meant that little redevelopment took place in the centre of Frome and as a result, many of its narrow medieval thoroughfares have survived, some with wonderful names like Pudding Bag Lane and Twattle Alley. The most impressive are Gentle Street, the steeply-sloping Catherine Hill, and Cheap Street, with its water course running down the middle. The bridge over the River Frome incorporates an 18th-century lockup gaol, close to which can be seen the Bluecoat School, and the Blue House, an elegant almshouse dating from 1726 which has recently been restored. Best explored on foot, the centre of Frome is now an attractive conservation area which contains an unusual number of interesting shops, cafés and residential buildings. For those interested in local history, there is an excellent museum (open Wednesdays, Fridays and Saturdays between early-March and end-November), and there is also an interesting arts and crafts complex, the Black Swan Centre, in Bridge Street.

To the north of Frome, the river winds towards its confluence with the Bristol Avon. Three miles downstream, the former wool village of BECKINGTON boasts one of the largest and most ornate Norman church towers in Somerset; the rest of the building is predominantly Perpendicular. The village contains some fine stone-built houses, including the early-Georgian Cedars, the 16th-century Abbey, an ecclesiastical guest house, or hospital, once run by the Augustinians, and Seymour's Court, a farmhouse once owned by Sir Thomas Seymour, the ambitious Lord High Admiral who married Henry VIII's widow, Catherine Parr. A lane to the southwest of Beckington leads to LULLINGTON whose Norman village church is worth a look for its remarkable carved north doorway, a wonderful accumulation of arched lintels and twisted columns crowned by a mysterious seated figure. A gateway on the southern edge of the village marks the start of the footpath to Orchardleigh Park, an imposing Victorian pile which was built in the 1850s. The lake in the grounds has an island in its western corner on which is perched a small church whose churchyard contains the grave of Sir Henry Newbolt, the author of Drake's Drum, who died in 1938. (Open at restricted times.)

Between the A36 and A361 a mile to the north of Beckington, the pretty village of RODE is the location of the famous Rode Bird Gardens. The seventeen-acre park is home to around 1200 tropical birds, many of which are allowed to fly freely. The grounds incorporate a miniature woodland steam railway, a pets' corner, and a series of lakes inhabited by flamingos, penguins and other water birds. There is also a captive breeding programme for rare and endangered species. (Open daily, 10am to 6pm, all year round.)

One of the finest medieval inns in Britain can be found in NORTON ST PHILIP, a lovely old village which lies a couple of miles to the northwest of Rode near the junction of the A366 and B3110 Bath road. The remarkable George Inn was founded as a guesthouse in the 13th century by the monks of nearby Hinton Priory, the second-oldest Carthusian monastery in the country (see chapter, 'Bath to Weston-Super-Mare'). The timber-framed upper floors were added in the 15th century when the building was also used as a warehouse for locally-produced woollen cloth. In 1668, the diarist Samuel Pepys stayed here with his family, recording the event, 'Dined well. 10 shillings'. Seventeen years later, the ill-fated Duke of Monmouth made the inn his temporary headquarters a few days before the Battle of Sedgemoor. Virtually unaltered since, the present-day George is a wonderful fusion of medieval stonework, oriel windows and timber-framing; there is also a superb courtyard and minstrels' gallery at the rear. A former wool village which once stood on the main Bath to Salisbury road, Norton St Philip also contains a fine mainly-Perpendicular church and a large number of 17th-century stone cottages. The ruined castle of Farleigh Hungerford lies close to the Wiltshire border, two-and-a-half miles to the northeast of Norton St Philip, details of which appear in the Wiltshire chapter, 'Trowbridge to Chippenham'.

Hidden in the lanes three miles to the west of Frome, MELLS must be one of the loveliest villages in northeast Somerset. Once the easternmost limit of the lands belonging to the mighty Glastonbury Abbey, Abbot Selwood drew up plans to rebuild the village in the shape of a St Anthony's cross (four arms of equal length) in the 15th century. Only one, New Street, was completed, and this architectural gem can be seen running south from St Andrew's Parish Church. The church itself is a magnificent example of Somerset Perpendicular, with a soaring 104 foot tower and spectacular pinnacled south porch. Inside there is a remarkable collection of memorials designed by some of the most acclaimed artists of the 20th century, including Lutyens, Gill, Munnings and Burne-Jones. One is to Raymond Asquith, the eldest son of the Liberal Prime Minister, Herbert Asquith, who was killed in the First World War. In the churchyard there is a memorial to Siegfried Sassoon, the poet and pacifist.

According to local legend, the Abbot of Glastonbury, in an attempt to stave off Henry VIII's Dissolution of the Monasteries, dispatched his steward, John Horner, to London with a gift for the King which consisted of a pie into which the title deeds of twelve manor houses had been baked. Horner returned to Somerset the rightful owner of the manor house at Mells, an episode which is recorded in the nursery rhyme Little Jack Horner. (The rhyme relates how he 'put in his thumb and pulled out a plumb', i.e. the deeds of Mells manor.) Despite the suggestion that he came by the property dishonestly, there is evidence that Jack paid over the sum of £2000 for the deeds of the manors of Mells, Nunney and Leigh-upon-Mendip. The one at Mells, which is not open to the public, remained in the hands of the Horner family until the early 20th century when it passed to the Asquith family by marriage.

In the centre of this attractive you will find **The Talbot Inn at Mells**. This traditional 15th century coaching inn, run by Roger and Bernadette Elliott, is very comfortable and welcoming. There are two comfortable bars, both serving excellent real ales with cosy open fires. The bar food is excellent, ideal for a quick snack or a special meal with freshly prepared dishes which include fresh game from the local shoot and fresh fish delivered each day. Outside is the Courtyard area and garden, both ideal for alfresco dining.

There is also some bed and breakfast accommodation here, with four en-suite bedrooms available. All the rooms are comfortable and individually furnished, in keeping with the traditional style of the coaching inn. Real ale, real food, real hospitality. Well worth a visit.

The Talbot Inn at Mells, Mells, near Frome
Tel: 01373 812254

The lanes to the south of Mells leads to the village of NUNNEY with its remarkable moated castle, details of which are included in the Wiltshire chapter, 'Westbury to the Dorset Border'. Midway between Mells and Nunney, there is an interesting vineyard and herb garden at WHATLEY. (Open Wednesdays to Sundays, 10am to 6pm between 1 April and 30 September.) Two miles to the northwest of Mells, Babington House stands at the end of a magnificent avenue of beeches; dating from around 1700, with a wing of 1790, the house and nearby Church of St Margaret form a perfect 18th-century composition. The church is a rarity in Somerset; built in 1750, it survives virtually unchanged, with its original timber panelling and box pews. These two buildings are all that remain of the medieval hamlet of Babington, a settlement which suffered as a result the 18th-century fashion for emparking, i.e. removing the dwellings of local inhabitants in order to create an uninterrupted view from the big house. The tower on the church at LEIGH-UPON-MENDIP (pronounced lye), two-and-a-half miles to the south of Babington, is modelled on its mother church at Mells; the interior however is less ornate, with a plain Norman font and simple pews.

CRANMORE, the eastern terminus of the East Somerset Railway, lies on the southern side of the A361 Frome to Shepton Mallet road, three miles to the southwest of Leigh-upon-Mendip. Originally a broad gauge railway dating from the 1850s, the present steam railway was founded by wildlife artist, David Shepherd, in 1975. Assisted by an enthusiastic team of volunteers, Shepherd has assembled a unique collection of steam locomotives, varying in size from the tiny Lord Fisher to the mighty Black Prince. An impressive replica Victorian engine shed and workshop has been built at West Cranmore, and there is also a railway museum, art gallery and restaurant. (Open Wednesdays to Sundays (weekends only in winter months), 10am to 5.30pm between March and December.)

The church at DOULTING, on the A361 a mile-and-a-half to the west of Cranmore, is unusual in Somerset in that it has a tall spire. Dating in part from the 12th century, the exterior is impressive, but with the exception of its splendid two-storey porch with its curious carving of the green man in the vaulting, the interior is over-restored and disappointing. The village dates back to the 8th century when King Ine of Wessex gave the local estate to Glastonbury Abbey after his nephew, St Aldhelm, the Abbot of Malmesbury and first Bishop of Sherborne, died here in 709. The saint's body was carried back to Malmesbury along a circuitous route which was marked by a series of stone crosses. The church, a statue, and the spring in the former vicarage garden are all dedicated to St Aldhelm; the spring was later incorporated into a holy well which became a place of pilgrimage in medieval times.

The great 15th-century tithe barn at the southern end of the village is a relic of Doulting's monastic past. (Under the tithe system, local farmers had to hand over a tenth of their output to the landowner.) The abbey's other main source of revenue came from the great quarry which lay to the north of the village. The cream-coloured stone from here was used in the construction of Wells cathedral and for later additions to Glastonbury abbey. The terrace of estate-style cottages near the church was built at the end of the Victorian era.

An important centre of communications since pre-Roman times, the lovely old market town of SHEPTON MALLET lies on the River Sheppey, a little to the west of the Roman Fosse Way, now the A37. The settlement's Saxon name, sheep town, reveals its main commercial activity throughout the medieval period, first as a centre of wool production, and later as a weaving town. In common with other cloth-making towns in Somerset, the industry reached its peak in the 15th century, and it was at this period that the magnificent parish church was constructed. The building has one of the earliest Perpendicular towers in the county and a remarkable wagon roof with some 350 carved oak panels and around 300 bosses, each fashioned to a different design.

Perhaps Shepton Mallet's most characteristic building is its 50 foot market cross. Constructed around 1500 and restored in 1841, it has been the town's commercial focus for almost 500 years. Several participants in the Duke of Monmouth's ill-fated 'Pitchfork Rebellion' were executed here on the orders of Judge Jeffreys in 1685. The curious roofed structure standing nearby is a fixed market stall dating from the 15th century which is the only surviving remnant of the medieval 'Shambles'. A lively weekly market is still held on the site every Friday. A lane running east off Town Street leads past the church to the grim walls of the old prison; the Domesday Book was brought here for safe keeping during World War II.

Those with an interest in the town's social and industrial past should make a point of visiting the local museum at the top of the High Street. Present-day Shepton Mallet is also a prosperous light industrial town with a good range of shopping and leisure facilities; perhaps its most distinctive employer is Showerings, the makers of Babycham.

Wells Cathedral

Each year, Shepton Mallet plays host to two famous agricultural shows: the Mid-Somerset Show which is held in the town on a Saturday in August, and the Royal Bath and West Show which is held over four days at the end of May on a permanent site beside the A371, a couple of miles to the south.   One of the most exceptional Perpendicular church towers in Somerset can be found a mile to the southeast of the showground in the lovely old village of EVERCREECH. St Peter's tower is a multi-tiered combination of tall pinnacles and traceried bell-openings which create an impression of great height. Inside, the roof of the nave is renowned for its gilded roof bosses and sixteen painted angels. The church overlooks a delightful square with a village cross which is surrounded by old stone cottages and almshouses.

To the north of Shepton Mallet, the Fosse Way ascends into the eastern margins of the Mendip Hills. The old brewing village of OAKHILL lies in the lanes near the junction of the A367 and A37; although the original brewery has long since disappeared, in recent years a new one has opened to provide the pubs and inns of the district with traditional ales. Oakhill manor is a small country mansion set in an attractive 45-acre estate which houses an extraordinary collection of models and pictures, most relating to historic forms of land, sea and air transport. The car park is connected to the house by a scenic miniature railway which incorporates a scaled-down version of the Cheddar Gorge. (Open daily between Easter and late-October.)

To the northeast of Oakhill, the Fosse Way continues as the A367 Bath road, and after three miles passes through STRATTON-ON-THE-FOSSE, a former coal-mining community and home of the famous Roman Catholic boys' public school, Downside Abbey. The original abbey was founded in 1814 by a group of English Benedictines who had settled in France, but were driven out by the French Revolution. As the school has expanded, the monastery has moved to a site on higher ground around the abbey church; this impressive building took over seventy years to complete and numbered among its architects, Sir Giles Gilbert Scott. On the opposite side of the main road, Stratton's parish church contains a number of fine 18th-century features which were added at a time when revenue from the local mines was at its peak. The last coal mine closed 1968.

Chewton Cheese Dairy at Priory Farm in **CHEWTON MENDIP** is one of the few remaining cheese-making dairies using truly traditional methods. Taking anything up to 18 months to mature at carefully regulated temperatures, you begin to realise what an art it is to make a Cheddar cheese. The length of maturation is what gives the cheese its distinctive thick rind. Milk pasteurisation gets underway around 7.30am, and the process continues throughout the day until the cheese is put into the press around 3pm. You can visit the dairy at any time of the day, though there are probably not many visitors for the 7.30 kick off! The whole process is fascinating.

There is a licensed restaurant serving coffee, lunch and cream teas, and a shop where Cheddar and a wide range of dairy produce can be purchased, together with cider, wines and preserves. There is even a secluded caravan park on the estate, but do make enquiries beforehand if you want to use this as your base for touring the area.

Chewton Cheese Dairy, Priory Farm, Chewton Mendip, Bath
Tel: 01761 241666

The former weaving village of **CROSCOMBE** lies a couple of miles to the west of Shepton Mallet on a loop off the A371 Wells road. Among its many fine stone buildings is the parish church, an imposing part-13th-century building with a tall spire, a rarity in Somerset. The interior contains a magnificent collection of Jacobean dark oak fittings carved in a variety of heraldic and pastoral designs. The medieval manor house behind the church has recently been restored by the Landmark Trust. The lanes to the southwest of Croscombe lead the village of **NORTH WOOTTON**, home of the Wootton Vineyard where the Gillespie family produce a range of prize-winning estate-bottled white wines which can be tasted and purchased. (Open Mondays to Saturdays, 10am to 5pm, all year round.)

A mile and a half to the southeast of North Wootton, another famous winery can be found in the scattered village of **PILTON**, just off the A361 Shepton Mallet to Glastonbury road. The extensive grounds of Pilton Manor, a former summer residence of the bishops of Glastonbury, have been planted with vines, mostly of the German Riesling variety, and visitors are welcome to stroll around the estate and sample the end product. The present manor house is an odd combination of architectural styles: largely Georgian, its central Venetian-style window is juxtaposed with turrets, pinnacles and castellations. Another legacy from the abbey is Pilton's great cruciform tithe barn which stands on a hill surrounded by beech and chestnut trees. Sadly, its magnificent arch-braced roof was destroyed by fire when the building was struck by lightning in 1963. More fortunate has been the roof of the parish Church of St John – a 15th-century masterpiece. The building's other noteworthy features include the Norman south doorway with its striking zigzag carving, the 15th-century stained-glass windows in the chancel, and the collection of early instruments which provided the congregation with musical accompaniment prior to the arrival of the church organ.

The sheltered south-facing slopes of the southern Mendips have become popular with the new generation of English vine growers, and another fine example, the Avalon Vineyard, lies near **EAST PENNARD**, two and a half miles to the south of Pilton. The owners produce a range of wines, ciders and mead, all from organic produce. (Open daily, 2pm to 6pm between 1 June and 31 August.) An unusual National Trust-owned property, a 15th-century five-bay barn, can be found in the lanes to the south of the village of **WEST PENNARD**. (Open by appointment only; admission free.)

GLASTONBURY, three miles further west, is a small town with an immense history. With a past shrouded in mysticism, it is a mecca for those encompassing such diverse beliefs as paganism, Christianity, Arthurian legend and the existence of UFOs. At one time, Glastonbury's dramatic Tor was surrounded by a great expanse of mist-covered marshland which was prone to seasonal flooding. One of the first outsiders to sail up the River Brue to land at the Isle of Avalon was the merchant and early Christian, Joseph of Arimathea, who arrived from the Holy Land around 60 AD. According to local legend, when Joseph was surveying nearby Wearyall Hill, he plunged his staff into the ground where it miraculously took root and burst into leaf. This he took as a sign to build a church, and a wattle and daub structure was subsequently constructed on the site of the present abbey ruins. (St Congar is said to have carried out a similar feat at Congresbury, sixteen miles to the north.) Joseph's staff grew into the celebrated Christmas-flowering Glastonbury hawthorn, and although the original is believed to have been felled by an overzealous Puritan during Cromwellian times (he was blinded by a flying shard of wood in the process), a lonely windswept ancestor can still be seen on the ridge of Wearyall Hill. (According to a different version of the legend, Joseph was accompanied on a visit to Glastonbury by his nephew, the young Jesus Christ, an occurrence which provided the inspiration for William Blake's hymn, Jerusalem.)

Glastonbury Tor rears up dramatically from the Somerset Levels, a landmark which can be seen from miles around (oddly, it is often less conspicuous from close by). The 520 foot conical hill has been inhabited since prehistoric times, and excavations have uncovered evidence of Celtic, Roman and pre-Saxon occupation. Perhaps because of its distinctive shape, its has long been associated with myth and legend. Depending on the context, the tor has been identified as the Land of the Dead, Celtic Otherworld, Druid's temple, magic mountain, Arthurian hill-fort, ley line intersection, and rendezvous point for UFOs.

Whatever its mystical qualities, the steep climb to the top is rewarded with a magnificent panorama across Somerset to Wells, the Mendips, the Quantocks, and the Bristol Channel. The view is most dramatic on a misty day when the tor is surrounded by a sea of silver cloud. The striking tower at the summit is all that remains of the 15th-century Church of St Michael, an offshoot of Glastonbury Abbey which fell into disrepair following the Dissolution of the Monasteries in 1539. In that turbulent year, the tor became a place of execution when the last abbot of Glastonbury,

Richard Whiting, and two of his monks were hanged near the summit for opposing the will of Henry VIII.

The wooded rise standing between Glastonbury Tor and the town centre is known as Chalice Hill after the well standing at the foot of its southern slope. According to legend, Joseph of Arimathea is supposed to have buried the Holy Grail (the cup used by Christ at the Last Supper) beneath the spring in the 1st century AD. The spring now lies in an attractive garden maintained by the Chalice Well Trust and is surrounded by a masonry structure which is thought to date back to the 13th century. The water has a high iron content which leaves a curious rust-coloured (some say blood-coloured) residue in its wake; it is said to have curative powers and flows at a constant temperature of 52°F at the rate of 25,000 gallons per day into a pool known as the Pilgrim's Bath. (Open daily, 10am to 6pm between early-March and end-October; 1pm to 3pm in winter.)

The dramatic remains of Glastonbury Abbey can be found to the northwest of Chalice Hill in the heart of old Glastonbury. If the legend of Joseph of Arimathea is to be believed, this is the site of the earliest Christian foundation in the British Isles. The first abbey is thought to have been founded by King Ine around 700 AD, and under St Dunstan, the 10th-century abbot who went on to become the Archbishop of Canterbury, it grew in influence so that by the time of the Norman invasion, three Saxon kings had been buried here and the monastery owned estates covering an eighth of the county of Somerset. The abbey continued to grow under the guidance of the Benedictines until a disastrous fire destroyed most of the site in 1184.

When the foundations of the replacement abbey church were being excavated seven years later, a wooden sarcophagus was found 16 feet down between the shafts of two ancient crosses; inside, the bones of a large man and a slender woman were discovered (one story tells of how the woman's long golden hair remained preserved until a monk touched it, transforming it to dust). A lead cross found nearby convinced the abbot he had recovered the remains of King Arthur and Queen Guinevere, although the discovery could be described as fortuitous, given the abbey's pressing need at the time for funds to pay for reconstruction. Glastonbury soon became a place of pilgrimage, and when the main part of the abbey had been

434

rebuilt in 1278, King Edward himself arrived to witness the final interring of Arthur's bones in a huge new tomb in the choir. By this time, the abbey had grown to a magnificent 560 feet in length, with a massive central bell-tower, twin west towers, a rare clock, and a series of shrines to the good and great.

After the Dissolution, the abbey was abandoned and it soon fell into disrepair; its walls were plundered for building stone and Arthur's tomb destroyed. Most of the remains that can be seen today date from the late-medieval period, the best-preserved being St Mary's Chapel, the abbey church, and a number of ancillary buildings. The finest of these is the 14th-century abbot's kitchen, a superb structure with a vaulted roof and a fireplace in each corner which has survived virtually intact. The gatehouse now houses an interesting museum which includes a model of the abbey as it was at the time of the Dissolution. (Open daily, 9.30am to 6pm (or dusk if earlier), all year round.)

The George and Pilgrims Hotel, 1 High Street, Glastonbury

In the days when Glastonbury Abbey was internationally famous for its wealth, architectural beauty and traditional reputation as an important centre of learning, visitors and pilgrims would flock to Glastonbury. The visitors were admitted to the Abbey for varying lengths of time, dictated by certain rules. Eventually the numbers of visitors increased so dramatically that a guest house was erected outside the Abbey walls under the supervision of an Abbey official.

This was 'The George' or 'The Pilgrim's Inn' which is now called the George and Pilgrims Hotel, and found by the Market Cross. It is thought to have been built around 1475. It is a highly ornamental building with an embattled parapet surmounted at each end by an octagonal turret rising from the base of the building. The mullioned windows were inserted at a later date and over the gateway there are three shields, one the St. George's Cross, the central one the Arms of Edward IV, and the third is blank. At one time there was also supposed to be a subterranean passage which led from the cellar of the Inn to the Abbey. Inside there are old timber beams adorned by carved angels and guarded by death masks of monks. The fireplace in the bar is surrounded by Delft tiles which are 200 hundred years old, but one is different, so see of you can spot it. The whole hotel, which has been run by Ann Wain for 3 years, is very comfortable, and you are sure to enjoy your stay.

A couple of doors away, the Tribunal is a handsome early-15th-century courthouse which now serves as the tourist information office. Look out for the two square panels above the doorway: each contains a royal Tudor emblem, indicating the king's justice was meted out inside. Glastonbury contains an unusual number of churches, the finest of which are St John's Baptist Church in the High Street with its imposing 134 foot tower, and St Mary's Roman Catholic Church in Magdalene Street which was built in 1939.

Glastonbury has been called the Ancient Avalon, the New Jerusalem, and the "Holyest Erthe" in England. It is a place of magical and natural enchantment, and attracts an ever-growing number of pilgrims and seekers. One reason for its appeal is immediately obvious in the quality of light and unusual landscape in the area.

In the centre of the town, next door to the Tourist Information Centre, you will see the Gothic Image book shop. Setting out from here you can enjoy a tour of ancient Avalon, travelling to some of the hills, holy wells, and ruins.

During the journey, with an expert tour guide, you will learn about the history, myths and legends of the area: the Celts, Druids, the early Christian period, Arthurian associations, and the flowering of medieval art and architecture. There are two types of tour, one is 3 hours long, and the other is only 1 1/2 hours, conducted in small groups in a private 8-seater Toyota Space

436

Cruiser twice daily from April to September. Ring ahead for full details of availability and prices. Fascinating!

Gothic Image, 7 High Street, Glastonbury
Tel: 01458 831453 Fax: 01458 831666

The abbey's principal tithe barn stands on its own to the southeast of the main monastic buildings. Although it is small for such a great estate, it incorporates some exceptional sculptured detail, including carved heads on the corner buttresses and emblems of the four Evangelists on the gables. The barn is now the home of the Somerset Rural Life Museum, an imaginatively-presented museum dedicated to the era of pre-mechanised farming. As well as a collection of historic farm implements, there are special displays devoted to cider making, willow shoot (or withy) cutting, peat digging and thatching. (Open daily, 10am (2pm Sundays) to 5pm, all year round.)

A delightful National Trust footpath to the east of Glastonbury leads to Gog and Magog, the ancient oaks of Avalon. This pair living antiquities are all that remain of an avenue of oaks which was cut down in the 1900s to make way for a farm. (One of the felled trees was recorded as being eleven feet in diameter and having over 2000 season rings.) Another historic attraction can be found in a field beside the Godney road to the northwest of the town centre. This was the site of a prehistoric lake village which was discovered in 1892 after it was noticed that a section of an otherwise level site was studded with irregular mounds. Thought to date from around 150 BC, the village was built on a series of platforms to raise it above the surrounding marshland. Artefacts recovered during site excavations can be seen in the town museum.

One of the greatest mysteries of the locality (and one which may stretch the mind to the margins of credibility) is difficult to observe except from the air. Much-loved and propounded by those with an interest in astrology, the Glastonbury Zodiac was brought to light in 1935 by Katherine Maltwood when she was researching a book on the Holy Grail. According to Maltwood, the twelve signs of the zodiac appear on the ground (in their correct order) delineated by streams, tracks, ridges and ancient boundaries, within a fifteen-mile diameter circle centred around the village of Butleigh, three miles to the south of Glastonbury. Its origins remain unexplained.

Whereas the growth of historic Glastonbury has been severely restricted (the centre is largely a conservation area), no such restrictions have applied to STREET, a modern town lying a couple of miles to the southwest whose population now approaches 10,000. The settlement takes its name from a Roman road which ran nearby and is centred around the part-14th-century parish Church of the Holy Trinity. However, it was in the 19th century that it began to grow from a small rural village to the light industrial town that we see today. One entrepreneurial Quaker family was largely responsible for this marked expansion: Clarks, the shoemakers. In the 1820s, Cyrus and James Clark began producing sheepskin slippers, and over the following century-and-a-half, the firm grew to become one the largest manufacturers of quality shoes in Europe. The company headquarters are still located in the town today.

Many of the older buildings in Street owe their existence to Clarks, including the Friends' Meeting House of 1850, the clock tower, and the original house in which the famous Millfield School was founded (the main part of the school is now located on the outskirts of the town). The oldest part of the Clark's factory has been refurbished as a fascinating shoe museum, containing displays of historic footwear, shoe-making machinery, fashion photographs and related exhibits dating from Roman times. The company also established one of the first purpose-built factory shopping centres in the Britain, the Clarks Village, in Street and elsewhere in the town, a great many other retail outlets claim to offer goods at 'factory' prices.

Despite rising to less than 300 feet at its highest point, the long low ridge of the Polden Hills seems to dominate the Somerset Levels to the south of Street. The conspicuous columnar monument which can be seen on the ridge above BUTLEIGH WOOTTON, a couple of miles to the east, is dedicated to Vice Admiral Sir Samuel Hood, a member of the celebrated family of naval officers who won a series of important maritime victories in the second half of the 18th century. Butleigh Court in BUTLEIGH is an impressive Victorian pile built in 1845 which was later damaged by fire and divided into separate residential units. BALTONSBOROUGH, in the lanes a further two miles to the east, is the birthplace of St Dunstan, one of the greatest figures in the Anglo-Saxon church (see Glastonbury Abbey). A fine example of a medieval church house adjoins the parish churchyard; a rare find in Somerset, this early village hall served the community as a brewery and social centre.

Shapwick Country House Hotel, Shapwick,
Nr Bridgwater Tel: 01458 210321

To the west of Street, the A39 runs along the foot of the Polden ridge through a strange heathland landscape. Like everything else in this part of the world, the roads are built on peat, giving them a curious lilting feel. Around the village of SHAPWICK, the surface of the ground is scarred by an extensive peat-digging operation which extracts the dark brown material in great quantities for use in suburban gardens.

On the site of a former 12th-century monastery, in 17 acres of meadowland is Shapwick Country House Hotel. This 16th-

Vicar's Close, Wells

century manor house, once a country retreat for the Abbots of Glastonbury, is now privately owned by Eddie and Pamela Barrett. Here is rural Somerset, the location enjoys unrivalled peace and tranquillity, yet at the same time is conveniently placed as a base for touring the area.

This hotel offers the discerning guest a comfortable homely atmosphere with a touch of luxury. The 15 bedrooms are all spacious and en-suite, and many of the public rooms are of historic interest. The candlelit dining room, featuring original exposed timber beams, offers intimate surroundings in which to enjoy the excellent à la carte cuisine. The menu, changes regularly and features fresh local produce, cooked and prepared on the premises. A fabulous place to stay.

Shapwick Heath nature reserve provides a safe haven for rare plants and wildlife, although to enter, it is necessary to obtain a permit from the Nature Conservancy Council in Taunton. No such restrictions apply to the public footpath which sets out across undamaged sedge moor to the northwest of the village. At **MOORLYNCH**, a mile to the southwest, the 16-acre Moorlynch Vineyard offers tastings and tours of the winery.

The Crown Inn, The Nydon, Catcott Tel: 01278 722288

Travelling through the village of CATCOTT towards BURTLE, you will find The Crown Inn, on The Nydon. This attractive inn dates back to the late 18th century and provides an ideal stopping place for families. The interior of the pub is cosy and comfortable furnished with wooden furniture and comfortable chairs sitting on

441

the stone floors. There is a skittle alley and in the lovely gardens there is a children's play area. The food is excellent, all home-cooked, and the menu changes every fortnight. The restaurant is very popular though, so it is advisable to book ahead.

A lane to the north of Shapwick leads to the village of **WESTHAY**, home of the Peat Moor Visitor Centre. The centre incorporates an imaginatively-presented museum which gives a fascinating insight into the history and ecology of the Somerset Levels. There are descriptions of commercial peat-digging throughout the ages, the special trades which have grown up in this unique environment, and the measures which have been taken to conserve the area's flora and fauna. There is also a reconstruction of a section of the oldest manmade trackway in the world, the 'Sweet Track'; dating from around 4000 BC, it was constructed of timber posts and ran across the Levels from the Polden ridge to the Isle of Westhay.

Rising to only 25 feet above sea level, the Somerset Levels cover an extensive area bordered by the Mendips to the east, the Quantocks to the west, and Ham-stone country to the south. It is an area which is now crisscrossed by a complex system of artificial drainage channels – ditches, rhines (pronounced reens) and drains in ascending order of size – but which for centuries lay for most of the year under a layer of standing water. Such stagnant conditions were ideal for the formation of peat, which is formed when a lack of oxygen prevents the normal decomposition of vegetation. Piecemeal drainage channels had been dug for centuries, but it was only in the last quarter of the 18th century that a coordinated system was proposed which included the construction of the great King's Sedgemoor Drain of 1794. Now half-tamed, the Somerset Levels, with their characteristic double rows of pollarded willows, have much to offer the bird-watcher, rural historian and casual visitor.

Two miles to the east, an unusual medieval building stands on the the northern side of the B3151 Glastonbury road, just to the east of **MEARE**. Prior to about 1700, the Abbot's Fish House stood on the edge of Meare Pool, a substantial lake over a mile-and-a-half in diameter which provided Glastonbury abbey with a regular supply of freshwater fish. Before the lake was drained, this plain, early-14th-century building was used for salting and storage; it has three ground-floor and two first-floor rooms, the latter being reached by way of an external staircase.

The B3151 to the north of Westhay leads to WEDMORE, the ancient capital of the marshes. In 878 AD, King Alfred brought the newly-baptised Danish King Guthrum to this remote village to sign the Peace of Wedmore, a treaty which left Wessex in Alfred's hands and gave East Anglia, East Mercia and Kingdom of York to the Danes. Wedmore's largely-Perpendicular parish church has a spectacular Norman south doorway which is thought to have been designed by the same craftsmen who built Wells cathedral. The main street, the Borough, contains some fine stone buildings, including the George, a lovely old coaching inn.

In the unusually named village of MARK, you will find The White Horse Inn. The pub has played a part in the history of the village for many years, originally thought to be the site of the Abbots of Glastonbury's 'High Hall'. The present building dating back to the eighteenth century was used partly as a Parish reading room and partly as a one room Cider house.

The White Horse Inn, Mark
Tel: 01278 641234

An interesting photograph on display in the Pub shows what happened when a local traction engine driver, in need of refreshment, stopped outside whereupon a small boy jumped onto the drivers seat, grabbed the controls and sent the machine into the 'Rhyne' or canal opposite. The boy jumped clear leaving his rather irate elders to set about getting the machine out.

Dramatic events of a different kind have taken place in the short time that new owners Mike and Chris McKenzie have been in residence. Refurbishing of the outside and inside have resulted in a cosy and welcoming atmosphere to be enjoyed by locals and visitors alike. Behind the bar is a range of award winning cask ales, fine wines and speciality Malt Whiskies. A surprisingly extensive menu awaits the traveller looking for more than liquid refreshment with the emphasis definitely on quality, and Mike's curries, recently entered for the National Pub Curry of the Year competition, have attracted a growing number of devotees. Also winning the coveted '1994 Brewmaster's Standard Award' makes the White Horse Inn definitely worth a visit.

In the Somerset Levels at WOOKEY is Fenny Castle House & Country Inn, run by Mary and Lesley Brown. The house stands next to the remains of a motte and bailey castle on the River Sheppey and is late Georgian, with a cosy old fashioned atmosphere. Food is served and menu specialities include sweetbreads, fresh river eel and venison. The inn also features relaxing gardens, function room and a skittle alley in which to try your hand at bowling. Accommodation consists of six en-suite rooms which are ETB 3 Crowns Commended.

A novel way of enjoying the beautiful countryside around Wookey, in grand style, is to take a horse and carriage tour run by Miss Brown in a 1910 French Wagonette. Surely a unique and memorable way to take in the Levels.

Fenny Castle House & Country Inn, Castle Lane, Wookey,
Nr Wells Tel: 01749 672265

To the east of Wookey, the old turnpike road across the low moors, now the B3139, leads past the restored water mill and craft workshops at Burcott to the ancient ecclesiastical centre of WELLS. With a population of under 10,000, this is the smallest city in England, and were it not for its cathedral and neighbouring bishop's palace, it would be unlikely to be more than an attractive market town (lively markets are still held in the square on Wednesdays and Saturdays). However, the magnificent cathedral of St Andrew, the first entirely Gothic structure of its kind in Britain, and its cathedral close make Wells one of the gems of north

Somerset. King Ine of the West Saxons, is believed to founded the first church here around 700 AD close to the point where a line of springs rises from base of the Mendips. After a diocesan tussle with Bath, the present cathedral was begun in the 12th century and took over three centuries to complete in a series of stages which incorporated the Early English, Decorated and Perpendicular styles of Gothic architecture.

The building's 13th-century west front is widely considered to be its crowning glory. Although defaced during the English Civil War, it incorporates over 100 larger-than-life-size statues of saints, angels and prophets who gaze down onto the cathedral lawn. The twin west towers were added a couple of centuries later; curious squat structures, they look as if they would benefit from the addition of spires. The cathedral's finest internal features are the beautiful and ingenious scissor arches at the east end of the nave which support the central tower, the great 14th-century stained-glass east window over the high altar, the sweeping chapter house staircase with its elegant branching steps, and the great 14th-century astronomical clock, one of the oldest working timepieces in the world, which shows the phases of the moon, the hours and minutes on separate outer and inner dials, and marks the quarter hours with a lively knights' tournament.

The 52 acre cathedral close, or Liberty, is a tranquil city within a city. To the south of the cathedral cloisters can be found the fortified Bishop's Palace, a remarkable medieval building surrounded by a moat that is fed by the springs which give the city its name. The palace is encircled by a high stone wall and in order to gain access from the town, it is necessary to pass under a 13th-century arch known as the Bishop's Eye and then over a drawbridge which was last raised for defensive purposes in 1831. Although still the official residence of the Bishop of Bath and Wells, many parts are open to visitors, including the bishop's chapel and Jocelin's hall. The broad palace moat is home to a number of swans which are famous for their ability to ask for food by ringing a bell on the wall below the gatehouse window. (Open Tuesdays, Thursdays, Sundays and Bank Holiday Mondays, 11am to 6pm between 1 April and end-October.)

Vicar's Close, the oldest planned street in Europe, can be found on the northern side of the cathedral green. This remarkable cobbled thoroughfare was built in the mid-14th-century (the ornate chimneys were added a century later) for cathedral officers and choristers, and is connected to the cathedral by a bridge leading to the chapter house stairs. Other noteworthy buildings in Wells include Llewellyn's Almshouses, the bishop's tithe barn, the Chain Gate, Penniless Porch, where beggars used to accost visitors entering the cathedral (a custom which generally seems to be back in fashion), and the part-15th-century parish Church of St Cuthbert, which has such a lofty tower it is sometimes mistaken for the cathedral. For those keen to find out more about the history of the locality, Wells Museum, near the west front of the cathedral, contains some interesting collections of locally-found artefacts. The splendid cathedral library also has a number of rare books and manuscripts on display. A pleasant undemanding walk offering a good view of the town from the east starts from Moat Walk and leads up onto the summit of Tor Hill.

The A371 to the northwest of Wells runs along the foot of the Mendip escarpment through an area which is known for its strawberries and soft fruits. The landscape is scattered with lovely old Mendip stone settlements, including WESTBURY-SUB-MENDIP, one of the earliest sites in Britain to be populated by humankind, RODNEY STOKE and DRAYCOTT. A lane to the east of Easton leads to WOOKEY HOLE, a series of vast underground caverns which were eroded by the River Axe over thousands of years. The core of the Mendips is composed of carboniferous limestone, a rock that is dissolved by the small amount of carbonic acid in rainwater. The effect is to turn cracks into fissures, and fissures into underground channels which occasionally form into immense subterranean caverns such as these. Wookey Hole was occupied by animals such as lions, bears, woolly mammoths and rhinoceros since the Palaeolithic Age, and by human beings during the Iron Age. A large cache of prehistoric mammals' bones were discovered in a recess known as the Hyena's Den, many of them showing the animals' teeth marks.

In total, there are over 25 caverns, although only half-a-dozen are open to visitors. The Great Cave contains a rock formation known as the Witch of Wookey which casts a ghostly shadow and is associated with gruesome legends of child-eating. The emerging River Axe has been harnessed to provide power for industrial use since the 16th century; the present building on the site was constructed in the mid-1800s as a paper mill, and in 1973, it was acquired by Madame Tussaud's who have installed a number of modern visitor attractions. These include an exhibition on the history of waxworks, a museum of Victorian fairground equipment, and a workshop where handmade paper continues to be produced. (Open daily, 9.30am to 5.30pm, all year round except December.)

About a mile to the northwest of Wookey Hole lies the National Trust-owned Ebbor Gorge, a national nature reserve which offers two scenic walks, the longer of which involves a certain amount of rock scrambling. The plateau of the Mendip hills, which in places rises to over 1000 feet above sea level, is a landscape unlike any other in Somerset. The ridges and valleys are broken by belts of trees and long stone walls which have been introduced by man to provide shelter and safe grazing. The scattered weatherbeaten settlement of **PRIDDY** is the highest village in the county. Once more important than it is today, its sizable part-13th-century church contains some interesting architectural oddities. The curious thatched structure on the green is a carefully-stacked pile of wooden hurdles; these were once used to construct makeshift pens for Priddy's sheep fair, a colourful event which still takes place annually on the Wednesday closest to August 21. An impressive prehistoric site lies within a mile of the village to the northeast. Thought to be Bronze Age or earlier, Priddy Circles are composed of a series of raised banks within ditches; the nearby tumuli are known as Priddy Nine Barrows.

Although it is hard to imagine today, the Mendip Hills were once an important lead and silver mining district, with the last mine at Priddy remaining open until 1908. Lead-mining activity was centred around **CHARTERHOUSE**, a remote village lying four miles to the northwest. The settlement takes its name from the Carthusian monastery at Witham Priory who owned one of the four Mendip mining sectors, or Liberties. The area had been known for its mines since the Iron Age, and such was their importance that the Romans made them state property within six years of their arrival in Britain. Under their influence, silver and lead ingots, or pigs, were exported to France and Italy, and the settlement grew into a sizable town with its own fort and amphitheatre, the remains of which can be still be out. Improved technology in later centuries allowed for the reworking of the original seams, and the area is now littered with dilapidated mine buildings and smelting houses.

A path from Charterhouse church leads up onto the 1067 foot Black Down, the highest point in the Mendips. To the northwest, the B3134 descends through Barrington Combe, a deep cleft which is said to have provided the Reverend Augustus Toplady with the inspiration for his hymn, Rock Of Ages. A much more spectacular ravine, CHEDDAR GORGE, carries the B3371 southwestwards onto the Somerset Levels. One of the most famous and most-often visited tourist attractions in Britain, its tall cliffs of curiously-weathered limestone are adorned with bands of precariously-rooted undergrowth. As well as being known for its gorge, Cheddar is famous for its caves and its cheese. Although much embellished by modern tourist paraphernalia, the two main show caves, Gough's and Cox's, are worth seeing for their sheer scale and spectacular calcite formations. (Open daily, 10am to 5.30pm, all year round.) An almost complete skeleton dubbed 'Cheddar Man' was discovered in Gough's cave in 1903 and now can be seen in the nearby museum. Starting from a little further down the hill, the 322 steps of Jacob's Ladder lead up the face of the gorge to the site of Pavey's Lookout Tower. An unusual old market cross stands at the centre of the old village; really two crosses in one, a hexagonal superstructure was added to the original 15th-century preaching cross a century later.

The term 'Cheddar' cheese refers to a recipe which was developed in the mid-19th-century by Joseph Harding, an educated farmer from near Bath who made the first scientific investigation into cheese-making. As the name refers to a recipe and not the place, the cheese can be made anywhere in the world; however, the area around Cheddar is filled with cheese manufacturers of varying size; from single farmhouses to substantial dairies. A number of these supplement their income by offering ancillary attractions such as guided tours, craft demonstrations, children's zoos and catering facilities.

To the west of Cheddar, the A371 skirts around the circular Cheddar reservoir before passing to the north of AXBRIDGE, a small town with a delightful centre which is worth making a detour to visit. Prior to the Norman conquest Axbridge was a fortified market town with its own mint, and in the late medieval period, it made its living from Mendip wool and cloth. Although nothing to do with the monarch in question, King John's Hunting Lodge in the Square is an exceptional example of a half-timbered merchant's house dating from around 1500. (Its name is a reminder that the Mendip hills were once a royal hunting forest.) Now owned by the National Trust, it was extensively restored in the 1970s and now houses an excellent local museum. (Open daily, 2pm to 5pm between Easter and end-September.)

On the square in the centre of Axbridge, opposite Kings John's Hunting Lodge, is **The Lamb Hotel**, managed by David and Sue Williams. The building in which the hotel is housed dates back to the 15th century, with the addition of an frontage which was added in the 1830s. The site is notable for having been the Guild Hall until the new town hall was built, also in 1830. The sign which hangs outside is also of significance in Axbridge and features a lamb and flag. This is the emblem of St. John the Baptist, to whom the parish church is dedicated, and which was also adopted as the Axbridge Borough crest.

The Lamb Hotel, The Square, Axbridge
Tel: 01934 732253

The Lamb Hotel, is much more of an inn than a hotel, having only three en-suite rooms available. Nevertheless, the rooms are good value, and comfortable - and haunted! The resident ghost is called Molly, she is believed to be friendly and her reasons for being here are unknown. The bar is quiet and has a very traditional atmosphere. You will find no juke boxes or fruit machines here, making the pub very popular with locals and visitors alike. A feature to look out for in here is the bottle collection embedded into the bar, it is both colourful and unusual. Bar meals are of course served, and because Sue is vegetarian, they are particularly well catered for.

Axbridge's magnificent parish Church of St John also overlooks the Square. A fine example of Somerset Perpendicular, it stands at the top of an impressive staircase and contains some exceptional monumental brasses and stained glass. Elsewhere in the town centre, there are an unusual number of handsome Georgian town houses. Those with an interest in tropical birds should make a point of finding the Ambleside Bird Gardens at LOWER WEARE, two miles to the west of Axbridge. (Open daily, 10am to 5pm between early-March and late-October.) A lane to the west of here leads to the hamlet of WEBBINGTON LOXTON, home of the Wheelwright's Working Museum and Gypsy Folklore Collection. (Open Wednesdays to Sundays (daily in July, August and September), 10am to 6pm, all year round.)

The A38 to the southwest of Lower Weare leads over the M5 to Brent Knoll, a conspicuous landmark which can be seen from as far away as South Wales. Before the Somerset Levels were drained, this isolated hill would almost certainly have been an island. It rises to 450 feet and is topped by an Iron Age hill fort which can be reached by way of the footpath which starts near East Brent church. King Alfred is said to have fought and won a battle against the Danes on the hill's southern slopes, and there are also stories that the knoll owes its existence to the Devil. The villages of Brent Knoll and East Brent both have exceptional churches. The one at Brent Knoll, to the west, has an interesting series of bench ends which tell the story of how a 15th-century parish priest won a quarrel with the abbot of Glastonbury. (The abbot is represented by a fox and the parishioners by a variety of animals, including geese.) The one at East Brent has a superb 17th-century plasterwork ceiling and a collection of carved bench ends which incorporate the abbot's coat of arms and initials.

On the outskirts of the village of LYMPSHAM you will find the delightful Hope Farm Cottages. Once a working farm, the four holiday cottages were once farm buildings which have been tastefully converted to provide first class accommodation. The

Market Cross, Somerton

cottages offer a high standard of decor and furnishings and are very well-equipped. The kitchens are all electric and come with fridge, cooker and microwave as standard. Each bedroom has a bathroom en-suite and all bed linen, duvets and towels are provided. All the cottages have two bedrooms and can accommodate up to four people. Other facilities on the site include a launderette, games room, pay phone and ample car parking. In an area that is renowned for its natural beauty, the 3 acre Hope Farm site is surrounded by picturesque countryside and open farmland. You will have to go far to equal Hope Farm cottages.

Hope Farm Cottages, Brean Road, Lympsham, Weston-super-Mare, Tel: 01934 750506

To the east of Lympsham, the lanes lead to BERROW and BREAN, two ancient settlements on the Bristol Channel which have been swamped by 20th-century seaside development. Both have part-13th-century churches which look out of place amongst the caravans and chalets. The sandy beach here is over five miles long, and at its northern end, the 320 foot high Brean Down juts out into the sea, an imposing remnant of the Mendip hills (another can be seen in the shape of the offshore island, Steep Holm).

Remains of an Iron Age coastal fort and a Roman temple have been discovered on the Down which is now a designated nature reserve under the ownership of the National Trust. The fortifications at the western end were constructed in 1867 and partially blown up in 1900 when a soldier accidentally fired his rifle into the ammunition store. The tidal range here is amongst the greatest in Europe, and the currents around the headland can be dramatic and dangerous.

Further south, BURNHAM-ON-SEA is a sizable seaside town with a wide sandy beach which at low tide seems to extend for miles. When mineral springs were discovered here in the late 18th century, an attempt was made to make Burnham into a spa town to rival Cheltenham. However, the efficacious effects of the waters were never properly demonstrated, and the town had to rely on its beach to attract visitors. (The curious square structure raised on stilts above the waves is known as the Low Lighthouse.) Thanks to its sandy foundations, the west tower of the part-14th-century parish church has a worrying lean. Inside there is a remarkable Jacobean altarpiece originally made for Whitehall Palace which was carved by Grinling Gibbons to a design Sir Christopher Wren. A stroll along the seafront to the southeast leads to HIGHBRIDGE, a small town which was once a busy coastal port at the mouth of the Glastonbury Canal. A couple of miles to the southeast, the enterprising owners of New Road Farm near EAST HUNTSPILL have introduced a number of impressive visitor attractions.

New Road Farm, New Road, East Huntspill
Tel: 01278 783250

New Road Farm is a typical lowland dairy farm run by Derek and Pauline Kidner. The farmhouse was built in the late 17th century and is now a listed building. The house has been extended over the centuries, but still retains its traditional character and all

Glastonbury Abbey

the rooms are beautifully decorated with antique furnishings. A part of the house is open as a tea-room, and although the family still live here, you are welcome to explore their home.

As well as keeping a variety of cows, other animals are farmed here too. Different breeds of pigs and a small flock of sheep containing a variety of breeds are kept on the farm. Hens are kept for their free range eggs, as well as several rare breeds which produce fertile eggs for sale, or hatched on the farm. There are also some goats, which apparently are all friendly!

In addition to the usual farm animals, the Kidners have some more unusual ones. Gordon and Bennet are two male foxes, brought to the farm at six months and sadly too tame to be let back into the wild. Sage the barn owl is one of a collection of owls and birds of prey, there are polecats and ferrets, a chipmunk, rabbits, tortoises which they breed, and badgers as well as the complement of cats and dogs.

The whole farm is well laid out, and will entertain children and adults for several hours. The visitor centre is excellent, and from there you can watch the blacksmith at work. The guidebook about the farm is well-written, and an ideal memento of your visit.

Bason Bridge Inn, East Huntspill, Highbridge
Tel: 01278 782616

Elsewhere is the village you will find a great place to stop for a drink and a bite to eat at the **Bason Bridge Inn**. The pub was taken over by present owners Keith and Ray Hobbs 8 years ago when it was somewhat run down. Over the years they have completely altered the place and can now offer accommodation in addition to a great pub. There are four en-suite rooms here, all clean and comfortable, and the location of the Bason Bridge makes it ideal as a base for touring the Somerset Levels. The bars are great too, serving real ales and a good range of bar food. The quality of the food is excellent, the portions are generous and are very good value. Should you require further entertainment, there are skittle alleys, pool tables and a darts board.

In **PAWLETT**, there is a great bed and breakfast at **Brickyard Farm**. The delightful property can be found near the river at the end of a cul-de-sac. The name originates from the time when it was owned by the foreman of the local brickyard. Now the home of Mr and Mrs Worgan, they have created a charming guest house and delight in welcoming guests. There are four letting rooms, which have views over the fields or the river, and one features a pretty cast iron bed. For those who prefer to be more independent, there are two self-catering chalets here too. The gardens are beautifully maintained and include a children's play area and a pond in which Mr Worgan keeps an impressive koi carp collection. He is very knowledgeable about the fish, so if you are interested, I'm sure he will tell you all about them. The river, which runs alongside the property, is particularly attractive to fishermen, as there is coarse fishing available. Guests can enjoy their own residents lounge and a big bonus, considering the remote location, is that there is a well stocked, licensed bar.

Brickyard Farm Guest House, River Road, Pawlett,
Nr. Bridgwater Tel: 01278 683381

To the south of Pawlett, the main roads cross the ridge of the Polden Hills into the low-lying area known as King's Sedge Moor. A field on the northern side of the village of **WESTONZOYLAND** was the site of the Battle of Sedgemoor, the last battle to be fought on English soil in July 1685. The well-equipped Royalist forces of James II defeated the followers of the Duke of Monmouth to bring to a bloody end what became known as the 'Pitchfork Rebellion'. Around 700 of Monmouth's followers were slaughtered during the battle, and several hundred more were brought to the churchyard at Westonzoyland where many were hanged; the Duke himself was executed on Tower Hill ten days later. However, it was during the infamous Judge Jeffreys' 'Bloody Assizes' that the greatest damage was inflicted: well over 1000 men were condemned to death and summarily executed, and another 600 transported to the colonies. Today, the site of the battle is marked by a stark memorial. Westonzoyland is also the site of a steam-powered pumping station which was built to pump water into the King's Sedgemoor Drain; now restored, it is open to visitors during the summer months.

Another interesting pumping station can be seen beside the River Parrett at **BURROW BRIDGE**, three miles due south; inside, there is a fine collection of Victorian pump engines. The conspicuous conical hill which can be seen nearby is known as Barrow Mump. This isolated knoll is rumoured to be the site of an ancient fort belonging to King Alfred, the 9th-century King of Wessex, who is thought to have retreated to this lonely spot to escape a bloody Viking incursion. It was during his time here that he sought shelter in the hut of a local Athelney family and was scolded for 'burning the cakes'. Barrow Mump is now crowned by the picturesque remains of a medieval church which can be seen from miles around.

The last thatched windmill in England can be found in the lanes, four miles to the east of Barrow Mump. Stembridge Tower Mill at **HIGH HAM** was built in 1822 and remained in use until 1910. (Open Sundays, Mondays and Wednesday, 2pm to 5pm between late-March and late-September.) The village of Stoke St Gregory, two miles to the southwest, is the centre of Somerset's wicker industry. The straight shoots of pollarded willows, or withies, have been cultivated on a substantial scale ever since the taste for wicker furnishings developed during the Victorian era.

After the withies are cut, cleaned and boiled, they are woven into a wide variety of baskets and other items using traditional methods which have been handed down for generations. Withies also provide the raw material for artist's charcoal.

The Somerset Levels are perhaps the most important area of Wetland left in England. Willow growing and basket making have long been a traditional Somerset craft and one of its oldest industries, once employing hundreds of local people. Today though much a smaller enterprise it is very much alive and well and even enjoying a revival. **The Willows & Wetlands Visitors Centre** is run by P. Coate and Son who have been growing willow for over 150 years. At the centre you can see the process that changes the willow into the beautiful finished baskets and furniture that can be purchased in the shop, and how they make the artists' charcoal that is found in nearly every school and college art class in the land. The Wetlands Visitors Centre shows how the landscape we see today has been created from the marsh and swamp, and highlights the wetland wildflowers, insects and birds that abound in this unique area.

Willows & Wetlands Visitors Centre, Meare Green Court, Stoke St Gregory, Taunton Tel: 01823 490249

West Somerset and Exmoor

Packhorse Bridge, Alreford

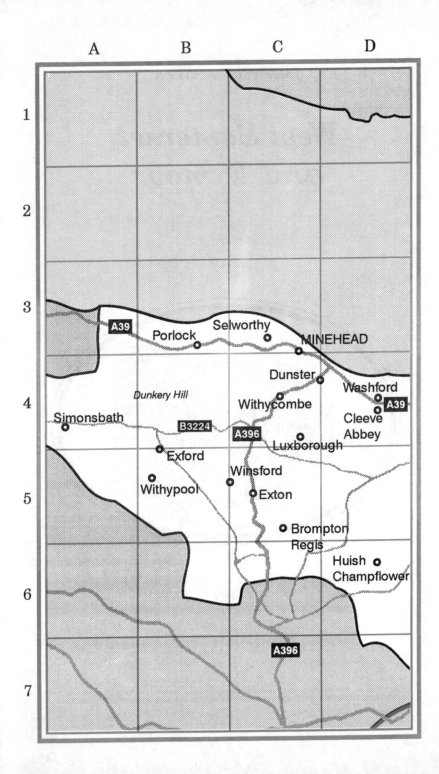

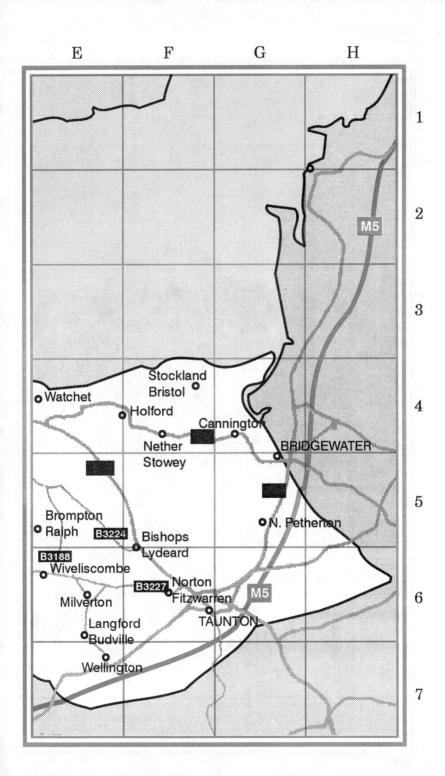

Dunster Yam Market

CHAPTER FOURTEEN

West Somerset and Exmoor

The ancient inland port and industrial town of BRIDGWATER stands at the lowest medieval bridging point on the River Parrett. Despite having been fortified since before the Norman invasion, the settlement remained little more than a village until an international trade in wool, wheat and other agricultural produce began to flourish in the late Middle Ages. During this period, Bridgwater grew to become the most important town on the coast between Bristol and Barnstaple, and the fifth-busiest port in Britain. The largely 14th-century parish Church of St Mary, with its disproportionately large spire, is the only building to survive from the medieval boom, the castle having been dismantled after the English Civil War and the 13th-century Franciscan friary and St John's hospital having long since disappeared. The oldest and most interesting part of the town lies between King Street and the West Quay, an area whose layout is medieval, but whose buildings are among the finest examples of Georgian domestic architecture in Somerset.

Prior to the construction of a new canal dock a short distance downstream, ships used to tie up on either side of the river below Bridgwater's medieval three-arched bridge. The last remnant of the castle, the Water Gate, can still be seen here on the West Quay, along with a number of fine Georgian residences, the most notable of which, the Lions, was built in 1725. After a long period of decline caused by a long-running war with the nation's continental trading partners, the town underwent something of an industrial renaissance in the 19th century. Glass manufacture had started the previous century, and a canal terminus, complete with docks, warehouses, brickworks and retractable railway bridge, was built between 1837 and 1841 a few hundred yards north of the old centre. Finally closed in 1970, the site has now been restored as a fascinating piece of industrial archeology and is well worth a visit. Bridgwater's manufacturers have long since relocated to the outskirts of town, and the most evident of these, a cellophane factory, makes its presence known to residents and visitors alike by its distinctive odour.

The interior of the parish church is worth seeing for its painting of the Descent From The Cross by an unknown Italian artist, and the fine Jacobean screen which extends across a side chapel. It was from the tower that the Duke of Monmouth is reputed to have spotted the approaching army of James II in July 1685; this supposed advantage gave him the inspiration to launch the unsuccessful surprise attack which led to his disastrous defeat in the Battle of Sedgemoor the following day. A bronze statue of Bridgwater's most famous son, Robert Blake, can be seen at the top of Fore Street. This celebrated military leader was born in 1598 in the house which is now the town museum. In his forties, he became an important officer in Cromwell's army and twice defended Taunton against overwhelming Royalist odds; then at the age of fifty, he was given command of the British navy and went on to win a number of important victories against the Dutch and Spanish, so restoring the nation's naval supremacy in Europe. The museum contains a three-dimensional model of the Battle of Santa Cruz, one of Blake's most famous victories, along with a collection of his personal effects. There is also a similar diorama of the Battle of Sedgemoor and a large collection of locally-discovered artefacts dating from the Neolithic period to the Second World War. (Open daily, 11am (2pm Sundays) to 5pm, all year round.) Also well worth seeing is Bridgwater's spectacular annual carnival which is held in the town on the first Thursday in November.

Situated on the west side of Bridgwater, with superb views to the Quantock Hills, is Woodlands, run by Richard and Diane Palmer. This spacious period house offers superb country house standard accommodation, at bed and breakfast prices and was once the residence of Round-the-World yachtsman Donald Crowhurst. There is a very relaxing atmosphere about the place despite its proximity to the town. The 4 bedrooms are superb, all well-equipped and three have en-suite facilities. The comfortable lounge/sitting room is for the exclusive use of guests, and has a selection of books, a TV and games for whiling away the evenings.

In the winter it is made even more cosy with an open log fire. Your hosts provide breakfasts that can only be described as gargantuan, and evening meals are by arrangement. The extensive landscaped gardens are well looked after and have a pond with Koi Carp. For those interested in wildlife, foxes, bats and badgers are frequently seen in the late evening. A great place to stay, where the service is always courteous, ideal for a quiet break.

Woodlands, 35 Durleigh Road, Bridgwater
Tel: 01278 423442

At DURLEIGH, in the lanes two miles to the southwest of Bridgwater, West Bower Farm is an extraordinary building which has been converted from a medieval gatehouse, its twin turrets having been incorporated into the large stone farmhouse behind. The nearby reservoir, which offers good freshwater fishing, is fed by the Bridgwater and Taunton Canal. Continuing westwards for two-and-a-half miles through the village of ENMORE, the small redbrick country mansion, Barford Park, can be found on the road to Four Forks. This delightfully-proportioned Queen Anne house is set in extensive grounds incorporating a walled flower garden, a water garden, an archery glade, and a large area of broad-leafed woodland. The interior contains some exceptional examples of Queen Anne furniture and is in daily family use. (Open by appointment only: telephone 01278 671269.

To the west of Enmore, the ground rises into the southern margins of the Quantock Hills, an Area of Outstanding Natural Beauty which stretches from Kingston St Mary, three miles north of Taunton, to Quantoxhead above the Bristol Channel. Rising to 1260 feet at the highest point, Wills Neck, the northern Quantocks are characterised by scattered woods and open heathland which supports one of the country's last remaining herds of wild red deer. The exposed hilltops are littered with Neolithic and Bronze Age remains, including around 100 burial mounds, many of which look like simple piles of rocks. The richer soil to the south sustains arable farms and denser woodland. This varied upland landscape, several pockets of which are owned by the National Trust, offers some excellent opportunities for walking and riding.

One of the loveliest areas in the Quantocks is around Fyne Court, the headquarters of the Somerset Trust for Nature Conservation near the village of BROOMFIELD. Leased to the organisation by the National Trust, the 26-acre grounds are a designated nature reserve which incorporates a walled garden, two ponds, a lake, and a small arboretum. The main house was built in the 17th century by the Crosse family, but was largely destroyed by fire in the 1890s. Its most illustrious occupant, Andrew Crosse, was an early 19th-century pioneer of electricity; known locally as 'the thunder and lightning man', one of his lightning conductors can still be seen on an oak tree in the grounds. According to rumour, one of his experiments created tiny live insects, a story which is widely believed to have given Mary Shelley the inspiration to write Frankenstein in 1818. After the fire, all that remained of the house was the library and music room, and these have now been converted into an impressive interpretation centre and eating place. (Open daily, 9am to 6pm, all year round; admission free.)

On the main street of the village of WEST BAGBOROUGH, you will find the only pub, The Rising Sun, run by Ken and Irene Oxley. The 16th century traditional inn is the hub of village life, boasting its own cricket team. Look out for the two cricket bats that are kept in special presentation cases, as they sport some very distinguished autographs. Village life aside, the pub is great for visitors in the area, offering quality home-cooked food, for which it is well-known, and bed and breakfast accommodation. The four rooms available are en-suite, and the location is perfect if you are wanting to explore the Quantock Hills. Back down in the bar area, you can enjoy something to eat from the very extensive menu with a many of the meals produced from local produce. The specialities are hearty casseroles and fruit dishes, but there is plenty of choice. Well worth a try if you're nearby.

The Rising Sun, West Bagborough, Nr. Taunton
Tel: 01823 432575

To the east and north of West Bagborough, the lanes undulate through some of the most beautiful upland scenery in Somerset. Throughout its history, this serene landscape has attracted Romantic poets and novelists including Wordsworth, Coleridge and Lamb. NETHER STOWEY, a peaceful village in the northwestern foothills of the Quantocks, is thankfully now bypassed by the main A39 Bridgwater to Minehead road. In Norman times it was the site of an early motte and bailey castle, the foundations of which can still be seen on the hill to the west of the centre. At the opposite end of the village stands Stowey Court, a substantial manor house which was begun by Lord Audley in 1497 shortly before he joined a demonstration against Henry VII's taxation policy. He was executed soon after. The clock tower in the centre of the village was erected in 1897 to replace a medieval market cross, a reminder that Nether Stowey was once a small market town.

A century earlier, a local tanner, Tom Poole, had lent the cottage at the end of his garden to his friend, Samuel Taylor Coleridge, who stayed there for three years with his wife and child. During this time he wrote The Rime Of The Ancient Mariner and sections of Christabel and Frost At Midnight, and was visited on many occasions by other literary figures of the day, including William Wordsworth and Charles Lamb, a colourful invasion which is claimed to have led the locals to believe they were harbouring a den of French spies. Coleridge's cottage is now owned by the National Trust and is open to visitors on Sundays, Tuesdays, Wednesdays and Thursdays, 2pm to 5pm between late-March and end-September.

To the south of the village, a lane leads up to OVER STOWEY, starting point for the Forestry Commission's Quantock Forest Trail, a pleasant three-mile walk which is lined with a selection of native and imported trees which have been planted since World War II. A little to the west of Nether Stowey, there is small privately-owned manor house which is only open for a few days each year. Dodington Hall is a Tudor gem set in attractive semi-formal gardens whose great hall features a splendid oak roof and a carved stone fireplace. (Open Sundays only, 2pm to 5pm between mid-May and late-July.)

Castle of Comfort, Dodington, Nether Stowey
Tel: 01278 741264

Castle of Comfort can be found set back from the A39 near the village of DODINGTON. The name Castle of Comfort features as far back as the Domesday Book, when there was a real castle on the site. The present building has a 400 year history and was once a coaching inn. Coleridge, the poet, used to live nearby, and is said to have composed his most famous work, The Rime of the Ancient Mariner, during stays at the Castle of Comfort. Apparently both Coleridge, his wife, and their friend William Wordsworth, used to drink at the Inn in those days.

With such a distinguished past, it is not surprising that this hotel offers such a high standard of comfort. The five en-suite bedrooms are all of a good size, and well-appointed, with two rooms featuring four-poster beds and the original fireplaces. The restaurant offers an à la carte menu with home-cooked food of a very high quality, and a good wine list to complement your meal. The bar is open all day, and in winter you can relax by the open fire, while in summer you may like to take your drinks into the garden. The gardens are attractively laid out, and the grounds lead directly to the woods where you may see deer. A relaxing atmosphere pervades this family owned and run hotel, and is a really special place to stay.

Further west, the A39 passes close to a number of charming rural villages, many of which allow access to the wooded combes and bracken-covered hillsides on the Quantocks above. A track from the village of HOLFORD leads up to a large Iron Age hill fortification known as Dowsborough Fort. Two of the most dramatic viewpoints in the Quantocks, Beacon Hill and Bicknoller Hill, lie on National Trust-owned land; on the latter can be seen a prehistoric livestock enclosure known as Trendle Ring. The view to the northeast takes in the angular shape of the Hinkley Point nuclear power station on the Bristol Channel coast.

The ancient village of STOGURSEY lies midway between the A39 and the coast. In the 12th century, this was the lair of the renegade lord, Fulke de Breaute, who along with a ruthless band of followers, terrorised the surrounding population until he was hunted down and brought to justice. The remains of his castle can still be made out. At KILVE, on the A39 three miles to the west, there is a delightful little church with a squat medieval-looking tower which probably dates from the 17th century as prior to 1636, the church bells were hung in a wooden structure in the churchyard. The nearby ruins are the remains of a medieval college of priests, or chantry, whose chapel stood on the northern side of the church.

A track beyond the churchyard leads down to a beach, a pleasant place despite its reputation as a favoured haunt of glats, conger eels up to ten feet in length which lie in wait among the boulders near the shore. Once known as 'St Keyna's serpents', local people used to search for them using trained 'fish dogs'.

From Kilve, a pleasant walk leads to **EAST QUANTOXHEAD**, a highly picturesque village containing an assortment of thatched cottages, a mill beside a millpond, and a handsome manor house, Court House, which stands within a beautiful garden on a rise overlooking the village and the sea. The manor has been in the same family bloodline since the time of the Domesday Book. In the 13th century, it passed by marriage to the Luttrells, subsequent owners of Dunster Castle, and the present house was built by succeeding generations of the family, mostly in the 16th- and 17th-centuries. The former estate church beside the house dates from the 14th century. Inside, there is some fine Renaissance woodwork, an imposing tomb chest commemorating two 16th-century members of the Luttrell family, and a rare 14th-century rood screen, one of the few examples in Somerset. Little remains of the village of **WEST QUANTOXHEAD**, or **ST AUDRIES**, two miles to the west, following an extensive redevelopment in the mid 19th century. Its few remaining features are a Victorian mansion, now a girls' school, a handsome neo-Gothic church, and a series of unusual gates, fences and walls which give the estate a flavour of organised respectability.

The stretch coastline between Quantoxhead and the bird sanctuary near **STEART**, ten miles to the east, is for the most part bleak and uninteresting. The sanctuary is located on the low peninsula between the Parrett estuary and the Bristol Channel, and from here is it possible to view the fast-flowing offshore tidal race, a dramatic and dangerous spectacle. From Steart, there is a footpath along the west bank of the Parrett all the way back to Bridgwater. Places of interest on the way include **COMBWICH**, once the lowest fording point on the river and the likely site of a great battle between the Saxons and the Danes, and **CHILTON TRINITY**, a village with a fine church which can be reached by taking a shortcut avoiding a major bend in the river. On the A39 three miles to the west of Bridgwater, the Heritage Gardens at Cannington College contain an impressive collection of rare and exotic plants, examples of which are on sale in the specialist plant centre. (Open daily, 2pm to 5pm between Easter and end-October.)

Another pleasant walk follows the towpath of the Bridgwater and Taunton Canal, a 14 mile inland waterway which was constructed in the 1820s and fully reopened in the summer of 1994

470

following several decades of neglect and a twenty-year programme of restoration. A relative latecomer when it opened in 1827, the canal was constructed as part of an ambitious scheme to create a water-borne route between Exeter and Bristol which avoided the treacherous journey around the Cornish peninsula. It was also used to carry coal and iron from South Wales to the towns of inland Somerset and to export wool and agricultural produce to the urban centres of Britain. The towpath winds its way through some of the most attractive countryside in the Somerset Levels, and the restored locks, swing bridges, engine houses and unique paddle-gearing equipment add interest to the walk. The canal also offers a variety of recreational facilities, including boating, fishing, canoeing and bird watching, and passes close to some attractive villages: at NORTH NEWTON, there is a small country manor, Maunsel House, which is occasionally open to visitors, and at CREECH ST MICHAEL, there is a part 13th-century church which is worth seeing for its fine wagon roof. At the canal's southern end, boats have access to the River Tone via Firepool Lock in the heart of Taunton.

TAUNTON, the county town of Somerset, has only been its sole centre of administration since 1936. (Previous county towns include Ilchester and Somerton.) The settlement was founded as a military camp by the Saxon King Ine in the 8th century, and by the early Norman period it had grown to have its own castle, Augustinian monastery and minster. An extensive structure whose purpose has traditionally been more administrative than military, the castle was the focus of important military sieges on two separate occasions during the English Civil War. Shortly after the ill-fated Pitchfork Rebellion of 1685, over 150 followers of the Duke of Monmouth were sentenced to death here by Judge Jeffreys during the Bloody Autumn Assizes. (His ghost is said to haunt the castle grounds on September nights.) Today, the much-altered castle houses the Somerset County Museum, an informative local museum containing a large collection of exhibits on the archeology and natural history of the county; there is also a special display on the Somerset Light Infantry. (Open Mondays to Saturdays, 10am to 5pm, all year round.) A section of the old monastic gateway known as the Priory Barn can still be seen near the county cricket ground.

Warm Summer evenings, and the slap of a leather ball on willow - cricket devotees will understand the lure of the game. At the Priory Barn, you can discover the **Somerset County Cricket Museum**, where fans of the game come to enjoy the nostalgic displays celebrating past glories. Housed in the historic old barn in the County Cricket Ground, the museum holds the 'hallowed' treasures of some of cricket's most famous sons, including press cuttings, international and county caps, photographs, and other memorabilia. If you become an associate Member you will be entitled to free admission and use of the lending library, and the subscription is only £5. The 'barn' is likely to have been a gate house or lodging house for the Priory, although the actual location of this remains something of a mystery. The smooth cricket ground that you can see today would once have been part of the Priory grounds, which probably stretched down to the river and provided a spot for cattle to roam and graze.

Somerset County Cricket Museum, 7 Priory Avenue,
Taunton Tel: 01823 275893

In common with many other towns and villages in the West Country, Taunton had a thriving wool, cloth-making (and later silk) industry during the late Middle Ages. The profits earned by the medieval cloth merchants went to build not one, but two enormous churches: St James' and St Mary's. Both have soaring Perpendicular towers which have since been rebuilt, and both have imposing interiors: the former has a remarkable carved stone font, and the latter an elegant painted roof adorned with angels. The

Packhorse Bridge, Alreford

town centre is scattered with other fine buildings, most notably the timber-framed Tudor House in Fore Street and the 17th-century almshouses. Taunton continues to be an important commercial centre with a lively weekly market and a thriving light industrial sector which benefits from some excellent transport links with the rest of the country. Other visitor attractions include Vivary Park, with its ponds, gardens and jogging trail, and the Brewhouse Theatre and Arts Centre.

The Brewhouse Theatre and Arts Centre was opened in 1977 after a concerted fundraising effort by numerous townspeople who were interested in the arts and felt that the county town of Taunton should have its own theatre. The modern auditorium seats 352 and the administration offices that adjoin it are housed in a Grade II listed building. There is a studio at the back of the building where visual art workshops take place and there is a gallery, where paintings and sculpture from local artists are displayed.

The Brewhouse Theatre and Arts Centre, Coal Orchard, Taunton, Tel: 01823 274608

There is a full programme of quality theatre, jazz, folk, dance, comedy, cabaret, children's show, drama and plays. You name it and they do it. Whatever your taste, there is sure to be something on that will appeal.

There is also a restaurant and bar, which offer wholesome lunches and snacks, as well as vegetarian, meat and fish dishes. All the sweets are deliciously tempting and home-made.

Lying on the south-facing foothills of the Quantocks just north of the village of CHEDDON FITZPAINE, the beautiful Hestercombe Gardens lie within easy reach of central Taunton. This beautifully-restored Edwardian garden is one of the finest examples in the country of the professional collaboration between the architect, Sir Edwin Lutyens, and the landscape designer, Gertrude Jekyll. Originally laid out in 1904, Hestercombe was restored in the 1980s by Somerset County Council using Jekyll's original planting scheme as a guide. (Open daily, 9am (2pm weekends) to 5pm, all year round (closed weekends in winter).

The sizable village of BISHOPS LYDEARD lies four miles northwest of Taunton, just off the A358 Williton road.

The Mount and Lydeard Crafts, The Mount, 32 Mount Street, Bishops Lydeard Tel: 01823 432208

In Mount Street, next to the Bird in the Hand pub, you will find The Mount and Lydeard Crafts, run by Jane and David Hinton. The handsomely proportioned house is Georgian, built of local red sandstone, and is an excellent example of a Somerset country gentleman's residence. Underneath is the craft shop, which was formerly the butchery for the village. The archway and stone-flagged passage, used by the animals, still exists.

The house is very welcoming, and all guests are immediately made to feel at home. There are 3 bedrooms with village or hill views, all delightfully furnished and decorated with fresh flowers. The day starts with an excellent cooked breakfast, using many locally produced foods, and includes home-made marmalade and jams. Evening meals can also be prepared by arrangement. On fine days, guests can enjoy afternoon tea in the pretty garden. A feature of this delightful area is the small water garden with its well-stocked fishpond. The Mount is ideally situated for walking in the Quantocks or driving further afield to Exmoor, Dartmoor or the sea to the north and south. Steam train enthusiasts will find the West Somerset Railway terminus within walking distance. The train whistle can be heard from the house as it leaves for the picturesque journey to Minehead.

Beneath the house, at street level, Jane and David have a craft shop, Lydeard Crafts, which you should make time to visit. In this fascinating shop there is an excellent selection of items which far exceed one's expectations. The range of crafts is impressive, some by nationally celebrated artists, all being made within a 10-mile radius of Bishops Lydeard.

Farmhouse cider has been made in the countryside around Taunton since the first professional cider-makers came over from Normandy with William the Conqueror. The damp fertile land in this part of Somerset is ideal for growing cider apples, and a number of producers, large and small, still operate in the area. One of the largest has its factory at NORTON FITZWARREN, a scattered village on the B3227, a couple of miles west of Taunton. There is also an early Bronze Age bank and ditch enclosure here, artefacts from which can be seen in the county museum at Taunton Castle. A producer of traditional farmhouse cider, R J Sheppy, has a forty-acre orchard beside the A38, three miles to the southwest of Taunton. Now well-geared up for visitors, members of the public can view the pressing room, barrel store and special museum dedicated to cider-making. TRULL, on a minor road a mile-and-a-half to the east, has a part-13th-century church which contains a remarkable carved-wood pulpit dating from around 1500.

The old market town of WELLINGTON lies beside the A38, six miles to the southwest of Taunton. Once an important producer of woven cloth and serge, the prosperity of the town owed much to Quaker entrepreneurs and later the Fox banking family. (Fox, Fowler and Co were the last private bank in England to issue notes, continuing to do so until 1921 when they were taken over by Lloyds.) The much-altered Perpendicular-style church at the eastern end of town contains the ostentatious tomb of Sir John

Popham, the judge who presided at the trial of Guy Fawkes. Another spectacular monument, that to the Duke of Wellington, can be seen on a spur of the Blackdown Hills, three miles to the south, more about which is said in our chapter on south Somerset. With its wide streets, neoclassical town hall and sprinkling of Georgian buildings, Wellington is now a pleasant and prosperous shopping and light engineering centre which benefits greatly from its close proximity to the M5.

The Vale of Taunton Deane, the broad valley between the southern Quantocks and the Devon border, contains some of the most fertile farmland in the county. Thanks to its prolonged agricultural prosperity, the area is dotted with fine country houses. In the lanes around the village of THORNE ST MARGARET alone there are three worthy of note: Cothay, described by Pevsner as 'one of the most perfect smaller English manor houses of the late 15th century', stands beside the River Tone, a mile to the west of the village; the slightly older Greenham Barton, a mile to the south, retains its early-15th-century two-storey porch and open hall (the windows were added a century later); and Wellisford Manor, half-a-mile north of Thorne St Margaret, is a handsome residence built of brick around 1700 in a style which reflects the contemporary architecture of nearby Devon.

The B3187 to the north of Wellington leads to the sizable village of MILVERTON, another community which was a prosperous weaving centre in the 18th century, a fact confirmed by its unusual number of elegant Georgian houses. The largely-14th-century red sandstone Church of St Michael contains some impressive internal features, including a Norman font with some fine cross and cable carving, a set of choir stalls carved with the twelve apostles, an impressive rood screen, and a good collection of carved bench ends. Another sizable village, WIVELISCOMBE, lies on the B3227 three miles to the west of Milverton. An ancient settlement with a strange atmosphere of remoteness, the Romans occupied a fort here for many years and left a quantity of 3rd- and 4th-century coins behind to prove it. In medieval times, the local manor house was a summer residence of the bishops of Bath and Wells. Its remains, including a striking 14th-century archway, have now been incorporated into some cottages near the church. The church itself was totally rebuilt of red sandstone in the 19th century in a curious

'Gothic' style which is part-Perpendicular, part-18th-century preaching house. During the Second World War, the crypt was used to store priceless historic documents and other ecclesiastical treasures which were brought here from parts of the country more at risk from aerial attack.

The B3188 to the north of Wiveliscombe passes to the west of TOLLAND, home of the delightful Gaulden Manor. The manor itself dates from the 12th century, although the present house is largely 17th-century. It once belonged to the Turberville family, a name borrowed by Thomas Hardy for use in his novel, Tess Of The D'Urbervilles. Still used as a family home, the house contains an exceptional collection of period furniture and fine china. The great hall has a superb plaster ceiling and fireplace, and the room known as the chapel a particularly fine oak screen. Set in a wooded combe, the house is surrounded by beautiful grounds containing the 'Little Gardens of Gaulden'; noteworthy features include the scent garden, butterfly garden, rose garden, bog garden and Old Monk's fish pond. (Open Sundays, Thursdays and Bank Holiday Mondays, 2pm to 5.30pm between early-May and early-September; also Easter Sunday and Monday.)

On the southern edge of MONKSILVER, three miles further north along the B3188 Watchet road, there is another handsome manor house which is worth a visit. Built in the middle of Elizabeth I's reign on the site of a monastic settlement, Combe Sydenham Hall was the home of Elizabeth Sydenham, second wife of Sir Francis Drake. According to local legend, Elizabeth was so weary of waiting for Sir Francis to return from his voyages around the world that she agreed to marry another. When she was on her way to the church, however, a meteorite flew down out of the sky and smashed into the ground in front of her, a sign, she thought, that she should wait on. The original 'meteorite', now known as Drake's cannonball, is on display in the great hall and is said to bring luck to those who touch it. The 500-acre grounds have been designated a country park and contain a working corn mill complete with water wheel, an Elizabethan-style garden, children's play area, woodland walks and deer park. (Open Sundays to Fridays, 10am to 5pm between early-March and end-October.) Close by, there is a trout hatchery originally constructed at the end of the 16th century which has been fully refurbished as a modern

478

trout farm. Visitors can purchase fresh rainbow trout, smoked trout and a series of other specialist food products made on the estate under the Monksmill label. Nettlecombe Court, one mile to the west, is an ancient manor which once belonged to the Raleigh family, ancestors of Sir Walter, and later passed by marriage to the Cornish Trevelyans; it is now a field studies centre which is open to visitors on Thursdays only by appointment.

The lanes to the east of Monksilver lead through the curiously-named village of STOGUMBER to Stogumber Halt, one of the ten stations on the privately-operated West Somerset Railway which runs between Bishops Lydeard, near Taunton, and Minehead. The longest line of its kind in the country, the railway was formed when British Rail's 100-year-old branch between Taunton and Minehead was closed in 1971. After a five-year restoration programme, the new company began operating a summer steam and diesel service which has grown steadily in popularity. Special attractions are the first class Pullman dining car and the Flockton Flyer, a steam locomotive which may be recognised for its many television and film appearances. (Services run throughout the day between mid-March and end-October.)

CROWCOMBE, perhaps the loveliest village in the area, is situated in the western foothills of the Quantocks, two miles east of Stogumber station. Once an important settlement on the road between Taunton and the Bristol Channel coast, the village has an impressive mainly-Perpendicular parish church with a fan-vaulted south porch, a superb south aisle and fine collection of bench ends, one dated 1534, depicting such curious pagan-looking figures as the green man, a mermaid, and a pair of naked men attempting to spear a dragon. There is also a striking 17th-century family pew of the Carews in the north transept, and an 18th-century screen, pulpit and altar designed by Thomas Parker. Parker was also the architect of Crowcombe Court, the now somewhat down-at-heel brick mansion which dominates the village, until he was dismissed for stealing coins discovered in the foundations of the previous house which had been declared treasure trove. The village also contains a rare part-Tudor church house, an early parish hall and brewery whose lower floor was later converted to almshouses and whose upper floor became a school complete with Jacobean mullioned windows.

The Carew Arms is a small and ancient village pub with home cooking prepared by the landlady Mrs Norma Bremner. There are few frills but the bedrooms are clean and comfortable and the company is good.

The pub stands at the south western end of the Borough of Crowcombe which itself dates back to the 13th century. It is known that there was an innkeeper in Crowcombe in 1620, and the earliest reference to this pub was in 1747. It was formerly known as the Three Lions or just "Lions" and the name was changed to the Carew Arms in about 1814. It is surprising that the pub existed at all, because although it stood on the main road between Taunton and Williton, a regular stage didn't run until the late 18th century. However part of the building is thought to have been used as a market house when a Thomas Carew revived the medieval market and fair in the 1760s, although the success of the market was of relatively short duration.

The development of the pub name is logical, albeit a bit backwards, as the coat of arms of the Carew family, Lords of the manor and builders of Crowcombe Court, included three 'lioncels' or young lions.

The Carew Arms, Crowcombe, Taunton Tel: 01984 8631

To the northwest of Crowcombe, the A358 runs along the foot of the Quantock ridge to its junction with the A39 at WILLITON. This former Saxon royal estate is now a sizable village on the busy holiday route to Minehead and the west Somerset coast. The manor was the home of Sir Reginald Fitzurse, one of Thomas

Becket's murderers, who sold part of it to pay for a journey of repentance to Rome and the Holy Land. The Knights Hospitaller then founded an institution on the land which continued to be known as Williton Hospital until the 17th century. The West Somerset Railway has its diesel locomotive workshops at Williton, and just off the A39 at Orchard Mill, there is a restored water wheel and museum of early farm and domestic equipment. (Open Tuesdays to Sundays, 10am to 6pm between early-March and mid-December.) A delightful small country manor house, Orchard Wyndham, is situated a mile to the southwest of the village. Built in the 14th century and much-altered since, it continues to be used by the Wyndhams as a family home after four-and-a-half centuries. (Guided tours available during August; telephone (01984) 32309.)

At WASHFORD, two miles to the west of Williton, a lane to the south of the A39 leads to the remains of Cleeve Abbey, the only abbey in Somerset which belonged to the austere Cistercian order. The monastery was founded in 1198 by the Earl of Lincoln in the beautiful valley of the River Washford, or vallis florida. Many monastic houses were allowed to fall into disrepair following Henry VIII's Dissolution in 1539; however, the cloister buildings at Cleeve were put to domestic use soon after and are now among the most complete in the country. Despite the cruciform abbey church having been reduced to its foundations, the refectory, chapter house, monks' common room, dormitory and cloisters remain remarkably intact. Most impressive of all is the great hall, a magnificent building with tall windows and a wagon roof which is decorated with busts of crowned angels, moulded wall plates, medieval murals, and a unique set of floor tiles in heraldic designs. The curved dormitory staircase with its archways and mullioned windows is particularly fine, and the combined gatehouse and almonry, the last building to be constructed before the Dissolution, makes an imposing entrance to the abbey precinct. (Open daily, 10am to 6pm between 1 April and 31 October; Wednesdays to Sundays, 10am to 4pm between 1 November and 31 March.)

To the south of Cleeve Abbey, the land rises into the Brendon Hills, the upland area within the Exmoor National Park lying to the east and north of the River Exe. During the mid 19th century, iron ore was mined in significant quantities above the village of TREBOROUGH and carried down a steep mineral railway to the coast for shipment to the furnaces of South Wales. At one time almost 1000 people were employed by Ebbw Vale company, strict Nonconformists who imposed a rigorous teetotal regime on their workers. (Those wanting a drink had to walk over the moor to Raleigh's Cross.) They also founded a miners' settlement, with three chapels and a Temperance hotel, which developed a reputation for the achievements of its choir and fife and drum band. Certain sections of the old mineral railway can still be made out, for example near the junction of the A39 and the B3190 to the east of Washford, and the two-mile stretch leading down to the coast at Watchet is now a pleasant footpath. The Brendon Hills also offer some fine walking, much of it through attractive woodland, and further south, the surprisingly well-assimilated Wimbleball and Clatworthy reservoirs offer some good facilities for picnickers, anglers and watersports enthusiasts.

WATCHET, on the coast to the north of Washford, has been a port since Saxon times. In the 6th century, St Decuman landed here from Wales, bringing with him a cow to provide sustenance, and in the 9th- and 10th-centuries, the town was important enough to have been sacked by the Vikings on at least three occasions. By the 17th century, Watchet was an important paper manufacturing centre, and by the mid-19th, around 30,000 tons of iron ore from the Brendon hills was being exported each year through the docks. Coleridge's imaginary crew set sail from here in The Rime Of The Ancient Mariner, the epic poem which was written when the author was resident in nearby Nether Stowey. Unlike many smaller coastal ports which fell into disuse following the arrival of the railways, Watchet docks somehow managed to survive. Despite the total decline in the iron ore trade, sizable cargo vessels continue to tie up here to be loaded with goods bound for the Iberian peninsula and elsewhere.

The scale of Watchet's parish church reflects the town's early prosperity; set well away from the centre, it contains several fine tombs to members of the Wyndham family, the local lords of the manor who did much to encourage the economic development of the district. One 16th-century family member, Florence Wyndham, had to be buried twice: the day after her first funeral, the church sexton went down to the vaults to surreptitiously remove a ring from her finger when the old woman suddenly woke up. In recent years,

Watchet has also developed as something of a coastal resort whose attractions include an interesting small museum dedicated to the maritime history of the port.

A more developed seaside resort can be found three miles further west at BLUE ANCHOR BAY, a broad arc of sand named after a 17th-century inn, not the colour of the sea. Sadly, this fine sandy beach is visibly marred by caravan sites and seaside attractions of the gaudier sort. The bay is well known for its fossils, both palaeontological and human. The atmosphere is very different at CARHAMPTON, a small inland village on the A39, one mile to the southwest, which was the site of a Viking victory in the 9th century. The original church was named after St Carantoc, a Celtic missionary who is said to have picked the sites of his missions by throwing his wooden altar overboard and following it to the shore. The present structure, though much restored, contains a remarkable 15th-century painted screen which extends across the entire width of the church. The old inn near the churchyard lych gate has the date 1638 set into its cobbled floor using sheep's knuckle bones. Each January, the villagers re-enact the ancient ceremony of 'wassailing the apple trees', when a toast is made to the most productive tree in the district and cider is poured onto its trunk, no doubt a custom of pagan origin. A local folk tale tells of mysterious Madame Carne, a Carhampton woman who died in 1612 after having done away with three husbands; according to the legend, she returned home after her own funeral to prepare breakfast for the mourners.

Lying a mile and a half to the northwest of Carhampton, DUNSTER has an almost fairy-tale appearance when approached along the A39. With its massive turreted castle rising above the trees and distinctive ruined folly on nearby Conygar hill, it is a place well-worth visiting, particularly out of season. The castle was founded by William de Mohun on a natural tor above the River Avill in time to be included in the Domesday Book of 1086. In 1404, it passed to the Luttrells for the then colossal sum of 5000 marks, about £3300, in whose family it remained for almost six centuries. (In 1975, Lt. Col. G W F Luttrell gave the property to the National Trust.) One of the last Royalist strongholds in the West Country during the English Civil War, the garrison only submitted after a siege lasting 160 days.

Gaulden Manor

The 17th century also saw some major alterations to Dunster Castle, and some of its finest internal features date from this period, including the magnificent balustraded staircase with its rich carvings of flora and fauna, and the dining room with its superb plasterwork ceiling. The banqueting hall contains a unique collection of 16th-century leather hangings, and there are also many fine examples of period furniture throughout the building. Further changes by Anthony Salvin in the 19th century completed the transformation from castle to fortified mansion. Work on the steeply-terraced garden with its striking collection of rare shrubs and subtropical plants was also carried out at this time. (Open Saturdays to Wednesdays, 11am to 5pm between late-March and end-October.) Dunster castle is set within an attractive 28-acre park containing an 18th-century flour mill which was built on the site of a Norman predecessor. Restored to working order in 1979, it continues to produce flour and other cereals for wholesale and retail sale. (Open daily, except Saturdays, 11am to 5pm between 1 April and 31 October.)

The village of Dunster has been described as a perfect feudal settlement. Its wide main street is dominated by the castle at one end and the octagonal Yarn Market at the other, a superb little building erected by the Luttrells around 1600 when Dunster was an important centre of the cloth trade. (The village even gave its name to a type woollen cloth which was known for its quality and strength.) The nearby Luttrell Arms is over a century older; a private residence which was converted to an inn around 1650, it has a fine 15th-century porch and a room lined with carved oak. It once belonged to the abbots of Cleeve, as did the 14th-century 'nunnery' in Church Street. The medieval village had its own monastic house, Dunster Priory, which was an outpost of Bath Abbey. All that remains of it today is the priory (now parish) church and a superb 12th-century dovecote which stands in a neighbouring garden and still contains the revolving ladder which was used to reach the roosting birds. (Open daily between Easter and mid-October.)

Dunster's parish church is perhaps the finest in west Somerset. Rebuilt of rose pink sandstone by the priory monks after 1100, its 100 foot tower was added in the 15th century at a cost of '13s 4d per foot, with an extra 20s for the pinnacles'. The church's most outstanding internal feature is its fan vaulted rood screen which extends across both nave and aisles, one of the longest and most impressive in the country. There are also some fine 15th- and 16th-century fittings, an unusual painting of the Brazen Serpent thought to be by Thornhill, and several monuments to members of the Luttrell family. On the southern edge of the village, the River Avill is spanned by the ancient Gallox bridge, a medieval packhorse bridge which is now under the care of English Heritage.

The West Somerset Railway terminates at MINEHEAD, a pleasant seaside town lying at the foot of the massive wooded outcrop known as North Hill, two miles to the northwest of Dunster. Despite its industrial-sounding name, this is one of the oldest settlements in the county, having been a busy Bristol Channel port since the time of the Celts. The old harbour lies at the foot of North Hill and has been described as one of the safest in the West Country. Merchandise to be landed here throughout the centuries include wool and livestock from Ireland, farm produce from Virginia, coal from the South Wales' valleys, and day-trippers from Cardiff and Bristol. Today, the merchant vessels and paddle steamers have all gone and the harbour is the peaceful haunt of sailing dinghies and pleasure craft. A good view of the old port can be had from the North Hill nature trail, a three-mile walk which starts near the lifeboat station on the harbourside. Minehead's parish Church of St Michael stands in a prominent position in the lee of North Hill. A substantial part-14th-century building, in past centuries a light was kept burning in the tower to guide ships into the harbour and provide encouragement for travellers on the moor. The interior contains a number of noteworthy features including a rare medieval prayer book, or missal, which once belonged to the Richard Fitzjames, the local vicar who went to become Bishop of London in 1506.

Minehead's 19th-century decline as a port was offset by its modest expansion as a seaside resort. The town went to great pains to attract a genteel clientele, and a local bylaw was in force until 1890 which forbad anyone over ten years of age from swimming in the sea 'except form a bathing machine, tent, or other effective screen'. The railway arrived in 1874 but did not inflict the monumental changes experienced by other resorts such as Torquay. During the First World War, holidaymakers were sheltered from the ravages of war at establishments like the Strand Hotel where they were entertained by such stars as Anna Pavlova and Gladys Cooper; then in the 1920s, improvements were made such as Blenheim Gardens, the impressive municipal park near the seafront which incorporates a model country town known as 'Little England' which has its own miniature railway and floodlights. In 1962, Minehead began to attract a new kind of holidaymaker when Billy Butlin opened a holiday camp at the eastern end of the esplanade. This and other popular attractions such as the Aquasplash Leisure Pool and Somerset World have made present-day Minehead into a family resort with a pleasant relaxed atmosphere.

A particularly fine walk sets out westwards from Minehead, over North Hill and on along the coast to Selworthy Beacon, part of the 12,400-acre National Trust-owned Holnicote Estate. The estate covers four-and-a-half miles of coastline between Minehead and Porlock Bay and extends over five miles inland to the 1700 foot Dunkery Beacon, the highest point on Exmoor. At Hurlstone Point, the South West peninsula coastal path curves inland to avoid the possibility of landslips in the soft Foreland Sandstone before dropping down to Bossington. (An alternative more arduous clifftop path is recommended to more experienced walkers only.) The estate also contains fifteen farms, many of them on the high moor, and a number of small settlements, including ALLERFORD, a lovely old village which has some fine stone cottages and a striking twin-arched packhorse bridge. The West Somerset museum is located in Allerford's old school. Its exhibits include a Victorian kitchen, laundry and dairy, and an old schoolroom complete with desks, books and children's toys. (Open Mondays to Saturday, 10.30am to 4.30pm between 1 April and 31 October.)

SELWORTHY, one mile to the east, is a superb model village of whitewashed cob and thatch cottages which was built Sir Thomas Dyke-Acland to house his retired estate workers. The churchyard at the top of the hill offers a fine view of Dunkery Beacon, and there is also a National Trust information centre which is open daily, 10am (2pm Sundays) to 5pm between late-March and end-October. From here it is possible to climb back to the top the hill for the return walk to Minehead, a round trip of about twelve miles.

487

Alternatively, both Selworthy and Allerford can be reached by car from the A39. For those preferring a walk on the high moor, a circular nature walk starts and finishes at the Webber's Post car park at the foot of Dunkery Hill.

A little further to the west, the A39 winds its way through the narrow streets of PORLOCK, an ancient settlement frequented by Saxon kings which in recent decades has become a popular tourist and riding centre. The streets are filled with lovely old buildings, most notably the 15th-century Doverhay Manor with its striking traceried hall window, and the largely-13th-century red sandstone parish church with its curious truncated shingle spire (the top section was lost in a 17th century thunderstorm). The church also contains an exceptional font and Easter Sepulchre, and the remarkable Harrington monument, a tomb composed of almost life-size alabaster effigies of Sir John Harrington, who was knighted by Henry V during the Agincourt campaign, and his wife, who lived on for over half a century after her husband's death in 1418. Porlock has long had the feel of a community at the end of the world thanks to its position at the foot of Porlock Hill, the notorious incline which takes the A39 onto Exmoor. The road rises 1350 feet in under three miles, and in places has a gradient of 1 in 4.

A less demanding toll road winds its way through the Lovelace estate from PORLOCK WEIR, a hamlet lying on the coast a mile-and-a-half to the northwest of Porlock. Although now only a tiny harbour populated by pleasure craft, this was once a thriving seaport. The Danes sacked it on a number of occasions in the 10th-century, and in 1052, Harold, the future king of England, landed here from Ireland to begin a career which ended at the Battle of Hastings. Now peaceful and picturesque, Porlock Weir offers a number of interesting attractions, including a working blacksmith's forge, a picture gallery, and a fascinating glass studio where visitors can see lead crystal being blown in the traditional manner. A submerged forest, a relic of the last Ice Age, lies a short distance offshore. From the harbour, a pleasant mile-long walk leads up through the woods to CULBONE church, the smallest church in England still in regular use. Measuring only 33 feet by 14 feet, this superb part-Norman building has a good 14th-century screen and some lovely old benches. The church is set in a delightful wooded combe which once supported a small charcoal-burning community.

From Culbone church, the footpath continues on to the Devon border at County Gate, one of several spectacular viewpoints on this dramatic stretch of coastline. Here, the great hog's back hills of Exmoor plunge into the sea, giving breathtaking views across the Bristol Channel to South Wales. One of the few Roman remains on Exmoor, a lookout station for observing cross-Channel raiding parties, lies on a headland to the north of the car park. To the south lies the scenic 'Doone Valley', a long steep-sided combe of green pasture and woodland immortalised by R D Blackmore in his classic romantic novel, Lorna Doone. The now-demolished medieval farm known as Hoccombe Combe is thought to have been the home of a wild and unruly Exmoor family whose real-life deeds provided the inspiration for the story. The charming 15th-century church at OARE was the scene of the heroine's interrupted wedding; inside, there is a fine set of 19th-century box pews and an unusual piscina shaped like a man's head.

The core of Exmoor National Park, 70% of which lies within Somerset, is a high treeless plateau of hard-wearing Devonian shale which has been carved into a series of steep-sided valleys by the prolonged action of the moor's many fast-flowing streams. Whereas the upland vegetation is mostly heather, gorse and bracken, the more sheltered valleys contain trees and cultivated grazing land. The wooded combes also provide shelter for herds of shy red deer which are free to roam, but seldom seen. Easier to spot are the hardy Exmoor ponies, now almost all cross-breeds, which tend to congregate at roadside parking areas where pickings from holidaymakers can be rich.

The moor is crisscrossed by a network of paths and bridleways which provide some excellent opportunities for walking and pony-trekking. Many of these follow the routes of ancient ridgeways across the high moor, passing close to a scattered assortment of standing stones, hut circles, barrows and other Bronze and Iron Age remains.

Some of the finest examples are the stone circle on Porlock Hill, Alderman's Barrow north of Exford, and the delightfully-named Cow Castle near Simonsbath. The remarkable clapper bridge known as Tarr Steps lies to the north of the village of HAWKRIDGE; a medieval packhorse bridge, it is composed of large flat stones placed across the top of upright stones. The

Roman relic known as the Caractacus Stone lies a couple of miles to the east of here near Spire Cross.

South Somerset

Cottages at Selworthy

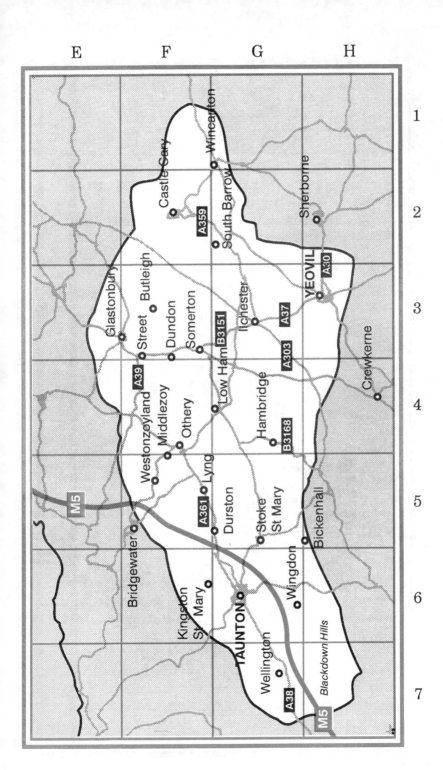

CHAPTER FIFTEEN

South Somerset

A good place to begin a tour of South Somerset is from the Wellington Monument, the conspicuous 170 foot obelisk which stands on a spur of the Blackdown hills overlooking the Vale of Taunton Deane. This striking landmark was constructed in honour of the Duke of Wellington on the estate bought for him by the nation following his victory at the Battle of Waterloo. (Despite his adopted title, the Duke had no connections with the locality and is known to have visited the estate only once in thirty years.) Conceived on a wave of enthusiastic public support, the monument's foundation stone was laid in 1817; however, when the necessary funds to complete the project were unforthcoming, a number of radical economies were introduced, including the redesigning of the structure to give it three sides instead of four and the cancelling of an ostentatious cast iron statue of the Duke which had been proposed for the top. The modified obelisk remained unfinished until 1854, two years after Wellington's death, when work on its plain triangular pinnacle was finally completed. Present-day visitors making the strenuous 235-step climb to the top are rewarded with spectacular views across lowland Somerset to Exmoor and the Mendips.

Most of the roads on the northern slopes of the Blackdown hills run from north to south, and so it is best to make for the A38 in order to progress eastwards.

The B3170 to the south of Taunton skirts Taunton racecourse, and a little further on, a lane to the west leads to Poundisford Park, a small H-shaped Tudor mansion which stands on the site of a deer park which once belonged to the bishops of Winchester. The house is renowned for its fine plasterwork ceilings and is set in delightful wooded grounds which incorporate a formal garden laid out in the Tudor style. (Open Wednesdays and Thursdays (also Fridays in

July and August), 11am to 5pm between early-May and mid-September.)

On the crossroads, at **STAPLE FRITZPAINE** you will find **The Greyhound Inn**. This 17th century hunting lodge is situated in the heart of an area of outstanding natural beauty, the Blackdown Hills. The Inn is renowned for its food and has two resident chefs preparing the à la carte menu for the separate restaurant area. The menu is outstanding, exciting and varied, featuring the best of fresh local produce and, wherever possible the dishes are totally hand-cooked. The beef that is used is reared on the family farm which is nearby. The à la carte menu is available only in the restaurant at weekends. On weekdays however, it is available in the bar, together with the bar menu and daily specials board. This inn also has other good facilities: there is a skittle alley and a beer garden with children's play area. The interior is really delightful, making visitors feel relaxed and at home in a period, rustic theme.

The Greyhound Inn, Staple Fritzpaine, Taunton, Somerset
Tel: 01823 480227

Another exceptional country house can be found at **HATCH BEAUCHAMP**, just off the A358 Taunton-Ilminster road two-and-a-half miles to the east. Built of superb honey-coloured limestone in two phases in the second half of the 18th-century, Hatch Court was designed in superb Palladian style by the Axbridge architect, Thomas Prowse. Among its finest features are the hall, with its cantilevered stone staircase, the curved orangery, with its arched floor-to-ceiling windows, and the semicircular china room, with its elegant display of rare porcelain and glass. There is also a fine collection of 17th- and 18th-century furniture, 19th- and 20th-century paintings, and a small museum commemorating Britain's last privately-raised regiment, the Princess Patricia's Canadian Light Infantry. Having just undergone an extensive programme of restoration, the grounds incorporate a walled kitchen garden, rose garden, arboretum and deer park. (Open Thursdays and Bank Holiday Mondays (plus grounds only on Fridays), 2.30pm to 5.30pm between mid-June and mid-September.)

The old ecclesiastical and agricultural centre of ILMINSTER lies near the junction of the A358 and A303, five miles to the southeast of Hatch Beauchamp. Meaning 'minster on the River Isle', the settlement takes its name from church which was founded here by the Saxon King Ine in the 8th-century. The borough was recorded in the Domesday Book as having a market and three mills, and over the following centuries it grew to become a thriving wool and lace-making town. This period of medieval prosperity is reflected in the town's unusually large parish church, a magnificent 15th-century rebuild whose massive multi-pinnacled tower is thought to have been modelled on Wells cathedral. The church interior is surprisingly plain, thanks to a Georgian restoration; however, it does contain a number of interesting tombs and monumental brasses. A stroll around the streets of the old town reveals a number of lovely old buildings, most of which are constructed of golden Ham stone; these include the chantry house, the old grammar school, and the colonnaded market house.

Dillington House, on the northern outskirts of Ilminster, is a handsome part-Tudor mansion which is the former home of the Speke family; it is now leased to Somerset County Council for use as an adult education centre. In the time of James II, John Speke was an officer in the Duke of Monmouth's ill-fated rebel army which landed at Lyme Regis in 1685. However, following its disastrous defeat at Sedgemoor, he was forced to flee abroad, leaving his brother, George, who had done no more than shake the Duke's hand, to face the wrath of Judge Jeffreys. The infamous Hanging Judge sentenced poor George to death, justifying his decision with the words, 'His family owes a life and he shall die for his brother.'

Three miles to the northeast of Ilminster, a lane to the east of the B3168 leads the beautiful National Trust-owned Barrington

Court Garden. The house was built in the 1570s from local Ham stone and displays the characteristics of the architectural transformation from Tudor Gothic (mullioned and transomed windows, buttresses) to Renaissance (twisted finials and chimney stacks). The garden was laid out in the 1920s in a series of themed 'rooms', including the iris garden, lily garden, white garden and fragrant rose garden. The celebrated landscape architect, Gertrude Jekyll, was brought in to advise on the initial planting and layout, and the garden remains the finest example of her work in the Trust's care. There is also an exceptionally attractive one-acre kitchen garden which, in season, produces fruit and vegetables for use in the restaurant. (Garden open daily, except Fridays, 11am to 5.30pm between late-March and end-September; house open Wednesdays only.) The nearby estate village contains some fine old Ham-stone cottages, and at WESTPORT, on the B3168 a mile-and-a-half to the north, is a former inland port which was built by the Parrett Navigation Company at the height of the canal era for the exporting of wool and stone, and importing of coal and building materials.

At SHEPTON BEAUCHAMP, one mile to the southeast of Barrington Court, the remains of a medieval 'open strip' field system can still be made out.

The Duke of York, North Street, Shepton Beauchamp
Tel: 01460 40314

In this tiny village you will find The Duke of York, a pleasant and comfortable traditional country pub. Roy and Jackie Spendlow

498

and their regulars will make you feel more than welcome should you decide to stop for a drink and perhaps a bite to eat. First class bar snacks are always available, but if you have more time to spare you could sample some of the delicious food on offer in the restaurant. There is also a skittle alley, a pleasant beer garden with swings for the children, and a games room. The simple ingredients of an enjoyable country pub consist of plenty of good food and drink in comfortable surroundings, convivial company and a friendly atmosphere. The Duke of York has all this and more, and we can guarantee that you will leave feeling relaxed and satisfied and glad that you dropped in.

Those with an interest in traditional cider making should head for DOWLISH WAKE, a pleasant community of honey-coloured Ham-stone cottages which lies in the lanes a mile-and-a-half to the southeast of Ilminster.

With a name like Perry, you could be forgiven for thinking that Perry's Cider Mills use pears for their cider. However it all becomes clear when you learn that the owners are Mrs. Perry and her sons, and yes, apples are the sole fruit they use here. This is the place to sample traditional farmhouse cider, and indeed the premises which date back to the 16th century have long been involved in its making.

The cider is pressed in the old thatched barn, and here visitors can look at many of the relics of a bygone age, with old farming tools and cider making equipment giving you a nostalgic insight into the processes once used.

In the new thatched barn, which was built in 1984, visitors can see a collection of wagons and farming equipment, together with the wooden barrels that are essential for the storing and maturing of cider. Made from locally grown apples from their own orchards as well as from other farms, the varieties used include Bulmers Norman, Somerset Red-Streak, Kingston Black, and the wonderfully named Brownsnout, to name but a few.

When the apples are picked, they are milled and pressed in the autumn and then the natural fermentation process takes place. Cows certainly benefit from this, as they are fed the pommace, or apple pulp, which is left over after pressing.

There is a shop on the premises which stocks pottery, corn dollies, baskets and other gifts, as well as cider. It is open all year round, and it is quite alright to sample the brews before you purchase. With medium sweet, medium dry or dry 'scrumpy' all available, you are sure to find a cider to suit your palate. There are absolutely no flavourings or colourings in Perry's ciders, just pure apple juice, and if an apple a day is meant to be good for you then a glass of cider is sure to be even better!

Perry's Cider Mill's, Dowlish Wake, Ilminster Tel: 01460 52681

Dowlish Wake's parish church stands on a steep rise at one end of the village, and inside can be seen the tomb of the intrepid Victorian explorer John Hanning Speke. After having travelled over 2500 miles to confirm Lake Victoria as the source of the River Nile, Speke returned to England a hero; however, on the very morning he was due to address the British Geographical Association on the subject, he accidentally shot himself while out partridge shooting.

On the main A358 at DONYATT, near Ilminster, and almost next-door to the Post Office, is Southway House. This is the home of David and Pauline Laughton, who have only just started offering bed and breakfast accommodation. They spent six enjoyable months decorating and furnishing the house, making it ready for entertaining. Guests are made to feel welcome from the minute they arrive, with tea, coffee or drinks in the visitors lounge or on the terrace. The two bedrooms each have colour TV, a radio and cassette player, with tapes provided. There are plenty of books, magazines too, for bed-time reading. One room is en-suite and the other has use of a private bathroom, but there are plans to extend the house and add more rooms. Breakfast can be served at any reasonable time, and special diets can be catered for. The gardens are great for relaxing in, or there is table-tennis for the more active. For comfortable, home from home surroundings, give this one a try.

Southway House, Donyatt, Ilminster Tel: 01460 52239

On the northern approaches to Chard, the A358 Axminster road passes close to two contrasting places of interest: on the west side of the road stands the Hornsbury Mill, a 200-year-old corn mill with a large water wheel which is still in working order, and on the opposite side of the road, the Chard Reservoir Nature Reserve offers a varied two-mile circular walk through swishing reed beds, broad-leaved woodland and open hay meadows. An important habitat for wildlife, the lake is home to a number of rare bird species, including kingfisher and great crested grebe.

CHARD, in the southwest corner of the county, is a pleasant light industrial town whose population of 12,000 has more than doubled since the Second World War. The town has Saxon origins, and by the 13th-century it was a prosperous wool borough with its own mayor, or portreeve, and burgesses. However, with the exception of the fine Perpendicular parish church, few buildings date from before 1577, the year of a devastating fire which razed most of the streets to the ground. (Perhaps this is how the town got its name?) Chard's reconstruction left it with some fine 17th-century buildings, including the court house and old grammar school, and there are also a number of striking Georgian and Victorian examples, most notably the neoclassical town hall of 1835 with its impressive two-tier portico. Despite its rapid postwar development, the centre retains its village-like atmosphere, in particular around the broad sloping main street.

A way to find out more about the town's social and economic history is to visit the award-winning **Chard and District Museum** in Godworthy House at the west end of the High Street, a large 'small town' museum housed in an attractive thatched building. The museum covers several aspects of local and social history and is sure to interest all ages. One exhibition is about John Stringfellow, a local tool maker who flew the world's first powered aeroplane. It was a ten foot, steam driven model, and the flight took place in Chard in 1848. Another local pioneer was James Gillingham, a Victorian shoemaker, who designed and built the first artificial limbs. One of Chard's local companies was Dening, who made farm machinery which was sold worldwide. There are displays of many of their designs, as well as some road making machinery made by Phoenix Engineering, Chard's oldest existing firm. Other displays include a blacksmith's shop, a 1940s garage, cider making and a 'touch and handle' collection for children. (Open Mondays to Saturdays (plus Sundays in July and August), 10.30am to 4.30pm between early-May and mid-October.)

Chard and District Museum, c/o Museum of South Somerset, Hendford, Yeovil Tel: 01935 24774

Those interested in animal welfare should make the trip to the Ferne Animal Sanctuary at **WAMBROOK**, a couple of miles along the A30 to the west of Chard. Founded during the Second World

War, the sanctuary specialises in animal rescue of all kinds. (Telephone 01460 65214 for opening hours.)

In the Hamlet of **HOWLEY**, off the A30, **The Howley Tavern** is ideal for a family to stop at. There is a lawned beer garden offering views over the valley which has a children's playground area. The tavern is a freehouse and offers real ale and a selection of good food. Bed & breakfast accommodation is also available with three en-suite letting rooms, one a family room.

The Howley Tavern, Howley, Chard Tel: 01460 62157

On the A30 three miles to the east of Chard lies **CRICKET ST THOMAS**, a former estate village which is now the home of one of Britain's least hidden places, Noel Edmonds' Crinkley Bottom television theme park (formerly the Cricket St Thomas Wildlife and Leisure Park). Although it may be hard to imagine it today, Cricket House was once the family home of great 18th-century naval commander, Admiral Sir Alexander Hood, and later of the Bristol chocolate manufacturer, F J Fry; today it is marketed as the 'Grantleigh Manor' of the BBC television comedy series, To The Manor Born. The grounds contain the tiny Church of St Thomas with its impressive monument to Admiral Hood, later Viscount Bridport. Other attractions include a horse stables, a children's adventure fort, a wildlife world, and an assortment of TV detritus designed for the very young. ('Open all hours.')

One of the loveliest country houses in England lies just across the Dorset border in the lanes to the south of Cricket St Thomas. Set in the beautiful valley of the River Axe, Forde Abbey was founded as a Cistercian monastery in the 12th-century, but took over 300 years to complete. Further additions were made in the early 16th-century; however, to prevent its destruction following the Dissolution of the Monasteries in 1539, the abbot made the difficult decision to offer the property to the crown. It is now the family home of the Ropers and contains a superb collection of period furniture, tapestries and paintings. The refectory, dormitory and chapter house (now a chapel) survive from the medieval monastery, and the whole structure stands within thirty acres of landscaped grounds containing lakes, a bog garden, nursery and walled kitchen garden. The estate is known for its pedigree herd of cattle and also incorporates a pick-your-own fruit farm. (House open Sundays, Wednesdays and Bank Holidays, 10.30am to 4.30pm between 1 April and 31 October; gardens open daily, all year round.)

Another delightful landscaped garden can be found beside the B3165, four miles to the east of Forde Abbey. The ten-acre Clapton Court Gardens are some of the most varied and interesting in Somerset. Among the many attractive features to be enjoyed are the terraced formal gardens, rockery, rose garden and water garden. The present owner, Captain Loder, acquired the house in 1978, and after much replanting and restoration work, he opened the grounds to the public. The estate incorporates a large wooded area containing a massive ash tree which, at over 230 years old and 28 feet in girth, is the oldest and largest in mainland Britain; there is also a fine metasequoia which is already over 80 feet tall, having been planted in 1950 from seed brought back from China. Many of the gardens' rare and beautiful plants are for sale in the plant centre. (Open Sundays to Fridays, 10.30am (2pm Sundays) to 5pm between early-March and end-October.)

The ancient former market town of CREWKERNE lies at the junction of the A30 and A356, two-and-a-half miles northeast of Clapton Court. Like Chard and Ilminster, the town developed as a thriving agricultural and market centre during Saxon times, and it even had its own mint in the decades leading up to the Norman invasion. The late-medieval boom in the wool industry resulted in the building of the magnificent parish Church of St Bartholomew, a structure of minster-like proportions which is one of the grandest of the many fine Perpendicular churches to be found in south Somerset. Unlike many of its regional counterparts, Crewkerne's textile industry was rejuvenated in the 18th- and early-19th-centuries when the availability of locally-grown flax led to an expansion in the manufacture of sailcloth and canvas webbing. (The sails for HMS Victory, Nelson's flagship at the Battle of Trafalgar, were some of the many thousands made here.) This renewed prosperity, which was helped by the development of the London-Exeter coaching route during the 18th-century, led to the rebuilding of old Crewkerne in Georgian style, and many elegant town houses and inns of this period can still be seen in the centre, most notably in Church and Abbey streets, now an Area of Outstanding Architectural Interest. The outskirts of the town, particularly to the north and south, are less appealing, having been given up to large-scale modern light industrial development. The A30 to the west of the town climbs onto the aptly-named chalk-topped ridge, Windwhistle Hill.

A lane to the northwest of Crewkerne leads to the former estate village of **HINTON ST GEORGE**, an unspoilt Ham-stone gem which for centuries was owned, and left virtually untouched, by the Poulett family. The Pouletts rebuilt Hinton House shortly after their arrival here in the 15th-century, and this late-medieval structure forms the core of the present-day mansion. Several ostentatious monuments to members of the family can be seen in the superb little 15th-century Church of St George which, with its pinnacled tower and imposing interior, is perhaps the most outstanding feature of the village. Another noteworthy building is the so-called priory, a 16th-century residence with a 14th-century window at its eastern end which may once have been owned by Monkton Farleigh Priory in Wiltshire.

Although now converted into apartments, Hinton House continues to be haunted by the ghost of a grey lady who is believed to be a young Poulett woman who died of a broken heart after her father shot dead the man with whom she was planning to elope. It is a tradition for Hinton children to beg candles to put inside their intricately-fashioned turnip and pumpkin lanterns on 'Punkie Night', the last Thursday in October. It is thought to be very unlucky to refuse them, as each lantern is said to represent the spirit of a dead person who, unless illuminated, will rise up at Hallowe'en.

The village of **MISTERTON** lies a mile to the southeast of Crewkerne. Set in two acres of garden in a quiet and peaceful part of the village is **Dry Close** which offers bed and breakfast accommodation. The 16th century listed, former farmhouse is so called after the field in which it was built. Later when the field was sold, the name changed to Exeter House but reverted to Dry Close in 1946. The accommodation comprises a twin which is en-suite and a twin and single rooms which have use of a private bathroom. There are two lounges for the use of guests too. The downstairs lounge is oak panelled and beamed and has an open log fire for winter warmth. The upper lounge has a TV and a range of books. The gardens are delightful in the summer months, and there is an unheated outdoor pool which guests are welcome to use. Facilities nearby include coarse and trout fishing, golf, horse riding and a tennis court.

Dry Close, Newberry Lane, Misterton, Crewkerne
Tel: 01460 73161

In the similar-sounding village of MOSTERTON, a mile and a half to the south, David, Benjamin and Simon Eeles produce a unique range of handmade stoneware and porcelain at the Eeles Family Pottery. At certain times, visitors can view the pots being thrown and decorated before they are taken for firing in a three-chambered dragon kiln.

The A30 to the east of Crewkerne crosses the upper reaches of the River Parrett before it is joined by the A3066 Bridport road. The delightfully-named community of HASELBURY PLUCKNETT lies half a mile south of this junction; another gem of a village, it has a large part-Norman church whose churchyard contains a series of unusual 'squeeze stones'. Returning to the A30 and continuing northeastwards, the magnificent Brympton d'Evercy manor house lies in the lanes to the north of West Coker, three miles from the centre of Yeovil. Norman in origin, but with major 16th- and 17th-century additions, the most outstanding part is the Jacobean south wing which was built of golden Ham stone to a design influenced by Inigo Jones. The house contains the longest straight single-span staircase in Britain and an unusual modern tapestry showing an imaginary bird's eye view of the estate in the 18th-century. The mansion, chantry or dower house, and Church of

St Andrew, with its sturdy square bell tower and fine collection of medieval monuments, make a delightful lakeside grouping. (Open by appointment only by telephoning 01935 862528)

With its 28,000 inhabitants and strategic position at the junction of several primary roads, YEOVIL is the largest centre of population in south Somerset. A modern light industrial town whose best-known employer is Westland Helicopters, it offers a full range of up-to-date shopping and recreational facilities. Despite its present-day character, Yeovil's origins go back to the time of the ancient Romans,. During the Middle Ages, a lively livestock and produce market was established in the town which continues to be held to this day (market day is Friday). The parish Church of St John the Baptist is the only significant medieval building to survive, most of Yeovil's older buildings having been destroyed in a series of town fires in the 17th-century. A substantial Ham-stone structure dating from the second half of the 14th-century, it has surprisingly austere exterior, given its exceptional number of windows (indeed, it is sometimes referred to as the 'lantern of the West'). Perhaps its finest internal feature is the plain brass lectern which is believed to date from around 1450; of the five still in existence, it is the only one to be found in a parish church.

During the 18th-century, Yeovil expanded rapidly as a coaching and industrial town whose output included gloves, leather, sailcloth and cheese, a development which was further enhanced by the arrival of the railway in the mid-19th-century. In the 1890s, James Petter, a local ironmonger and pioneer of the internal combustion engine, founded a business which went on to become one of the largest manufacturers of diesel engines in Britain. Although engine production was eventually transferred to the Midlands, a subsidiary set up to produce aircraft during the First World War evolved into the present-day helicopter plant. A fascinating museum documenting the social and industrial history of south Somerset is situated in Wyndham House, Hendford. (Open Tuesdays to Saturdays, 10am to 4pm, all year round; admission free.)

The original inspiration for the Museum of South Somerset came from Alderman W.R.E. Mitchelmore, the Mayor of Yeovil between 1918 And 1921. He was fascinated in local antiquities and in particular the Roman site at Westland, discovered in 1923.

507

Since moving to its present site in the old coach house of the Manor House at Hendford in 1965 the museum has gone from strength to strength; the history of South Somerset now being experienced in the splendid displays of the recently refurbished museum. In an imaginative and exciting way the story of rural life through the ages is told. Visitors will discover artefacts of a past and passing age set in scenes that vividly recapture the atmosphere of their time. Certainly the place to visit if you'd like to learn more about this lovely area, the museum is open Tuesday to Saturday between 10am to 4pm. Admission is free and there is a small shop.

Museum of South Somerset, Hendford, Yeovil Tel: 01935 24774

One and a half miles south of Yeovil, a turning to the east off the A37 leads to Barwick Park (pronounced Barrik), an estate dotted with bizarre follies which are said to have been built by the local landowner, George Messiter, to employ out-of-work glove-makers in the 1830s. Arranged at the four points of the compass, the folly to the east known as 'Jack the Treacle Eater' is composed of a rickety stone arch which is topped by curious turreted room. According to local lore, it is named after a foot messenger who ran back and forth to London on a diet of bread and treacle. The estate also contains a grotto and a handsome church with a Norman font and an unusual 17th-century transeptal tower. The renowned Worldwide Butterfly and Lullingstone Silk Farm can be found in the grounds of Compton House, a couple of miles across the Dorset border to the east of Yeovil. (Open daily, 10am to 5pm between Easter and late-October.)

The village of MUDFORD lies on the A359 to the north east of Yeovil and here you will find The Half Moon Inn opposite the church.

There has been an tavern on the site for 700 years, although the buildings you see today only date back to the 17th century. The Inn comprises a cosy and comfortable lounge bar and a lively village bar. As well as providing a good choice of liquid refreshment the inn has two restaurants, one exclusively for non-smokers, serving food that ranges from bar snacks to a full à la carte menu.

AA listed, 3 Crown ETB approved and open all year the motel accommodation is within the grounds of the inn and all the rooms are on ground floor level, facing on to a courtyard area which has plenty of seating. Each has additional sofa beds, remote controlled colour television, tea and coffee making facilities, direct dial telephones and showers en-suite. Of the eleven rooms, nine are twin-bedded and two are doubles. One room has been specially design for the disabled.

The inn offers special two-day bargain breaks for two, which include bed and breakfast and à la carte evening meals at a very reasonable price - ideal for a short break.

The Half Moon Inn Motel and Restaurant, Main Street, Mudford, Yeovil Tel: 01935 850289

Four miles to the west of Yeovil, and just south of the A3088 Martock road, lies the superb, if popular, Elizabethan mansion, Montacute House. 500 years before present house was constructed, the nearby hill was the location of a controversial castle built by

509

William the Conqueror's half-brother, Robert, Count of Mortain. The Saxons were angered by his decision to build on the site, for they believed it to be a holy place where King Alfred had buried a fragment of Christ's cross. In 1068, they rose up and attacked the castle in one of the many piecemeal revolts against the Norman occupation; however, the attempt failed and the uprising was ruthlessly put down. Ironically, a subsequent Count of Mortain was found guilty of treason and forced into founding, and then donating all his lands to, a Cluniac priory on the site now occupied by Montacute village. The castle has long since disappeared, as has the monastery, with the exception of its part-12th-century priory church which contains some striking monuments to members of the Phelips family.

Work on the present Montacute House was begun in 1588 by Edward Phelips, Queen Elizabeth's Master of the Rolls. The building is a Renaissance masterpiece, constructed of golden Ham stone to an 'H-shaped' floor plan and adorned with open parapets, fluted columns, twisted pinnacles, oriel windows and carved statues. The long gallery, one the grandest of its kind in Britain, houses a fine collection of Tudor and Jacobean portraits which are on permanent loan from the National Portrait Gallery in London. Other noteworthy features include the stone and stained-glass screen in the great hall, and Lord Curzon's bath, an Edwardian addition which is hidden in a bedroom cupboard. An established story tells of how Curzon, a senior Tory politician, waited at Montacute in 1923 for news that he was to be called to form the new government, a call which never came. Now owned by the National Trust, the house stands within a landscaped park which incorporates a walled formal garden, a fig walk, an orangery, and a cedar lawn formerly known as 'Pig's Wheaties's Orchard'. (House open daily except Tuesdays, 12 noon to 5.30pm between late-March and end-October; grounds open all year round.)

The lanes to the west of Montacute lead to **STOKE-SUB-HAMDON**, another attractive village with a fine part-Norman church in its eastern part, and the remains of a late-medieval priory in its western part. The latter was built in the 14th- and 15th-centuries as the chantry chapel of the now-demolished St Nicholas college of priests. The remains, which include an impressive great hall, are now under the ownership of the National

Trust. (Open daily, 10am to 6pm, all year round; admission free.) To the south of the village lies Ham Hill (or Hamdon Hill), the source of the beautiful honey-coloured building stone of which so many of the surrounding villages are constructed. Although only 400 feet above sea level, this solitary limestone outcrop rises abruptly from the Somerset plain, creating a magnificent viewpoint over the surrounding farmland. This was the site of a substantial hill fort during the Iron Age which was subsequently overrun by the Roman legions. The new occupants then built their own fortification here to guard the Fosse Way and its important intersection with the Dorchester-Bristol Channel road at nearby Ilchester.

The Romans discovered that the Ham Hill's soft even-grained limestone made a highly attractive and flexible building material which was ideal for constructing their villas and temples. Many centuries later, the Saxons and then the Normans came to share this opinion, and throughout the Middle Ages, extensive quarrying activity took place which reached its height in the 17th-century, by which time a sizable settlement had grown up within the boundaries of the old Iron Age fort (only a solitary inn remains today). A war memorial to the 44 local men who died in the First World War stands at the summit of the hill which in recent years has been designated a country park. The view, the old earthwork ramparts, and maze of overgrown quarry workings combine to make this an outstanding picnic and recreation area.

St James's Cottage, 31 St James's Street, South Petherton
Tel: 01460 240460

The village of **SOUTH PETHERTON** is just half a mile north of the A303 between Ilchester and Ilminster. In the centre, near the Market Hall and the church is **St James's Cottage**. This delightfully picturesque 16th-century thatched cottage is the home of Richard and Ann Sheridan who offer bed and breakfast accommodation. All guests are made very welcome from the tray of tea when you arrive to the morning paper with your breakfast - all included in the price. There are only two letting rooms, one double en-suite and one twin with private bathroom. Guests also have their own sitting-room with TV and Hi-Fi and are free to explore the garden. Breakfast is served in the conservatory, and in winter the sitting-room is warmed by a log fire. Richard and Ann, who are both keen cooks, can also provide evening snacks and picnic hampers. A delightful place to stay - home from home.

The lanes to the north of South Petherton lead to **EAST LAMBROOK**, a charming hamlet with a beautiful garden which is open Mondays to Saturdays, 10am to 5pm between 1 March and 31 October.

East Lambrook Manor Garden is signposted off the A303, just beyond South Petherton. The garden was created by the Late Margery Fish who lived at The Manor from 1937 until she died in 1969. Now a grade 1 listed garden, it is both a traditional cottage-style garden and an important collection of plants and in addition is a National Collection Holder of Geranium (Cranesbill) species. The garden was made famous through the writings of Margery Fish and the story of her creation of East Lambrook Manor Garden is told in her first book, 'We made a garden'.

East Lambrook Manor Garden, near South Petherton
Tel: 01460 240328

The lovely Ham-stone village of **MARTOCK** lies on the northern side of the A303, two miles due east of East Lambrook. The town is surrounded by fertile arable land, and in the 17th- and 18th-centuries, it was renowned for the wealth of its farmers who made a comfortable living producing large quantities of wheat, beans and other cash crops. The impressive part-13th-century parish church reflects this prolonged period of prosperity; a former abbey church which once belonged to the monks of Mont St Michel in Normandy, it boasts one of the finest tie-beams roofs in Somerset, almost every part of which is covered in beautiful carvings. Opposite stands the handsome part-13th-century Treasurer's House, one of three exceptional houses in Martock. Recently refurbished by the National Trust, it incorporates a medieval great hall and cross wing, and a kitchen annexe which was added around 1500. (Open by appointment only; telephone 01985 847777.) To the southwest of the church stands the Old Court House, a former parish building which served the locality for 200 years as a grammar school; to the west, Martock's 17th-century manor house is the former home of Edward Parker, the man who exposed the Gunpowder Plot after Guy Fawkes had warned him against attending Parliament on the fateful night.

In the village you will find Michael Burton, Silversmith, at The Pig under Tree. He creates flamboyant and classical bespoke silverware that make perfect and unusual gifts or additions to any home. He is well worth seeking out to admire his craftsmanship.

Michael Burton, The Pig under Tree, Martock

It's worth making a diversion to see the enchanting National Trust-owned Tintinhull House Garden which lies on the northern side of the A3088, a couple of miles to the east of Martock. Laid out in the early-20th-century, the garden is divided into a series of distinctive 'rooms', each with its own planting theme. These include a pool garden with a delightful lily- and iris-filled pond, a kitchen garden, and a sunken garden which is cleverly designed to give the impression it has many different levels. (Open daily except Mondays and Fridays, 2pm to 6pm between late-March and late-September.) The garden is set in the grounds of Tintinhull House, an early 17th-century farmhouse which was given a spectacular west front around 1700. Sadly not open to the public, the house overlooks an attractive three-sided green which forms the centre of the sprawling village of Tintinhull. A number of other buildings of interest are also to be found here: Tintinhull Court, a part-medieval rectory which was remodelled in the 17th- and 18th-centuries, the Dower House, which was built for the Napper family in 1687, and St Margaret's Parish Church, a rare example in Somerset of a rectangular single-cell church.

The low-lying land to the northwest of Martock is crisscrossed by a network of drainage ditches, or rhines (pronounced 'reens'), which eventually flow into the rivers Parrett, Isle and Yeo. The ditches were originally cut in the early 1800s and are often lined with double rows of pollarded willows which have come to characterise this part of Somerset. Despite having to be cleared every few years, they provide a valuable natural habitat for a wide variety of bird, animal and plantlife.

Located on the B3165, in the village of LONG LOAD, between Long Sutton and Martock, you will find Amberley. This farmhouse-style detached house with far-reaching views is the home of Jean Jarvis, and has a very welcoming atmosphere. The house is comfortably furnished and decorated and the bedrooms are well-appointed. Guests also have use of the lounge with TV, the conservatory and are free to explore the garden. Jean is a great cook and prepares typically English meals.

Amberley, Long Load, Langport
Tel: 01458 241542

An interesting way to discover more about this unique wetlands environment is to call in at the Thorney Moor Farm Park on the southern side of the village of MUCHELNEY. (Open Tuesdays to Sundays, 10am to 6pm between early-March and end-October.) Also located nearby is the thatched workshop of the potter, John Leach, whose grandfather, Bernard, established the famous Leach Pottery at St Ives in Cornwall in the 1920s. (Open Mondays to Saturdays, 9am to 5pm (1pm Saturdays), all year round.)

Here, in ancient farm buildings, you will find Muchelney Pottery, set up in 1964. John Leach, with the help of his wife Lizzie, and assistant potter Nick Rees, operates his kiln and workshops here as well as a shop from which you can buy his products. As well as producing the classic Muchelney tableware range, John also creates individual pots, each signed with his own seal, and understandably more expensive. Common to all the pots is the distinctive flame marking, a unique characteristic of the wood-fired kiln. The workshops can be viewed by prior arrangement and the kiln firing on advertised open days.

Muchelney Pottery, Muchelney, near Langport
Tel: 01458 250324

Muchelney itself is the location of a part-ruined Benedictine abbey which was first established by the Saxon King Ine in the 8th-century. The monastery grew throughout the Middle Ages to rival the great abbey at Glastonbury; however, after its dissolution in 1538, the building gradually fell into disrepair and much of its fabric was removed to provide building material for the surrounding village. Notwithstanding, a substantial part of the original structure remains, including the abbot's lodge and south cloister, and the site is now under the protection of English Heritage. Muchelney contains two other buildings of note: the parish church, which has a remarkable illuminated nave ceiling dating from the early-17th-century, and the Priest's House, a late-medieval 'hall' house with large Gothic windows which has recently been refurbished by the National Trust. (Open Sundays and

Mondays only, 2pm to 5pm between late-March and end-September.)

The privately-owned Midelney Manor can be found at DRAYTON, a mile and a half to the west. Originally an island manor belonging to the abbots of Muchelney, this handsome 16th- to 18th-century manor house has been owned by the Trevilian family since around 1500. The estate incorporates the unique 17th-century Falcons mews, a heronry and a series of delightful gardens and woodland walks. (Open Thursdays and Bank Holiday Mondays, 2.30pm to 5.30pm between late-April and end-September.)

One of the finest examples in the county of a late-medieval 'Somerset' tower can be found on the church at HUISH EPISCOPI, one mile to the north of Muchelney. This exceptional honey-brown structure is adorned with the most ornate tracery, pinnacles and carvings, and is perhaps at its most impressive in high summer when viewed through the surrounding greenery. The church also boasts an elaborate Norman doorway which shows signs of having been affected by the fire that destroyed much of the rest of the building in the 13th-century, and a window in the south chapel which was designed in the 19th-century by Burne-Jones.

Almost adjoining Huish Episcopi to the west is the pleasant former market town of LANGPORT. The old part of the town stands on a rise above an ancient fording point on the River Parrett, just downstream from the points where it is joined by the Isle and Yeo. Defended by an earthwork rampart since Saxon times, by 930 it was an important commercial centre which minted its own coins. The town's east gate can still be seen today, a curious structure which incorporates a 'hanging' chapel, so-called because it stands above the arch on an upper level. The tower of Huish Episcopi Church can be seen through the barrel-vaulted gateway, and a little to the west, Langport's own parish church is worth a look for its beautiful stained glass and 12th-century carved lintel over the south doorway.

The strategic importance of the Langport Gap has twice made it the site of important battles: the first involved Geraint, King of the Dumnonii in the 6th-century, and the second, the Battle of Langport of July 1645, gave Parliament almost total control of the South West. During the 18th- and 19th-centuries, Langport flourished as a banking and distribution centre, and the local bank, Stuckey's, became known for its impressive branch buildings, many of which can still be seen in the surrounding towns and villages trading under the banner of NatWest. At the time of its amalgamation in 1909, the bank had more notes in circulation than any other in the country except the Bank of England.

One of the few claims that the village of ALLER can lay to fame occurred in 878AD. It was in the church that King Alfred converted Guthrum the Dane and his followers to Christianity following a battle on Salisbury Plain.

In the village today, and opposite the garage, is Aller Pottery run by Bryan and Julia Newman. This working pottery is open Monday to Saturday from dawn until dusk. There you can watch the potters at work and purchase the results of their efforts in the shop. The pottery specialises in Stoneware, a hard and durable ceramic, and creates a wide range of decorative and useful items, from casseroles to lamp bases, so you are sure to find something in the shop that appeals. They use clay dug in Cornwall and Dorset, and a variety of glazes to create a range of subtle colours and finishes.

Aller Pottery, The Pottery, Aller, Nr Langport Tel: 01458 250244

The B3153 to the east of Langport leads to SOMERTON, a fine old town built of bluish lias limestone which was the capital of Somerset for a time under the West Saxons. (It was also the location of the county gaol and meeting place of the shire courts between 1278 and 1371.) The original settlement grew up around an important crossroads to the northwest of the church; however, a redevelopment towards the end of the 13th-century expanded the town and created the present open market place with its 17th-century 'town hall' and distinctive market cross. (Somerton's roots as a market town are revealed by such imaginatively-named streets as Cow Square and Pig Street, now Broad Street.) All around, the handsome old shops, inns and residential buildings create an air of mature prosperity, an atmosphere which is enhanced by a number of other fine buildings, including the 17th-century Hext almshouses and the part-13th-century church, with its a magnificent 15th-century tie-beam roof and unusual transeptal south tower.

The B3151 to the southeast of Somerton leads to the village of KINGSDON, a mile to the east of which lies the delightful National Trust-owned country house and garden, Lytes Cary. This late-medieval manor house was built by succeeding generations of the Lyte family, the best-known member of which is Henry Lyte, the Elizabethan horticulturalist who translated Dodoen's Cruydeboeck from the Dutch to create the book which became widely known as Lyte's Herbal. Dedicated to the Queen, it went on to be reprinted several times as an interest in kitchen gardening began to develop. The present garden is an enchanting combination of formality and eccentricity: there is an open lawn lined with magnificent yew topiary, an orchard filled with apple, pear and quince, and a network of enclosed paths which every now and then reveal a glimpse of the house, a lily-pond or a classical statue. The house was built over a long period and incorporates a 14th-century chapel, a 15th-century hall and a 16th-century great chamber. (Open Mondays, Wednesdays and Saturdays, 2pm to 6pm between late-March and late-October.)

From Lyte's Cary, the B3151 continues southwards to ILCHESTER, a pleasant, if unexceptional, small town which, like Somerton, is a former county town of Somerset. In Roman times, the settlement stood at the point where the north-south route between Dorchester and the Bristol Channel crossed the Fosse Way. However, it was during the 13th-century that the town reached its zenith as a centre of agriculture, administration and learning. Roger Bacon, the celebrated scholar, monk and scientist was born here around 1214 and went on to predict the invention of the aeroplane, telescope and steam engine. He was eventually confined for his outspoken ideas, and if he were alive today, he would no doubt be quietly satisfied by the existence of the aircraft museum at nearby Yeovilton. To accompany Ilchester's medieval status as the county town, a substantial gaol was built which remained in use until the 1840s; another indication of its former status, a 13th-century mace thought to be the oldest staff of office in England, can be found in the town hall. Today, Ilchester is bypassed by the A303 and most of the tribulations of the outside world.

Ilchester Museum, High Street, Ilchester Tel: 01935 841247

In the centre of the town, by the Market Cross, you will come across the Town Hall and Community Centre. The small **Ilchester Museum**, can be found in this building, occupying a single room. The museum tells the story of the history of Ilchester from Pre-Roman times to the discoveries of the 20th-century, which include a Roman coffin and a skeleton. Other exhibits nay explain why the town has had three gaols and how it comes to have the oldest mace in the whole of Europe. The museum is, however, only open on Thursdays and Saturdays from May to September.

Liongate House, Ilchester, Nr. Yeovil Tel: 01935 841193

Liongate House, a Grade II listed Georgian house, is in the centre of Ilchester, adjacent to the site of the last of Ilchester's gaols. The house retains many of its original features, in particular the stone fireplaces in the major rooms. There are 10 letting rooms, four of which are en-suite, and another four with en-suite toilet. The largest en-suite room can be used as a self-contained family suite, incorporating a sitting room and kitchen. All rooms have drink making facilities and colour TV and are attractively decorated and furnished. Breakfast is served in the vaulted dining room where the walls are adorned with prints from an exhibition on the town's prisons. The garden is large and is dominated by a large copper beech tree. Guests are free to wander at will, but be careful not to fall into the raised pond where John and Marlene keep koi carp.

On the B3151, which is the old Fosse Way, you will find the **Podymore Inn**, in the village of PODIMORE. The unusual name of both village and the inn, although spelt differently, means 'Moor of the Frogs'. Originally built in the late 18th century the building was formerly a cider house and called The Butchers Arms. In later years, the local cider gave way to beers and real ales, and in 1930 the name was changed to Podymore Inn.

The Podymore Inn, Podimore, Ilchester Tel: 01935 840484

This pub offers great home-cooking and a variety of real ales, and hosts Jan and Graham Bailey have created a welcoming air, making it ideal as a stopping point for individuals or families. The bright and cheery interior is made more cosy in the winter months, when the stone fireplace houses a roaring log fire. The restaurant doubles as the skittle alley, and is known to the locals as Doc's Bar, in memory of 'Doc' Love and Ben Casey, who lost their lives in the Falklands War. The food available is reasonably priced, and is home-cooked, traditional pub fare. The pub has good relations with the Royal Naval Air Station which is not far away, and has several fantastic photographs of the planes decorating the walls.

Those with an interest in the history of flight should make for the **Fleet Air Arm Museum** at **YEOVILTON**, on the B3151 three miles to the east of Ilchester. The museum is one of the world's leading aviation museums housing the equipment, records and documents of the Fleet Air Arm's history. There are 83 aircraft in the collection, and over 40 are on display.

Fleet Air Arm Museum, Royal Naval Air Station Yeovilton, near Ilchester Tel: 01935 840565 Fax: 01935 840181

Many exhibitions illustrate the history of Naval aviation in graphical and dramatic form: World Wars I and II; Wrens; Kamikaze; Korean War; recent conflicts; Harrier 'Jump' Jet (the history of VSTOL); Concorde 002 (the British Prototype). In addition there are displays of weapons, medals and memorabilia, which bring to life the exciting history of Naval aviation, and the men and women who were part of that history.

A major new exhibition, recently opened, is the 'Ultimate Carrier Experience'. A Flight Deck built on land, with steam catapult, deck landing sight, and 11 carrier-borne aircraft parked on the flight deck. Also included are Island, Flyco, Goofers Deck, Operations Room, Control Centre, Workshops, Living Quarters (wardroom and mess-decks) and a scissor lift.

Visitors will join the ship via a helicopter simulation, as it proceeds on a mission of mercy. They will see the entire operation unfold, using the latest in audio-visual and interactive technology. You can also watch the modern Naval Flyers train from our airfield viewing galleries.

Facilties include free car parking, licensed restuarant, gift shop, baby care room, children's adventure playground, access for the disabled and a dog exercise area. (Open daily, 10am to 5.30pm (4.30pm in winter), all year round.)

Catch the spirit of Naval Aviation at the Fleet Air Arm Museum.

Run by Richard and Helen Crang, **Courtry Farm** is a working farm of beef, sheep and arable crops that can also offer fine farmhouse bed and breakfast. The main farmhouse is 17th century and has a typically delightful interior full of traditional features. Accommodation consists of two self-contained ground floor bedrooms with tea making facilities and TV. Outside there is a full sized tennis court and garden which guests are more than welcome to use. For walkers the Leland Way passes through the farm and the farm is surrounded by accessible fields to explore. Close to the Fleet Air Arm Museum, Courtry Farm can be found in the village of Bridgehampton.

Courtry Farm Farmhouse B&B, Bridgehampton, Yeovil
Tel: 01935 840327

Another interesting museum can be found beside the A359 on the northeastern edge of **SPARKFORD**, five miles to the east of Yeovilton. Perhaps the largest example of its kind in the United Kingdom, the Haynes Motor Museum is a unique collection of over 200 veteran, vintage and classic cars and motorbikes from the 100 year history of the motor vehicle. Nearly every exhibit is driven at least once every six months around a specially-constructed one-kilometre demonstration road. Special collections include Jaguars, Minis, Chevrolet Corvettes and red-painted sports cars. (Open daily, 9.30am to 5.30pm, all year round.)

The Sparkford Inn, Sparkford, Yeovil, Somerset Tel: 01963 440218

Just off the A303 in Sparkford is **The Sparkford Inn**. The establishment dates back to the 15th Century and was once a coaching inn serving the needs of travellers. Now a free house, it is owned and run by Nigel and Suzanne Tucker. Although the main road no longer passes the front door, travellers in need of refreshment are still offered a warm welcome. The comfortable lounge bar boasts four real ales which change regularly, and an excellent selection of bar meals are available. There is also a dining room, with a full à la carte menu prepared by resident chefs Sean Bradford and Bill Budd each evening. They also offer chef specials and a carvery at lunch times although on Sundays you will need to book. Fish also feature on the menus, usually freshly caught and landed at St Ives.

This pub also caters very well for children (and parents!). A great fun idea is the indoor, soft playroom called 'Snakes and Ladders'. The room is open every weekend and school holiday lunch times, and furthermore it is supervised so mum and dad can have a quiet drink. Outside, also for the children, although parents may be tempted, is an adventure trail. It is fully enclosed with a deep bark base for a soft landing. If you're having so much fun here that you can't tear yourselves away, Nigel and Suzanne can also provide bed and breakfast.

Midway between Ilchester and Wincanton, the A303 passes along the northern edge of Cadbury Castle, a massive Iron Age hill fort which is also rumoured to be the location of King Arthur's legendary Camelot. The hilltop site was in fact occupied for some 5000 years, from the middle to the Neolithic period around 4000 BC right up to the 13th-century. Heavily fortified throughout the Iron Age, the Romans are thought to have carried out a massacre here around 70 AD in response to the revolt by the Britons. As well as uncovering a wealth of Roman and pre-Roman remains, a major archeological excavation in the 1960s confirmed the existence of a substantial fortification dating from around 500 AD, the time when Arthur would have been spearheading the British resistance against the advancing Saxons. (Contrary to myth, it is likely that this would have been a timber structure and not the turreted stone castle of the storybooks.)

The easily-defended hilltop site was refortified as a defence against the Danes during the reign of Ethelred the Unready. The poorly-advised king also established a mint here around 1000 AD, most of the coinage from which was used to buy off the Viking invaders, the origin of the term Danegeld. (As a consequence, most of the surviving coins from the Cadbury mint are to be found in museums in Scandinavia.) The mile-long stroll around the massive earthwork ramparts demonstrates the site's effectiveness as a defensive position: troop movements to the north and west would have been seen in plenty of time, and the important route into the Heart of England, the Fosse Way, would have been clearly visible five miles away to the northwest. Another magnificent view of south Somerset can be had from the summit of Corton Hill, the site of an ancient beacon which can be reached by following Halter Path Lane from the village of CORTON DENHAM, two miles to the south.

Near to Cadbury Hill in Camelot country is Barrow Farm, a working dairy farm, where Penny Trott offers warm and charming bed and breakfast in her 17th-century farmhouse.

There are two comfortable rooms with tea making facilities and a TV is available to guests in the lounge. Penny provides a full traditional breakfast and can also prepare packed lunches on

524

request. Barrow Farm also offers self-catering accommodation for up to seven people in Richmond House, almost opposite the farm, and adjacent to the church. The house has its own gardens and swimming pool as well as access to the farm fields. Barrow Farm is on the South Somerset Cycle Route, and would make an ideal rest stop for cycle tourers, or anyone exploring the area for that matter. Discover the farm in North Barrow, two miles from the A303 or from the B3135 via Lovington.

Barrow Farm B&B, North Barrow, Castle Cary Tel: 01963 240244

Aptly named, Quiet Corner Farm is tucked away on the fringe of HENSTRIDGE, off Oakvale Lane. The farm is the home of Brian and Patricia Thompson who offer farmhouse Bed and Breakfast Two Crowns Commended standard.

The 18th century stone farmhouse can accommodate up to six guests in very comfortable rooms, with a guest's sitting room and a Sunroom where you can take breakfast. There is a pretty garden and cider apple orchards and paddocks where visitors can make friends with the sheep, the award-winning Shetland ponies and Truffles, the little pig.

Quiet Corner Farm, Henstridge
Tel: 01963 363045

The self-catering cottages can each accommodate 2 to 4 persons and are of a Four Key Highly Commended standard. Both have been converted from old stone barns and have a traditional feel.

525

The A357 to the north of Henstridge passes close to the old cloth-making and coaching centre of WINCANTON. Standing on a draughty hillside above the River Cale, the town lies almost exactly half way between London and Plymouth, and in the heyday of the horse-drawn carriage, up to twenty coaches a day stopped in the town which offered stabling for over 250 horses. Now it is a peaceful light industrial town whose old sector contains a surprising number of fine Georgian town houses, some of which were constructed to replace earlier buildings destroyed in a town fire in 1747. The parish church is a Victorian rebuild whose most interesting feature is a medieval carving of St Eligius in the north porch. Wincanton's renowned National Hunt racecourse can be found beside the B3081, a mile to the north of the town centre.

For those of you that enjoy caravanning there is a fine and peaceful site at Wincanton Racecourse. The site has 50 pitches which are all on grass and 18 have electrical hook up facilities. There are free showers, a television room and sinks for dish and clothes washing as well as vegetable preparation. The town is just one mile away and offers every additional amenity you could need.

Wincanton Racecourse Caravan Site, The Racecourse,
Wincanton Tel: 01963 34668

Racing began at Wincanton in the 18th century and started on the present course in 1927, only pausing for the Second World War. Today you can enjoy National hunt jump racing in season, which runs from October to May. The second meeting in October features the Desert Orchid S.W. Pattern Steeplechase, at which Desert Orchid still parades. If you have remembered your clubs there is a challenging nine hole pay and play golf course.

Hadspen Garden & Nursery is a five acre Edwardian garden which features a two acre curved walled garden with extensive colourful borders, a woodland of fine mature specimen trees and a meadow of naturalised flowers and grasses. As well as the nursery there is a small tea shop. (Open Thursdays to Sundays and Bank Holiday Mondays, 9am to 6pm between 1 March and 30 September.)

Hadspen Garden & Nursery, Castle Cary Tel: 01749 813707

526

The lovely little town of CASTLE CARY lies to the west of the A371, one-and-a-half miles to the northwest of Hadspen. Once the site of an impressive Norman castle, this has now all but disappeared and today, the town has the atmosphere of polite rural calm. The streets contain a number of exceptional old buildings, including a distinctive beehive-shaped lock-up gaol dating from the 1770s, a handsome 18th-century post office, and a splendid Victorian market hall which incorporates a 17th-century colonnade.

In the centre of Castle Cary, opposite the George Hotel, is the Castle Cary District Museum housed in the Market House. The present building was built in 1855 on the site of a Tudor building and incorporates the Castle Cary lock-up. The exhibits in the museum are mainly agricultural implements and period household artefacts. (Open daily between April and September.) The rectory at Ansford, on the northern edge of Castle Cary, is the former home of the 18th-century diarist, James Woodforde, whose life seemed to revolve around the consumption of lavish meals.

Castle Cary District Museum, c/o Museum of South Somerset, Hendford, Yeovil Tel: 01935 424774

The remarkably well-preserved former clothing and ecclesiastical centre of BRUTON lies on the A359, three miles to the northeast of Castle Cary. More a small town than a village, a priory was established here in the 11th-century on the south bank of the River Brue. The former great church, St Mary's, is a fine Perpendicular structure with a soaring 100 foot west tower and a

527

rare second tower which was built over the north porch in the late 14th-century. The interior is unusually light and spacious, and contains a number of memorials to the Berkeley family, the local lords of the manor who also owned the land on which London's Berkeley Square is built. A walk around the streets of Bruton reveals a surprising number of historic features. The curious little square building across the river from the church is the Patwell Pump, a communal parish pump which remained in use until the early 20th-century, and a little further downstream, a 15th-century arched packhorse bridge stands beside a ford and just above the site of the part-16th-century King's School. The High Street is also lined with exceptional old buildings, including the Pharmacy, with its elegant 18th-century façade, and the intriguingly-named Sexey's Hospital, a 17th-century almshouse which was founded by one of Elizabeth I's auditors, Hugh Sexey. Perhaps Bruton's most distinctive building, the Dovecote, stands on the crest of a hill to the south of King's School; built in the 15th-century, it may once have doubled as a watch tower and is now under the ownership of the National Trust.

Claire de Lune, 2-4 High Street, Bruton Tel: 01749 813395

In the centre of Bruton, it is difficult not to notice Claire de Lune as it is painted bright blue. The building was once the old Post Office and stands at the hub of a major conservation area. The façade dates from around 1770, and became listed in 1953. It is difficult to believe that it fell into such disrepair that it was nearly demolished. Thankfully it was rescued and restored using old postcards and drawings. Today, it is a wonderful restaurant specialising in French cuisine. Although much of the interior is fitting to the period of the original building, featuring exposed beams and a stone inglenook, it has been tastefully decorated with a French theme. Families are welcome, and in addition to the à la carte menu, which changes regularly, there is a children's menu.

At the west end of town, at the bottom of the High Street, you will find **The Old Forge**, the home of Chris and Christine Dunn. Converted from 15th century cotton and silk mill workers' cottages, the Old Forge offers extremely comfortable bed and breakfast accommodation. There are three rooms - one double/family en-suite, a double and a twin. All rooms offer tea-making facilities and TV. There is a wide range of games and books available and guests have use of the lounge/dining room. Off-road parking and secure parking for cycles. The Mill On The Brue Activity Centre lies a short distance downstream from the town centre; set in twenty acres of countryside around a converted farmhouse and barn, the centre specialises in residential activity holidays for children between the ages of 8 and 14.

The Old Forge, 89 High Street, Bruton Tel: 01749 812585

For those keen to explore this beautiful part of Somerset on foot, the Leland Trail long-distance footpath begins at King Alfred's Tower, part of the glorious National Trust-owned Stourhead estate which lies just across the Wiltshire border, six miles to the east of Bruton. The 25-mile trail passes through the wooded hills and valleys of Camelot country and takes in Bruton, Castle Cary,

Cadbury Castle and Tintinhull on its way to Ham Hill. A further long-distance footpath, the Liberty Trail, then continues southwestwards through the Ham-stone country of south Somerset and finally passes out of the county near Forde Abbey.

Tourist Information Centres

AMESBURY
Redworth House, Flower Lane, Amesbury Tel: 01980 623255

BATH
The Colonnades, 11-13 Bath Street, Bath Tel: 01225 462831

BRADFORD-ON-AVON
The Library, Bridge Street, Bradford-on-Avon Tel: 01225 865797

BRIDGWATER
50 High Street, Bridgwater Tel: 01278 427652

BRISTOL
14 Narrow Quay, Bristol Tel: 01179 260767

BRISTOL AIRPORT
Bristol Airport Tel: 01179 474444

BURNHAM-ON-SEA
South Esplanade, Burnham-on-Sea Tel: 01278 455485

CHARD
The Guildhall, Fore Street, Chard Tel: 01460 67463

CHEDDAR
The Gorge, Cheddar Tel: 01934 744071

CHELTENHAM
77 The Promenade, Cheltenham Tel: 01242 522878

CHIPPENHAM
The Neeld Hall, High Street, Chippenham Tel: 01249 657733

CHIPPING CAMPDEN
Woolstaplers' Hall, High Street, Chipping Campden
Tel: 01386 840101

CIRENCESTER
Corn Hall, Market Place, Cirencester Tel: 01285 654180

COLEFORD
27 Market Place, Coleford Tel: 01594 836307

DEVIZES
39 St John's Street, Devizes Tel: 01380 729408

GLASTONBURY
The Tribunal, 9 High Street, Glastonbury Tel: 01458 832954

GLOUCESTER
St Michael's Tower, The Cross, Gloucester Tel: 01452 421188

MALMESBURY
Town Hall, Market Lane, Malmesbury Tel: 01666 823748

MARLBOROUGH
Car Park, George Lane, Marlborough Tel: 01672 513989

MELKSHAM
The Roundhouse, Church Street, Melksham Tel: 01225 707424

MERE
The Square, Mere Tel: 01747 861211

MIDSOMER NORTON
Wansdyke TIC, South Wansdyke Sports Centre,
Rackvernal Road, Midsomer Norton Tel: 01761 412221

MINEHEAD
17 Friday Street, Minehead Tel: 01643 702624

NEWENT
The Library, High Street, Newent Tel: 01531 822145

NORTHLEACH
Cotswold Countryside Collection, Northleach
Tel: 01451 860715

PAINSWICK
The Library, Stroud Road, Painswick Tel: 01452 813552

PODIMORE
Somerset Visitor Centre, Forte Services (A303), Podimore,
Nr. Yeovil Tel: 01935 841302

SALISBURY
Fish Row, Salisbury Tel: 01722 334956

SEDGEMOOR SERVICES
Somerset Visitor Centre, Sedgemoor Services, M5 South,
Nr. Axbridge Tel: 01934 750833

STOW-ON-THE-WOLD
Hollis House, The Square, Stow-on-the-Wold Tel: 01451 831082

STROUD
Subscription Rooms, George Street, Stroud Tel: 01453 765768

SWINDON
32 The Arcade, Brunel Centre, Swindon Tel: 01793 530328

TAUNTON
The Library, Corporation Street, Taunton Tel: 01823 274785

TETBURY
The Old Court House, 63 Long Street, Tetbury
Tel: 01666 503552

TEWKESBURY
64 Barton Street, Tewkesbury Tel: 01684 295027

TROWBRIDGE
St Stephen's Place, Trowbridge Tel: 01225 777054

WARMINSTER
Central Car Park, Warminster Tel: 01985 218548

WELLS
Town Hall, Market Place, Wells Tel: 01749 672552

WESTBURY
The Library, Edward Street, Westbury Tel: 01373 827158

WESTON-SUPER-MARE
Beach Lawns, Wester-super-Mare Tel: 01934 626838

WINCHCOMBE
Town Hall, High Street, Winchcombe Tel: 01242 602925

YEOVIL
Petter's House, Petter's Way, Yeovil Tel: 01935 71279

Index

A

B

536

W

Y

THE HIDDEN PLACES

If you would like to have any of the titles currently available in this series, please complete this coupon and send to: **M&M Publishing, Tryfan House, Warwick Drive, Hale, Altrincham, Cheshire WA15 9EA**

	Each	Qty
Scotland	£5.90	____
Northumberland & Durham	£5.90	____
The Lake District & Cumbria	£5.90	____
Yorkshire & Humberside	£5.90	____
Lancashire & Cheshire	£5.90	____
North Wales	£5.90	____
South Wales	£5.90	____
The Welsh Borders	£5.90	____
Thames & Chilterns	£5.90	____
East Anglia	£5.90	____
The South East	£5.90	____
Dorset, Hampshire & the Isle of Wight	£5.90	____
Heart of England	£5.90	____
Devon & Cornwall	£5.90	____
Set of any five titles	£20.00	____

TOTAL: £

(Price includes Postage and Packing)

NAME..

ADDRESS ....

....

.... POSTCODE ....

Please make cheques payable to: M&M Publishing